BETTY CROCKER'S

Starting Out

Golden Press/New York
Western Publishing Company, Inc.
Racine, Wisconsin

Illustrated by Ray Skibinski and Loring Eutemey
Cover photograph by George Adams

First Printing, 1975
Copyright © 1975 by General Mills, Inc., Minneapolis, Minnesota. All
rights reserved. No portion of this book may be reprinted or reproduced in
any form or any manner without the written permission of the publishers,
except by a reviewer who wishes to quote brief passages in connection with
a review.

Printed in the U.S.A. by Western Publishing Company, Inc.
Published by Golden Press, New York, New York.

Library of Congress Catalog Card Number: 74-27726.

Golden and Golden Press® are trademarks of
Western Publishing Company, Inc.

Contents

Foreword

Starting out—it means a lot of things. One of the first is establishing a household of your own. Whether you're a young married or a career-single living alone or "sharing"—whether it's a starting again, to go with a new part of your life—whether you're moving into your first home or to different or larger quarters—it's an important and challenging step you're taking. And the first thing we want to say is, "Congratulations and best wishes to you in your new life!"

If all we could offer were best wishes, however, there'd be no reason for this book. We want to be helpful in more tangible ways. It takes a lot of different abilities, talents and bits of know-how to establish and maintain an efficient and happy household of your own. Some know-how involves the purely practical side of life—like finding a place to live and financing it. Other abilities involve the aesthetics of living: choosing furniture, decorating your place so it reflects you. Both aspects are equally important. What this book offers you is a kind of consulting service that covers both the practical and the aesthetic side, a store of ready material that you can call upon for advice and information whenever you want.

What's really involved in starting on your own? What goes into setting up your own household? Much of the advice that's available in print is concerned with the mechanics of housekeeping. That's useful information, of course, and it hasn't been bypassed here. But it overlooks a lot of information that is very likely to be the information you need most, and that *isn't* so easy to find in book form. And that's what we want to offer you.

Finding a place of your own that works for you; being able to furnish it so it's both comfortable and attractive; caring for it with a minimum of wasted effort; managing finances to get the most out of the money available; knowing enough about food, meal-planning and preparation to eat healthfully every day and entertain easily—it seems to us that these are all involved in living an independent life successfully. So these are the major areas covered in *Starting Out,* and there's a fact-packed chapter on each of these topics waiting for you here. As an added bonus, each chapter includes a special Handbook that zeroes in on information of particular interest and help to starting-outers.

But just presenting facts isn't enough. If our consulting-service-in-book-form is going to be really useful, you have to be able to find the specific information you want, when you want it. That's why each chapter of *Starting Out* is divided into several sections, all clearly headlined. (You'll find that those headlines function like an information-retrieval system, incidentally.) There's a detailed table of contents at the beginning of each chapter that shows you just what's included there, and a complete index at the end of the book. There are margin notes and sketches to highlight special points of interest. And you'll also find lots of beautiful color pages full of decorating ideas and entertaining ways.

We're really proud of those color pages! They include living rooms, bedrooms, bathrooms, kitchens, dining areas . . . space-making ideas, unusual color schemes . . . window treatments, wall treatments. Whether you're traditional or tomorrow-minded, whether you favor the formal or the casual approach to living—you'll come away with ideas you'll want to use in your home. The point is, these pages should give you ideas and suggestions that you can take off from and adapt to your own particular tastes.

What we've tried to do is to make *Starting Out* a book you'll read, then refer to again and again. It's not an easy matter, developing the skills to live independently. No one does it overnight. It's a growing forward, really—and like all growing, it takes time and patience. You won't achieve the abilities all at once, but the problems won't crop up all at once, either. You may get discouraged and think you'll never find a place that you like and can afford. Or furniture you've ordered may not arrive on schedule. More seriously, you may find it quite difficult to manage the details of housekeeping—or you may have problems managing money. But there's usually a compensating triumph or two to balance each difficulty. And remember—the ultimate point of this information is to enable you to get more out of your home, more for your money, and more enjoyment out of your life. Because you're starting out, there'll be change in your life, and change implies problems as well as joys. We hope this book will be helpful in smoothing out, or even avoiding, some of the problems that can crop up. Even more important, we hope that we'll be able to help you realize some of the very definite satisfactions inherent in your new life. That's what *Starting Out* is really all about.

Betty Crocker

1 Looking for a Home of Your Own

1 Looking for a Home of Your Own

HOW TO BE A SUCCESSFUL HOME-HUNTER

BASIC DECISIONS TO MAKE

HOW TO CHECKLIST ANY AREA
YOU'RE CONSIDERING

SHOULD YOU RENT AN APARTMENT?
THE PROS AND CONS

HOW TO TRANSLATE APARTMENT-FOR-RENT ADS

WHEN TO START LOOKING FOR AN APARTMENT

HOW TO BAG THAT APARTMENT:
TRIED AND TRUE TECHNIQUES

CHECKLISTS, CHECKBOOK AND AN OPEN MIND:
BE PREPARED—BRING THEM WITH YOU!

HOW TO CHECKLIST BOTH BUILDING
AND APARTMENT

A TYPICAL LEASE

YOUR LEASE: KNOW WHAT YOU'RE SIGNING!

OUTLINE OF POINTS TO WATCH FOR
IN YOUR LEASE

SOMETHING SPECIAL: BUYING YOUR OWN HOME

SUCCESS STORY: MOBILE HOMES, CONDOMINIUMS,
COOPERATIVES, TOWNHOUSES

HANDBOOK ON HOW TO MOVE

TEST YOUR KNOW-HOW

STAY AHEAD OF THE MOVING GAME!

PACKING LIKE A PRO

MOVE-IT-YOURSELF: SOME HELPFUL
HOWS AND WHYS

YOU'RE MOVED IN!

TO BE A SUCCESSFUL HOME-HUNTER:
KNOW WHAT YOU WANT,
KNOW WHAT'S AVAILABLE

Close your eyes and daydream a little about your first home together. What will it be? A modern apartment with a sweep of picture window and a plant-filled terrace? A handsome town-house with a private patio for outdoor entertaining? Let your mind browse around a little. This kind of daydreaming is valuable because it begins to bring into focus the kind of surroundings you want to live with.

Like marriage itself, however, you can't stop with daydreams. To find a place to live, you have to turn dream into reality. You have to take a longer, harder look at that ideal home and begin to match it up with what's actually available in your area. You have to have specific ideas about how many rooms you want, what you can pay, what features are important and what are extras.

The fastest and best way to size up your local real-estate situation is to start reading real-estate ads. You'll find some pointers on how to decipher real-estate language later on in this chapter. If you read the ads carefully, you'll soon get a sense of whether or not your area is a tight market. Housing situations vary widely from area to area. It's important to know what you're facing because you'll then know what compromises are necessary when it comes to matching up your dream with reality.

Your first home may not be your long-range "ideal." Probably you'll find something that meets *most* of your requirements. If you live in a tight housing area, however, you may have to settle for what you can get and then use brains and ingenuity to make it work for you.

Most young couples start out renting, so this chapter offers lots of pointers on finding apartments. If you're thinking of a rented house or of buying, however, you'll find specific suggestions for these situations, too. Just remember—whether you settle into a neat new apartment, a gem of a house or a 1-room walk-up with iffy plumbing—*it's yours*. When you walk inside and close the door—you're home!

MAKE THESE BASIC DECISIONS FIRST

Before you seriously start considering whether to buy or rent, whether to look for an apartment or a house, there are several important questions you should talk over. They sound simple, but your answers may very definitely affect the type of housing you opt for. Also, don't be surprised if you find that the two of you have slightly different ideas in this basic area. What you'll really be talking about is the kind of overall life-style you both enjoy. So it's worth taking the time to figure out together-decisions based on these leading questions.

Are you a city person? Let's face it, some people are born cityites, happy nowhere else. They sleep blissfully through traffic noises, like the bustle of a metropolis, and can take their trees framed in concrete. Others want the greenery-scenery and quieter ways of the suburbs. Both types of life have built-in advantages and drawbacks. What's important is that you weigh the pros and cons realistically before deciding which way of life will work best for both of you.

Of course, your job or study situation may make the decision for you. If one or both of you are running a heavy schedule of night classes, for instance, or often work after-hours at the office, you'll probably want to live as close as possible to your school or job. Or one of you may simply detest the whole idea of commuting. Apart from special setups like these, here are some of the other factors you might think about when it comes to making up your mind whether to be a cityite:

☐ Concentrating your life-style in the city (both living and working there) offers conveniences that may be just the ones you're looking for. Basic services are all close at hand. Usually, there's a food store, a dry cleaner, a launderette within easy walking distance. Many neighborhood stores are set up to handle phone orders and deliveries. If you've never coped with running a home before, it can be very comforting to know that a quick trip around the corner or a fast phone call will handle the laundry or produce a dinner in minutes. If you're trying to combine a job and home-making, conveniences like these can help avoid many a minor crisis.

☐ City living makes spur-of-the-moment fun much easier, too. Films, concerts, restaurants—whatever you enjoy when you go out together—are usually right there in your neighborhood or just a short bus ride away. Once again, couples busy combining career-making with homemaking may find impromptu going-out almost the only kind possible.

☐ You'll probably find a wider range of apartments-for-rent within city limits. While it's true that more and more rental units are being built in suburban and rural areas, most cities still offer you more of a choice.

☐ Public transportation in most cities is adequate and fairly cheap. This saves you the expense of buying and maintaining a car. And city bus fares usually run a lot lower than other means of transportation. Best of all, when you're using public transportation, you can project pretty exactly what each week's transportation will cost you. When you're coping with a brand-new budget, it's really helpful to have expenses like this nailed down.

Life in the suburbs or exurbs offers more than just scenery, however. You'll breathe less polluted air, worry less about street crime, enjoy a stronger sense of community in the suburbs. If commuting is involved, the fact that golf, tennis courts, swimming and winter sports are closer to home may more than make up for that extra traveling time. Suburban housing usually offers its own advantages, too.

☐ Rental apartments, where they are available, are usually cheaper in the suburbs than equivalent quarters in the city.

☐ Suburban apartments often feature some appealing extras, like larger and airier rooms, terraces or gardens, a swimming pool.

☐ If you're a confirmed car buff, parking, garaging and maintaining that car will certainly be simpler and less expensive in suburban areas. The same is true for motorcycles, incidentally.

☐ And—new homemakers—the suburban apartment is easier to keep clean! You just won't have the same amount of soot and dust that filters through city windows to settle down on sills and form a film on tabletops.

What kind of neighborhood do you like? While you're mulling over the advantages of city versus suburb, give some thought to the question of neighborhood, too. Each section of a city, each suburban area, usually has its own distinctive "flavor." To be happy in your new home, you ought to feel comfortable in your surroundings, find them congenial.

You may be the type who enjoys the adventure of fixing up a big old apartment in a tumbledown area—and also enjoys the saving in rent. Or this might strike you as a foolish economy. You may prefer an apartment building or suburban area where there are lots of other young couples for company. The question of companionship is worth thinking about, particularly if you enjoy community-oriented activities.

This question of flavor is more than a matter of whether or not an area is reasonably safe and well kept up. One young couple found a great "buy" in a rented apartment in a beautifully run but very conservative building. The catch? It was definitely not a

City or suburban living? Weigh the advantages of each before you make your move.

building where wearing jeans, carrying bundles through the lobby, or playing a stereo late at night were possible. In this case, the rent was cheap because the apartment was part of an estate. But the "flavor" of the building was all wrong for this couple and they moved as soon as they could.

Conservative, nonconformist, all one age-group or mixed young-and-middle marrieds—individual areas and apartment buildings come in many flavors. All that's important is that you both have some idea of the aura you like around you—and keep this in mind when you start actively home-hunting.

How much room do you need? "As much as I can get" is one way to answer this question. And, in fact, it's usually very near the truth for most new home-lookers. Although we've divided it into two topics, the question of living space is very closely related to how much you can pay. Usually, smaller quarters cost less than larger ones. If your budget is limited, you'll probably have to settle for less space than you'd really like. The only way around this problem is to look for quarters in an older apartment building or try to find an older house to rent or buy. Here, however, you may be faced with the problems of repairs, higher upkeep and a neighborhood that may not be ideal. In most cities, mid-rise apartments are cheaper than buildings with elevators, but don't forget—you're going to have to lug groceries and laundry up and down those stairs!

If you have some pressing need for a generous-sized apartment or house—if one of you works at home, for instance, or if you plan to start your family right away—it may be worth stretching your budget or settling for an older neighborhood to gain extra space. Otherwise, you'll probably settle for a 1-room studio, 1-bedroom apartment or small house. Given a choice between one large room and two smaller ones, take the two, unless the 1-roomer is large enough to be divided into several areas. Living together without ever being able to put a wall between you can cause a bad case of "cabin fever" in almost any twosome.

Smaller quarters have some things going in their favor, too. You won't need as much furniture. And you'll have less area to clean. But here's a note of warning: Although they're easier to clean, smaller quarters are usually harder to keep tidied up than larger ones. You really have to be pretty well-organized to keep them looking neat. Built-ins that you can put together yourself, furniture pieces that provide storage as well as seating or table space, pegboard "storage walls"—these can all help you make the most of minimal space.

You'll find some helpful hints on how to organize your space, and special space-making decorating ideas on pages 191 through 210 in this book. If you're not the born-neat type, however, this tidying-up problem is one you might just as well face before you start looking for quarters. After talking it over, you two just might decide to try for older-but-larger housing.

How much should you pay? There is really no easy rule of thumb to use in deciding what share of your income to allot for housing. Surveys of consumer finances have shown that if you are in a high-income group you'll allot a smaller share of your budget to rent or house payments than if you are in a lower-income group. Some experts on family management suggest that you allow 20 to 30% of your net income for housing. Others claim that the amount you can spend depends on how much you must spend for all your other living needs. In fact, they suggest you figure these needs out first and then work back to arrive at a realistic housing figure. This last really seems to be the most sensible approach.

Rentals and the cost of houses vary widely from one section of the country to another. Just to give you an idea of the range that exists, let's take the example of a 2-bedroom unfurnished apartment. According to real-estate ads in leading newspapers from each of the following areas, this is what you would find. Rentals in major cities on the West and East Coasts run up to 50% higher than rentals in the Southwest, up to 66% higher than those in the Deep South or Midwest. And those higher coastal rentals usually don't cover "extras" like swimming pools, tennis courts, carpeting and utilities. These are often included in your rent in those other areas. Of course, there are always lucky "finds" even in the hub of a megalopolis. If you run across one, you're entitled to feel smug. But don't bank on being lucky!

Other basic costs like food, transportation and clothing also vary from area to area. The best advice: Try to size up your area realistically; be a bit cautious about rent.

When you start thinking about how much you can pay, or want to pay, to keep a roof over your head, here are some of the facts you should think about before arriving at a specific figure:

CHECK:
- [ ] the general cost of living in your area
- [ ] how tight the housing situation is—the law of supply and demand will drive prices up where housing is short
- [ ] whether you'd rather scrimp on rent and have extra money available for other things, or vice versa

The one thing you must remember is that your rent per month, or your mortgage payments, will not be your only housing expenses. Even in a rented apartment, you'll have to freight your own telephone bills, for instance. Buying your own home? Taxes, insurance and other related costs have to be budgeted for. See

HOUSING EXPENSE
Your needs and the area you live in determine the share of income spent on housing.

page 18 for a specific breakdown on related costs for apartment-renting; check pages 36 and 37 for similar details on home-buying. But aside from allowing for these necessary expenses, there are other important reasons for trying to hold down your housing costs.

You want to be able to enjoy your new home. This means having enough money to furnish it attractively, to splurge on a steak or roast-for-two once in a while, to have friends in occasionally. No home is going to be a pleasure if you have to sit up nights worrying about how to pay for it. Also, if you've chosen an apartment or house in a neighborhood that's way over your head financially, your chances of making friends and sharing activities with your neighbors are going to be slim to say the least. If you both enjoy eating out occasionally—and most people do—that's another expense you have to allow for.

One more point about housing costs. In some areas (usually in the larger cities, where housing is in great demand), just looking for an apartment can be expensive. If you're tracking down leads on your lunch hour, it may mean taking taxis fairly frequently until the search is over. You may occasionally want to take friends to lunch to get their ideas and suggestions on how to go about looking or to see if they've heard of any vacancies. You might have to figure on laying out more than one month's rent as security, too (see page 31). While all these are one-time rather than regular monthly expenses, it's still money out-of-pocket. It's money you won't have in your budget as an extra cushion.

To sum it all up, the whole subject of deciding how much you'll pay for housing calls for common sense. It also calls for cooperation between the two of you in making the decision.

CHECKLIST ANY AREA YOU'RE CONSIDERING TO SEE "WHAT'S IN IT FOR YOU"

Even if you know the area quite well, and particularly if you don't, it pays to walk or drive through it once with your eyes wide open. Look for essential services and conveniences—the "availables" that make the difference between easy living and a daily hassle with homemaking needs. Look for "extras," too—entertainment facilities, special-interest shops, landscape features—things that will add to your enjoyment of the area. Be really hard-nosed and self-oriented about it. After all, you're the ones who have to live and pay rent there. Don't let other people's opinions affect your judgment. If your overall impression isn't good or if a lot of the services you want seem to be lacking, skip it. On the other hand, if it seems to offer most of what you're interested in, don't be dissuaded by others.

Before you start on this "let's be sure tour," think about the things you want to look for and jot them down! A written checklist can save you an awful lot of wasted time and energy. To help you get started, we've compiled a basic list you can work from. You may not agree with the order of importance in which we've listed the services and conveniences, but the list does cover all essentials you'll want to consider. You can copy our list and just juggle the order around, or make up your own list with this one as a guide. Once you have your checkpoints down on paper, however, stick to them. Compromise only if there's a reasonable alternative to what you've listed.

Don't depend on memory. Take your checklist with you!

Check: What Conveniences Are Available?

One or two of these you may be able to live without—most you'll want to have within easy reach. You'll miss them if they're not!

STORES
- [ ] supermarket or grocery
- [ ] drugstore
- [ ] dry cleaner
- [ ] shoe repair
- [ ] launderette
- [ ] barber shop, beauty salon

ENTERTAINMENT
- [ ] movies
- [ ] theaters
- [ ] restaurants
- [ ] sports facilities (list your favorites)

CULTURAL AND RELIGIOUS
- [ ] churches
- [ ] library
- [ ] museums
- [ ] community house
- [ ] adult education facilities

MUNICIPAL AND HEALTH
- [ ] police department
- [ ] fire department
- [ ] hospital
- [ ] medical care
- [ ] dental care
- [ ] ambulance services

CHILD CARE (IF NEEDED)
- [ ] day-care center
- [ ] public parks
- [ ] nursery schools

Check: What Are The Transportation Facilities Like?

Whether you train it, bus it or drive your own car, you want to be able to get around your area quickly and comfortably. You also want to be able to get to job or studies with a minimum of hassle, so these are all factors you'll have to think about:

PUBLIC TRANSPORTATION
- ☐ how frequent
- ☐ how crowded
- ☐ how expensive
- ☐ how lengthy a trip to job or school

PRIVATE TRANSPORTATION
- ☐ how crowded the roads are
- ☐ how expensive (tolls, gasoline bills)
- ☐ parking facilities available
- ☐ service garage
- ☐ how lengthy a trip to job or school

Note: It's a good idea to plan a "dry run" of either public or private transportation facilities and check out these lists for your-self. You might decide that you just couldn't take that subway crush every day or that the commute by car is too expensive, and start looking in another area.

Check: Is It A Safe Neighborhood?

This is worth checking out carefully, particularly in big cities and in many low-rent areas. Fear is an unpleasant companion.

SAFETY FACTORS
- ☐ Can you walk around the area after dark?
- ☐ Is there a high burglary rate?
- ☐ Is there a high crime-against-persons rate?

Note: If you know people who already live in the neighborhood, they're your best source of information. Otherwise, a talk with building superintendent/managers, local shopkeepers or the local police might answer these questions.

The safety factor is particularly important if you're both work-ing or studying. You may be coming home separately, after dark, *and* your home may be vacant for many hours during the day, a fact that makes it particularly vulnerable to robbery.

Check: What's The Pollution Picture?

Most large cities, and some suburban areas, have definite pol-lution problems and are a long way from solving them. However, some areas are making greater strides than others and it's worth checking out.

POLLUTION PROBLEMS

☐ Is there a factory or industrial facility nearby?

☐ Is garbage collected regularly?

☐ Are the streets reasonably clean?

☐ How noisy is the area?

☐ Do local buildings have their chimneys capped? (You'll live with a layer of soot over everything if they don't.)

So far you've more or less set the foundation for home-hunting. You've decided where you want to live, how much room you need, how much you should pay, and you know how to check out an area you're interested in. Along about now you're ready to get down to specifics. But you still may not be quite sure what kind of housing you really prefer if the choice is up to you. If you've settled on a suburb, both rental and "buy" situations may be available. Ditto for many cities. So what we've done in the next sections of this chapter is to cover most of the important information about all the major housing setups—renting and buying, apartment and house. Each situation is clearly headlined so you can find just what you're looking for. You'll find most of the information you'll need here.

We've also tried to cover it "as it is" in most parts of the country. There are always special-situation areas, of course, but in most cases you'll be aware of these localized problems if you live in, or are moving to, such an area. A summer or winter resort, for example, will have a very different rent or buy setup than will other places. There are special housing situations connected with special career fields, too. Military personnel, those connected with government projects (such as aeronautics research) and people in move-around businesses (like construction engineering) face very particular housing problems. Here, you'll get the best advice from those in your own field and from the company or agency for whom you work.

Apart from special situations like these, we've tried to provide good, useful, specific pointers about the most usual housing situations; we hope this information will help you choose a real-life home that comes close to matching your dream house.

SHOULD YOU RENT AN APARTMENT? HERE ARE THE PROS AND CONS

The practical advantages of renting an apartment when you're starting out are real and rapidly seen. You can sum them up in just two words: *cost* and *convenience*. You'll get less of the first and more of the second if you end up as "the couple in 5B." That is, it usually costs you less to rent an apartment than to buy.

And there's a high degree of convenience offered. There are disadvantages, too. But let's look at the bright side first.

These are the cost-cutters you have going for you—and they can help put a real glow of health on a slender budget over a full year or two:

☐ You're not committed to any large investment of capital when you rent an apartment. Usually, your rent ends up costing less-per-month than carrying charges and upkeep would come to if you bought.

☐ You can budget your housing costs almost to the penny because your rent is set for the period of your lease. Your heat and hot water (and sometimes air conditioning) are included in the rent. You have no real-estate taxes to pay, and some rentals even include gas and electricity. If you do have to pay for utilities, you can usually get a fairly accurate estimate of what they'll come to from the rental agent, superintendent/manager or local utilities office.

☐ You are in no danger of suffering a loss of capital due to the apartment depreciating in value. If the building does devaluate, that's the owner's headache, not yours.

☐ Your basic appliances (range and refrigerator) are supplied. Many of the new buildings feature dishwashers as well. And a lot of apartment buildings offer garbage disposals and laundry facilities for tenants.

And you get a helpful helping of conveniences, too. There may come a time when these won't seem quite so important. But for many starting-outers they're what tip the scale in favor of apartments. First and foremost, there's usually a superintendent/manager on the premises to cope with minor disasters like leaking faucets, stopped-up drains and appliances-on-strike. Of course, some superintendent/managers are more efficient and more cooperative than others. If it's at all possible, try to get a line on the disposition and know-how of yours-to-be before signing the lease. You can always ring a tenant's bell, explain that you're thinking of moving in, and pop the question. If the "super" isn't a gem, you'll hear about it!

Many apartment buildings have attractive gardens and landscaped areas—but you don't have to take care of them. Also, there are no porches or stoops to sweep, no storm windows to put up or take down, no furnaces to cope with, no basement to be cleaned out. Right there are hours of extra time added to your year. Apartment buildings come with incinerators or garbage-collection arrangements built in, too. This also can be a great convenience and a time-saver!

At the end of your lease, you're free and clear; you can move away or stay, as you wish. Often, you can arrange an apartment-swap right within the building if you need larger quarters. Of course, there'll be an adjustment in rent—upward!

Unless you live in a very tight housing area or sublet, you can count on fresh paint, refinished floors and an overall cleaning. Even with a sublet, you can sometimes insist on a painting or at least have it done by the landlord at a reduced rate.

The drawbacks? You're not full "master of the house." No matter how long you live in it, a rented apartment never becomes "yours" in terms of ownership. This has definite disadvantages, which some personalities feel more keenly than others.

☐ The rent you pay out is gone forever. In financial language, "you are not building any equity." If the building increases in value, all you gain is a higher rent. If you own your own home, however, and decide to sell, you *may* get a price for it that is higher than what it has cost you in mortgage payments (including both principal and interest).

☐ Apartment leases do impose certain restrictions. For more details on these, see the section on leases further on in this chapter. Also, you are somewhat dependent on the goodwill of your landlord. This can sometimes be a problem.

☐ Essentially, you are sharing a building with other people. You have to take their rights into consideration when it comes to keeping pets, playing your stereo, and giving late-night parties. Even if none of this presents a problem, some couples just don't like the idea of sharing a building with others. This can be a difficulty if you have always lived in a private home.

☐ There is one more objection that can be made to apartment-renting. If your business or hobby requires extensive alterations to rooms, an apartment is probably not for you. Or if you like caring for a garden and generally "puttering" around a house, you'll feel deprived in any apartment setup.

HOW TO TRANSLATE APARTMENT-FOR-RENT ADS

Reading the "for-rent" ads in most newspapers can be a dizzying experience. You may end up wondering what's happened to your eyeballs and to your understanding of the English language! For instance, here's one you almost have to see to believe:

70-80's E. WHY PUFF STAIRS?

75 E. "Elev 2" a throbber	$225
82 (Lex) "Georgian Elev twnhse"	$190
81 E. "Award winning elev 2"	$197

Fortunately, most apartment descriptions are not this open-ended, although the abbreviations and some of the terminology can be confusing until you get used to them.

Apartment terms vary from area to area—but they all apply to the number of rooms in the apartment, not to the square footage. A "studio" is a 1-room apartment the whole country over. But in one city it might be barely large enough to swing a cat in; elsewhere it might be large enough to house an elephant. Also, unless otherwise specified, all apartments include a bathroom, which is not counted in describing the number of rooms. Kitchens, on the other hand, are included in the room-count. Apart from the size of the rooms, certain terms are fairly standard.

APARTMENT-RENTAL INFORMATION

Terms	Translation
An efficiency, studio, bachelor or 1½-room apartment	All mean about the same thing. You'll get: • a large room • a small separate kitchen or a pullman kitchen against one wall • a bathroom
A 2½-room apartment	You'll get: • a large room • a small separate kitchen • a sleeping alcove or small dressing room • a bathroom
A 3½-room apartment	You'll get: • a living room • a separate bedroom • a separate kitchen • an extra dining alcove or foyer as part of the living room • a bathroom
1-, 2-, or 3-bedroom apartments	You'll get: • a living room and kitchen • the number of bedrooms specified • a kitchen • a bathroom (unless otherwise specified)

Terms	Translation
Duplex and triplex apartments	You'll get: • a 2-floor or 3-floor apartment
Garden/patio apartments or efficiencies	In the suburbs this means: • an apartment in a 2- or 3-story building that is built around a courtyard or pool. Sometimes, rather misleadingly, it just describes a standard apartment building in a suburban-greenery setting. In the city this means: • a ground-floor apartment with access to a backyard.
Luxury (or "executive") apartments	This usually means: • an apartment in a new high-rise building that features a doorman, elegantly furnished lobby, full service in terms of a resident superintendent/manager, and usually, some extra features such as a roof-pool, sauna, gymnasium or tennis courts.
Brownstone apartments	This is a city term and means: • a 4- or 5-story private house that has been broken up into several apartments. All apartments above the ground floor will be walk-ups. Depending on your point of view, these apartments have a lot of charm or are just renovated old buildings. They are usually quite expensive.

Fitting the furniture to the apartment: a warning! Because room sizes and wall space vary so from apartment to apartment, don't rent or buy your larger pieces of furniture until you've signed your lease. In fact, it's best not to buy really oversized pieces until you're settled for good or are sure they will fit through doors and into elevators. If you're inheriting furniture, measure before you move it! If it won't fit into the elevator, very few moving men will huff and puff it up the stairs for you.

WHEN DO YOU START LOOKING FOR AN APARTMENT?

CHECK:

☐ If it's an unfurnished apartment, are you planning to furnish it before you move in?

☐ Do you have to vacate present quarters by a certain date?

☐ Are apartments hard to find in your area?

☐ Are you an optimist or a pessimist?

☐ Do you like to have things "settled" or are you the "last-minute" type?

Seriously, these are all factors that more or less affect the one big question: "When do we start looking?" Obviously, if you plan to have all or most of your furnishing/decorating done before moving in, you'll want to take possession sooner than if you plan to "camp out" in the apartment while collecting furnishings. Again, you may live in a "tenants' market," and apartment-hunting may consist of picking up the local newspaper, checking out the ads that look interesting, and signing up for the one you like the best. In other areas, you might have to figure on several months of pavement-pounding and hide-and-seek with apartment ads before finding anything even possible in terms of price and comfort. In fact, you might even have to make the wedding date and plans contingent on finding that apartment. These are the two extremes, of course. If your situation lies somewhere in the middle, these timing tips may be helpful.

The 1st and the 15th—check these dates. Most leases start as of the first or the fifteenth day of each month and end on the same dates, so these are the big move-out times each month. More apartments become available. Even if you start looking around the 15th of one month, you may be able to take possession, or move into the apartment, by the first of the following month.

April and September are move-out months. Many leases, particularly long-term ones, start at the beginning of May or October, and you get a lot of moving out in the preceding months.

One month's notice—at least. Most leases require this, so you can be reasonably sure of being able to move in within a month once you find an apartment that will become vacant. Of course, some people give more than the required notice, so you can start looking more than one month ahead of your target date for actually moving in.

An extra month's rent—to be sure. You may want to pay an extra month's rent if you find something you like ahead of time and want to cinch it down. On the debit side: This is an extra expense. On the credit side: You can start moving your things in sooner, can furnish in a more leisurely way.

If time is no problem. You can put your name down on a list for an apartment in a new building not yet completed. Caution: You run the risk of the building not being finished on time! Some existing apartment buildings also maintain future-tenant lists, but this is not nearly so usual.

Armed with this timetable and some knowledge of your own plans and local housing conditions, you should be able to set up a rough starting date for your apartment search. Good hunting!

HOW TO BAG THAT APARTMENT: TRIED AND TRUE TECHNIQUES

"Luck and legwork"—that's how one junior executive described his hunting technique in a city famous for its housing shortage. It's a bit general, but it does include the one major element involved in any search for an apartment. Even where housing is relatively easy to find, you'll have to do some looking around to find what you want at the price you want to pay. The choosier you are, the harder you'll have to look. And in some areas, you'll grab what you can get and count yourself lucky if it comes anywhere near being what you want or need.

There *are* standard approaches to apartment-hunting that work! You may be able to think up a few new ones to add to our list, but these are the ones you should certainly try first:

For-rent ads—how to make them work harder for you. Pick the local paper that seems to have the largest and widest selection of apartment-for-rent ads. Then jot down the areas in which you're interested in living—or those that you definitely dislike. If you're home-hunting in a new town, it will save time to circle these locations on a local map. Then check each newspaper ad that sounds interesting against these "target areas." Another time-saver: Using your map, try to memorize the names of major streets in these sections. You'll be able to cross off a lot of ads without checking back with the map each time.

When you're making a phone appointment to see an apartment, try to get answers to these questions—they'll save a wasted trip.

☐ How much is the rent, if not specified in the ad?
☐ Where is the apartment located—near the elevators or stairway? Near the incinerator?
☐ What floor is the apartment on?

☐ Is it in an old or a new building? What facilities does the building offer?
☐ When is the apartment available?

Get to the real-estate section ahead of time, make the call first, be first in line to see the apartment—that's often what's involved in snaring quarters in the bigger, more congested cities. The Sunday papers generally have the largest listings of apartments. Often, you can secure the real-estate section from a friendly newspaper stand on Friday evening or Saturday. This puts you one jump ahead of the mob. Another way to get a head start: Many metropolitan papers put out early daily editions—Wednesday's edition would be available by about 11 PM on Tuesday, for instance. These editions are well worth a late trip to a newsstand!

Early editions give you a head start!

Word of mouth—tell the world you're looking. Tell your relatives, friends, business or college acquaintances. Tell local shopkeepers, your banker, "baker and candlestick-maker." The wider you spread the word, the more people you have going for you. Since this is the most effortless way to find an apartment, you might just as well make full use of it. The drawback? It may take some time, time you may not have.

Don't forget the printed word—notices and ads. Take advantage of typewritten notices. Post them on the employees' bulletin board at work, or in the rest rooms. Check stores in your local shopping center. Many have bulletin boards for just this kind of thing. Or ask a store or dry cleaner to post one in a window. If it's a small town, ask about putting one up in the post office.

If the situation is really tight, you might try running your own apartment-wanted ad in a local paper. Usually the cost is not too heavy. Be sure to check, though, and also—be wary of listing your own phone number. You might collect a lot of crank calls. If possible, give a post office box number or see if the paper has an arrangement for receiving replies.

Try a street-to-street search—it can pay off. If you have one or two areas that are real favorites, it may pay you to tour through them looking for vacancy signs, for new buildings that are accepting rentals, for a friendly local shopkeeper who knows of a vacancy coming up.

In big cities like New York, Chicago, Los Angeles—check with building managers and doormen. They usually know who's planning to move out almost before the tenant himself does. And they often know well before the owner or real-estate agent! But beware of those who ask for a small fee. You can easily be cheated—and you're perpetuating a system that makes it tough on everyone.

If you're really well-organized, you might combine this apartment-hunting with your checklist-the-neighborhood tour. If you decide that you like what you see, it will save you a second trip to the area.

Use an agent if time is tight. It's sometimes worth it, even if you end up paying a fee. In some areas, you may not have to pay at all (it will be paid by the owner) or you may split it with the owner. Just be sure you know what you're getting into, though. Most importantly: Be honest with the agent about how much you are willing to pay for rent. Otherwise, you waste his time and yours. Even an agent can't guarantee results in tight housing areas. You may end up having to call him every day. And when he does have something for you, he may have notified several other clients as well. Also, most agents tend to handle the more expensive types of apartments and buildings. What are the advantages, then? They *do* take some of the look-load off you. And —if an agent comes up with a winner, he'll handle the lease for you. This includes acting as go-between in any hassles you may have about painting, decorating or repairs.

You'll pay the agent the first month's rent and security. After that, usually, you'll pay rent directly to the landlord or his agent. The agent's fee usually reflects the ups and downs of the apartment market. It can range from a flat registration fee to one full month's rent or 10% of the first year's rental. In some cities, you'll find apartment-locator services. These work on the same basic principle, but they usually advertise as a "free service to tenant" or "with no finder's fee."

See page 31 for definitions of "rent" and "security."

CHECKLISTS, CHECKBOOK AND AN OPEN MIND: BE PREPARED—BRING THEM WITH YOU!

It does happen—sometimes you're expected to vote "yes" or "no" on an apartment right while you're standing there because the next taker is poised in the hallway ready to grab said apartment. If you're the type who likes to make leisurely decisions, don't panic! A nice-guy landlord or building manager should give you a little time to talk it over, take measurements, get the "feel" of the place. But in tight rental areas, he may not hold it for you if you leave the premises. At the very least, he may ask for a deposit which is not returnable if you decide against the apartment. When faced with this kind of "executive decision," say "no" if you have any doubts about the apartment at all (unless, of course, you're absolutely desperate, in which case you might just as well have agreed to take it over the phone!). This brings up another point about apartment-hunting.

If it's at all possible, look together! You'll save time in the long run. You'll both see the apartment under the same circumstances. You'll get a feeling for each other's reactions. You can talk it over after you've seen it. If you *have* to give an instant answer, you can decide on it together. When your looking is a little more leisurely and involves several trips back, you can split these up. But shared first impressions are really valuable.

Face it—you may have to put down advance deposits on other items such as gas, electricity and a phone. So check that checkbook balance and make sure it will take the strain! If you usually keep a balance just big enough to cover normal weekly or monthly expenses, you may have to swing funds in from your savings account.

CHECKLIST BOTH BUILDING AND APARTMENT: WILL THEY FILL THE BILL YOU'LL BE PAYING?

Once again, it's a question of knowing your own needs and measuring them up against what the building, and the specific apartment you're looking at, have to offer. Making these lists may seem like a lot of work, but it's better to do it now than spend time later regretting your choice. And remember—a checklist is only helpful when you have it with you. Once you've made your lists, group them in a notebook or folder and take them along when you look!

Check: What Necessities And Niceties Does The Building Offer?

Apart from a general impression of whether or not the building is clean and well kept, there are very specific things to look for and ask about. Most probably, you'll be shown through the building by the superintendent/manager. If not, ask to meet him. Find out whether he's assigned to the building full-time or whether he covers several buildings. Another thing to check out carefully is the security system. Most cities require that the front entryway be adequately lighted at night. What other security measures exist? Is there an intercom and/or a security locking system? Ask to see the laundry facilities. If they're adequate and cleanly kept, life will be a lot pleasanter. Ditto for garbage facilities. Most newer buildings have some kind of incinerator installation. Ask whether it's a full system or a "dump spot" arrangement. If it's the latter, make no mistake: You'll have roaches. If it's not an incinerator building, ask how often garbage is collected and just how it's taken care of. Look at the condition of the halls as well as the lobby. Many a building will splurge on front-lobby decorations and skimp on cleaning and waxing hallways. And don't forget to ask about storage facilities and mail-and-package distribution. As time goes on, you'll have some things to store; you'll want to make sure they're safely kept. As for mail and packages—you may both be out a good part of the day and you won't always want to rely on your neighbors for deliveries. Many buildings have a mail-and-package room.

There's something else it's best to find out about before signing a lease: How does the management feel about children and pets? This is essential if you're thinking about starting a family in the near future or have stepchildren who will be visiting. If you're a pet lover it's important, too.

Now for the "extras." If you have a car, check on the garage facilities. Are they inside or outside? What's the cost? If not available, is there a commercial garage nearby? What are the street parking regulations? When it comes to those much-advertised pools, saunas and recreation rooms, there are a couple of hard-nosed questions to ask. Are they included in your rent or will you have to pay a separate membership fee? At what hours are they open? And if this kind of thing doesn't interest you at all, then skip any building that has them. Inevitably, they'll up the rent you'll be paying!

Obviously, you wouldn't want to write all this down on a checklist. Once you have these factors in mind, just jot down a quickie reminder list like this one:

QUICKIE LIST: FOR THE BUILDING
☐ superintendent/manager available
☐ security systems
☐ laundry facilities
☐ garbage disposal system
☐ condition of halls and lobby
☐ storage and mail facilities
☐ attitude toward children and pets
☐ garage
☐ pool, sauna, recreation room

What Is The Apartment's Livability Rating?

Turn yourself into a real snoop once you're inside the apartment. People aren't going to go out of their way to point out disadvantages. It's up to you to find them. Basically, you want to look at the apartment from two viewpoints: What is it like structurally, and what's in it?

From the structural point of view—you'll want to check on walls and windows. What shape are the walls in? Do they need plastering, painting? If this work is needed, will it be done before you move in, and who'll pay for it? Also check to see that you have enough wall space for essential items of furniture like beds, a bureau, a sofa. Some apartments can be awfully cut up. When it comes to windows—are there enough of them, is there cross-ventilation, do they open and close easily? What's the view like? You can get pretty sick of staring out at a blank wall or fire escape. A rear apartment will be darker than a front one—but it will also be quieter and it's usually cheaper. And you can sometimes brighten it up with a gay color scheme. A word of advice: Always try to see an apartment during daylight hours. Its faults show up more clearly. While you're checking windows, look to see if the apartment is air-conditioned. Is it central or are there individual window units? If the latter is true, they'll end up as part of your electricity bill. Electricity? How are those lighting fixtures and outlets, by the way? Are there enough of both?

Don't forget closets. How many are there? How big are they? What shape are the floors in? Can you get by with small area rugs or will you have to cover the whole floor with carpeting? Whip out your tape measure while you're there (you should have it with you) and take a few basic measurements. Now close your eyes and open your ears. What do you hear? Traffic noises, the neighbors' voices, sounds of the elevator going up and down? If you find them disturbing, better pass up the apartment—these are the sounds you'll live with.

Now check what's in the apartment. What are the major appliances like? Is there a dishwasher? Take a look at the kitchen cabinets and decide if they're adequate. Turn on a water faucet. Does the "hot" run hot and the "cold" cold? Do they drip? Flush the toilet, run the bathtub. Low pressure or gurgling pipes can be a real nuisance. Look at the shades and/or blinds, too. They should be clean and in good repair. If carpeting and draperies are provided, be sure to make a note of the color scheme. Do you find it pleasant or a pain? Can you work around it? In some new buildings different apartments have different color schemes. You may have a choice.

Of course, there's always a chance that you'll find an apartment that falls far short of providing the items we've listed but has some special feature you feel makes up for its lacks. Maybe it has wood paneling, a working fireplace or an absolutely beautiful view. The compromises you make are purely personal. But try to look at those compromises realistically. Project how you'll feel after six months or a year of inconvenience. Then make your decision. Another word of warning: If you're looking at an apartment that is still occupied by a tenant, try to visualize it empty of furniture. That decorating scheme may cover a lot of flaws. Or it may be so different from your own taste that you're put off by it. This may take X-ray eyes, but it's worth the effort.

**QUICKIE LIST:
FOR THE APARTMENT**

Structural:
- ☐ walls and wall space
- ☐ windows
- ☐ air conditioning
- ☐ lighting fixtures and outlets
- ☐ floors
- ☐ noise
- ☐ basic measurements
- ☐ existing damage

What's in it:
- ☐ major appliances—dishwasher
- ☐ kitchen storage space
- ☐ plumbing
- ☐ window shades/blinds
- ☐ color scheme

A TYPICAL LEASE

The front names the leasing parties, the length of the lease and the amount of the rent. Read the back carefully—it usually spells out all the rules and regulations you're agreeing to. Note that we show the simplest lease form. Some run several pages long. You should read *all* the pages before signing!

A Lease

Made and executed between ....
Landlord, of ....
and ....
Tenant, of ....
this .... day of ...., 19...........

In consideration of the rents and covenants hereinafter expressed, the said Landlord has Demised and Leased, and does hereby demise and lease to the said tenant the following premises, viz: ....
....with the privileges and appurtenances for and during the term of
.... from the .... day of ...., 19..........
which term will end ....

And the said Tenant covenant that he will pay the Landlord for the use of said premises, the ....rent of .... Dollars ($...........................), to be paid ....

And provided said Tenant shall fail to pay said rent, or any part thereof when it becomes due, it is agreed that the said Landlord may sue for same, or re-enter said premises, or resort to any legal remedy. ....

The .... agree to pay all .... taxes to be assessed on said premises during the term of this lease ....

The said Tenant covenant that at the expiration of said term he will surrender up said premises to the Landlord in as good condition as now, necessary wear and damages by the elements excepted ....

In witness whereof the parties hereto have hereunto set their hands and seals the day and year first above written.

.... Landlord

Witness: .... Tenant

YOUR LEASE: IT'S BINDING, SO KNOW WHAT YOU'RE SIGNING!

Ignorance
of the
lease is
no excuse!

When you take a look at your first lease you may wonder if the landlord wants you as a tenant at all. The document seems to be full of don'ts. And the do's smack more of chores than pleasure. *The most important thing to remember about any lease is that it is written to protect the landlord's rights, not the tenant's.* Nevertheless, once you've signed it you are legally bound to adhere to all the stipulations it sets forth. So it pays to go over it carefully and understand what each and every paragraph means. If you have any questions, ask before you sign. Also, have a lawyer check over the lease. It's cheap insurance against a possible mistake. Nine times out of ten you'll sign a standardized lease form because most localities have them. They do vary from one part of the country to another, however. It pays to check the proper city authorities to see if such a standardized lease is available and to pick up any booklets they may have on tenants' and landlords' rights for that community. Also, in many areas, tenants' groups are forming to act as a helpful clearinghouse for advice and information.

Even on a standardized lease, you can make changes if both you and the owner agree to them. But make sure they are written on the lease and initialed by both parties. Never settle for verbal changes. And make sure that changes are worded exactly. Example: You ask the landlord to paint the kitchen cabinets and fix the leak under the sink before you move in. He says yes—perhaps even adds a note to the lease stating that "general repairs will be made." Absolutely useless, legally. The notation should spell out exactly what work is to be done, that it is to be done to your satisfaction, and should name a date by which it is to be completed. Sounds like nit-picking? What isn't on that paper doesn't have to be done!

In the few instances where a lease is not required (if you're moving into a very small building or into an apartment in someone's house), be sure to talk out what is expected of each side. Make certain you agree on all points before you move in. If possible, try to get some sort of written agreement that sets forth the major points of your arrangement.

The lease form reproduced on the previous page will give you an idea of what one looks like physically. But we repeat: If you can get hold of an actual lease form and read it through before you start apartment-hunting, you'll be that much ahead of the game. It will give you something to check your own lease against. Wherever the two don't agree, ask why. You may get some information you might not have thought to ask for—and it may turn out to be pretty important to you.

HERE'S AN OUTLINE OF POINTS TO WATCH FOR IN YOUR OWN LEASE

Use this list as a map to guide you through the jungle of jargon that most leases feature. These are the usual points at issue.

Check The Big Four First

RENT

How much is it, and how is it to be paid? Check clauses referring to non-payment.

Watch for this one: a clause stating that the landlord can raise your rent if his taxes go up. In rent-controlled areas: Check to see that the rental charged is the legal rate.

RENEWAL

Check for an automatic renewal clause, i.e., the lease renews itself unless you notify the landlord otherwise. The clause may require as much as three months' notice, in writing!

SUBLET

A clause you want and the landlord probably doesn't. Without it: You can be held for the full rental if you move before the lease expires. If a new tenant can be found immediately, the owner may release you from this obligation, retaining the security to pay for repainting. With it: You find the new tenant, subject to the landlord's approval; are liable for damage or rent default; the landlord retains your security. Or the landlord may find his own tenant, release you from the original lease, and return your security.

SECURITY

Usually it's required; usually one month's rent, sometimes two. This must be paid in advance, cannot be used in lieu of the final month's rent. Your security is returned after you vacate your apartment, which must be left "broom clean." The owner will deduct the amount he thinks fit for light damage, above normal wear and tear. For severe damage, most states prohibit a landlord from retaining the whole security and state that the matter must be settled in court. Don't confuse security with rent paid in advance; they're two different things.

Clauses To Discuss Or Play By Ear

ACCESS

Note this: The landlord has access to the premises, with due notice, any time within reasonable hours of the day. If you change locks, give him or his agent a duplicate key.

> Generalities
> are made
> to be
> broken.

LIABILITY OR DAMAGE

It's best to consult a lawyer if a claim arises due to lease clauses dealing with liability for injury or damage, fire or theft. Rules vary from city to city, can be interpreted in many different ways.

REPAIRS

Study this part of the lease carefully. State laws vary widely; individual landlords can insert specific clauses into a lease. Here are the basics to look for in most, but not all, cases: The landlord is responsible for keeping roof, exterior walls, plumbing and wiring, grounds, hallways and entrances in good condition. Ditto each apartment with regard to hidden defects (such as faulty wiring) not obvious to the tenant, or general wear and tear on appliances. The owner is also responsible for any violations of local housing laws.

If damage is due to the tenant's willful negligence or carelessness, the tenant must have the repairs done and pay the bill. Document any existing damage to avoid having to pay for it later. Sometimes all of the above, including keeping the apartment safe and sanitary, are passed on to the tenant and specified in the lease. Where the landlord fails to make agreed-in-writing repairs: Some states allow the tenant to withhold the rent; others to pay rent into an escrow fund; others to make repairs himself and bill the owner or deduct this amount from the rent. The tenant can also go to court.

CARPETING

Usual clause: Cover at least three-quarters of floor space with carpets or rugs. In reality: It depends on how soundproof the building is and what floor you're on. On the ground floor you may not need any. If the building is very badly soundproofed, even three-quarters covered may not be enough.

MUSICAL INSTRUMENTS

One of the oddballs: You can't *practice* voice or an instrument in an apartment. But you can *play* an instrument (or presumably sing in the bathtub). Two ifs: If it doesn't disturb the neighbors, and if it's during specified hours. Question: Would you rather hear Leontyne Price practice or your neighbor sing?

ALTERATIONS

There's much variation among states and individual landlords. For rented property: Alterations are anything glued, nailed or cemented to floors, walls or ceilings that may cause damage when removed (e.g., wall paneling or floor tile, but not a free-standing room divider). Permission to make alterations: Get it in writing; check on what happens when you move. Often alterations become the property of the landlord. Or the owner may insist you restore the apartment to its original condition. Rare case: the landlord who'll agree to alterations and pay for removing them. Usually, the owner specifies "no alterations" so he has no headaches.

PAINTING AND DECORATING

Usually, the landlord will repaint the apartment every two or three years, will also polish/sand floors. If yours isn't due for a painting: The owner may go halves on the cost of the paint or refund the whole amount if you do the work yourself. To substitute dark colors for standard apartment pastels, you may have to pay extra and agree to restore walls to a lighter shade before leaving.

Wallcoverings, too, will have to be removed and walls left in original condition. Nailholes: You'll have to fill them in since, technically, all leases ban driving nails into walls. But who can live without pictures and mirrors?

PETS

Most leases: No pets allowed. You have to horse-trade it out with the landlord. Most are reasonable, some are not. More agree to cats and birds than to dogs.

PESTS

The landlord is usually not responsible for bugs, vermin or insects on the premises. Some may provide free exterminator service.

UTILITIES

If utilities are included in the rent, make sure this is stipulated in the lease. Otherwise, if the building changes hands, you could have trouble.

There's lots to check in a lease, right? And most of it's unfamiliar territory. So—make sure! Make a double-check list and go through it to see that you haven't forgotten to eagle-eye anything important.

QUICKIE LIST: TO DOUBLE-CHECK THE LEASE

- ☐ rent
- ☐ automatic renewal clause
- ☐ sublet
- ☐ security
- ☐ repairs
- ☐ alterations
- ☐ carpeting
- ☐ painting and decorating
- ☐ music
- ☐ access
- ☐ pets
- ☐ pests
- ☐ liability or damage
- ☐ utilities
- ☐ swimming pool—if one is involved, make sure rules for its use (including any possible fees) are attached to lease

Personality Profile Of Landlords: How Pleasant And Pliable Are They?

"Not very," some who've had a bad experience will say. Others sail through a lease with not a ripple of "landlord trouble." A landlord's profile-in-public probably has a lot to do with what the real-estate market is like at that time and place. He'll be a lot pleasanter if he's got extra apartments to get off his hands than if they're in demand!

Taking On A Sublet: Wise Or Foolish Move?

Sublets are a quite-common situation in sections of the country that have a rather transient population. Under certain circumstances they can be desirable, offering these advantages:

If you're looking for a short-term arrangement, it's often better to live out the remainder of a lease than sign up for a full-term one. This is particularly true in areas or buildings where two- or three-year leases are usual.

Very occasionally, you can pick up a real deal in terms of the cost. If neither the original tenant nor the landlord can find a sublessee who will pay the full rent on the apartment, the original tenant may settle for accepting less than the original rent from you. He himself then makes up the difference to the landlord.

Watch out for these two disadvantages—first, make absolutely sure that the sublet is legal. This means that the original tenant has the right to sublet and that the landlord agrees on you as the incoming tenant. *Always* pay your rent to the landlord or his agent, never to the tenant himself. You have no guarantee that he'll pass it on! Secondly, face the fact that you may not get painting or repairs done as you would on an original lease. Often this can be worked out, but sometimes not.

What About Renting A Furnished Apartment?

Here you may or may not have a lease. In any event, you'll be responsible for the rugs, draperies and furniture. Any damage done beyond "reasonable wear and tear" you must pay for. So look things over pretty carefully. Then list any existing damage that you don't want blamed on you and have the landlord or his agent sign it.

Suppose You Decide To Rent A House?

In general, this is much like renting an apartment. You can rent furnished or unfurnished. And you will have a lease. There are some additional considerations, however.

You can arrange a straight rental or a rental with an option to buy. Sometimes your rental will apply toward the purchase price. An option to buy usually raises your rent because the owner is, in effect, taking the house off the market until you decide.

Other questions you want answered: Are you responsible for the upkeep of the house, including major repairs? Are you responsible for the upkeep of the grounds? Will the landlord furnish the major appliances? Who will pay the utility bills?

IT'S SOMETHING SPECIAL: BUYING YOUR OWN HOME

For many people this is the dream come true—owning their own home. No matter what shape it takes, how much it costs, it's always a big investment—of funds, time, interest and emotion. This is one step you really can't afford to stumble over. So read up, ask questions, become as much of an expert as you can before you actually start looking at homes-to-buy. *Right off the bat, let us tell you that this section is not a primer on "How To Buy A House." That subject is a book in itself.* We'll try to give you a thought-provoking overview of what's involved—some idea of the areas you'll have to investigate and of how to go about it. With this as a starting point, you can check your local library for books and articles on specific aspects of home-buying. You'll have some idea of what questions to ask your banker, your lawyer and personal friends. And you can begin doing some basic arithmetic.

Today, variety spices the home market. Don't decide on a house before surveying the whole scene. There are several different types of housing you might be interested in buying. You might even consider an apartment. Your choice includes:

- townhouses
- patio homes
- clusterhomes
- houses
- mobile homes
- apartment condominiums
- apartment cooperatives

We'll give you some pointers about each of these. But first we'll cover some of the main factors that are involved in any type of buying situation.

First, The Matter Of Mortgages And Mortgage Money

Very few people pay for their homes in cash. Usually, they finance part of the purchase by means of a loan called a mortgage. What exactly is a mortgage? A conventional mortgage means that you borrow a certain amount of money from a lending institution and that you put up the home that you are buying as security or collateral. If you default on your payments, the lending agency has the right to take over the property. Basically, there are three different types available to you:

☐ the conventional mortgage extended by banks and other lending institutions

☐ the mortgage insured by the Federal Housing Administration (called an FHA mortgage)

☐ the mortgage guaranteed by the Veterans Administration (called a VA, or GI, mortgage)

Essentially, the money still comes from local banks or lending institutions on all three. However, interest rates on the FHA and VA mortgages are generally lower due to the fact that the government agency involved will guarantee payment of the mortgage loan to the lender in the event of the borrower's default. This is not always attractive to the lender because of (1) the substantial paper work involved for the lender, and (2) the lower yield. FHA will normally insure up to 100% of a mortgage and VA, 90%.

Where do you go for a mortgage? Savings and loan associations and mutual savings banks are most often the sources for home mortgages. Commercial banks can generally offer rates on home mortgages that are competitive with savings institutions. However, since such loans are not their chief area of business, commercial banks usually limit these to existing customers of their bank. If you have life insurance, you can also approach your insurance company about a loan. A good way to get mortgage advice: Ask your realtor or agent to suggest local lending institutions that, in his experience, are most cooperative. Always try to check more than one source. Interest rates do vary from one institution to another, even at the same time.

Figuring up how much you can pay? A word of caution: Even with a mortgage, you will still have to come up with a cash down payment. The amount will vary. The larger the down payment the less your mortgage will cost you in the long run. However, don't strip yourself bare to lay out that cash! You should retain some savings to cope with emergency expenses.

When you're estimating how large a mortgage you can carry, it also pays to be conservative. Remember, your monthly mortgage payment is not your only housing expense. You face what are called total carrying charges and this is what you'll really have to come up with each year until the mortgage is paid off.

How do you figure your total carrying charges? They include:

☐ your monthly mortgage payment

☐ other housing expenses like insurance, taxes, repairs, maintenance, and operating costs such as utilities

---

MORTGAGE POINT SYSTEM

Sometimes discount points are used to increase the cost of FHA and VA loans. A "point" is equal to 1% of the amount of the home loan. The buyer pays one point; the seller's points are set by the lender.

Basically, you want to figure out what these two combined figures amount to. There are general rules of thumb that help you do this. You can check the actual arithmetic shown below.

Rule: Take a home purchase price that sounds possible. (We've worked it out on the basis of $30,000 for easy figuring.) Then subtract the amount of the down payment. (Figure 10% as a rock-bottom *minimum*. You may have to pay 25% or even more, as this figure varies locally.) Now take 1% of that remainder. The figure you get is roughly what you can expect to pay *each month* for that house for all your housing expenses.

$30,000 purchase price
10% of $30,000 = $3,000
$30,000 minus $3,000 = $27,000
1% of $27,000 = $270
$270 = monthly carrying charges on
$30,000 house

How do you figure your monthly mortgage payment? Your monthly payment depends on the rate of interest you are paying on the amount borrowed and the length of time of the mortgage. It also includes paying back (or amortizing) that loan. A look at the chart below will give you an idea of mortgage payments-per-month based on amounts of $1,000 and $10,000.

Don't forget: On the longer-term mortgages, you are paying less per month, but you are paying more for the loan in the long run. Some actual figures? At 8% on a $10,000 loan for 15 years, you will repay a total of $16,602.60. The same loan for 25 years will cost you a total of $23,157.00. All you do is multiply the monthly repayment figure by the number of months involved (180 and 300 in this case) and see what you get!

MONTHLY MORTGAGE PAYMENT RATES

Terms:	7½%	8%	9%	10%	10½%
on $1,000					
and $10,000					
15 years	$ 9.28	$ 9.56	$ 10.15	$ 10.75	$ 11.06
	92.71	95.57	101.43	107.47	110.57
20 years	8.06	8.37	9.00	9.66	9.99
	80.56	83.65	89.98	96.51	99.86
25 years	7.39	7.72	8.40	9.09	9.45
	73.90	77.19	83.92	90.88	94.45
30 years	7.00	7.34	8.05	8.78	9.15
	69.93	73.38	80.47	87.76	91.50

Note: This is a sample range. You may pay a higher or lower rate.

Suppose you want to figure backwards. You know how much you can afford to lay out each month. Now—how large a mortgage will that pay for? Take the terms you might reasonably be offered (interest rate and length of time). Check our chart for the monthly payment on $1,000 at those terms. Now divide this into the amount-per-month you estimate you can pay and multiply that figure by $1,000. You'll find that payments of $200 per month for a 20-year mortgage at 9% will support a mortgage of roughly $22,000. If you could get a 20-year mortgage at 8%, your $200 per month would freight a loan of roughly $23,800. (Bear in mind that this is mortgage payment only, not your entire monthly housing cost—see pages 36 to 37.)

Be aware that some mortgages have a penalty clause that adds to the cost if you pay off the mortgage ahead of time. Try for one with no prepayment penalties or very mild ones. Due to upward-mobility moving or business relocating, chances are you'll pay off that loan ahead of time. That's what the statistics show, anyway. The mortgage arrangements for mobile homes are usually a little different. We'll talk about those in the mobile home section.

Doing your homework: check out the construction. Obviously, you want a soundly built home that will be dry and warm in winter, reasonably cool in summer, and require a minimum of repairs. You should look over any house you're interested in yourself. Check to see that the foundation is free of cracks, the basement dry, floors even and the attic properly ventilated. Walls should be smooth; windows and doors should be set squarely, and open and close easily. Check for signs of roof leaks. Rap your knuckles against an inside wall. Is the house reasonably sound-proof? Are the closets and storage space adequate? Ditto the heating and hot water unit—what type of fuel will you use?

If you have any doubts about the house, have it checked over by a professional. There are appraisers and licensed professional engineers who will give you a written report on its condition. Their fee is usually not exorbitant. Ask your broker, a bank dealing in mortgage loans, a local home-builders' association, or check the classified phone book, to get the name of such a professional. In the margin is a checklist of basic house checkpoints which a professional report or your own observations should cover. Don't forget: The appraisal you'll get from a bank or insurance company will state only whether or not the house is worth what you're paying. It won't give you a point by point checking of the house.

Basic Figures That May Help You Interpret A Report
These will give you some idea of whether or not the home you're considering has adequate basic services.

**QUICKIE HOUSE-LIST:
MAKE SURE
THESE ARE CHECKED**
- [ ] foundation
- [ ] basement
- [ ] floors
- [ ] walls—interior, exterior
- [ ] insulation—soundproofing
- [ ] roof
- [ ] windows and doors
- [ ] closets and storage
- [ ] heating
- [ ] plumbing
- [ ] electrical system

The heating system—its capacity is rated in British Thermal Units (BTUs). One BTU equals the amount of energy needed to raise the temperature of one pound of water by one degree—from 39 to 40 degrees Fahrenheit. Figure 50 BTUs per square foot of heated living area (average wintertime heat-loss in northern United States).

Room-unit air conditioners—capacity is rated in tons. One ton supplies 12,000 BTUs an hour. You need one ton of capacity for each 500 square feet of floor area.

A septic tank—a 3-bedroom house requires a septic tank with a capacity of 900 gallons.

The electrical system—with all the electrical appliances in home-use today, home wiring should be capable of handling 240-volt current with a strength of 150 amperes.

Some Open Talk About "The Closing" Or "The Settlement" Or "Taking Title"

This is the moment when ownership actually passes into your hands. This has been a real horror experience for many a home-buyer who was running tight on cash. Be prepared to have it cost you! Here are some of the things you may pay for:

- [ ] your down payment (minus any deposit you've made)
- [ ] title insurance
- [ ] mortgage service charge
- [ ] hazard insurance on the property
- [ ] property survey
- [ ] appraisal report
- [ ] prepaid interest
- [ ] tax on mortgage

Some of these costs are set by law, some by custom, some are up for grabs. To give you an idea of why some of these additional cost items are necessary, we'll explain three in more detail.

[ ] **Title insurance** includes a search of the mortgage and tax records of the premises to be purchased. This insures the lender that his mortgage lien is not primed by any other, and insures the purchaser against any other claims of ownership. Prior liens (i.e., back taxes) must be paid by the seller or buyer of a property at the time of closing. The cost for this search and insurance is normally based on a percentage per $1,000, multiplied by the amount of the mortgage loan. (In addition, the title agent is usually paid a small gratuity.)

□ **The mortgage service charge** is normally a flat fee charged by a lending institution and/or its law firm to close a number of mortgage loans, as in a housing development or condominium, where the documentation is standardized.

□ **Hazard insurance** on the property insures the purchaser and lender against (most commonly) fire and malicious mischief, but not against force majeure. All lenders will require hazard insurance; depending on the location, insurance against flooding, hurricanes and earthquakes is normally excluded from such policies.

Note: There's no general rule that governs the total charges. One survey showed these costs varying from an average of $165 in one area to almost $2,000 in another. But remember: You can ask what the exact costs will come to at the time you make the appointment for the closing! Just announce that the settlement can wait until this advance statement of charges is in your hands, in writing. Also remember: a certified check for the down payment balance!

Just a word of warning! Real-estate law is a legitimate, full-time branch of the profession, and the importance of an attorney so trained is often overlooked by prospective home-buyers. The help of such an attorney is especially essential where purchase of a condominium or co-op is concerned because of the enforced togetherness imposed on the unit owners. See pages 42 through 44 for more details on these situations.

SUCCESS STORY: MOBILE HOMES, CONDOMINIUMS, COOPERATIVES, TOWNHOUSES

Suppose you're interested in owning your own home but don't want to take on the responsibility of a house just yet. You have several other choices open to you. Each has its advantages—and some drawbacks. We'll hit the high spots of both.

Mobile homes are an alternate idea in housing.

What is a mobile home and what is it not? This is an alternate concept in housing—a completely factory-built home designed for year-round living. It has a structural frame or chassis which supports the walls, floor and roof. If you choose carefully, you can select one that looks very much like a conventional house. *But*— the mobile home has an underneath running gear which provides wheels and brakes for transportation. This means that it can be towed to the dealer's, or to your own prepared homesite, as a unit. Once at the site, it is anchored to sturdy concrete piers and—

there's your new home! Complete with appliances and furnishings. Don't confuse a mobile home with a trailer, however. "Mobiles" are designed to be installed at a site and lived in there. You cannot tow one behind your own car. They are not recreational vehicles.

Some facts and figures on mobile homes—there are several varieties available in a wide price range.

☐ SINGLE-WIDES—the most usual is a 12-foot-wide by 65-foot-long unit with 744 square feet of living space. Some 14-foot-wide units are now being manufactured, as more and more states allow passage of these extra-wides over state roads.

☐ EXPANDABLES—made with telescoping additions that add 60 to 100 feet to the room in which they are located.

☐ DOUBLE-WIDES—built and towed separately, joined together at the site to make a single living unit. They can be separated for towing to a new location.

There are some essential "extras" you'll have to buy. These include steps with handrails for every outside door, skirting to conceal the wheels, supports or piers that act as the foundation. Over-the-roof ties are desirable everywhere, essential in high-wind areas.

The typical mobile home offers a living room, equipped kitchen, separate dining room or dinette, one or two bathrooms, up to three bedrooms, hardwood cabinets and closets. It will be centrally heated and have a hot water heater. It will include both built-in and freestanding furniture, floorcoverings, curtains and draperies. If you prefer, you can usually get a mobile home unfurnished at some reduction in price. You can also buy optionals like air conditioning, dishwashers, garbage disposals, laundry equipment—even fireplaces, trash compactors and intercoms.

Once you own it, where do you put it? You can sometimes position your mobile home on your own private plot of land. Many rural areas and smaller towns permit this, most larger cities don't. So remember to check local zoning restrictions. The other choice: to locate in a mobile-home park owned by the dealer or in one of your own choice. These vary widely in desirability, so again, check before you buy!

Mobile-home construction and design standards are improving all the time. More than 65% of the homes produced conform to American National Standards Institute requirements (ANSI A119.1). These models carry a blue and silver seal. In terms of design, the old "trailer look" is rapidly disappearing. More designers are getting interested in mobile homes, and their influence is becoming apparent. One manufacturer's line was designed in conjunction with the Frank Lloyd Wright Foundation. More of this can be expected.

What are the basic advantages? They're easily summed up. The purchase price is usually well below that of a site-built home. Their "package" aspect (fully equipped and furnished) lets you project your costs almost exactly. They can be moved to another site and are usually easier to sell than a house. This flexibility is often an advantage. Many different types of layouts are possible. Mobile-home manufacturers will be happy to send you brochures showing the different floor plans they can offer you.

What are the disadvantages? Aside from the fact that you may not care for their rather functional design and that you are sometimes required to live in a mobile-home park, there are two financial drawbacks. First, mobile homes have a much more rapid rate of depreciation than you would expect. This doesn't mean that they literally fall apart. It means that on the open market they tend to be thought of in much the same way as a secondhand car. One banker estimated that within the first year a new mobile home depreciates 20 to 25% of its wholesale cost, up to 10% of its remaining value for every year thereafter. In a sense this is an unfair depreciation rate, but it is a fact so keep it in mind.

The financing arrangements work against you, too. Very often you must finance a mobile home as you do a car or a boat—that is, under a chattel mortgage. The Federal Truth-in-Lending laws now require lending institutions to publish the true annual rate of interest on such mortgages—and it's usually a whacking 12% or more! This doesn't stack up very well against home mortgage loans.

Very importantly, in a home mortgage loan, your monthly payments keep reducing the principal of the loan. So you are paying interest on a constantly shrinking amount. With a mobile-home chattel mortgage, the monthly payments *do not* reduce the amount on which you are being charged interest—although, of course, you are repaying that loan. This is what accounts for the difference in interest rates between conventional and mobile homes.

Condominiums and cooperatives: other choices in housing.

Condominium, cooperative: what's the difference? For the buyer, the most obvious difference between these two types of ownership lies in the fact that you can get a bank mortgage on a condominium apartment and you can't on a cooperative. What's the reason? Essentially, when you buy into a cooperative building you're buying shares in a corporation. The builders, usually, have already financed the building through a bank mortgage of 70 to 80% and raise the rest of the money by selling equity shares in the corporation to tenant-owners like yourself. This means that you own X number of undivided shares in the corporation, but you do not own the apartment itself. In return for your shares, you are assigned an available unit of your choosing. You are responsible for your share of maintaining the total building as well as your quarters.

Note: New York State has a special law allowing commercial banks and savings and loan associations to make co-op loans. In other states, you have to arrange a personal loan if you cannot pay for the co-op in cash.

Advantages to a cooperative? A certain portion of your monthly payments are tax deductible (this is not the case when you rent an apartment). Also, the blanket mortgage, which the co-op developer or association can obtain, can be refinanced (useful in event of default) and the corporate (group) ownership will always be looking to its own best interests in maintaining the operations and condition of the premises and related facilities. Then too, you and the other owners have the say-so about any plans for the building. If you all agree, you can redecorate the lobby or put in a sauna—and assess yourselves the money to pay for it. The disadvantage: If the corporation defaults in its payments because some individual tenant-owners have defaulted, it affects the occupancy and title-to-property of *all* the cooperative owners. This rarely happens, but it's always a possibility.

In a condominium you receive a deed to your apartment—in effect, you actually own a specific amount of steel, brick or concrete enclosing a certain area. You can apply for a mortgage on this property just as you can for a house.

A warning: Condominium purchase is infinitely more intricate than co-op buying. Because there is no corporation (each dweller being owner of only a specified area—with the exception of common facilities), each purchaser is on his own when it comes to obtaining mortgage financing and dealing with the developer.

Advantages to a condominium? Apart from the financing, there are two other pluses. Part of your monthly payments are tax deductible. And—since each unit is owned and financed separately, a default in payment by one tenant does not affect the others. Some people also like the idea of owning a specific apartment. Psychologically, they feel that it is more "their own" than a comparable apartment in a cooperative.

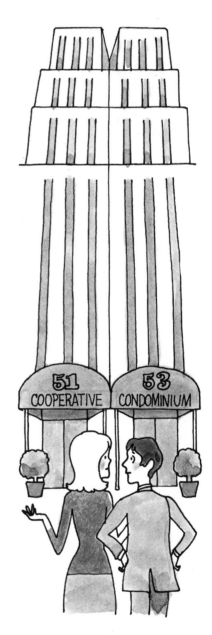

The disadvantages: The land on which a condominium is built might only be a leasehold and the related recreation and common facilities may be leased to the condominium association by the developers. In each case, the purchaser is not directly an "owner." He can face substantial increases in costs to preserve his rights. Because a condominium is not managed as a corporation and all ownership is separate, built-in obsolescence may become a problem since, usually, no common fund will exist with which to make repairs, replace items and/or effect changes to the premises.

Suppose you're trying to decide between two apartments—one a co-op, one a condominium. How do you decide which is the better buy for you? The best advice is: Consult the experts. Both condominiums and co-ops have some built-in problems. These are different from those encountered in single-home ownership and an experienced real-estate source (broker and attorney) should always be consulted prior to the closing. Show him the contracts and documents connected with each. These can be very complicated indeed! Tell him what your financial picture is and let him decide, and explain, why one may be a better deal than the other. While most cooperatives and condominiums are honestly conceived and organized, there are some buyer-bewares around. Unless you're a real expert, you may not spot the money-traps buried in the legal jargon and fancy figure work.

Townhouses—what does this new type of housing offer? Townhouses combine some of the advantages of both houses and apartments. Basically, they consist of a series of 2- or 3-story living units adjacent to each other, with a common wall between every unit. *But—the purchaser acquires title to his home and to the land on which it stands.* Unlike condominium apartments, no other townhouse can be built above or below you. With a townhouse, all the traditional chores of homeowning—chores like lawn mowing, snow shoveling, outdoor maintenance—are contracted out by the owner association. Today's townhouses often feature basements, garages, setback entrances, parcels of land for patios, and landscaped open areas. If you don't object to neighbors close by, townhouses can offer a pleasant and convenient alternative to owning a conventional house.

Patio homes and clusterhomes are other new varieties of own-your-own-land housing. With both, homes are set close together to make more land available to the community for open-space parks and recreational areas. Once again, these open areas are maintained by owner associations to relieve individual owners of this responsibility.

With a
townhouse:
You own
your own
land.

HANDBOOK ON
How to Move

We want our "starting out" advice to be as useful to you as possible. So—when we were putting our heads together about what needed to go into this book, we talked to a lot of newly marrieds and a lot of "old hands," too. Certain topics kept coming up as being particularly valuable info to have. Our sources said things like: "I wish I'd known about this," or, "I looked in all kinds of books but couldn't really find what I wanted," or, "I finally found what I needed to know, but wow! Did I have to do a lot of digging!" Well—how much nudging did we need?

Right away, we decided to take those "problem" areas and do a real job on them. The result? You'll find a special Handbook section in each chapter of this book. And each Handbook covers one of the areas our sources mentioned as being of particular interest or as being particularly hard to find out about.

High on the list of "needed to knows" was the problem of moving. And particularly the problem of do-it-yourself moving. One woman recited an epic disaster of her cross-country trip with a hired trailer. Neither she nor her husband had known about the payment arrangements for this kind of thing. They hadn't checked out their car properly before starting the trip. They didn't really know how to pack up a trailer. So—there was a last-minute scramble for cash, they had to stop for several impromptu repackings, they suffered through a major car breakdown. A whole number! Granted that this was a basket-case situation. But in milder forms, it's not uncommon. Well, we really dug into the topic for you and this Handbook on How to Move is the result.

We hope it will give you pointers on how to handle whatever type of move you're faced with—just across the street *or* across the country. Read it through, perhaps make notes as you go, and rely on the fact that the information is as accurate as digging and checking can make it.

TEST YOUR KNOW-HOW ON THIS PICTURE QUIZ

How many moving do's and don'ts can you identify in these pictures? Look them over, then read through the nuggets of know-how on the following pages. Chances are you'll end up so full of new information you'll want another crack at the quiz.

This Handbook brings you the advice of working moving men, home economists, house-and-home editors—a wide range of experts on "how to move." Basically, much of their advice boils down to the advantages of proper planning, preparation and packing. Easy enough to say—but how do you go about doing all this? Read on and find out. Whether you're moving your share of a "singles" apartment, transporting donations from family and friends, or coping with a full-scale move, this kind of know-how can make it much easier on you. There's a lot to remember in even the simplest move, so we've supplied a number of checklists to help reduce the brain-strain. You'll find plenty of pictures, too, to help show you just how to go about packing various household items as well as efficient methods of loading up your car or a rented trailer or truck. Should you decide to use a professional moving service, you'll find some useful advice on how to plan this kind of move as well. We hope we've given you most of the pointers you need for a successful (and relatively painless) move.

STAY AHEAD OF THE MOVING GAME!

One of the cardinal rules of moving is: Do as much as far ahead of time as possible. Don't let the chores pile up into a last-minute scramble. Plan out what you have to do, make a realistic schedule for yourself, then hold to it. You can use the timetable below as a starter. We've tried to cover all the important things. If you have any special "to do's" of your own, just add them to this list.

Four to six weeks ahead of time—in fact, the sooner the better—start making these basic arrangements and phone calls:

☐ Contact telephone company; arrange for service. Phone installations can lag behind orders. Give as much notice as possible. Call the telephone company's business office or go in person. A deposit may be necessary if you have never had your own phone before. Telephone "extras" available include: color phones, wall phones, princess models, jacks for plug-in phones, extra-long cords, push-button dial phones and, of course, extension phones. Remember, you pay for these niceties. Some costs (installation fees and extra-long cords, for instance) are one-time charges. For others, you'll be billed extra each month. Ask what the charge will be; think about whether or not it's worth it. The telephone representative will name a date for installing your new phone. Note it down on your calendar so you can arrange for the serviceman to be let into the premises. Give over-the-phone instructions about where the instrument is to be placed. Better yet, be there yourself or ask a friend to stand in for you.

☐ Remember, you'll have a change of address. Notify the post office; fill out a change-of-address form for forwarding mail. **Caution:** If you check "forward all mail," you'll pay additional postage on second class and bulk items. Maybe you'll want to settle for "first class only."

☐ While at post office: Pick up free change-of-address cards. Mail them to friends, business associates, firms with whom you do business. Most computerized bills (credit cards, insurance payments, bank loans, etc.) have an area on the return envelope or on the bill itself to indicate change of address. Use it as you're paying bills.

☐ Magazines want six weeks' notice. A bound-in change-of-address form to fill in is included in each issue. Usually, you're asked to paste on your subscription label as well. Allow four to eight weeks for the new address to become active.

☐ Visit your branch bank. Notify them of your address change; transfer savings and checking accounts to branch near your new address. Or close out accounts and transfer to another bank.

(Usually, the bank will handle most of the transfer details for you—a big saving in time and effort!) Arrange for new joint accounts if you've decided on these. Have a bank loan? Make sure the loan department also has a record of your address change.

☐ Notify your personnel department. If you're continuing on at the same job, make sure personnel has your new address. Note for newlyweds: Your "married" status may change your withholding and medical insurance arrangements. Personnel will have all necessary information and forms.

☐ Notify superintendent/managers of your moving date. Many buildings require an appointment ahead of time to avoid conflicts with other move-ins or move-outs.

☐ Ask stores for a delivery date. Make sure someone is available to accept deliveries of furniture and other packages too large to be held at post office or in building package room.

☐ Check local motor vehicle bureau. Find out proper procedures for changing your address on license and car registration. Yours may be one of the states that can penalize you for failure to notify.

☐ Start clearing out closets and cabinets. Most people are amazed at how much "junk" accumulates. Be ruthless. Give it away, throw it away, but don't move it!

About two weeks ahead of time, you'll be heading into the home-stretch. Now's the time to defrost the refrigerator, clean the oven so you just have a quick wipe-off at the last minute. There are other plan-aheads you can do now, too.

☐ If necessary, arrange your utility "turn off" and "turn on" and/or the date for your billing to end. A deposit may be needed if you've never had an account before. For a house: If you heat as well as cook with one type of fuel, there may be a lower rate for this heavier consumption. Check it out.

☐ Start packing books, dishes, glasses, out-of-season clothing—all items you can daily-live without.

☐ Arrange to board out pets with friends or a kennel while you move. If they're coming with you, remember a traveling case. You may want to "board out" plants, too, and pick them up after you're moved. They don't take to life-in-a-van. Moving long distance? Give plants away; you'll all be happier.

☐ Bring in car for a checkup. Particularly important if you're using it to move with.

If you're heading into an apartment, make sure that you understand what the landlord will do about painting and repairs. If he's

FOR NEW WIVES
Remember to include your new name when you notify your bank, your personnel department and the motor vehicle bureau of your change in address.

painting for you: Have you selected your colors, set a painting date? Always check on the job after it's finished. Sloppy work or wrong colors? Complain now, not later.

If you're heading into a house—does the water have to be turned on? Have you notified the water company? What about garbage collection? It pays to arrange this ahead, too.

Type up this quickie version of the lists we've just given you and stick it in your bureau mirror, beside the phone, anyplace you'll see it often.

QUICKIE LIST: WON'T GO AWAY TILL IT'S ALL CHECKED OFF!

☐ Have you called the phone company?
☐ Did you pop by the post office?
☐ Were those change-of-address cards you were busy writing yesterday?
☐ Magazines and bills—you did fill in the change-of-address section!
☐ Don't break up with your bank—see them today.
☐ Forget personnel and they may forget you!
☐ Talk to the superintendent/manager today.
☐ Call and ask when they'll deliver the chair.
☐ While you're up—phone the motor vehicle bureau.
☐ Let's start those closets and cabinets!
☐ Don't forget your refrigerator and range.
☐ The utility companies want to hear from you.
☐ START PACKING!
☐ Maybe your mother will take Rover for a while.
☐ Remember the car checkup!
☐ Movers contacted or van rented?

The day before you move! Panic—you'll never get it all together. Why didn't you pay more attention to the list? Relax—it's usually not as bad as it looks. True, you may have to abandon perfect packing in favor of less exquisite scoop-and-stuff methods that will fill up those boxes fast. There's greater danger of breakage and loss but it can't be helped now. Time to call on friends, too. Every pair of hands is valuable. Look at your list, see what isn't done, then start assigning jobs all over the place. Just remember —only *you* can do the bank and banks have a habit of closing earlier than other firms. Need cash for Moving Day? You probably will. Buy traveler's checks—they're not that expensive and they're much safer than charging around with cash. Don't worry, you'll get it all done. But planning makes it easier.

PACKING LIKE A PRO

In addition to this advice, check local movers for the booklets on packing and moving that they may distribute. If you have any specialized items like a very large mirror, one or two really good paintings, a mobile or a piece of antique furniture, it might be wise to check your phone book. There are specialists in packing and moving fragile objects or works of art. Otherwise, plenty of newspaper and sturdy cartons should see you through. Plus some expertise like the following:

Turn yourself into a pitch-out artist; go through your apartment like a disposal machine and get rid of anything that's too damaged, too dirty or too disagreeable to use in your new quarters. Keep asking yourself: Will I use it? Would it be cheaper to replace it than move it? Be honest and you'll save packing time and moving money.

Stock up on the packing supplies you need. These include gummed labels, felt-tipped marking pens, masking tape, loads of newspaper, perhaps a roll of corrugated paper or bubbly plastic if you're packing dishes and glasses.

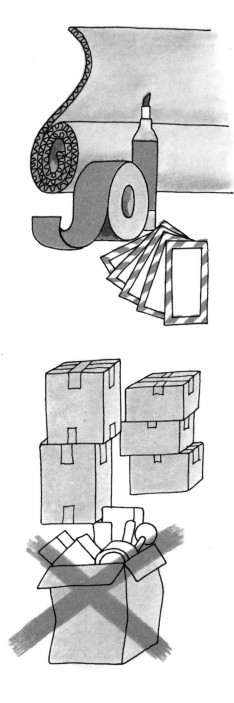

Make sure box tops don't bulge, but lie flat so boxes can be stacked one on top of another. Tape them tightly closed with masking tape. Boxes from the liquor store are better than cartons from grocery stores or supermarkets because they're usually heavier—and liquor stores open theirs neatly with a razor and leave the tops hinged on. Start collecting these as soon as you know you'll be moving.

Other types of containers—inexpensive trunks are handy hold-alls for fragile items. Use them as end tables, bedside tables, extra seating afterwards. Some moving experts suggest taking drawers and using them as separate "holders." Others advise against it, say drawers sometimes burst apart. If you opt to use them, don't pack them brimful of very heavy objects.

Don't pack books in anything larger than a liquor carton or the box will be too heavy to lift. If you're moving a long distance, consider sending books railway express. It's cheaper than vanning them because they're both bulky and heavy. Remember: Weed out as you pack. If you haven't read it and don't want to, or can't even remember how it landed on your shelves, pitch it, don't pack it! Pack records the same way. Weed out here, too.

Pack food in cartons, not shopping bags—the bags burst too easily. Don't pack spoilable foods or liquids at all. Ditto makeup. All three can be "messies."

Convertible sofas: remove the mattresses when you get ready to take them out of the building. Then tie the frame with rope or tapes so the sofa won't fall open while being carried. More on how to move them in the section on packing a truck (pages 55 to 56).

Take light bulbs out of lamps and try to resist the temptation to pack them. If you must bring one or two along, bring them in the car with you or in your personal luggage.

You can't pad mirrors too heavily—few people realize how fragile they really are. Just setting one down too heavily on the edge of a stair step can shatter it. Professional movers' padding can be rented. If you're moving an expensive mirror yourself, the padding is worth pricing out.

Dressers and desk drawers: tie them tightly so they won't fall out. Or take them out and carry them separately (this makes extra trips, however).

Leave clothing on hangers; tie ten hangers together. You can lay one or two groups of hangers flat out on a blanket, fold the blanket up over them, and lay them on the top of the load in the car or truck. Or stick a broom handle from window to window in the back of your car and hang clothing on this makeshift "closet bar." Wardrobes take up too much space for cars or small trucks.

Rugs: roll and tie. But beware! If they're so long you have to fold them in the car or truck, they'll take up an awful lot of room. You might have to figure on a special rug run.

Dishes, cups and glasses: use lots of paper. Stuff crumpled sheets into cups and glasses before wrapping each in additional paper. Lay a small, lightly crumpled piece on top of each plate before further wrapping. Pack plates in center of cartons; place cups and glasses in the corners. Or fill the corners with soft things like washcloths, socks, stockings, underwear. They'll fill in empty space and help cushion plates against possible bumps and jolts.

Kitchenware and appliances: stack and stuff. The more things you can nest together the better—smaller bowls and pots in larger ones; kitchen knives and utensils in the taller containers; securely taped spice boxes in the smaller containers. When packing cartons, put the heaviest items at the bottom, the lighter on top. Fill in the corners with more small, soft things.

Sheets and towels make good stuffers to layer in between flat, fragile things like pictures and mirrors, and to roll up other "delicates" in. And—you're managing to pack up the sheets and towels at the same time!

Birds, fish, reptiles: The cage or tank menagerie is better left behind if you're moving any distance. For short hauls, empty fish tanks to one-third full (fish will get adequate oxygen as long as there's wide water *surface* exposed to the air). Take tanks or cages in the car with you or "up front" in the truck. If you decide to leave them, find homes for them before you go! One apartment building manager nearly died of fright when he uncovered a box left in the hallway by departed tenants and found himself eyeball-to-eyeball with a large, round python. This was inhumane for both super and snake.

Furniture legs: take them off when you can—off tables, sofas, beds. It makes them easier to carry through doorways, helps prevent damaging or breaking them.

Stereo components: consult the experts in the shop where you bought them or call the local manufacturer's representatives for advice on how they should be packed. Always carry them on the front seat with you, or under the seat, where they're protected from harm.

Mark each carton. As you close it up, mark on the outside what room it's going into (kitchen, bedroom, living room). You might also indicate what's in it: "kitchen—dishes" or "kitchen—pots," for instance. This makes unpacking much easier.

Try to group all the packed cartons in one place, as close to the front door as possible. They'll be easier to move out. And your chances of forgetting one are lessened.

Save one carton for things you'll want to unpack immediately— two towels and washcloths, a change of clothing, the coffeepot, coffee, a couple of mugs, two forks and spoons. These are the things you'd probably be packing last, anyway.

MOVE-IT-YOURSELF:
SOME HELPFUL HOWS AND WHYS

When it comes to a do-it-yourself move, the first thing to decide is whether or not it's a good idea at all. This usually depends on how much stuff you have to move and how far you have to move it. If you're traveling any distance and need a hired truck or van, the chances are you won't save as much as you think. But if you're just changing neighborhoods or are trading suburb for city, it can be worth it. You'll be able to move on your own schedule, there'll be less chance of the stuff getting lost, and it'll probably cost much less. But it's hard work and things can get broken.

Here's the easiest move of all: You have a couple of cartons, an extra lamp, your stereo equipment and the cat. All of it goes in your own car. If you have to, you make a second trip. No real sweat for anyone.

But suppose you also want to move a convertible sofa, a bureau, maybe a washing machine. One answer that's becoming popular is the combination move.

Combination moving: Good in mid-rises and high-rises which have the problem of stairs and elevators. Here, you move the smaller stuff yourself, hire a professional to handle the heavy pieces. This kind of gives you the best of both situations. It's particularly useful in cities, where moving can be more of a problem all around.

Facts/figures: renting a truck or trailer. They're available for rent in all sizes by the hour, day or week. Usually, the larger trucks are in better shape than the smaller ones. If you're renting a small one, look it over pretty carefully; check wheels and brakes. Also, reserve well in advance if you're moving during a peak season. Otherwise, you may not get the size truck you want. Companies tend to advertise the smaller, cheaper sizes, but actually have fewer of them on hand than of the larger, more expensive models. If you're renting a trailer, always check to see whether or not the hitch is included in the cost of the rental or if it's an "extra." Also, make sure that your car can take the hitch.

One-way rentals are usually calculated on set mileage and a given number of days. Round-trip rentals charge you on an hourly or daily basis, plus mileage. You also pay the gas, state taxes or fees, tolls, parking and insurance. Always check to see what the renting company's liability covers for collision, loss or damage. Check your own insurance for coverage of household goods and personal effects. You may need a special floater to cover the load. Check with your insurance agent if there's any question.

You'll have to pay in advance the total estimated amount of the trip, plus a deposit that you'll get back (less any additional charges) once the truck is delivered at your destination. At least one major truck-rental company will also give you a refund for unused mileage on one-way rentals. Most will accept any insured credit card. This includes all the major bank and charge cards. Remember: You can also rent most types of moving equipment like dollies, hand trucks, ropes and pads. And large cartons and wardrobes, if you need them.

How To Load Your Car, Trailer Or Truck More Efficiently

First bit of advice—you're way ahead of the game if your own car is a station wagon or if you have the use of one. For a short-distance move, you might even consider renting a wagon. It can considerably reduce the number of trips you make. And here are some other time- and step-savers:

☐ When you're estimating how large a truck you need: A small power truck will take 1½ rooms of furniture. Less than that? Use a trailer or station wagon. More? Use one of the larger models.

☐ Try to park your car or truck as close to your front door as possible. Ask a friend to function as "truck watcher." This will prevent stuff from being stolen, also means you can double-park if you have to.

☐ As a general rule of loading: Put the heaviest pieces in first (toward the front), the lightest last. If the load shifts, it will then move further *into* the truck rather than back out.

☐ Make sure that the load is stabilized inside your car or truck so it won't shift. Treat the inside of the vehicle as though it were a packing carton. Wedge things into the corners and around the sides of the load. If your own stuff won't fill the space, use rented moving pads and torn up cartons—or try to borrow some old blankets or bedpads from friends.

☐ Don't put fragile things under heavier objects. Keep them toward the top of the load. Again—wedge them tightly so they won't shift!

☐ Stack pictures and mirrors against the sides of the truck or trailer. Then put heavy objects against them to brace them upright. Or place paintings over the top of the load, but not mirrors!

☐ Beds go on top of the car or truck, securely tied. Turn the soft side of the box spring toward the roof.

☐ Slide the mattresses into the center of the truck; put mirrors or pictures between them. Nervous about those beds on the roof? If your truck is large enough, you can slide the beds inside it, soft sides in. Then pack around the legs.

☐ Refrigerators and washing machines—think over carefully. If they have to go up or down flights of stairs, it might pay to have a professional move them. Otherwise, see if you can rent a "reefer dolly" to help slide them down stairways.

☐ To move out that convertible sofa, lay a mat or a thick blanket flat on the floor. Flip the sofa onto its side, on the mat. Now use the mat as a dolly. Drag it along the floor and the convertible will slide right along with it. Beats using a dolly because there's less chance of the sofa slipping and you don't have the width of the dolly to bother about. Caution: Don't pull the mat across cement. It will get too ripped up. If you can't remove the sofa legs, flip sofa onto its side as quickly and smoothly as you can to avoid cracking off those legs.

☐ To get the convertible into the truck, let a mat hang out the back like a skirt. As you shove the sofa up into the truck, the mat will slide along under the sofa and make the shoving much easier.

☐ Tables go into car or truck upside down so you can pile stuff on top of them.

☐ Tie bicycles to the back of the truck or put 'em "up top" if you have room. Another idea: If you're moving within the same city, ride them over to your new home a day or so before The Move and arrange to leave them there. Make it an occasion—bring lunch and picnic on the way!

☐ The well-dressed mover covers up to protect against bumps, bruises, scratches. The costume includes long pants, a sturdy long-sleeved shirt and gloves. *Very important:* Never wear sneakers! They provide no protection should you drop something heavy on your foot. Instead, wear a heavy boot or work shoe, preferably with a tread-sole.

☐ To warm up those lower back muscles: Do 25 of these bend-overs before you begin lugging stuff around. The exercise: Place hands on hips; with shoulders back, bend forward and out as far as you can; straighten up and repeat. Those back muscles are the slowest to warm up and they take the brunt of the work. So it pays to pamper them a little. Even if you're not lugging the heavy pieces around, just the bending and lifting involved in carrying out the lighter cartons and "knickknacks" can make itself felt.

Trailer/truck: it's a different kind of driving than you may have been used to. First of all, check your route. Some highways are closed to trailers or trucks. Check out any special rules and regulations that may apply and make sure you meet them all. Your local motor vehicle bureau will give you the information you need.

Ideally, you should take any rented rig for a dry run around the block before loading up and taking off. You'll get the feel of the machine and you can make a last-minute check-out on brakes and lights.

CHECKLIST: THE SAFE-NOT-SORRY TRIP
☐ Do you have your important papers with you? Driver's license, registration, traveler's checks, insurance policies—they should be in the car with you. Ditto jewelry and other small valuables.

☐ Have you checked the tires, the gas and oil? How about the spare? Is it in good shape, filled with air?

☐ Have you got a basic tool kit with you? This includes a jack that works!

☐ Have you got your handyman items with you? Flashlight, screwdriver, hammer, pliers, scissors, first-aid kit, paper towels and tissues—they might come in handy on the way. And you'll probably want them when you get there.

Using A Professional Mover: What's Involved?

We'll give you a brief overview of the professional-mover situation. For more details, check your library and a paperback bookstore for both books and consumer reports written specifically on moving. Here are some of the basics it's helpful to be aware of:

☐ Try not to move at the peak season—Memorial Day to Labor Day.

☐ Always ask several companies for estimates—they're free. Ask for both time and cost projections. Also for the number and type of cartons needed. Most companies charge for these.

☐ Make sure the estimator understands how much, and what, is to be moved. Write up an inventory list for him or show him what's going.

☐ Ask about extra insurance—cost and availability. Most companies will only assume a minimum liability for damage. You have to pay for extra coverage. Ask your insurance agent for advice.

☐ Try to arrange for a morning move. The men are fresher and this fact alone can save you time and money. Be very wary of evening moves. The van may not show up at all.

☐ Think twice, and then a third time, before you take an "iffy" item with you. Professional moving is expensive. The more things you move the more it costs!

Paying for your move: prepare ahead. Moving companies won't take credit cards or personal checks. It's certified check, money order or cash only! Have it with you—allow 10% over the written estimated amount. In some areas, the men may expect to be tipped, too, and this is an added expense. If in doubt, ask beforehand. A wise word: Know exactly where you want the larger pieces of furniture placed. Movers will put them where you want them—but indecision can be expensive when you're paying people by the hour!

ABOUT TIPPING
It's illegal to tip in moves that cross state lines. Moving intrastate? Check your state's regulations. Tipping may be illegal here, too.

A reliable moving company: how do you find one? The best way is to get a recommendation from someone who has actually used their services. Check this list for other ideas:

☐ Check out the classified section of your telephone directory.
☐ Try to choose a company that has been in business a long time.
☐ Check references with the Better Business Bureau.
☐ Ask superintendent/manager for names.

Note: Always check the classified listing of a company against the regular phone book. You may find that they are actually located out of town and you'll end up paying extra travel-time charges.

If you are involved in a "company move," you probably won't have to pick up all the moving costs. The company may pay it all, including having your packing done professionally. Make sure you understand what you are responsible for.

Don't Overlook These Don'ts!

☐ Don't pack important papers, jewelry or other small valuables in with other "shippables." Put them in a briefcase or manila envelope and transport them personally.

☐ Don't pack inflammables—paint, cleaning fluids, oily or greasy rags, aerosol cans. Get rid of them before you go. But remember—never dump items like this down an incinerator! Leave them out where they can be seen and collected by the garbage collection service or superintendent.

☐ Don't make informal arrangements with friends to take over your old apartment. In the long run, it's safer to notify your landlord that you're moving out; then recommend your friends as possible new tenants. Remember—you're responsible for the rent and for the condition of the apartment as long as your name is on that lease! And good friends don't *always* make ideal tenants as far as the landlord is concerned.

A day or so before you're ready to move out, check this chart for last-minuters that ought to be done. We've broken them down by the kind of move you're making, so it's easy to spot the do's that apply to you. Once again, you may have a few special chores of your own. Maybe it's picking up a pair of glasses at the optometrist's, or returning a book borrowed from a friend, or arranging with a local charity to pick up clothing or furniture you're discarding. Whatever your "specials," add them to our collection. Then show the complete list around to family and friends and ask: "Can you think of anything I've forgotten?" You may pick up another item or two that you hadn't thought of. Many heads are better than one (or two) when it comes to this kind of list!

THE FORGET-ME-NOTS

To Do:	Moving from Previous Apt.	Moving from School, Parents	Local	Long Distance
Cancel deliveries of milk, newspapers.	☐		☐	☐
If necessary, make sure utilities, phone, water are turned off.	☐		☐	☐
Collect from cleaner, laundry, shoemaker.	☐	☐	☐	☐
Return library books.	☐	☐	☐	☐
Return library card.	☐	☐		☐
Close local charge accounts.	☐	☐		☐
Collect prescriptions from local drugstore.	☐	☐		☐
Pick up film being developed.	☐	☐	☐	☐
Do you have checks, cash for "Moving Money" and "extras"?	☐	☐	☐	☐

FINALLY, YOU'RE MOVED IN. NOW—TAKE A BREATHER!

The last box or shopping bag is in. You stagger through the door, close it behind you and—! You're attacked by a case of compulsive energy or paralyzing panic. Don't give in to either. Sit down, take it easy, go out for a victory hamburger—or a celebration dinner if you can afford it. Do anything that will give you a little break. You may have three shopping bags of bare essentials or an apartmentful of furnishings that need organizing. Whichever extreme or in-between you're facing, remember these two sanity-savers:

☐ **You don't have to do it all at once!**
☐ **Eventually things will get sorted out!**

Right now, relax a little. You're not wasting time. You're getting ready to tackle unpacking in a more efficient and timesaving way. In addition to taking this breather, it's also helpful to have a "plan for settling in" worked out ahead of time. Here are some suggestions for spacing out the jobs to be done:

Do "first things first." When you walk in the door, check to see that utilities and phone are working (if you haven't had a chance to do this before moving in). If not, you'll have to resort to emergency measures—as far as the utilities go, anyway. Check our other "firsts" listed in the margin.

Get to these within the first few days. There's no panic if you don't get quite through this list, but you'll be more comfortably settled if you do.

☐ Order newspaper and milk deliveries (if you want them).
☐ Put in food staples and meal-makings for a week's menus.
☐ List the hardware items you need (things like extension cords and picture hooks) and buy them.
☐ Comparison shop neighborhood food stores; try to find at least one that stays open late.
☐ Locate a dry cleaner, a laundry, a launderette if you need one. Arrange a pick-up schedule if you want home delivery.
☐ Start comparing dry cleaners, laundries and shoe repair shops.
☐ Find out which stores will accept or cash checks.
☐ Select a drugstore and make a note of their telephone number; drop off any prescriptions you've brought with you.
☐ Arrange for household insurance. If you've received a lot of wedding presents, you may have already taken out a floater policy. This is usually a short-term arrangement, however, and doesn't replace regular household insurance.

Check these out within the first few weeks. In addition to any of the above points that you may have missed, here are other "do's":

☐ Locate a local doctor and dentist. Ask those you have been using for recommendations or call the county medical and/or dental society.
☐ Don't forget about a vet if you have pets—again, check your previous veterinarian or a local professional society.
☐ Get a library card and/or check out local lending libraries.
☐ Open charge accounts with local stores. Don't forget about bank accounts if you haven't already done this.

And remember—don't load up each day with so many chores that you don't have time to say "hi" in the elevator, chat with a neighbor, ask someone in for coffee or a beer. It's your neighborhood now—join the group!

CHECKLIST
☐ Buy light bulbs (if these are needed).
☐ See that your name is on the mailbox; arrange to have it put there.
☐ Have additional keys cut and/or arrange for any special locks.
☐ Arrange with superintendent/manager or garbage collection service to dispose of packing boxes and cartons.
☐ Put in a few simple meal-makings, enough for breakfasts and quickie dinners for a day or two.

2 Putting Your Home Together: The Furnishings

2 Putting Your Home Together: The Furnishings

BIG AND LITTLE BASICS:
CHOOSE BOTH WITH CARE

You've found a place to live—four walls and a roof you can call your own. But so far, it's just that—a place. Now *you* have to turn this space you've leased or bought into a home. Your home! Ideally, you want it to do two things. Most importantly, you want a home that comforts you and lifts your spirits. You also want your home to say something about both of you—the kind of people you are, the things you're into, what you like and value. The furnishings you choose, whether bought or borrowed, will do a lot to create this special place.

If you've always lived at home, you may have taken furniture and home furnishings pretty much for granted up until now. Your parents had a comfortable assortment of tables, chairs, dishes, glassware, linens, cooking utensils. Even if you weren't crazy about the stuff, it was there. If you've been living in your own singles apartment, you've already collected some basics that can come with you. But singles furnishings tend to be a little catch-as-catch-can. "Some things old, some new, some borrowed, some make-do" is the usual formula. You'll probably want to add furnishings that have a more permanent character now. Whatever your situation, we've gathered together enough bedrock fact and information in this chapter to help you pick with a wise eye when you do buy.

Face it—you won't be able to get everything you want. You'll make compromises and you'll probably make some mistakes, too. Almost everyone does. But thinking, planning, reading and looking before you buy will cut your margin of error.

Remember, too, that the more you have to compromise on the bigger basics the more important the little ones become. If you have to settle for hand-me-down furniture that isn't really "you," then have fun with things like sheets and towels. Maybe you'll sleep on stripes or a wild geometric—or put together a red, white and blue bathroom. Just make sure that there are some things around you that you really like and that really do represent you!

"I KNOW WHAT I LIKE"—BUT DO YOU?

Knowing one's own tastes can be a knotty issue. Some of us seem to be born with a strong sense of personal style and will head right for the furnishings that reflect or enhance our own personalities. More of us kind of mill around searching for identity in tastes. We pick something because it's "what we had at home" or because it's exactly the opposite of what we grew up with. We imitate friends—or we settle for something safe and sane, but dull. We're the types who can be all mod-and-vinyl one minute, into curlicued "oldies" the next. When there are two people involved who don't know what they like or are afraid to take a stand, the results can be pretty muddled.

How do you find out where your taste really is and, since you're just one half of a twosome, whether or not your tastes agree? Talking together can certainly help. Talk about the kinds of things you like to do. Talk about the way you think you want to live. Then try to think about your preferences in terms of the kind of furnishings they'll require. Maybe you're both book and record buffs. That means bookcases, good reading chairs and lamps. Maybe one of you really sees housework as a drag. In furnishing terms, this might translate into easy-care modern—and a minimum of that. Do one or both of you enjoy do-it-yourself projects? Then you can think about unfinished furniture, built-ins, more expensive fabrics for draperies or slipcovers you'll be making yourself. This kind of mental exploring can be both rewarding and fun.

Looking at furniture together can help, too. Stroll through the shopping section of town. Look at items in those store windows. Point out the pieces you like, the ones you don't. When you're at parents' and friends' homes, cast an inquiring eye around. But don't take things for granted this time. Try to decide in your own mind what you like about their rooms and what *doesn't* come off for you. Don't be afraid to admit to yourself that *there are* things you don't like. Because something suits them doesn't mean it will suit you or fit into your new life.

Make up your own "what do you like" game! If your strolling time or window-shopping facilities are limited, try this shortcut. Settle down with a pile of magazines—some on decorating, some fashion mags, maybe one on boats or cars, too. Go through them together, pointing out which items appeal to you, which don't. Then do the same thing with the furniture and room-arrangement Handbooks (pages 131 through 148 and 191 through 210). You should soon get an idea of whether you like things simple or lush, dramatic or subdued, contemporary or traditional. You'll also find out where you're together, where apart in tastes. Better to find out now than hassle it out after your furnishings are delivered!

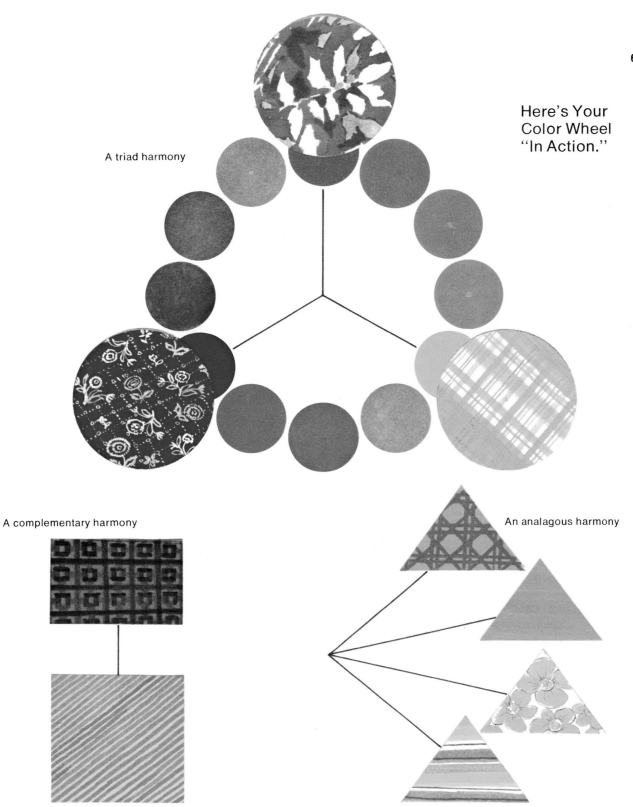

Here's Your
Color Wheel
"In Action."

A triad harmony

A complementary harmony

An analagous harmony

Use this standard palette of colors to plan out successful color harmonies like those outlined on page 157. Our fabric swatches show you three basic color schemes translated into prints and solids. **The circles show a triad harmony—** combining three colors equidistant from each other on the wheel (red, yellow and blue, in this case). **The rectangles show a complementary harmony—**colors directly opposite each other on the wheel (here, a purple and red-purple print with a yellow and yellow-green stripe). **The triangles show an analagous harmony in action,** combining colors that lie next to each other. (Our example shows a red-orange and orange bamboo print; a solid orange; a yellow floral print; a yellow and yellow-green stripe.)

woven slats

cork

fake fur

basket weave

caning

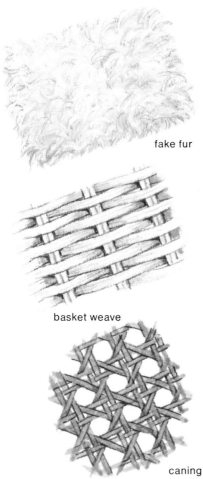

bamboo

parquet

Star The Naturals With The Neutrals For Dramatic Effect!

Vivid accents can be the secret of your success here. A touch of yellow? A flare of orange? Choose whatever appeals. You're following one of nature's own decorating

ewood

fruitwood

maple

knotty pine

birch

walnut

mahogany

schemes, with colors from wood brown to sand beige and white, and natural textures featured. There's harmony in these. But even nature can be improved upon, with accent colors!

Where Do The Colors Come From? A Red, White And Blue Poster!

This sprightly bedroom/work area is both efficient and eye-appealing. What's the secret? The bold, clearly defined color scheme (taken from the dominant accessory in the room) pulls it all together.

THE BEST ADVICE ON FURNISHING YOUR HOME: START WITH A PLAN AND STICK TO IT

Once you know what you like, it's time to decide what you need and can afford. And here's where thinking and planning ahead really pay off. Sure, it's fun to feel like a collector—to fall in love with an item and grab it while you can. Maybe a Chinese birdcage will absolutely make your living room. But it could also be an awful headache to work around. When we stress planning (and we do), we're not trying to take all the fun out of buying. We're just trying to help you make sure that, along with an occasional flyer, you'll have what you need to pull together a workable home.

"Plan it out—fine," you say. "But how?" Well, there are some fairly simple guidelines for buying furnishings successfully. They take a little time, but honestly, they beat snap decisions in the long run. You'll find these basic buying rules below, plus some specific pointers on putting them into practice.

Remember: home essentials include more than furniture! A sofa, tables, chairs, bureaus—furniture usually looms so large in a budget it's easy to forget the small necessities. But they, too, have to fit into your buying plan. The best way to start thinking it all out is to start with a list like this one:

CHECKLIST: BASIC HOME FURNISHINGS

- ☐ tables
- ☐ chairs
- ☐ sofas
- ☐ floorcoverings
- ☐ window coverings
- ☐ beds
- ☐ mattresses
- ☐ bureaus
- ☐ bed linens
- ☐ blankets
- ☐ towels
- ☐ table linens
- ☐ dishes
- ☐ glasses
- ☐ flatware
- ☐ pots and pans
- ☐ major appliances
- ☐ small appliances
- ☐ kitchen utensils
- ☐ basic supplies (kitchen and cleaning)

Now you can start filling in what you have, what you need, what you think you can do without. You might decide to scrap bed frames, for instance, and settle for mattresses on the floor or on a homemade platform. Or you might decide to dress your windows with hanging plants and skip standard window coverings. There are lots of substitutions and replacements you can take advantage of. But before you can start planning them out, you have to know what you'll need. And that's where an advance-planning list like this one comes in handy!

Plan a time when you can sit down together and list any furniture or household items you already own, or know you can beg or borrow from friends and family. If your budget is up to it, you can get choosy about this list and decide to take only hand-me-downs you really want in your home. Even if you opt for whatever comes your way, try to make sure that all the larger items are in usable condition or can be made so with little cost or effort. They're a false economy otherwise. Another pointer: When you check off the items you have, or can inherit, fill in a description of them—color, size, whether they need repairing or recovering. If you luck into two maroon armchairs in good condition, for instance, there's no sense in losing your heart to that purple sofa you saw on sale. Better to choose something that will work well with the two "freebies."

Don't blow your budget on one or two items. Spread it around throughout all the categories. You're aiming for as put-together a look as possible. True, an antique table is a long-range investment. But if buying it leaves you so broke that you have to set it with jelly glasses—and they sit under stark bare-bulb lighting—it's not doing much for you now!

When you have to settle for stopgap items, put your head into it. Try to plan out items that can live on in other parts of your home after you can afford to replace them—folding camp chairs can move from living room to porch, a redwood picnic table might go from dining area to family room to backyard. If you can manage this, even your substitutes will pay off. Try to make your home furnishings budget as long-range as you can. List the items you know you must buy during the first year. But also try to project what you might want to add after that.

Become an information sopper-upper. Look for magazines and books on home furnishings and decorating. Collect manufacturers' booklets, read newspaper ads, look at tags and tickets on items in the stores. Above all, ask questions! If you're dealing with a reputable store, the salesman shouldn't mind. If he seems to, switch to another salesman. You really do have that right! And always get a salesman's name. If you find you need more information, you can ask for him over the phone and perhaps save yourself a second trip to the store.

Get organized with your information. Start a notebook or folder. Enter store names, salesmen's names, facts on prices and sizes. Include fabric samples if you're checking these out. In other words, don't trust to memory. Write it down! If all this sounds like a lot of work—well, it is. But furnishing a home is a big investment, and it really doesn't pay to make mistakes you can avoid by thinking and planning.

SOME TIPS ON TIMING

Well-timed buying can save on disappointments and on money. It's sometimes possible to walk into a furniture department and order a piece "right off the floor" for immediate delivery. More often, the piece will have to be ordered or, at the very least, delivered from the warehouse. This usually means waiting anywhere from three weeks to three months or more for the piece to arrive. This shopping-in-advance applies to most major furnishings—furniture, floorcoverings, mattresses—sometimes fabrics and draperies, too. If you "special order" furniture in a particular finish or specially chosen fabric, you're particularly apt to run into delays.

Keep those clearance sales in mind when you time your buying! February and August are the big months for clearances in home furnishings. Of course, individual stores may run special sales at other times too, so always check your local newspaper before you buy. (See pages 128 through 130 for more information on sales.)

Another tip on timing: Be sure to get a delivery date from the store and arrange to be there or have a friend in your apartment or house on that day. If it's a large piece that's arriving, try to notify your apartment superintendent/manager, too.

PLANNING THE PAYMENTS

Arranging to pay for what you buy is, of course, the most important part of the whole process—and sometimes the hardest! If you can pay by cash or through a regular charge account, you'll save yourself the cost of carrying charges or interest rates. Most people use some form of credit, however, for major furnishings. Credit-buying can include various store payment plans, the use of credit cards or a cash loan from a bank or other lending institution. Just make sure that you understand what the terms of any credit plan really are—and how much it's adding to the cost of the item. (See pages 273 through 276.)

Special dollar-savers in the home furnishings field include buying "seconds"—i.e., sheets, towels, et al., that have slight imperfections not severe enough to seriously affect their wear or appearance. Other savers: buying furniture that has been used as a floor sample, and ordering unfinished furniture, then painting or finishing it yourself. Then there's the whole field of secondhand furniture, which runs the gamut from almost-antique to Salvation Army and thrift shop buys. Included here are the finds you can pick up at garage sales and the sales that people who are relocating a whole household sometimes offer. You can often find announcements of these in your local newspapers. Secondhands can offer real value if you know what you're doing. Check our tips on furniture construction (pages 73 through 76) before you plunge too deeply into the secondhand field, however.

And for good measure, measure large pieces of furniture before you buy so you know they'll go through doorways, up stairways and fit comfortably against walls.

THERE'S MORE TO FURNITURE THAN A "PRETTY FACE"

Style and design: These catch the eye and attract you to a piece of furniture. Obviously, they're important. Given a choice, who wants to keep looking at something that's ugly? But furniture is to use as well as to look at. Any major pieces you buy will probably be with you for a long time. So you want them to keep their looks, to stand up under normal wear, to "work." You want legs that are firm, drawers that pull easily, upholstery that won't rip, fray or sag after a few months. This means that sound construction and quality materials must lie behind the design. Even if you think of a piece as "temporary," you still want to be sure it will give good service while you have it. If you're planning to refinish "found furniture" or slipcover family castoffs, you'll want to be sure they're worth the time and trouble. Learning to look further than the surface will help you choose pieces with a long life-span.

Basically, furniture falls into two categories: wood furniture, which people in the business call "case goods," and upholstered furniture. Case goods includes items like tables, chests, desks, dressers—the cabinetry pieces that are made entirely of wood. If you can, choose case goods and upholstered pieces in the medium or upper price ranges and skimp somewhere else. It's usually false economy to settle for the cheapest here. If you do, you're almost bound to sacrifice looks as well as wear.

For those areas where you have to fill in with penny pinchers, there's a whole new world of "throwaway" furniture you might consider. The plastic inflatables and pieces made from paper or cardboard belong in this category. Even here, however, there are different grades of quality available and it pays to do some looking, checking and comparison shopping.

How do you look behind the "looks"? There are several ways you can help protect yourself against bad buys. Most importantly:

☐ Deal with reputable stores and manufacturers. They've built their reputations by selling sound merchandise and standing behind what they sell.

☐ Learn to look for those written warranties and/or guarantees.

The National Association of Furniture Manufacturers' Seal of Integrity is a major protection.

☐ Try to check out all pieces yourself for soundness of construction and materials. The following pages checklist specific things to look for in both wood and upholstered furniture. Look the lists over carefully and put the suggestions to use. Don't be afraid to handle pieces—lift them up, look at the backs, pull out drawers. A good store wants you to be satisfied.

CHECK THESE NITTY-GRITTIES IN WOOD FURNITURE

Some of these may seem like picky points to fuss about, but they're all-important to the basic functioning of a piece. Believe it—a sticky drawer or squeaky hinge can drive you up the wall after a while! And they're not always easy to fix.

Check: Drawers, Doors And Handles

Drawers should fit perfectly and slide back and forth easily. One sign of good workmanship is a center glide on drawers. Dust panels between drawers are another good feature. They help to seal off each unit. If the piece has doors, check these out, too. They should fit together smoothly and stay closed when you want them closed, open when you want them open. If they swing open or closed on their own, that's a sign of poor construction.

The handles, pulls and hinges—all the hardware on a piece—should be set on straight, should be in scale with, and complement, its basic design. Pulls and handles should be easy to find and to use.

Check: Joints And Joinings

Really give these the eagle eye. Our sketches show you what to look for. In general, all the sections of a piece should be joined firmly and securely. One way to tell: Put your hand on top of the surface and rock the piece back and forth. If it's well made, it will remain rigid under your hand. What kind of joinings do you look for when you're testing out a piece?

☐ On medium- to high-priced furniture, look for mortise and tenon or double dowel joining; they hold the outer frame securely together. Dovetail joints are usual on drawer corners.

☐ All joints should be glued and fastened together with screws; they give extra stability.

☐ Underneath chairs and tables—or wherever extra strength is important—joints should be reinforced with corner blocks that are glued and fastened with screws.

Drawer with center glide.

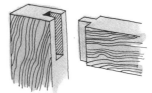
Mortise and tenon joining.

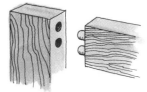
Double dowel joining.

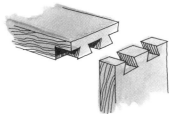
Dovetail joint.

Reinforced joint with corner block.

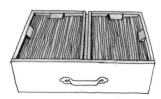

Dust panel.

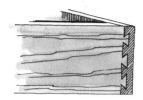

Dovetail joint.

Hidden areas should be neatly finished.

Ill fitting back corner panel.

Check labels.

Check: The Hidden Areas

They may not show, but the way they're finished off tells a lot about the manufacturer's standards in general. All the unexposed parts and underneaths of wood furniture should be clean, smooth, well sealed and stained to match the rest of the piece. Back panels should fit well and be smoothly finished, too.

Check: Surface Finishes

Any finish should be smooth and free from rough spots. Finishes are available in a wide variety today and do all kinds of things—from changing the color and sealing the wood to resisting heat, alcohol, water and other surface stainers. These new super finishes are even performance rated; manufacturers who use them will add a special tag to the furniture to identify them. Check these tags or ask a salesman what the finish will do and how to care for it.

Check: All Tags And Labels

They're there to give you information and to protect you—so read them. Be especially careful of any tag that reads "oak finish" or any other wood finish. It usually means that a cheaper wood has been finished to look like a more expensive kind. Obviously, softwood with an oak or mahogany finish won't hold up as well as these harder, more expensive woods. When you see this sort of label, try to find out what wood the piece is really made of. Special note: Don't confuse the above with tags that tell you a particular wood has been finished in a color different from its natural shade. For instance: Mahogany is a dark reddish wood, but today it's often finished in a soft brown color. This doesn't affect the basic qualities of the wood at all.

Another point: Plastics that imitate woodgrain are being used a lot today for tops and decorative parts of furniture. Some purists dislike this, but actually the process has been so perfected that even experts can find it hard to tell the difference. If it's obvious to your own eye, chances are it's an inferior piece.

When You're Buying Secondhands

The same construction checkpoints apply. In fact, details like the type of joinings become even more important because you're dealing with a piece that's already had a bit of wear and tear. And—you don't have a store name to protect you. You won't have the tags to identify the type of wood and/or finish, either. The best rule of thumb here: If the finish is in reasonably good shape and the piece still seems to be sturdy and "together," it's probably worth buying. Another point to keep in mind: Softer, cheaper woods are usually lighter in weight than the harder, more expensive varieties. So try "hefting" those secondhands to get an idea of their basic quality.

Special for do-it-yourselfers: This tip about wood weights applies especially to you. If you're hoping to find "good wood" under those layers of gunk, check the weight! And remember another work-saver: Don't strip off old paint in layers. Choose a hidden spot and work your way down to the original wood. If you don't like what you see, you've saved yourself the trouble of stripping the whole piece.

LOST IN THE "WOODS"?
FOLLOW THIS GUIDE . . .

You'll hear a lot of phrases flung around about furniture woods and how they're used. It's useful to know what they really mean when you come up against them in an ad or on a label. First and foremost—what kinds of woods are you most apt to find in the furniture you buy? Here's a list of the most popular kinds used in America today, with some hints about the types of furniture they're used for:

WALNUT—The great variety of figures in the grain and the hardness of this wood make it ideal for contemporary and modern furniture; it takes the new oiled finishes well.

PECAN AND HICKORY—These are hard, tough woods; look for them in Spanish, Mediterranean and Italian designs.

OAK—An old favorite, back in style for country Spanish-, Italian- or French-style furniture, oak is so resistant to stains it needs less care and attention than other woods.

MAPLE—"The" wood for Early American furniture; its fine, even texture makes it ideal for painted or enameled finishes, too.

MAHOGANY—Since it's easy to cut and carve, it's seen mainly in traditional (particularly eighteenth-century English) designs— occasionally used for contemporary furniture.

TEAK AND ROSEWOOD—These "exotics" are seen mostly in imported Scandinavian contemporary and other modern designs. A heavy residue of oil in rosewood makes high-luster finishes possible.

FRUITWOOD—Today, this usually identifies a finish rather than a particular wood. Golden-brown in color, a fruitwood finish is often used on French Provincial furniture designs.

Now for some construction terms—on the following page, you'll find a description of the ways in which these woods are made into furniture.

☐ SOLID WOOD FURNITURE is labeled "solid" if all exposed surfaces are of the solid wood named. It's easy to repair or refinish.

☐ VENEERED PLYWOOD is made from three, five or seven layers of cabinet-grade plywood laminated together—it's labeled "genuine" if all exposed parts are made of the wood named.

What "makes" plastic furniture? Plastic can be molded, cast or cut into any desired shape. Well-made "plastics" are unbreakable, dent- and scratch-proof, lightweight and easy to clean. *And* they're available in a wide variety of colors, styles and prices.

IN UPHOLSTERED FURNITURE: TAILORING AND COMFORT ARE CLUES TO QUALITY

When you're choosing an upholstered sofa or chair, remember that most of the basic construction is under wraps. You're really relying on the store's or maker's integrity. Check what does show on the surface, though; it's often a clue to the quality of workmanship in the piece. You want "yes" answers to these questions.

CHECKLIST: FOR TOP-NOTCH TAILORING
☐ Do hems and pleats hang straight and even?
☐ Is cord or welting smooth and firmly stitched?
☐ Is weave of fabric even with frame?
☐ Is fabric pattern centered and matched at seams?
☐ Are zippers and fasteners concealed?
☐ Is the fabric itself sturdy and of good quality?
☐ Is the fabric treated for stain- or soil-resistance? Is it treated against mildew, shrinkage, fading or wrinkling?
☐ Are the areas in the back and under the cushions covered with good-quality fabric?
☐ Do the cushions fit snugly against each other?

CHECKLIST: FOR BUILT-IN COMFORT
☐ Can you sit comfortably in it with your feet on the floor? The height and depth of the seat should be such that you can do this —a seat slanting backward is usually more comfortable.
☐ Are the arms the right height for you? Try them out. Elbows should rest comfortably on the arms, without your feeling that you're stretching or stooping; keep in mind the height of the person who'll be using the piece most often.
☐ Are the springs, padding and filling firm and resilient? The firmer and denser the springs—and the more padding—the better the quality. Check the seat deck to make sure there are no lumpy stick-outs.

IDEAL COMFORT
Provide a "favorite chair" for each of you—each chair chosen to fit specific height and arm requirements.

A note on fillings: The most commonly used for pillows are urethane or rubber foam and Dacron polyester, or Acrilan acrylic fiberfill.

The Dacrons and Acrilans can be used alone or wrapped around a foam core for more luxurious seating. Down or feather fillings are usually used only in the most expensive furniture.

If a cushion is well filled, it'll be resilient and bounce back into shape quickly. Most common fillings for platform seats: rubberized hair; rubberized sisal, flax or cotton; rubber foam; polyurethane foam. The foams have the advantage of being non-allergenic and are also moth- , mildew- and insect-repellent—an advantage in damp climates.

TODAY'S BEDTIME STORY
TAKES MANY DIFFERENT FORMS

Variety is the key word when it comes to the range of beds and bedding available today. From conventional beds-with-headboards to way-out waterbeds, you have a wide choice of types and sizes. Big news is the no-headboard bed, the trend toward the wider-and-longers and the continuing popularity of the double-duty varieties. For starters, here's a chart of the conventional bedsteads-with-headboards that are available, with the mattress size each takes:

BEDS WITH HEADBOARDS

Type	Mattress Size	Description
Twin	39x75″	Standard twin sold singly or in pairs.
Full	53x75″	Accommodates two people (but not each in twin-size comfort).
Extra length	80″ long	Available in twin- or full-size widths.
Queen	60x80″	Essentially an extra-large double bed.
King	72 to 78x80″	Ideal sleeping for two (if you have room for the bed).
Hollywood	Equals two twin-size	Two twin-size bed frames attached to a single headboard.

Note: Sheets, bedpads and blankets are easy to find for these sizes. Other mattress sizes available: 30x75″; 33x75″; 36x75″; 48x75″ (¾ size); 72x84″ (California King-size).

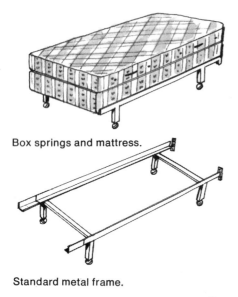

Box springs and mattress.

Standard metal frame.

Wallpaper behind bed simulates a headboard.

You've just seen all the basic sizes in conventional beds. Now consider some of the variations available using these standard-size mattresses and springs.

Money-saver: springs and mattresses in metal frames. Here, spring and mattress are fitted into a standard metal frame that adjusts in width and length to suit any size. Advantages: These frames are much less expensive than conventional bedsteads, but offer just as much support. They can be attached to a headboard later. Check to make sure that the frame has wheels, casters or glides. The casters at the foot of the bed should be of the locking variety, to "anchor" the frame.

Another idea: Put springs and mattresses right on the floor or on a sleep platform you build yourself. Cover with a bright-dyed fitted sheet or slipcover.

Ideas to use instead of headboards. If you're long on looks and short on cash, make a fake-it headboard. Put up a strip of wallpaper, swag a length of fabric, or "frame" your bed with strips of molding. If you're really talented, try a paint-it-yourself mural behind the bed. These ideas are just starters. You'll probably come up with some of your own that are better than ours!

Beds that double as furniture. These changeabouts can turn a living room, dining room, even a foyer into a bedroom or guest quarters. They're highly styled, comfortably designed, sturdily made. They come in all sizes—from Queen-size sofas to open-up hassocks, with all stops in between. Reliable brands feature real bedding mattresses. Sofa beds have a new type of construction that allows comfortable sitting along the whole length without any feeling that there's a convertible underneath. When buying any model, be sure to check the mechanism, look for the same tailoring details you would on regular upholstered furniture, check to see that corners are rounded to prevent bruises and that front legs are capped to protect carpeting. Make sure the piece has a tilt mechanism for easy cleaning (convertible sofas are heavy!). Optional but nice: tilting headrests for TV-watching or reading.

What's up with waterbeds? Beware of the cheaper varieties and those being sold without frames. If you want a waterbed, you have to be willing to freight all the necessary parts: a strong, well-fitting frame that sits squarely on the floor; a thermostatically controlled heating element approved by a certified testing laboratory; a water bag of heavy-gauge vinyl. Some floors can't take the weight of a waterbed, so *always* check with your landlord before you go ahead and buy one!

Swag of fabric is another idea to "fake" a headboard.

Take A Firm Stand When You Buy Springs And Mattresses

Be firm about quality, about testing out springs and mattresses for comfort right in the store—and, most important, choose ones that will support your body firmly without giving in to body weight. Serviceable springs and mattresses will cost you a fair amount of money, so you want them to last and to provide comfortable, healthful sleep. Like upholstered furniture, their basic construction is "hidden," so the safest course is to stick with a reputable manufacturer or store.

What's the inside story? Mattresses come with two types of inner construction: innersprings and all foam. All-foams are made of foam rubber latex or synthetic foam. Lighter in weight than innerspring mattresses, they should be at least 4 to 6 inches thick and made of high-density foam. For innersprings, most experts agree that a count of 250 to 300 coils is the minimum for sound construction. There should be firm layers of insulation between the coils and the outside ticking—either cotton felt with an insulator pad, cotton felt with a foam pad, or all-cotton felt that is covered and then compressed. Box springs should have at least 63 coils (for a standard full-size mattress) and can go as high as 70-, 80- or 88-coil construction. The box spring provides the right degree of resiliency and firmness to the mattress, so it's just as important as the mattress. Both mattress and spring should have side supports to prevent sagging. These will give you edge-to-edge support so that every inch of sleeping surface lies comfortably flat under you.

What's up top? When it comes to tickings, you can indulge a taste for florals, stripes or abstracts. You also have a choice of mattress finishes—that is, you can choose one that is smooth, tufted or quilted. Smooth tops have a soft, pillowy feel. Tufting features cords stitched through the mattress for extra firmness. Quilting is the most expensive finish and offers the most luxurious surface. All are equally "good"—it's a question of personal choice.

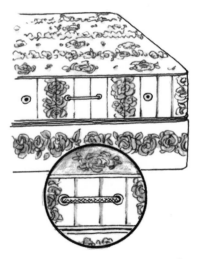

Side vents and handles on an innerspring mattress.

Signs of extra quality: Vents along the border of an innerspring mattress allow the mattress to "breathe" and stay fresh. Side handles will make the mattress easier to handle when you want to turn it.

Special note: Don't skimp by putting a new mattress on top of a hand-me-down box spring. Most manufacturers match up mattresses and box springs to bring out the best in both. It's wise to buy yours in matched sets. This way, you'll get a bonus in comfort and in wear. And you'll have the added luxury of ticking that pairs up!

Mattress Insurance: A Well-Fitting Mattress Pad

Buying new mattresses and skipping mattress pads is a foolish economy! And not all pads are the same. Most important: Look for the letter "T" on the label. It means the pad has been treated for flame-retardancy. Also look for: a minimum-shrinkage label, neatly stitched quilted design and taped, double-stitched edges. Check out the filling, too. Whether it's bleached cotton or a synthetic fiber, it should be evenly distributed throughout the pad. How to tell? Hold the pad up to the light. Lumps and bunches will show up. Some pads or mattress covers are plastic coated so they can be sponged off and there are plastic zip-ons that will guard a mattress completely. These have a rather crackly feel under the sheet, however. Keeping pads in place can be a problem. The cheaper ones come with elastic corner bands that have a tendency to tear loose or stretch out. Combination pad and mattress covers go on over the mattress like a fitted sheet. Look for sturdy binding or elastic on these because they get a lot of wear and tear.

LOOKING INTO THE PILLOW PICTURE

Filling	Description	Comparative Cost	Sizes
All down	Very soft, with little buoyancy.	Most expensive.	Standard (20x26")
Feather and down	Ideal combination for sleeping comfort—soft and buoyant—duck or goose feathers are best.	Less expensive than all down.	Queen-size (20x30") King-size (20x36")
All feather	Slightly firmer than feather and down, but very satisfactory—duck or goose feathers are best.	Least expensive of the natural fillings.	Bolster sizes (20x36", 20x44", 20x62")
Foam	Highly resilient, resistant to mildew and germs, non-allergenic. Can be washed at home. Some people find them too "bouncy."	Less expensive than natural fillings.	Note: This variety lets you choose a pillow that's in proportion to your bed size!
Synthetic fiberfill	Firm, non-allergenic, but without much feeling of buoyancy. Can be washed at home.	Least expensive of all fillings.	

Hand-test all pillows. They should be free from lumps and should spring back into shape after squeezing. Ticking should be firmly woven cotton and, ideally, seams should be piped. Have down and feather pillows washed occasionally by a professional laundry. Air all pillows when you change the cases.

FLOORCOVERINGS:
BETTER FASHION, BIGGER VALUES
THAN FLOORS EVER SAW BEFORE

Tile or pile . . . plain or patterned . . . painted or parquet! What's afoot today is almost limitless.

The good-wood floor in a handsome parquet pattern is still considered a decorating delight in itself. Wood not so good? A coat of white or brightly colored paint will perk up wooden floors that are past their prime. See pages 162 and 163 for some special decorative effects you can achieve with painted floors.

When it comes to floorcoverings, today's "versatiles" can lay the groundwork for a room's color scheme or act as accents. They'll cover messy old flooring or set off sophisticated tiles. They'll plush up porches, patios, kitchens and bathrooms. Along with their really splendid good looks go useful virtues like muffling sound, resisting soil and mildew, cushioning footsteps—*and* they meet basic flammability standards so they're not fire hazards! In fact, they're available in such a range of sizes, shapes, types and price lines—and they can help bring about such varied effects— that trying to choose what you want from available selections can be like starving to death in front of a smorgasbord table. To choose successfully, you have to think out your floorcovering needs before that trip to the store! You have to balance out what you want these coverings to look like with what you want them to do in any particular room. Once we've told you something about the different types of carpeting and rugs available, you can check our information on page 87 for suggestions on which types do best in specific areas—and why. In addition to this "placement" chart, however, you should do some *now* and *future* thinking.

Think about your here and now. How big is your overall furnishings budget? How important will floorcoverings be in your decorating scheme and what do you hope they'll achieve? If you're counting on carpeting to disguise warped floors and cracked walls, for instance, then a good hunk of the budget is headed that way.

Other questions to keep in mind: Do you want to take them with you when you move? Are you planning on moving in the near future? Is the floorcovering you're looking at easy to install and pick up again?

Think about your tomorrows. If your personal taste or decision runs to expensive wall-to-wall carpeting you'll want to take with you, here are some points you should keep in mind: Are your present rooms oddly shaped? If so, you'll lose a lot of carpeting when you recut to suit new rooms. How do you plan to use the carpeting in new surroundings? Are you choosing a color and pattern that will lend itself easily to new color schemes, a different room? Can the carpeting transfer from living room to bedroom?

There are so many types of adhesives and backings available for today's floorcoverings that you can plan almost any kind of future for them. But thinking ahead will make the transformation come off better.

HOMING IN ON CARPETS AND RUGS

Here's a brief review of today's all-star cast of carpets and rugs. Use this as general background knowledge—but don't forget to check with your salesman about new developments and refinements in the field. Manufacturers are working constantly to improve their products and bright newcomers appear on the scene regularly. Another happy note: The range available is wide enough to cover even tight-budget buying!

For a real spread of color and comfort: wall-to-wall. Here, the carpeting is custom cut to snug up right to the walls; then it's secured in place. Advantages: a smooth, draft-free feel underfoot, a unified look *and* only one kind of surface to clean. This unbroken stretch of color and texture will make a small room look larger, too. It's the most expensive carpeting to lay and to pick up, however. You also face the possibility that the landlord or incoming tenant will consider it a "permanent improvement" and insist that you leave it behind when you move.

Dollar-saving alternative: foam-backed carpeting. This is like regular broadloom, but it features a high-density foam rubber or vinyl foam backing so (if you're at all handy) you can cut it and lay it yourself. It gives you a saving on installation costs and it's easy to pick up and recut when you move.

Mobile carpeting: the room-size rug. Carpeting is cut to rug size and bound all 'round. This usually leaves a border of bare floor showing—nice if your floors are in good condition. Moving? You just roll it up as you would a regular rug and into the truck it goes. Readily available in standard sizes like 5x7', 9x12', 12x15',

12x18'—or you can special-order your choices cut from the roll and bound. Two great advantages: They can be turned to distribute the wear evenly and they can be sent out for cleaning.

Put carpet tiles down plain or in a pattern. These handy squares of carpeting let you plan your own design. They're easy to work with if you plan to do-it-yourself and they come with a wide range of backings. Some you lay without an adhesive or with double-faced tape. Some are self stick or have a release adhesive —so they go down and come up easily. One big plus here: You can replace individual squares that get worn or badly soiled.

The "put me anywhere" type: indoor-outdoor carpeting. It's a real toughie that weathers rain and sun on your porch or patio, can also take the wear and tear of kitchen, bathroom or basement. No scrubbing or waxing with this one. Stains—even hot grease—just wipe away! And don't think it's drab because it's so practical. Quite the contrary—it comes in a kaleidoscope of colors. Warning: There's also a wide variance in quality and performance between individual brands—so ask before you buy!

How To Figure It Up: Quantity And Cost

A little simple arithmetic will show you how much carpeting you'll need for any room. Most carpeting is sold by the square yard, and here's how to figure that out:

1. Measure the length and the width of the room, in feet.
2. Multiply the length by the width, still in feet.
3. Divide this figure by nine to turn feet into square yards.

Example:

For a 12x15' room—

12x15'=180'; 180÷9=20 square yards

Usually, carpeting comes in 12- or 15-foot widths and some styles are also available in 9- or 18-foot widths. This means that you can choose carpeting in a width that will adapt to the width of the room, with a minimum of cutting or wastage. Where exact fit is most important—in wall-to-wall installations—the store you buy from will measure your room for you, and figure out the cost of installation and padding as well. Carpeting you buy already cut and bound as a room-size rug is usually priced as a unit rather than by the square yard.

Carpeting comes in three grades and price ranges: economy grade, medium grade and top quality. When you're considering which to buy, don't judge solely on the basis of price, however. Pattern and color, the durability of the carpeting, the reputation of both the manufacturer and the retail store you're buying from —these are all factors to be considered, too.

Some manufacturers are even producing the same texture and color carpeting in all of the three grades. You can get an "all together" look at minimum cost by using the economy grade in light traffic areas like bedrooms or guest rooms, the medium grade in the living room and dining room and the top grade in heavy traffic areas like a hallway, stairs or living room (if your living room tends to take a lot of to and fro movement). This across-the-board look can really help a small apartment or house to look larger than it is. It also helps achieve the unified look that ultra-sophisticated contemporary aims for. Practically speaking, the denser the pile the longer the carpet will keep its looks and feeling of luxury. Remember, too, that *both* very light and very dark shades show dirt quickly. To cut down on cleaning, head for medium-solid tones or a tweedy or many-color pattern. Texture also affects the practicality of carpeting, with the top-duty rating going to twists, loops, shags and textured types. With these, however, you should consider their cleaning practicality as well as their wear. See page 90 for a complete rundown on textures. A general rule of thumb: Skip the economy grade if you're going to the expense of installing wall-to-wall. If your rooms boast finished floors, choose a good room-size rug instead that can be turned to equalize wear. If your rooms feature subflooring only, then you'll need to get wall-to-wall carpeting—even if you'd prefer something else.

How To Be A Quality-Counter

If you're thinking about buying carpeting, make these quick quality-checks first:

☐ The denser the pile the better the wear. In high-density pile, the fibers are closely packed to form a tight, cohesive mass. The height of the pile alone has little to do with carpet wear—it's purely a matter of what you think looks good. To judge pile density, bend the carpeting back on itself. If the backing shows up clearly between the rows of pile, the carpeting is probably not dense enough to wear well. Be particularly careful with low- to medium-priced shags. Many of these have a self-colored backing which tends to conceal gaps—these can be the result of skimpy construction.

☐ A good backing is important to the life of the carpet, too. The backing can be made of jute, cotton, raft cord or polypropylene. It's there to provide a firm foundation and prevent stretching, shrinking, buckling. All tufted and knitted carpets, and many woven types as well, have an added coating of latex on the backing. To check for this, run your hand across the backing. If it feels "rubbery," it's latex coated. Also check the label to see what the backing is made from.

Tightly packed loops are an indication of high quality in carpeting.

□ Special note for tufted carpeting: Most good-quality tufted carpets have an extra layer of backing-fabric laminated to the primary backing to lend greater strength and longer life. Tufting is the most widely used construction method today, so be sure to ask about double-backing when you're checking carpeting. (See chart on page 89 for description of tufting and other carpet construction terms.) Don't feel self-conscious about all this checking. Any good store wants you to be satisfied.

These Undercover Agents Help Protect Carpets And Rugs

Not just a "nice extra," not a "let's do without it" . . . good-quality padding, backing or underlaying can add years to a carpet's or rug's life-span. With wall-to-wall, it's essential—and it's almost as important for room-size or area rugs. What does it do? It adds softness and comfort, helps absorb the shock and pulling of hard leather heels and soles. Choose from three types: felted, usually made of hair or hair and jute; foam or sponge rubber; or felted hair with a rubber coating. Felt gives a firmer feel, sponge is bouncier underfoot, and rubber-coated hair combines the advantages of both. It's not good business to lay new carpeting on old padding, so count up the cost of carpeting *and* backing when you're figuring costs.

For good quality, choose a 40-ounce felted padding or a ⅜-inch-thick sponge cushioning. These are suitable for normal home use. While we're on the subject: If you go in for casual cotton throw rugs, be sure you anchor them in some way! Your rooms can turn into a skating rink otherwise. Thin sheets of rubber backing can be ordered cut to size, or you can use strips of the double-faced backing tape that's available in most rug or hardware stores. Both work well.

FYI: A Résumé Of Rugs

How is a rug different from carpeting? Usually, a rug is made as a single design, complete within its own borders. Carpeting is manufactured in continuing lengths which are cut into rolls. From ancient times on, rugs have been prized as works of art and today rugs from every part of the world are available.

Area rugs, most popular and most versatile, come in all colors, patterns and sizes. Real or fake fur, wool, cotton, nylon—the whole range of fibers is there to choose from. Enjoy a sleek Scandinavian design, Mediterranean with a touch of Marrakesh, traditional Navajo or Hopi—the choice is almost endless. These small-to-middling rugs are attractive against wooden floors, doubly dramatic shown off against vinyls, tiles or brick. Some serve as handsome wall hangings. Most live a long life, going

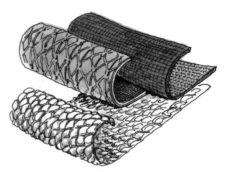

Types of carpet padding (from top to bottom): felted; felted with rubber coating; foam rubber.

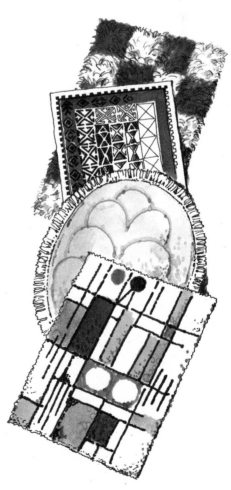

Variety of area rugs.

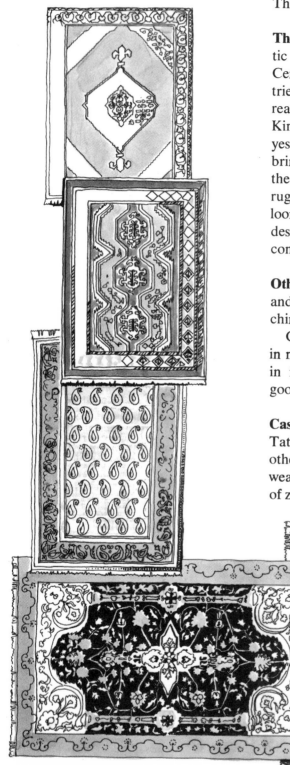

easily from room to room as your home grows in size and scope. This is one reason for their popularity.

The fabulous Orientals are here for your choosing, too. Authentic Orientals may be woven in India, Pakistan, China, Japan, Central Asia, Persia (Iran), Turkey or other Near Eastern countries. They feature hand-knotted construction, and this is the reason they wear so well. Famous names in Orientals: Sarouk, Kirman, Tabriz, Kashan, Hamadan, Shiraz. They're expensive, yes—but they usually grow in beauty and value as they age, bringing high prices as semi-antiques or "used" rugs. If you like the look but can't go the price—cheer up! Fine American-made rugs in Oriental patterns are now available. They're machine loomed, much less expensive and just as colorful and intricately designed. Remember: Orientals don't show dirt easily and they complement any decor from medieval to tomorrow!

Other varieties include the pale and stately French Aubussons and Savonneries. Once handwoven in France, they can be machine-made today, but still must be specially ordered.

Country-style hooked, braided and rag rugs are also with us in machine-made versions, as a popular do-it-yourself project or in inexpensive handmades imported from the Orient. They're good with early American or any informal decor.

Casual cover-ups blend in well with contemporary surroundings. Tatami mats; hemp squares; matchstick runners; grass, sisal or other fiber rugs; rice paper scrolls—take your pick. Most won't wear as well as the more traditional coverings, but they bring a lot of zing to a room!

Some examples of Oriental rugs (from top to bottom): Tabriz; Shiraz; Kashan; Saruq; Kirman.

ALL CHARTED OUT FOR YOU:
THREE PAGES OF VITAL STATISTICS
IN EASY-TO-TAKE CHART FORM

RUGS VS. CARPETING: ROOM BY ROOM

Type	Room or Area	Reason Why
Wall-to-wall*	Halls Stairways Living room Den Guest room Bedroom	Reduces noise and chances of tripping; gives a look of luxury wherever wear and tear is not too heavy.
Room-size rugs	Living room Dining room Bedrooms Playrooms	Give the carpeted look but can be turned to equalize wear, can be sent out to be cleaned —so they're ideal for heavy traffic rooms, rooms where spills are apt to happen.
Area rugs	Living room Dining room Bedrooms	Add color and excitement, yet pick up for cleaning easily—heavily patterned ones tend not to show dirt.
Orientals	Living room Dining room Bedrooms—you can even cut worn ones into runners for stairs.	Adapt to any type of furniture—don't show dirt—are easier than carpeting to home-shampoo.
Hooked, braided, rag rugs	Living room Dining room—good for bedrooms if large enough to cover areas where you'll be walking, or if they're put down over carpeting.	Wear well, don't show dirt, clean easily— unless heavily padded, they don't block out drafts as well as others.
Carpet tiles*	Living room Dining room Hallways Bedrooms Playrooms	Offer advantages of "laid" carpeting with added plus that individual tiles can be replaced when soiled or damaged.

Note re installation: For safety's sake, it's best to have a professional install carpeting on stairways. In fact, all wall-to-wall benefits from professional handling. Have the usable scraps left for possible patching or small area rugs. Carpet tiles, on the other hand, are ideal for do-it-yourself decorating.

FACTS ABOUT FIBERS

Fiber	Looks	Wear	Soil and Crush Resistance	Price Range
Acrylics	Look and feel of wool.	Good to excellent	Resist soil, clean easily, resist crushing.	Medium to high

Some trademarked names: Acrilan (Chemstrand); Creslan (American Cyanamid); Orlon (DuPont); Zefran and Zefkrome (both DuPont and Dow Chemical); Dynel (Union Carbide); Verel (Eastman Chemical).

Fiber	Looks	Wear	Soil and Crush Resistance	Price Range
Nylons	Take wide range of clear colors—slightly shiny unless delustered.	Excellent	Soil quickly unless delustered, but clean easily —stain resistant—resist crushing.	Medium to high

Some trademarked names: Caprolan (Allied Chemical); Celanese Nylon (Celanese); Cumuloft (Chemstrand); DuPont Nylon (DuPont); Enkaloft (American Enka); Nyloft (Firestone).

Fiber	Looks	Wear	Soil and Crush Resistance	Price Range
Polyesters	Very resilient, look like wool.	Good to excellent	Almost uncrushable—resist soil, clean easily.	Medium

All polyester fibers are labeled as such by manufacturers.

Fiber	Looks	Wear	Soil and Crush Resistance	Price Range
Polypropylene	Used in indoor-outdoor carpeting—looks like nylon.	Excellent	Resists soil, moisture, stains, abrasion—crushes easily, so best in flat constructions.	Medium

Fiber	Looks	Wear	Soil and Crush Resistance	Price Range
Wool	Wide color and style range.	Good to excellent	Good crush and soil resistance; needs moth-proofing.	Medium to high

Blends: Characteristics of fiber blends depend on the fibers used and the percentage of each fiber included. Usually, a fiber must represent at least 20% of a blend before its characteristics become apparent.

THE PROCESS: HOW CARPETS ARE MADE

Name	Process	Look	Advantages
Tufted	Made on a multi-needle machine that attaches pile yarns to a pre-woven backing, which is then latexed. May have a second backing laminated to primary one for extra strength.	Majority of today's carpeting is made by this process; the closer the tufts the better except in shags, which are made to look shaggy.	Speed of process cuts costs, saves you dollars.
Woven	Made on looms; pile and backing produced simultaneously. Standard weaves: velvet, Axminster, Wilton.	Velvet: smooth-surface pile, looks like tufting. Axminster: thick, high pile; intricate pattern, many colors. Wilton: long-wearing, luxurious; often sculptured or embossed.	Oldest method — pile yarns and backing are interwoven in one operation; good quality, but expensive.
Needle-punch	Web of loose fibers interlocked with felting needles, then compressed and backed with foam or latex.	Simulates a felt; often used in tiles and indoor-outdoor types.	Low cost.
Flocked	Electrostatically charged fibers adhere to adhesive-coated surface.	Simulates rich velour fabric.	Fairly new process; good looks at low cost.

Note: When you talk about the general "style" of a carpet, you're really talking about the texture and pattern rather than the actual manufacturing process by which it was made. Texture, pattern (and color, of course) are the aspects of carpet that directly affect your decorating scheme and help set the mood of a room—so they're important factors to keep in mind. On the following page, you'll find some commonly used terms that describe a variety of the textures and/or patterns available in carpets today.

COMMON TERMS YOU'LL SEE AND HEAR: WHAT THEY MEAN

Term	Description
Broadloom	Not a weave; refers to any seamless carpet made on looms 6 to 18′ wide.
Pile	The wearing surface of a carpet; may be loop, cut or a combination of loop and cut.
Shag	Any carpet in which pile is long enough and widely enough spaced to give a shaggy effect. In moderate depths, it's called "shag-plush," "plush-shag" or "splush" carpet.
Plush	A deep pile construction—not to be confused with velvet, which is woven.
Loop pile	Surface tufts are left uncut. Today, they wear especially well because of a special tufting process that packs loops tightly together.
Sculptured or embossed	A pattern or texture with varying pile heights to simulate hand-carved effect. Related terms: high-low, hi-lo, cut and loop, cut and uncut.
Random sheared	Loops are clipped at random to make cut-pile areas. Tip shearing produces similar effect.
Twist	Tightly twisted yarns in a cut-pile surface, with a curled or "frieze" look.

Note: This list may not include all the terms used by stores and manufacturers. However, it does include the most commonly used terms—the ones you'll often see in carpet ads and read about in home furnishing magazines and articles. Familiarize yourself with this list and you'll be able to "talk carpets" fairly knowledgeably—and know what you're getting for your money!

THE NEW "SMOOTHY" FLOOR TILES ARE BEING USED MORE AND MORE

Linoleum used to be an "ugh" word. But today's linoleum tiles and their glamour cousins—the asphalts and vinyls—are out of the kitchen and showing up all around the house. Sophisticated colors and patterns have made them real "decorator" floorings. Many are designed to "put down yourself." All offer long wear and resilience, along with a sleek modern air. The disadvantages? You'll need a special OK from your landlord to install them—*and* you'll have to leave them behind when you move! Terrazzo, mosaic, wood, brick, marble—these are just a few of the effects you can achieve with these up-and-comers. Take a quick look at the chart on the facing page to see what's available in this field. Choose the one that suits you best—from both a practical and a financial point of view.

FLOOR TILES: THE CITY-COUNTRY SLICKERS

Type	Advantages	Special Care
Vinyl (also available in planks and rolls)	Great natural beauty.	Don't use water; dry mop only. Clean with solvent-base polishing wax or self-polishing wax.
Vinyl asbestos	Grease-resistant; can also withstand alkaline-base cleansers like ammonia, baking soda, borax.	Damp mop. Use self-polishing or polishing wax. Protect against dents with furniture glides.
Linoleum (also available in planks and rolls)	Grease-, oil- and abrasion-resistant.	Dry or damp mop. Use polishing or self-polishing wax, steel wool for stains.
Asphalt	Grease-resistant types available; low-cost but noisy.	Dry or damp mop. Use self-polishing or buffable water-base wax. Avoid solvents and strong cleansers.
Rubber	Quiet and dent-resistant, but slippery when wet.	Dry mop. Use self-polishing or buffable water-base wax (two thin coats rather than one heavy coat).

Always check to see what type of subflooring is necessary for the type of tile you're interested in.

WINDOWS ARE WHAT YOU MAKE THEM

A sweeping view of the sun setting behind trees or city lights frosting a night sky—you may luck into a home with broad picture windows that frame a scene like one of these. In that case, your window-dressing problem is easy. More likely, though, in at least one room your windows will be small and uninteresting. Here's where window dressing becomes an art.

Usually, you can't rebuild the window—but you *can* plan an arrangement of curtains, draperies, shades or shutters that will make the most of what you have. Take a good look at what's there. Then decide what you want your windows to do: show off or hide a view; become a dramatic accent in the room; or blend gracefully into the wall. Do you need to control the light they admit or the ventilation they provide? You may even want to "create" a window where there really isn't one. All this you can do by planning out the right window treatment for your own situation. Let's start with a quick look at the usual types of curtains and draperies. You'll probably include some of these in your window scheme whether you make them yourself, buy them as ready-mades, or have them custom-tailored.

Draperies. Use alone or with shades, blinds or sheer curtains . . . with or without a valance. How to hang them: as draw draperies, full enough to close across the glass, or as side panels only. Can hang from the ceiling or from the top of the window on traverse rods or on poles and rings. Can be extended across more than one window; can be mounted beyond the sides of the window casing to make the window look larger; can cover an entire wall. Lengths: to the floor, to the apron or to the sill (but measure exactly, please, or they'll look awful!).

Casements or glass curtains. Usually hung close to window without draw pulls. Use alone or with draperies. They can be straight panels or shirred. They now come in colors as well as white and

Floor-length draperies with formal valance.

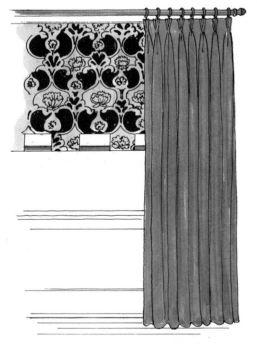

Floor-length draperies hung on brass pole from ceiling, with no valance, a shade instead of curtains.

Café curtains.

Sheer glass curtains.

Ruffled curtains.

off-white. They control light, add privacy, lend a finished look. Lengths: short or floor length.

Café curtains. Panels hung from a rod placed across the middle of a window. Can have one or more upper tiers and/or a top heading. Lengths: sill, apron or floor length—can include tiers of different lengths. Lend an easy, informal look.

Ruffled. Very feminine in look, with ruffled rather than straight hems. Usually sheer or medium-weight fabrics shirred on a single rod and tied back or overlapped. Can have valance. Used in bedrooms, kitchens, bathrooms, informal living or dining rooms.

Now it's time to take a look at the windows themselves. The informative sketches on these two pages can help show you what kind of windows you're working with and alert you to some of their positives and their pitfalls. Note our clues here for practical new ways with windows.

Sash window with hourglass (top and bottom rod) arrangement.

Use ornamental grillwork or fabric across a wall and picture window to unify wall and window.

Bay window.

Dormer window.

Clerestory window.

GETTING TO KNOW YOUR WINDOWS

Window Type	Description	To Keep in Mind
Picture	One large, fixed pane; or one fixed pane with adjustable side panes.	Treatment depends on the "picture" you see through it. Poor view? Block it off, make it part of the wall with ornamental grillwork. Good view? Make the most of it with wide-set, sideswept sheers.
Casement	Double or single windows that swing in or out.	If windows open in, you may want a floor-to-ceiling, wall-to-wall treatment set far enough in front of the windows to allow you to open them behind the draping.
Sash	Two frames, one above the other. Open from top or bottom.	If windows are paired, you might unify them with a single valance, formal draperies and glass curtains. Or close out view but allow for ventilation with an hourglass (top and bottom rod) treatment.
Bay or bow	Three or more windows, angled to form a recess in the wall. Called a bow when the recess is in the form of an arc.	Often have a built-in window seat under them, so short, ruffled curtains to match the seat-covering might be in order. Or try bright-colored shades topped with a broad painted strip as a "pretend" valance.
Dormer	Usually small and vertical, set into an alcove or projecting gable.	Since the shape is vertical, you might cut the height with tiered curtains or an awning-type valance.
Jalousie	Constructed of glass slats that all open and close by means of one crank.	The slats form their own design, so you might plan a painted or fabric border-treatment in a solid color.
Clerestory	Shallow windows placed high in a sloped ceiling or set close to the ceiling for privacy.	Since a view is not the object here, shades patterned to match ceiling panels or matchstick hangings painted to match the walls can help to create unity.
Sliding glass doors	May be part of a glass wall or can be set into a solid wall.	Choose curtains or draperies that draw or can be pulled across the expanse.

Window Type	Description	To Keep in Mind
French	Full-length windows that open like doors. Sometimes called "French doors."	Quite formal in looks, take well to a full-length curtain and swagged drapery effect.

Facts About Fibers, Finishes And Weaves

How easy will it be to take care of? How will it wear? In curtains and draperies, the answer depends on a combination of the fiber, the weave, the finish and the dye used in or on the fabric. First, some facts about weaves, finishes and dyes—then a fiber-fact-and-laundry-hint chart.

Weaves can be plain, twill, satin or variations of one of these. Closer-woven fabrics usually wear better, resist stretching and sagging, are easier to work with if you sew-your-own.

Finishes can be applied to achieve a variety of results: to improve or change appearance; add body, luster, crispness; make moth- , water- or shrink-proof; make stain- or soil-repellent. Read labels carefully to see what finishes have been applied, what they do, if they're permanent. If not, ask if they can be reapplied and how big a deal this is.

Dyes can be added to fibers or to solutions from which man-made fibers are spun; to yarns before spinning into fabric; to the woven fabric. Read labels to see whether fabric is colorfast to sun, heat, laundering, dry cleaning.

For natural fibers (wood, silk, cotton, linen), follow instructions on tag or instructions on soap or detergent box for specific fiber. Remember: With both natural and synthetic fibers, the weave or the finish may require special handling—so *check those tags!*

Brief note: rods and fixtures. Listed below are some of the basic types of rods, with the fixtures they take:

☐ traverse rods (for draw draperies or curtains)
☐ extension rods (extend to accommodate a variety of window sizes)
☐ straight metal rods (have to be cut to order)
☐ cafés (come in various lengths and thicknesses)
☐ poles and rings (available in wood and metal, in various lengths and thicknesses)

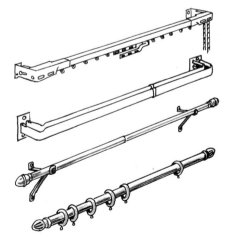

From top to bottom: traverse rod; extension rod; café rod; wooden pole with rings.

FIBER FACTS AND LAUNDRY HINTS

Name	Characteristics	Care
Acrylics (Trade names: Orlon Acrilan Zefran Creslan)	Strong, yet soft and silky —drape well, wash easily, dry quickly. Almost shrink-proof.	If no specific instructions, wash as wash-and-wear. Use lukewarm water, heavy-duty laundry powder, bleach—can use cleaning fluids on grease stains. Wash colors separately, as whites tend to pick up colors. Use softener. Drip-dry or tumble at synthetic setting. If you iron, set at "rayon" or "synthetic."
Polyesters (Trade names: Dacron Kodel Vycron Fortrel)	Crisp to the touch, resilient; resist moisture so there's no stretching or sagging in damp weather. Polyester curtains are outstanding for dainty appearance and easy care.	Don't need ironing if correctly laundered. If no specific instructions, wash as wash-and-wear or dry-clean. Special washing tip: Use bleach occasionally on whites. Any bleach may be used, unless tag warns against chlorine bleach.
Glass cloth (Trade names: Fiberglas PPG Beta)	Fireproof and almost chemical-proof. Anti-static; mildew-, rot- and insect-resistant. Won't stretch, sag, wrinkle or shrink. Caution: has high tensile strength, but cannot take abrasion. Don't wring or twist, don't secure with clothespins, always hang just short of floor or sill. Cover tip of curtain rod with cloth before slipping curtain over it.	Recommend hand washing. Use hot suds with mild soap or detergent. Two rinses. Squeeze! Don't rub, twist or mangle. Roll gently in towel to remove excess water, rehang while damp. Smooth hems with fingers. *Never iron, never dry-clean!*

If You Make Your Own:
Dress Fabrics And Sheets Are Sew-Practical!

Planning to stitch, staple or tape together your own window dressings? Be sure to check out dress goods departments and counters. Prices are lower than for drapery goods and often the look is "the height of fashion." Mad madras, dizzy denims, checks, stripes—in corduroys, cotton suedes, solids and patterns. You'll find the whole range here. Only difference: Fabric widths are narrower than in regular drapery goods. If width is a problem —or if you want to save on hemming, or just don't find what you want in dress goods—amble over to the sheet department. Some of the really dramatic draperies and curtains are made from today's brilliantly designed, easy-care sheets!

Today's Ready-Mades Are Really Something Special!

They come in such a range of colors, sizes, styles and fabrics that it's almost like working with custom-mades. Some are by famous-name designers. Some come as match-mates, too—matching draperies and bedspreads, matching curtains and quilts, matching cafés and studio covers. For bedrooms, some curtains are matched to sheets and pillowcases. For patio doors, there are special one-way draw panels on the market. Here are lists of some of the standard lengths and widths available in curtains and draperies:

One-way draw curtain for patio door.

Lengths	Widths
24″	48″—single
30″	width
36″	72″—width
45″	and a half
54″	96″—double
63″	width
72″	144″—triple
81″	width
90″	

These sketches, all done from ready-mades bought from a department store, will give you an idea of the effects you can achieve.

Draperies and curtains in living room.

Matching café curtains and studio bed cover.

Matching spread and draperies in bedroom.

Shade stenciled by hand.

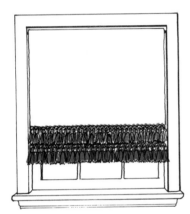

Shade trimmed with fringe.

Shade trimmed with decorative tape.

Shades Of The Present: New And Different

Formal, casual, colorful, crazy—shades have come a long way from the off-white conventionals of a few years ago. Today, they come patterned, printed, trimmed, textured—to go up almost anywhere a curtain or drapery would. Convenience note: You can choose shades (white or in colors) coated in wipe-clean vinyls for the easiest upkeep ever!

What's your stock in shades? Like curtains and draperies, stock shades come in a wide selection. Sizes? Most run 72 inches long and are available in widths from 23 to 36 inches. Adjustable brackets are also available; these can further "customize" the size range. Choose translucent shades to act as room dimmers or opaque ones to block out light more completely. Most stock shades come with a straight or scalloped hem. All it takes to trim them to a custom-look is a bit of mind-stretching plus easily available materials and/or trimmings. Here are some starter suggestions for shades:

Op arts. For spray-painted designs, use only cloth-base shades (not vinyls). Here are some methods of producing op art designs on shades. Lay a pattern out with masking tape and spray-paint the entire area; remove tape and your design will pop up "in relief." Or cut a stencil from cardboard or poster board and use it with spray paint. Or try a print-your-own design, using colored ink, fabric or food dyes, or one of the plastic-enamel paints. Almost anything will serve as a printer: different-size tin cans for circles, boxes for squares, or cut your own design into the cut side of a halved raw potato. Hint: Get a book on nursery school arts and crafts from your public library. It'll give you some tips on making printers! Other ideas: Use a standard office rubber stamp or one of the new "kooky" rubber stamps to get an unusual effect; tie-dye a cloth shade with fabric or food dye; stripe it by using spray paint and two pieces of straight-edged cardboard as "shields."

Trimmings. Beaded eyelet, fringe, ball fringe, sequin strips, cut-out wallpaper appliqués—shade trimmings are limited only by your own head and how skillful you are with your hands.

Taping. You'll find a wide variety of decorative tapes available in local stores. Some come with stick-on backs. Others have to be glued or sewn on. The solid-color plastic tapes can also help create mini-masterpieces in shade art.

The custom-made shade can be cut and designed in a variety of sizes, styles and materials. If you're match-minded, have one made to match drapery, bedspread or upholstery fabrics you're using. This type of shade is then laminated for easy care. You can also use one of the available make-a-shade kits to make your own and then laminate them yourself. The instructions that come with the kit will show you just how to put the shade together—and may include suggestions for easy-care finishes.

New Ways With Shades: As Camouflage Or Instant Art

Today's shades can be so decorative that they're often used "up on the wall" to create a number of different effects. Appliquéd with an Oriental scenic paper or spray-painted with an Oriental design, shades can be trimmed and hung as handsome wall scrolls. They make easy roll-up-and-take-with-you "pretend" headboards when hung on the wall behind your bed. They can be used to hide (or replace) ugly doors or close off cluttered shelves from sight.

The window that wasn't there exists because "you made it happen" with a shade, some strips of molding, a bracket shelf and a cheery planter. A sheer-fantasy window like this can create wall interest where there was none, or give you a reason to group or pair off pieces of furniture. Or it can add a feeling of "outside" in an inside windowless room.

The bamboos, woven woods and verticals. Most exotic of the window-shaders, they're available today in natural finishes or a variety of colors. Again, you're almost sure to find a stock width you can use—and some of these are available in plastic versions that are a snap to care for. Now for some vital statistics on the group. The split bamboos and matchsticks come both as roll-ups and as vertical traverse curtains. Ditto the woven woods. Vertical venetian blinds (very sophisticated!) are available in a range of cloths and plastics. Standard venetian blinds come in aluminum, steel, plastic and woods, in a variety of colors, and have matching or contrasting tapes.

The Inside Story On Shutters: The New Versatiles

Once you had to have these wooden beauties made; now they can be bought in combinations of stock sizes that fit almost any window. They're available in a variety of styles, too—some are designed to be filled in with fabric! They're usable on most types of windows (with the exception of casements that open inward and windows that open with a crank), but do require a framing of wooden strips to which the shutters can be hinged.

Like shades, shutters have more than one decorating talent. They can close off a storage corner (or create one), hide shelving, divide a room into defined areas. And they too can be turned into an attractive headboard!

THE "WHAT, WHERE AND WHY" OF SHEETS, TOWELS, TABLE LINENS

You might also call this section "Hey—what's happened to the hope chest?" The fibers and finishes available in linens today help you get by with fewer, also mean your linens will last longer, be easier to care for. You can go way out on color and pattern or do interesting things with bright whites in combination with colors. You can treat yourself to signed designer "originals" or buy thrifty seconds or sale specials. Even budget-muslin comes gussied up these days! You don't have to give up a closet to linens anymore, either. The following pages include some helpful hints on space-saving (or space-making) ways to store your linens.

Budget note: Today's Bridal Registry or linen shower can help take the place of yesterday's hope chest. If someone asks you what you want (or if you plan to use a Registry), don't forget to mention linens. Even with today's "wash 'em in the machine" varieties, linens can mount up into a sizable item if you're starting from scratch. For sheets and towels, you might specify a particular color or pattern. With table linens, you'd probably mention the general types you want.

What's New In Sheets? The Blends, The Beauty

Certainly the first thing that'll strike your eye at the bed-linen counters is the range of color and pattern. You'll find everything from tiger stripes to garden flowers, with deep-toned solids and modern abstract designs in between. Often, you can color-coordinate a solid with a print. (Idea: When picking prints, try to match print to personality. Don't burden an outdoorsy personality with a Victorian posy print, for instance!) You'll find whites available too, of course—many with decorative borders. Advantages of each? Color can give a lift to your bedroom decor and to your spirits. Whites are usually cheaper, are "safer" if you buy before you're sure of your bedroom color scheme, and are adaptable in case you change that color scheme later on.

The new easy-cares result from a blending of cotton fibers with polyesters, rayon, nylon or Dacron. (Ratio: 50% cotton and 50% Dacron, for instance.) Result: They'll stand up to repeated washings, retain their "whiteness" or color, will not need ironing. Some easy-cares feature additional stain- and soil-release finishes. This means they'll release most stains—even oil-based stains from hair oil or hand lotion—when washed at home with regular detergents. These finishes also lend sheets added resistance to staining from most water-based or oily materials. And this resistance will last through many launderings.

Decorating With Things You Love.

Fragile treasures are safe inside their own light box, built right into a bookcase. Check hardware stores for lighting ideas and fixtures.

Build your own catty-corner display table to show off treasures you like to use occasionally.

Use "little collections" and a runner to decorate that dining table between meals. Display the "littles" on trays so you can move them easily to another spot when it's time to set the table.

Dramatize A Kitchen—With Color, Texture, Pattern.

Small and dull becomes small, sleek and sophisticated! Choose a "wild" color, lavish flooring (you don't need much—so splurge) and a wide peel-off stripe to modernize old fixtures.

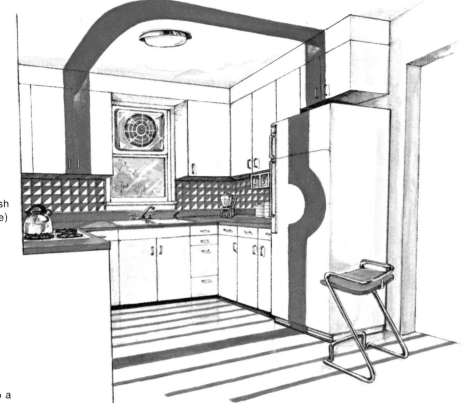

A big old monster can be transformed into a showplace. Use new, do-it-yourself brick wall facing (sold at lumberyards), "antique" accessories, a wooden table—country charm itself.

Decorating With Plants: Three Ways To Create An Indoor Landscape.

"Curtain" a window with plants and planters. They let in the light, create a pretty view—and they'll fit another window if you move.

Little plants, big plants, hanging plants, floor plants. All together, they create a room divider that's refreshingly different, looks great from any angle.

Use an indoor tree as the main point-of-interest in a room. Just one, combined with some interesting furniture, can give the effect of a whole garden in very little space.

Quilt, Canopy Or Cover-Up —Fabric Adds Extra Dimension To Walls.

Cover-up caper! Hide tired walls behind a sweep of fabric staple-gunned at ceiling height. Our chair rail adds a Shaker-style touch.

Quilts are fun whether you opt for traditional or modern or both. Mount them on a wall with wooden dowels for a personality-plus wall decor.

Define a dining room in very simple terms. Create a gay fabric canopy— add a matching wall panel applied via staple gun or fabric paste.

Always rub sheets together before you buy. If a powdery residue appears, it may mean that the manufacturer added a kind of starch to the finishing process to disguise poor quality. Hold sheets to the light, too. The weave should be even, without thick or thin spots, knots or slubs. Also test the firmness of the selvage.

Muslin vs. percale. It's a matter of thread count. Muslins with a thread count of 140 threads per square inch will give good wear. Percales are lighter in weight and smoother than muslins. A 180-count percale will give excellent wear; a 200-count will give even better wear. In general, percales are more expensive.

Sizing up sheets. Getting a good fit depends on knowing your mattress size. Sheets should allow for a 10-inch tuck-in on each side and at top and bottom. For fitted sheets, measure the length, width *and depth* of your mattress. There's a big difference between an innerspring and a foam mattress; fitted bottoms come made especially for each type. In general, these sizes apply.

SHEET SIZES: FOR COMFORT, CONVENIENCE

Type of Mattress	Flat Sheet Size (after hemming)
Daybeds, cots, bunk beds	63x108″
Single	63x108″
Twin	72x108″
Extra-long twin	72x120″
Double	81x108″
Extra-long double	81x120″
Queen-size	91x120″
King-size	116x120″
California King-size	112x124″

How many are "enough"? The old rule of thumb was six sheets per bed: one set on the bed, one in the closet, one in the laundry. If you have the easy-cares and launder at home or at the launderette, you'll probably be able to get by with four sheets per bed, however. If you run into a problem, you can always add another set. People used to figure on a total of six pillowcases, but you might try four and add extras if you have to.

Space-saving stowaways. If closet space is tight, you might design a bedroom storage-wall to hold sheets, books, magazines—perhaps a small TV set and anything else you need or think will look good on those shelves. Another solution: Use the space under the bed. You can buy large, flat containers especially made for such storage, although any large, flat box will do. Or turn a small trunk or footlocker into a bedside table and use it as storage space. Today, these trunks come in bright colors and shiny finishes; they're quite inexpensive, too. When you move, they make helpful carryalls and can always be shifted to living room, den or playroom to use as extra tables.

What's New In Towels? Colors And Coordinates

Today's towels take the lighthearted approach, too. Striking colors and color combinations crop up everywhere and the "completely coordinated" look is big news. This can mean towels, bed linens and spreads, blankets and shower curtains, as well as bathroom accessories like hampers and tissue boxes. You'll also find a new feeling to towel surfaces. Check the chart below for a description of these newcomers. Then check the chart on the facing page for a rundown on towel sizes.

TYPECASTING TOWELS

Type	Description	Comments
Terry	The basic weave common to all towels.	Closeness of loops and tightness of weave (not the thickness of the towel) produces the drying power.
Velvet or velour	Achieved by shearing the loops after weaving.	Gives a luxurious, decorator look.
Combination	Terry on one side, velour on the other.	Happy combination of brisk-rubdown terry on one side, decorative velvet or velour on the other.
Jacquard	Design is woven right into the towel.	Design appears on both sides. Towel usually has a textured surface.
Printed	Pattern is printed on towel rather than woven in.	Pattern appears only on one side, may not be as permanent as a jacquard, particularly in cheaper grades.

Note: All towels are made of cotton; the weave or pattern constitutes the difference.

Sizing up towels. Although sizes tend to vary from one type and quality to another, the following are the most usual.

TOWEL SIZES: THE WHOLE RACKFUL

Type	Size
Bath	22x24″ to 27x50″
Hand or face	16x26″ to 16x30″
Guest or fingertip	11x18″ to 13x20″
Washcloth	12x12″ or 13x13″
Bath sheet	34x66″ to 36x72″
Tub mat	20x30″ to 22x36″
Bath mats or rugs	These vary widely, but here are some sample sizes: 20x36″, 23x35″, 24x42″, 27x48″; 24″ or 30″ round

How many towels are enough? Towels are usually sold in sets, although you can also buy them individually. A set includes: bath towel, hand towel, washcloth. Again, tradition says three sets per person plus two or three tub mats and an assortment of guest towels. With a home washing machine or handy launderette, we suspect you could shave this to two sets per head plus a couple of extra washcloths as "spares."

Space-saving stowaways. Like sheets, towels need not take up valuable closet space. Here are some ideas: Inexpensive ready-made bathroom shelves are available that utilize the space above the toilet tank. Or add towels to your bedroom storage wall, to an under-bed container or storage-chest night table.

Blankets: Better Bed-Mates Than Ever

Here too, manufacturers offer you a combination of beauty and practicality. Wide ranges of colors, designer prints, summer-winter weights, new "suede" finishes, new thermal weaves—these are some of the news highlights in this field. The chart on the following page gives you a look at the big blanket-picture.

Comforter/quilts do double duty. They serve as lightweight, super-warmers at night; combined with a dust ruffle, they can double as a bedspread during the day. They're available in twin- (72x84″), full- (80x90″) or Queen/King-size (105x90″). Favorite filling today: Dacron, which is light, warm and washable. Down, feather and down, and cotton are other, less common, possibles.

BLANKETING THE NEWS IN BLANKETS

Constructions	Fibers	Sizes
Conventional nap—available in all types of fibers. Weight is not important for warmth, but a dense nap is necessary to trap air and retain body heat. Acrylics function as well as wool, but rayon tends to mat down.	Wool Acrylics Rayons Cottons	65x80″, 84″ or 90″ for twin-size bed 72x90″ for twin- or full-size bed 108x90″ for Queen- or King-size bed
Bonded plushes—created by bonding nylon fibers to polyurethane foam. They're lightweight, machine washable, resist shrinking and shedding. They also resist the tendency to "pill" that characterizes some other types of synthetic fiber blankets.		
New thermal weaves—a crochet-like weave that creates thousands of thermal air pockets, which act as insulation. Available in synthetic and cotton fibers. They're warm in winter, especially if used with a light blanket or spread over one. Used alone, they're cool in summer.		
Electric blankets—with heating unit in use, they're light-but-warm winter snugglers. Without unit, they make an ideal summer blanket. Heating units are available in single or dual controls. With duals, each of you can dial the degree of warmth you wish. Many electrics come with fitted corners for extra convenience. Caution: Never dry-clean an electric blanket. Hand- or machine-wash, following tag instructions to the letter.	100% acrylic fiber or rayon blends	

Table Linens Match Your Life-Style

Whether it's dinner for two or entertaining friends, eating times focus on friendly informality today. Guests come prepared to serve themselves; to eat from coffee, card or occasional tables; to substitute floor cushions for chairs; to barbecue outdoors, or indoors around the fireplace. But because occasions like these are informal doesn't mean that they're sloppy. There's a whole spread of up-to-date table setters available. Not only do they handle at-ease situations beautifully, but they're easy on the upkeep, too!

The place mat goes everywhere. Most versatile of all "linens," these are unbeatable on conventional dining tables, individual TV tables, card tables—anyplace that anyone ever thought of using as a dining surface! You'll see them in cork, vinyl, cotton, cotton-and-synthetic blends, woven wood, paper—the list is almost endless. Now you can buy linen place mats individually, with napkins to match or contrast. It'll probably be more convenient, though, to pick wipe-clean types and pair them with color-coordinated easy-care napkins. In this case, easy-care can include no-iron varieties. You have a choice of shapes, too. Rectangles and ovals are the most usual, but you'll also find special shapes designed to match up with different-shaped tables—round, square or free-form, for instance. Often, a change of napkin will change a mat from formal to informal—a boon if space or money is tight. So look at what's around, then set your table with whatever appeals!

Tablecloths, too, have moderned up! Of course, you can still buy a formal damask or linen if you wish. But there's a lot else going for you, too. Synthetic fibers; natural fibers with no-iron, soil-release finishes; vinyls (both wipe-off and machine washable). The choice is wide, wide; so is the range of sizes and shapes. Squares, oblongs, ovals, rectangles are all available in so many sizes it's hard to generalize. As a rule of thumb: Your cloth should be large enough to cover the tabletop, with an overhang of 10 to 16 inches. Here's a list of some of the tablecloth sizes listed in a large department store's mail-order catalog:

52x52″ square	60x108″ rectangle
54x54″ square	62x102″ oval or rectangle
52x70″ oval or rectangle	68x82″ oval
52x90″ oval or rectangle	70x90″ oval or rectangle
54x72″ rectangle	70x108″ rectangle
58x88″ oval	60″ round
60x80″ rectangle	70″ round
60x90″ oval or rectangle	90″ round

Want to add on to the size of your table? Have your lumberyard cut a piece of plywood to the desired size and shape; top your table with this whenever you need extra seating or surface area.

Napkins are newsy, too. No-iron is the big news here. Dinner-size napkins (17x17″) are popular, but you'll also find the smaller luncheon size available. Ecology note: Paper napkins become prettier every day; only you can weigh out their practical advantages against your own ecology-sense. Possible solution: Use the absolutely no-iron terry fingertip towels instead.

DINNERWARE: FORMAL OR CASUAL—
LET YOUR LIFE-STYLE SET THE PATTERN

Formal patterns and matched sets of dinnerware are still very much on the scene. And they help create an air of caring and of gracious homelife. But today, there's also a trend toward the "modular" approach to table settings. Contrasting solid colors, light and dark shades of one color, solids and patterns, even two or more patterns are often combined on the same table. And the effect can range all the way from formal sophistication to "wild and way out." This mix-and-match look offers some very real advantages when you're starting out. You can achieve variety with a limited number of pieces—a definite plus when storage and budget are limited. It also allows you to make the most of hand-me-down china (which often can't be matched) by filling in with pieces of a different style or pattern. Whichever approach you decide to take, keep the following points in mind when you're buying dinnerware.

Useful Tips On Buying Tableware

☐ Consider the general "look" your home will have. Is it traditional . . . modern . . . country-style . . . citified? Your tableware should help carry out the general feeling of your home. At the very least, it shouldn't conflict!

☐ Keep your glassware and silver in mind. All the elements on a table should work together. You might combine wooden-handled stainless with one of the traditional English floral china patterns—but not with a formal gold-banded design! Keep this point in mind if you're mix-matching china patterns, too. They don't have to be of the same type or period, but they should share a common feeling to look well together.

☐ Try to buy "open stock" patterns—that is, patterns in which you can buy individual items and that will be stocked by the store for several years to come. Ask your salesman about this. If you're planning to set your table all in one pattern, consider starting off with a "starter set." These can have as few as sixteen pieces, as many as forty-five. Most starter sets include the basics for four place settings (see details on this on page 112). These are often specially priced, so they're cheaper than individual pieces bought separately would be.

☐ Will it be easy to store? Odd shapes, raised edges, heavily embossed borders—these will all make tableware harder to store and to fit in a dishwasher.

☐ Does it handle easily? The only way to find out is to pick up a piece or two in the store. Are cup handles large enough and conveniently placed? Ditto for cream pitchers, coffeepots and teapots, if you're investing in them. Other points about these: Will

Size up its
personality.

they pour easily and will they clean out easily? Round shapes are usually better than squarish or hexagonal in this respect.

☐ Always ask if a pattern is dishwasher-safe. Even if you don't own a dishwasher now you probably will someday, and you undoubtedly don't want to be stuck with pieces that have to be washed by hand.

Check it
out for
practicality.

We've charted out the basic ways in which china, glassware and table linens can be combined in mix-match (or modular) arrangements. We'll leave specific colors and patterns up to you. But this chart will give you the framework for planning out some interesting combinations using your own linens, china and glassware.

TABLE OF CONTENTS: FOR MIX-MATCH TABLEWARE

Dinnerware	Glasses	Linens
Patterned plates. Bowls, cups and saucers pick up one of the pattern colors.	Matched to solid-color bowls, cups and saucers.	Matched to solid color.
Patterned plates. Bowls, cups and saucers in a contrasting solid color.	Matched to contrasting solid used in bowls, cups and saucers.	Matched to solid color.
Solid-color plates. Bowls, cups, saucers (and possibly salad plates) in contrasting solid.	Matched to contrasting solid used in bowls, cups and saucers.	Matched to either solid color. Or patterned in matching or complementary colors.
Plates, bowls, cups and saucers in light and dark shades of the same color.	Matched to one solid color. Or in an in-between shade of the same color. Or in a complementary color.	Matched to any of the solid colors used in plates or glasses. Or patterned to match one of the solids or to include two of the solids.
A pattern-on-pattern combination. A stripe with a floral, for instance. Same basic color appears in both patterns.	Matched to basic color in patterns. Or in a contrasting color.	Matched to one of the predominant colors, or to background color if it's the same in both prints.
Two patterns combined. Predominant color in one contrasts with predominant color in other. Note: Single-color patterns are safest here.	Matched to one of the predominant colors. Or use a clear glass.	Matched to one of the predominant colors, or to background color if it's the same in both prints.

CHECKLIST

Place Setting:
☐ dinner plate
☐ salad/dessert plate
☐ fruit/cereal bowl
☐ cup and saucer

Serving Pieces:
☐ sugar bowl
☐ cream pitcher
☐ platter
☐ vegetable dishes
☐ gravy boat
☐ coffeepot

Basic Dinnerwares: China And The Other Choices

You'll still hear the word "china" used to describe all kinds of dinnerware—most of which isn't china at all. Listed below, a mini-dictionary of dinnerware descriptions:

Fine china (porcelain): made of fine clays, fired at high temperatures for added strength. Fine; translucent; looks fragile, but resists chipping and cracking well.

Bone china: same as above, except that animal bone ash is added to clays to produce a stark white color.

Earthenware: thicker, more porous than china. Opaque; usually features colorful glazes. In general, chips and cracks more easily than china, although some finer qualities have a hard, strong body and last well.

Pottery: heavier, less expensive type of earthenware; less resistant to chipping and cracking. Both pottery and earthenware are usually available in more informal types of dinnerware.

Ironstone: type of earthenware, usually the most durable. Look for casual designs here.

Stoneware: a glassy-finished, opaque ceramicware, usually quite strong and thick. Usually seen in grey, buff or brown "country casual" designs.

Ovenware: type of clayware designed to withstand oven heat.

Melamine: plastic dinnerware that resists chipping and breaking. Available in a range of colorful and attractive styles.

Glass: newest dinnerware. The glass, which is opaque, looks like china, but is guaranteed to resist breaking, chipping and cracking for a specified number of years. Dishwasher- *and* oven-safe!

The Question Of Quantity: What's Enough To Get By With?

We've already mentioned the advantages of starting out with a starter set, which usually consists of four place settings. What's in a place setting? See the list in the margin for a description of a basic place setting. Our margin list also includes a listing of some serving pieces that are sometimes included in a starter set. If you've got a bit more storage space than average or have a little more dinnerware money in the budget, you might buy one of the sets that include place settings for six. If you're going mix-and-match, buy six of each: plates, bowls, cups and saucers.

Some other items you can add later on: soup plates, small side bowls, bread-and-butter plates, luncheon-size plates (smaller than dinner-size), fruit bowls.

Table-fashion note: Even if you choose to set your table all in one pattern, you can still pick your serving pieces in an alternate color or pattern or in a different material—silver or ovenproof ceramic or glass, for instance. Ovenproof serving pieces are particularly practical. They save a lot of washing up and they make warming and reheating-to-serve-again much easier!

Entertaining "extras": Not all of these are necessary, but we bet you'll end up wanting some of them, depending on the type of entertaining you do.

☐ LARGE SALAD BOWL, with or without matching individual bowls. These are available today in the classic wooden versions, but also in glass and a variety of clear or opaque plastics. Use them for green salads, of course. Use the glass or plastic ones to serve crunchy-crisp raw vegetable strips (kept alive and blooming on a packing of cracked ice). Don't forget to buy salad servers when you buy the bowl, by the way!

☐ LARGE, OVENPROOF CASSEROLE DISH and/or ovenproof skillet. The bigger the better with these if you go in for mini mob scenes.

☐ SEVERAL SMALLER OVENPROOF CASSEROLES. Use these when the crowd is smaller, or for side dishes. We've already mentioned that these can double as traditional vegetable dishes.

☐ A SOUFFLE DISH AND RAMEKINS are both good thoughts in this whole oven-to-table field. Individual baked-in-a-ramekin dishes are great for brunches, sit-around-the-TV suppers—anytime when the crowd is not too large.

☐ PIZZA PAN AND CUTTER; FONDUE POT AND ACCESSORIES are bright ideas. Both make possible highly specialized but easy-on-the-hostess types of food. Of course, they happen to be favorite foods with guests, too!

☐ A CHAFING DISH, with a bright flame burning underneath, really does a number for a buffet table (even if you're featuring canned meatballs inside it!).

☐ THE ELECTRIC HOT TRAY can be a dinner-saver for a new cook. If all courses don't "come out on time," you can often keep the early-readies warm and inviting on a hot tray while the other foods finish cooking.

☐ A LARGE BREAD BASKET; A HANDSOME COFFEE WARMER (or electric pot) are almost "musts" these days.

☐ A GOOD-LOOKING SET OF MUGS is practically pure "plus." Mugs are easy-to-hold for soups and don't need saucers for coffee; they're great for ice-cream desserts and for soft drinks, too!

GOOD NEWS IN GLASSWARE: A PALETTE OF COLORS—PLUS THE PLASTICS!

Glasses no longer have to line up like soldiers on guard—different heights but all dressed the same! Here too, the trend is toward informality and mix-match. Of course, there's nothing wrong with having all your glassware in one pattern, but storage space, budget and breakage often make this impossible. You may settle for having each type of glass (tumbler, juice, wine goblet) in a different style, with six or eight of each type on your shelves. More good news! Color is coming up strong in contemporary glassware; plastic is perfectly acceptable; and you don't *have* to serve wine in a stemmed glass.

The Question Of Quantity: Barest Basics

If you're *really* squeaking by on the mini-est minimum, you can settle for six large tumblers and six smaller ones—in plastic! You serve water and long drinks in the larger size, shorter drinks, juice and wine in the smaller. Choose the right plastic and you'll get good looks as well as durability. Good plastic glasses (like all good glasses) are expensive—but they pay for themselves in length of service. You can choose them in a color to coordinate with linens and dishes or in go-with-everything clear. Colors seem to be favorites in plastics, but it's a matter of personal taste.

If you have room for more—here's a traditional starter set (although you don't need to choose it in a traditional type of glass). Buy four or six of each.

☐ water tumblers
☐ all-purpose wine glasses
☐ juice glasses
☐ stemmed sherbet or champagne glasses
☐ stemmed water goblets

Add these at a later date if life leads you into a heavy entertaining scene and schedule:

☐ cordial glasses
☐ sherry glasses
☐ old fashioned glasses
☐ brandy glasses

Buyer's guide note: You can choose your starter set, or any glassware you buy, in a range of different qualities.

CRYSTAL really refers to the clearness and brilliance of the glass. It is usually used to describe the finest-quality, most expensive grade, known as lead or flint glass.

LEAD GLASS has a brilliant shine and will take deep cutting or etching that, as with a diamond, adds to its sparkle. Tap the edge of this glass and it rings like a bell.

LIME GLASS, most popular for general use, is a medium-grade glass, slightly yellower in color than its more expensive cousin. Held up to the light, it should be colorless, transparent and have a minimum of imperfections. Check for smooth, regular edges. In stemware, stems should be firmly and smoothly joined to base. Colored glass should have luster and be even in tint.

BARGAIN-STORE GLASSWARE is being made in better designs all the time. With a little searching, you can find patterns (often copies of more expensive brands) with true good looks.

THE NEW PLASTICS are available in different grades, too. Usually, the more expensive the "glass," the thinner and more lustrous the plastic will be.

If you're a treasure-hunter, you can set your table with one-of-a-kind finds. Elaborately cut crystal, old pressed glass, Bohemian glass (in which the cut design shows up "clear" against a background of rich red, dark blue or green)—you can still search out old or interesting glassware like this in antique shops, thrift shops, flea markets. They're rewarding items to collect and the price is usually within reach.

FROM STERLING TO STAINLESS: FLATWARE IS A MATTER OF PERSONAL CHOICE

You have an across-the-board choice when it comes to selecting your flatware. Sterling, silverplate, stainless—even goldplate and new plastics! It's just a matter of what you think looks best with your dinnerware, linens and general decor. It's pattern, not price, that will probably indicate which type of flatware you'll want. Some stainless is as expensive as sterling; silverplate can be less expensive than either. If you favor very contemporary designs, you'll probably head for stainless or plastic. If you're middle-of-the-line, you'll find a wider selection in sterling or plate. The term flatware, incidentally, covers the knives, forks and spoons you will find in a place setting as well as serving pieces like forks, spoons, sugar tongs, gravy ladles. Hollowware refers to silver or metal pieces like vegetable dishes, teapots or coffeepots, even candlesticks.

Facts about sterling. It's usually the most expensive—and the classic—choice. Sterling is solid silver with 7½% copper added for hardness. If kindly treated, it will last many lifetimes. Wash it in the dishwasher (*except for old, hollow-handled knives!*) or with soap/detergent and water. Dry with a soft cloth if you hand-wash. It's available in a range of finishes, from shiny-bright to mellow. If you decide on sterling, you really *can* use it every day. Daily handling and rubbing in time work up a beautiful soft finish called a "patina."

What will sterling cost? Price varies with design and weight. The heavier the pattern the more expensive. Today, many people prefer luncheon-weight knives and forks to the larger and heavier dinner size. The luncheon-weights seem more suitable to our less-formal life-style and are less expensive as well! When comparison shopping on sterling, make sure you're comparing dinner against dinner, or luncheon with luncheon pieces.

Facts about silverplate. It looks much like sterling because it features a thin coat of silver over silver nickel or other metal base. The silver grade depends on the thickness of the plating: XXXX (quadruple); XXX (triple); XX (double)—these are some of the standard ratings. In finer designs, spot overlays reinforce areas that get the hardest wear—the base of the bowl in spoons, for instance. Some silverplate is guaranteed for lifelong service, as is sterling.

Facts about stainless. This is a solid metal that's almost completely stain proof. It wears well, doesn't tarnish—so it doesn't have to be polished. As with silver, weight is the sign of quality—the heavier the piece the better! The price range is enormous—all the way from discount-store kitchen sets to Scandinavian imports that are designer inspired. There's nothing temporary about the latter! If you invest in these, you'll want to keep them for a lifetime. But some couples do invest in a good-looking but cheaper stainless pattern while they're deciding on a sterling pattern or accumulating place settings. The stainless can always be used later for cookouts or picnics.

Facts about some other possibilities. We've already mentioned the ultra-modern "plastics" that are available. These range from patterns that combine plastic handles with stainless steel blades, tines or bowls to all-plastic designs. Most of these entries are very handsome and very practical—but not always very cheap. A real "exotic" is goldplate. To make this, a layer of gold is electroplated onto a metal base, a process much like that used for silverplate. Prices run about double what silverplate costs, but are not exorbitant. Another good way to get "the golden look" is with dirilyte—an alloy that combines aluminum, copper and nickel for a light, strong, gleaming-golden service.

Some practicalities. Just as for dinnerware, it's best to buy flatware from open stock. Many traditional patterns have been on the market for as long as seventy-five years; this is eminently practical when it comes to filling in on extra pieces and "losables" like teaspoons.

Remember that the simpler patterns are easier to clean and will probably be more adaptable to changes in dishes, linens, decor. However, if an ornate pattern is what you want, have it by all means, and ease up on the cleaning by keeping the flatware in a silver chest or wrapped in treated silver-cloths. This is good advice to follow for any silver, incidentally.

You can buy flatware as sets, as individual place settings or as individual pieces. The most usual for starting-outers is to invest in four, six or eight place settings, then add settings as they're needed.

Each Place Setting Usually Consists Of:
☐ knife (luncheon- or dinner-size)
☐ fork (luncheon- or dinner-size)
☐ teaspoon
☐ salad/dessert fork
☐ soup/dessert spoon (or second teaspoon)

Other basics you'll need almost immediately:
☐ 2 tablespoons or serving spoons
☐ carving set
☐ 1 sugar, sauce or relish spoon

Other pieces you can add from time to time, depending on your needs, might include: additional teaspoons, cocktail forks, iced tea spoons, butter knives, cake server, berry spoon, gravy ladle.

Collector's note: Unearthing individual pieces of old silver has become a hobby with many. Some look just for serving pieces to mix in with their regular pattern; some collect old spoons; some go all the way and put together a tableful of flatware, each piece one-of-a-kind!

CHECKLIST: A QUICK COUNT OF YOUR BASIC LINEN, TABLEWARE AND FLATWARE NEEDS

LINEN

sheets—2 sets per bed	bedspreads
pillowcases—2 per pillow	towels—2 sets per person
mattress pads	tub mats
blankets or comforters	place mats, tablecloths, napkins

CHINA

dinner plates
salad plates
fruit/cereal bowls
cups and saucers
serving pieces

GLASSWARE

large- and small-size tumblers
        or
tumblers and stemmed glasses

FLATWARE

knife and fork
teaspoon
salad/dessert fork
soup/dessert spoon
  (or second teaspoon)
serving pieces

Note: Buy all of the above in quantities of four or more.

LOOK WHAT'S COOKING IN KITCHENS AND KITCHENWARE!

Designers are planning kitchens that cover the range from all-along-one-wall pullman setups to kitchens that function as complete family rooms. Big or small, kitchens are looking brighter, functioning better every day! Appliances, cabinets and equipment come in a spectrum of colors. Decorative wallpapers and carpeting underfoot? You can have these, too. And if you plan and buy wisely, you can turn even a standard small apartment kitchen into an attractive, smoothly working space.

Buying Plan: Don't Skimp On Essentials; Do Stick To The Essentials

You can really go hog-wild on pots, pans, kitchen appliances and gadgets. If you do, chances are that a lot of what you buy will become prize dust-collectors and space-consumers. The better way: Figure out a few basics that can serve more than one purpose and then add to these as you find out what kind of cooking and entertaining you're actually doing. This doesn't mean you skimp on quality. Good pots and pans are a wise investment. They're easy to take care of, they'll last much longer than poor-quality utensils, and food cooks better in them. A good heavyweight pot with a tight-fitting lid and an ovenproof handle will do much more for you than its "tinny" poor relation, no matter how cheaply priced the latter may be. The same goes for appliances. Steer away from the so-called "bargains" in those you do buy. But make sure that the appliance you want is something you'll really use more than once or twice. An electric popcorn popper is great if you're big on popcorn. But if popcorn is a passing fancy in your life, what else can you do with the electric popper?

Up-To-Date News On Pots And Pans

A lot of today's kitchenware is so well-designed and eye appealing that you can almost class it as tableware. In fact, many pieces are planned to go from range to table. Keep this cook-and-serve factor in mind when you buy. It's a lifesaver, especially if storage space is limited *and* if dishes are done by hand! There's a wide variety of cookware available—in many different kinds of materials, with many different linings and finishes. Each type has its own advantages. You'll find a performance-rating chart of the most popular types below. Here are some basic pots and pans, identified by size and type:

1½-qt. saucepan (covered)	8″ open skillet
2-qt. saucepan (covered)	10 to 12″ skillet (covered)
3-qt. saucepan (covered)	5-qt. Dutch oven (covered)

PERFORMANCE-RATED: POPULAR TYPES OF COOKWARE

Description	Performance
Stainless steel:	Lightweight, durable, easy to clean. Resists staining, pitting, corroding.
aluminum clad	Rapid, even heating; reduces chances of heat spots developing.
copper clad	Excellent for low-heat cooking; bottoms require some care. May have a radiant or copper core added for additional heat conduction.
Cast aluminum	Heavy-gauge, durable, retains heat well. Excellent for most cooking needs.
Stamped aluminum	Fairly lightweight; inexpensive. Conducts heat well but dents easily, loses shape quickly. Best used for baking utensils.
Porcelain enamel:	
on heavy-gauge aluminum	Gives an attractive, easy-clean finish to the aluminum.
on steel	Offers a nonporous surface that resists odors and stains. Some enamels may chip or craze when exposed to sudden high heats.
on cast iron	Heavier, more durable than porcelainized aluminum or steel. Higher-priced but worth it because it can be used on the range top, in the oven and at the table. Can also be used for food storage.
Glass	Sometimes designed for use on top of range but most often for casseroles, pie plates and other baking dishes. May crack if subjected to temperature extremes. Good for cooking, serving and storing.
Glass-ceramic	Opaque type of glass. Can be used over flame or in the oven. Will withstand extreme temperature changes. Cleans easily.

PERFORMANCE-RATED: POPULAR TYPES OF COOKWARE

Description	Performance
Cast iron	Heats easily, retains heat for a long time. Excellent for long, slow cooking. Usually available in black, with no special finishes. Must be seasoned. Used for skillets, baking pans, Dutch ovens, griddles.
Tinned copper	The traditional beauty of copper on the outside, lined with tin. Like all copper it's a fast heat conductor, can create hot spots with high heat. Copper can also be lined with stainless steel. Some brands have a core of other metals to make heat distribution more even.
Ceramic	Colorful pottery, glazed on the inside. Conducts heat poorly, can be fragile. Used for casseroles, for slow oven cooking. Cleans easily. New pottery dishes are available that will withstand a moderate gas flame but not the heat of an electric unit.
Non-stick finishes	Two varieties available. The cheaper type is applied to surface, will eventually wear away and need resurfacing. The better type is fired on, guaranteed for life of the pan. Always follow manufacturer's directions for initial seasoning and general care.
Terra cotta bakers	Unglazed pottery with a tightly fitting lid. Allows you to bake vegetables, chicken, meats with the addition of a minimum of water or shortening.

Note: Special utensils (usually paper or glass) designed to be used in microwave ovens are available. When you invest in one of these ovens, be sure to ask about suitable cooking utensils.

CHECKLIST: PICKING THE BEST PAN FOR THE JOB AT HAND

In general, a good cooking utensil should be strong, easy to clean, spread the heat evenly, and create no hot spots. Here are some specifics to check out:

☐ Bottoms—should have allover contact with the heat source.

☐ Sides—should be straight or rounded; sloping sides can contribute to heat loss.

☐ Lids—should fit well, but not so tightly that they are difficult to remove when pot is hot.

☐ Handles—should be heat proof and easy to grip, with no danger of their turning in your hand. They should also be long enough to make sure your hand won't touch the sides of pots when you grasp them.

☐ For quick, top-of-range cooking, look for a medium-weight pan that's a fast heat-conductor.

☐ Corners—should be rounded so there are no hard-to-clean crevices for food to lodge in.

☐ Knobs on lids—should be heat resistant as well as easy to grip.

Note: If you invest in a smooth-top range, in which the heat source is located under smooth ceramic glass material, check to see if the manufacturer recommends any particular type of cooking utensils.

Other pointers to bear in mind when you're choosing utensils:

☐ For simmering or slow cooking, look for a heavier-weight pan that will retain heat and steam so there's no loss of liquid or flavor.

☐ For oven cooking, make sure pan handles and lid knobs are ovenproof.

☐ For easier storing, make sure pots stack together easily. Try to include one or two range-to-table types to cut down on the number of utensils you need.

KITCHEN LISTS: A POTPOURRI OF ESSENTIALS AND EXTRAS

ESSENTIALS

set of covered saucepans
(1-qt., 2-qt., 3-qt. or Dutch oven)

2 covered skillets (8″ to 12″)

casseroles (20-oz., 1-qt., 2-qt.—
preferably oven-to-table)

roasting pan with rack

baking pan (8x8x2″ or 9x9x2″)

baking pan (13x9x2″)

2 round layer pans (8 or 9x1½″)

pie plates (8″ and 9″)

cookie sheets (at least 2 without sides)

muffin pan

loaf pan (9x5x3″)

pot holders

meat thermometer

knives (see information on
following page)

knife-sharpener

wooden spoons

metal spoons

rubber scrapers

flexible metal spatula

can opener

bottle and jar opener

measuring cups
(for dry and for liquid
ingredients)

measuring spoons

mixing bowls

long-handled fork

juicer

cutting board

grater-shredder

strainer or sieve

vegetable parer

vegetable brush

rotary beater

kitchen scissors

rolling pin and cover

pastry cloth

tongs

timer

electric mixer

toaster

NICE BUT NOT NECESSARY

Dutch oven

coffeepot

teapot

tea kettle

omelet pan

griddle

double boiler

individual baking dishes
(2 or more)

6 custard cups
(6-oz. size)

2 custard cups
(10-oz. size)

tube pan

jelly roll pan
(can double as extra cookie
sheet)

food chopper or grinder

electric knife-sharpener

gelatin molds
(individual and 4-cup size)

ring mold

ladle

wire whip

pizza pan and cutter

soufflé dish

biscuit cutter
(2-inch or set of rounds)

apple corer

pancake turner

slotted spoon

deep fat thermometer

candy thermometer

salt and pepper set for range

canister set

cake safe

colander (can use as sieve)

utility tray

refrigerator containers

electric knife

mallet

funnel

ice-cream scoop

cheese slicer

electric carving knife

baster

poultry shears

ALSO NEEDED
(if you don't have a dishwasher or garbage disposal)

dish drainer and dishpan

plastic garbage pail

Re Knives: Some Of The Fine Points

Good knives will do their job quickly and efficiently, will be comfortable to handle and, given reasonable care, will last for years. Good knife blades are made from "carbon steel"—steel that contains a high content of carbon, sometimes with vanadium and chromium added. Also available: polished, stainless steel blades that have a high carbon content and so combine the edge-holding qualities of carbon with the good looks of stainless. The handles are of wood or high-quality plastic and are fastened to the blade with rivets. Always handle a knife before you buy it to make sure that it fits your hand and that you feel comfortable using it.

Electric knives offer their own advantages: quick, neat, effortless carving or slicing at the push of a button. They do an especially nice job on large birds like turkeys, firm cheeses such as

Swiss or Edam, and those hard-to-cut fruits and vegetables like pineapples and turnips.

To keep knives in good condition, protect them from nicks and scratches by keeping them in a rack or box. Always use a wooden cutting board (a protection for counter tops, too, by the way) and don't expose the blades to high heat or an open flame. Use a good steel, stone or electric knife-sharpener to hone the cutting edge. A professional sharpening from time to time is a good idea, too. Another point: Most knives do better if they're washed by hand rather than in the dishwasher.

A starter set of knives. There's really no such thing as an all-purpose knife. To be well equipped in the knife department, invest in one or more of each of the following basic types:

☐ PARING KNIVES—used for paring, peeling and small slicing jobs. These come in a variety of shapes with both rounded and pointed tips. Blades usually run from 2½ to 3 inches long. Pick the one or two from this category that seem to fit your hand most comfortably.

Paring knife.

☐ UTILITY KNIVES—the in-between size you'll use for cutting and slicing jobs that are smaller than out-and-out carving. Again, they're available in a variety of shapes, with straight or serrated edges. It's just a matter of finding the shape you like best.

Utility knife.

☐ FRENCH CHEF'S KNIFE—the heavy triangular blade puts a lot of heft behind this one. It's great for chopping.

French chef's knife.

☐ CARVING KNIFE—usually has a long, curved blade to help you slice meat in wide, even slices.

Carving knife.

☐ SLICING KNIFE—comes with a serrated or "toothed" edge to use on crumbly things like bread or cake.

Slicing knife.

APPLIANCES: THE PROS AND CONS

An appliance is like a political candidate. Some will vote for it, some against. The trick is to decide which of these electrical helpers will be really useful for *you!* To be useful, an appliance must do a job that needs doing and must do it faster and more efficiently than you can yourself. With that as a rule of thumb, here are some details on the more common appliances, both big and little:

Cooking appliances. Several of these reflect the trend to cook "right at the table." They do their jobs neatly and quickly and are available in designs that are dressy enough to come out of the kitchen. We've listed the ones that most people find they really have a use for.

ELECTRIC SKILLETS. They'll do anything that a regular skillet will do, and they have the advantage of controlled heat so you can dial the right temperature for any particular job. The heat-control units are detachable so the pan can be washed. They're available with both regular and non-stick finishes.

ELECTRIC COFFEE MAKERS. Again, you have the advantage of controlled heat; you brew the coffee, then keep it warm once it is made. These are available in a range of sizes from 2-cup to giant party models that will brew a gallon or more.

TOASTERS. You have your choice of the traditional pop-up type or the oven type that will do small baking jobs as well as toasting.

BROILER-OVENS. These will do almost anything that the oven and broiler of a full-size range will do. They offer fast, clean cooking and can be used on porches or patios as well as in kitchens, dining rooms, family rooms.

MICROWAVE OVENS. This type of oven cooks with high-frequency microwaves and cuts cooking time down to a fraction of what it is in a regular oven. Some models combine microwave cooking with a conventional heating unit. Always follow manufacturer's directions for operating and cleaning your microwave unit. This is absolutely essential.

MIXERS. Basically, one of these gives you something to take the elbow grease out of mixing, beating and whipping batters, soft doughs and potatoes. They really do the job better than you could do it by hand and are almost essential. They're available in both freestanding and hand models. Freestanding units come complete with their own mixing bowls. They take up more room than the hand models, but they usually have a little more power—and you don't have to stand and hold them. Check to see that bowls fit neatly under the mixer, that beaters eject easily, that controls are easy to reach. The hand mixers store away easily in a cupboard or up on the wall. They can be brought right to the stove for in-the-pot beating; they're easy to clean. Check to see that the unit is not too heavy for comfort, that it offers at least five speeds, that the beaters eject easily, and that the unit feels comfortable in your hand.

BLENDERS. They'll chop, puree, liquefy and blend. They can greatly reduce preparation time for many recipes, and if you're into making your own vegetable juices and extracts, this is especially for you.

Household helper appliances. We'll give you a rundown on the most basic. There may be others you'll want to acquire as you go along, but these are almost essential to start out with.

STEAM IRON. Even in this wash-and-wear age, clothes often need an occasional touch-up with an iron. Some of your garments or household denims may need more than that! Today's steam and spray-steam models help you do it like an old pro. Just dial the degree of heat indicated for the type of fabric you're ironing—you're all set.

VACUUM. You have your choice of upright or canister types. Both do a good job—although the uprights may be slightly better for pile or twist carpeting. The canisters, however, are lighter in weight and easier to carry around than the uprights. It's really a matter of personal preference. "First" homes can often get by with what's called an electric broom.

ELECTRIC BROOM. This is really a mini-vacuum with a fair amount of suction. Electric brooms are very light, easy to store and relatively inexpensive. If you invest in a regular vacuum at a later date, you can always use this one for little in-between jobs or as an "upstairs" vacuum. The safest way to choose among upright, canister or electric broom is to decide after you've chosen your carpeting.

Major appliances—full-size and compacts. If the range, refrigerator and dishwasher are already "there when you get there," you'll probably face standard models of each. If you're faced with buying any of these "majors" yourself, your preliminary detective work should include: reading up on various consumer reports and buyer's guides; talking to friends or relatives who have recently bought appliances; and above all, doing business with a reputable store. Many people today, however, are adding to their basic appliance setup by investing in one or more of the new "compacts" now available.

The new compacts include small spin-dry washers or even washer-dryer combinations that can be fitted into kitchen or bathroom; convertible dishwashers that can be left portable or be built in under a counter; and small wall refrigerators. These last are real space-savers since they hang up on the wall. They're adequate for a couple or small family and can always be used as an "extra" in a family room, game room or den later on. Although less expensive than their major cousins, compacts should be bought with care. A faulty or inadequate appliance can be very aggravating to deal with—as well as being an expense.

Buying by brand. Manufacturers have a large investment in their brand names and they know that the best protection for that investment is a satisfied customer. Many large stores have also developed store brands which they are anxious to protect. You are always safest buying "branded" items like these rather than unknown "specials." Sometimes the store brands run a little cheaper than the nationally known items, but beware of any merchandise that costs a great deal less than the average. You run the risk of getting an inferior product.

Wooden table used as "work island."

Fold-down wall shelf.

Kitchen counter with pegboard.

Plan Your Kitchen
As A Time-And-Motion Expert Would

Large and modern, or all-on-one-wall compact, your kitchen will function better if you position your cooking equipment, utensils and supplies efficiently. One industrial efficiency expert has pointed out that homemakers will often buy the expensive equipment they need (and some that they don't), but will balk at investing in two or three duplicate sets of minor items like measuring cups and spoons. Instead, they'll eventually clock miles of extra steps walking cross-kitchen to fetch that one precious set! Not sensible—but to see what is, take a look at the chart on the facing page; it covers the three basic work centers in any kitchen. And we've included lists of the equipment that does best stored in or near each area. And yes, there are duplicates included. The closer you can come to following this chart, the more efficient your kitchen work will be. Directly below, you'll find some helpful ideas for making the most of the kitchen space you have.

Cramped For Kitchen Work Space?
Try These Place-Makers!

If you have room and money enough to put in an "official" work island and extra built-ins, by all means do. If not, here are some emergency measures that are penny saving and purely practical. Properly done, they're also attractive.

In larger kitchens—add a table. It can be a simple thrift shop "find" or attic reject. Strip it down to the bare wood or paint it a color that complements your kitchen decor. Put it smack-dab in the center of the kitchen, where it can function as an island that's accessible from all sides. Or "store" it against a wall when you're not using it.

In tiny kitchens—try a fold-down shelf. This plunks up against the wall, out of the way when not in use—folds down to make work space for a mixing-bowl operation or other food-preparation activity. If you have enough wall space, include a couple of these fold-downs—the additional work area created will be worth its weight in gold!

Swing a counter-cabinet vertically against the wall. This will make more of the top surface available for use—and will make it accessible from two sides. Paint the back a bright color and fit it out with pegboard or magnetic hooks to add to general storage facilities.

Good rule of thumb: Even if you can't follow the arrangements detailed in the chart opposite, at least try to put pans and saucepans near the range, and keep dishes and glasses near the sink or dishwasher.

THREE BASIC KITCHEN WORK CENTERS

Activity	Appliances and Location	Equipment and Supplies
Food preparation	Refrigerator-freezer	Baking utensils and equipment
Activities like: measuring and mixing preparing meats grating/slicing cheese, onions, etc.	Note: Properly placed equipment helps cut down on the number of times you have to open refrigerator and/or freezer doors.	Mixing bowls and spoons Measuring cups and spoons Cutting board Kitchen scissors Grater Storage bags and foil Knives and sharpener Ice bucket Food grinder Molds, ramekins, custard cups Paper towels
Cooking and serving	Range	Saucepans, skillets, roasting pans Cooking forks and spoons (wooden and metal)
Activities like: baking, roasting, cooking on top of the range placing food on platters and in serving dishes	Note: Grouping equipment near the range can help prevent accidents.	Cooking thermometers Casseroles Ladles, tongs, spatulas Pot holders Poultry shears Cooling racks Measuring cups and spoons Electric mixer, other small electric appliances
Cleanup	Sink, dishwasher, garbage disposal	Saucepans (most often used with water) Can opener Knives Juicer Coffeepot Vegetable brush Strainer
Activities like: opening and disposing of cans washing vegetables scouring pots and pans	Note: Try to think out all the activities that require the use of water, then group the necessary supplies near the sink.	Measuring cups and spoons Paper towels Soaps, detergents, cleaners, cleanser-pads Dish towels Sponges Garbage can and/or wastebasket

Shelves put up across window.

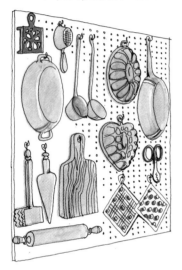

Pegboard kitchen storage wall.

Room divider that creates a breakfast nook.

New Storage Ideas Keep Things Out In The Open

Of course, you want to make the most of the cabinet space you already have. Adding hooks and small racks to the insides of the doors and investing in small, commercially sold storage aids like plate racks, turntables and stackable storage bins will help a lot here. In addition to these, we've sketched a few ideas that can put "free space" to work for you.

Shelves, hooks and racks. These come in so many sizes you can fit them in almost anywhere. Some spots for shelves you may be overlooking: above your sink, across a window, around your range. Magnetic hooks will grip the side of a refrigerator and are handy for light objects like pot holders or a memo board. Overhead pot racks turn ceiling space into a storage area and are really one of the handiest ways to store saucepans and skillets. (That's why restaurants use them!)

Hold-everything pegboard. You can turn a kitchen wall into a whole storage unit with pegboard and an assortment of the specialized hooks and holders designed to be used with it. Here again, you have the advantage of the utensils being in sight and easily reached.

Room dividers. Use one to create a breakfast nook in the kitchen or as a partial wall between kitchen and dining area. Store skillets, saucepans, casserole dishes, plates and glasses here. All the stored items will be reachable from either side of the divider.

Wooden dressers and wardrobes. These two can provide attractive and useful storage space in your kitchen or placed near the kitchen door in the dining area. Their drawers will also hold place mats, napkins and small trays in addition to cooking and serving utensils.

EXTRA DIVIDEND DEPARTMENT: HOW TO MAKE SALES PAY OFF

Buying "bargains" can get to be one of the most expensive hobbies around. Some shoppers really get hung up on sales—just can't pass up an item if it's reduced! If you evaluate them carefully, however, price reductions *can* help you stretch the budget. Here's some advice it pays to follow:

Basic rules for playing the sales game. Before you grab that "big bargain," always ask yourself these questions:

☐ Are you buying the item because you want it or need it—or because it's on sale?

☐ Can it be returned? The key words "final sale" written on the ticket usually mean it can't be returned. Double-check by asking!

☐ Is it damaged or badly out-of-date? Most imperfect merchandise will be marked as such, so check the ticket for descriptions like "irregular," "soiled," "floor sample." In sheets, towels and blankets, "irregular" can mean anything from almost invisible variations in weave to badly pulled threads that will definitely reduce wear. If the damage is not too severe, irregulars can be good buys. If the merchandise is in fairly good shape, it may be a "find."

Understanding the language of sales. Most stores advertise a variety of sales, so it pays to know just what each type of reduction means. Here are some key phrases and a translation of same:

☐ "REDUCED FROM STOCK" OR "REDUCED" means that the store is temporarily offering merchandise from their regular stocks at a reduced price. At the end of the sale, the merchandise will again be sold at the regularly quoted value. This assures you that the item is of standard quality, really did sell at the higher price, and will be available to fill in with at a later time.

☐ "SPECIAL PURCHASE" means that a group of items have been specially bought by the store for this particular sale. For some reason, the store has been able to buy the merchandise at a reduced price and is passing on the saving to you. The catch: Less reputable stores may feature inferior merchandise (which never sold at the quoted value) as a price reduction. Doing a little comparison shopping on your own should help here.

☐ "CLOSEOUT" means that the store or manufacturer is discontinuing a certain item and is reducing the price in order to sell all existing stocks. The disadvantage: No more will be available should you want to match up or fill in at a later date.

☐ "HOLIDAY SPECIALS" may be stock-reductions, special purchases or closeouts. Or they may be "loss leader items"—merchandise on which the store is shaving its normal margin of profit in order to encourage shoppers to come into the store. The store's hope is, of course, that you will buy other items while you are there.

☐ "WAREHOUSE SALE" usually includes larger items of merchandise (like furniture, carpeting or major appliances) that are offered for sale at the retail store's warehouse rather than at the store itself. The customer must arrange, and pay for, delivery of the goods. The store passes on to the customer the savings it effects on handling, inventory and shipping costs by selling the item right from the warehouse. The store may also reduce its actual margin of profit on the item as an added inducement to help move the item quickly.

A calendar of sales arranged alphabetically. This list shows the times of year when you are most apt to find particular types of house-and-home merchandise on sale. In general, look for white sales in January, May and August—and in February in some stores. February and September are most often the months for housewares sales. Both white sales and housewares sales include a variety of items—and the variety may differ slightly from one store to another.

appliances (small)	Jan.
bedding and bedspreads	Jan., Feb., May, Aug.
blankets	Jan., Feb., May, Aug., Nov.
china	Feb., Sept.
dishcloths and linens	Jan., Feb., May, Aug.
coffee makers (electric)	Jan., Feb., Sept.
cooking utensils	Feb., Sept.
curtains and draperies	Jan., Feb., May, Aug.
cutlery	Feb., Sept.
floorcoverings and rugs	Jan., Feb., July, Aug.
furniture	Jan., Feb., Aug.
glassware	Feb., Sept.
housewares	Feb., Sept.
mattresses	Feb.
refrigerators	June, July
washing machines	July

Final thought on furnishings: Don't overlook your Bridal Registry when it comes to planning your furnishings. You can list your preferences in tableware, glassware and dishes; your needs in small appliances, cooking utensils, even smaller pieces of furniture. It can save duplications and the embarrassment of receiving gifts you really don't want.

HANDBOOK OF
Furniture

Furniture styles are no mystery. They simply reflect how people live and what their interests are (or were) at different times, in different places. During the seventeenth and eighteenth centuries, for instance, the wealthy nobles lived in large palaces staffed with many servants. Tastes ran to elegant fabrics and ornately carved and decorated furniture.

Today, we live in much smaller homes and welcome the freedom that more casual living brings us. We favor simpler, less elaborate-looking furniture and fabrics that are easy to care for. Modern furniture designers create to satisfy these tastes and preferences. Often, they adapt styles of the past to the present. These adaptations retain the graceful lines and gracious looks, but simplify the decorative elements. Furniture designers work with new materials, too—plastics and metals molded into simple flowing shapes, many of which are multipurpose to increase the livability of our smaller rooms.

As you browse through the following pages, you'll be seeing pieces from the famous periods of furniture design *and* examples of how these "looks" are interpreted today.

We don't claim we'll turn you into a furniture expert. But you will get some idea of the tradition that lies behind even the most contemporary pieces. And you'll have plenty of examples of fine design to comparison shop with.

This should make it easier to separate the good from the gimmicky when you start selecting and collecting furniture for your own home.

Armoire: Louis XIV.

Detail of carved and painted door (Sun King motif): Louis XIV.

Torchère: Louis XIV.

THE TRADITIONAL FRENCH LOOK

The Mood It Creates: richly formal or gracefully elegant; creates a highly "fashioned" room, often with a minimum of furniture.

The term "traditional furniture" usually means designs based on furniture styles of the seventeenth and eighteenth centuries. In France, this period begins with the **Baroque** style of Louis XIV—elaborate, imposing, heavily ornamented with carving, marquetry and inlay. The curvaceous, "extravanganza" look of the Louis XV **Rococo** style followed. Here, exotic woods such as purpleheart and tulipwood replaced the walnut favored in the earlier period. The **Classic Revival** marked a swing away from elaborate curves and ornamentation, and toward the straighter lines and more restrained approach of classical Greece and Rome. Outlines were chiefly rectilinear, legs were straight, and the circle, oval and ellipse replaced the sinuous curve found in Rococo furniture. This classical influence continued through the eighteenth century, moving from the almost direct classical copies of the **Directoire** period to the highly formal grandeur of the **Empire** style, a style that reflected the triumphant victories of France under Napoleon and his empire.

Armchair: Louis XIV.

Secrétaire: Louis XV.

Console: Louis XV.

Chaise longue: Louis XV.

Lady's bureau: Louis XV.

Armchair: contemporary adaptation of Louis XV.

Armchair: Directoire.

Table: Directoire.

Cylinder-top desk: Directoire.

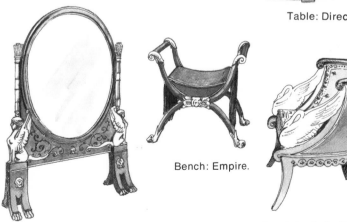

Cheval glass: Empire.

Bench: Empire.

Gondola chair: Empire.

Armoire: French Provincial.

THE FRENCH PROVINCIAL LOOK

The Mood It Creates: informal, hospitable, cheerful; combines sturdy construction with graceful lines.

Originally, **French Provincial** furniture was made by local cabinet-makers in the smaller cities and villages. It represented their interpretations of the designs popular at court. These local artisans adapted the designs of Paris to suit the simpler lives and country homes of the French nobility and middle class. The style most frequently copied was the **Rococo** look of Louis XV. The ornamentation typical of this style, however, was simplified in the country. Provincial furniture was generally of solid wood with little or no veneering used. Favorite woods: oak, walnut, beech, elm, wild cherry. The pieces were practical, solid and sturdy. Most typical were the tall cupboards called armoires; these were used to store clothing, linens, china and glassware. Today's provincial furniture still features walnut and fruitwoods and harmonizes well with woolen fabrics, printed cottons and linens. It is a favorite for bedrooms, dining rooms and informal living rooms.

Dining table and chairs: contemporary adaptation of French Provincial.

Commode: French Provincial.

Sofa with caning: French Provincial.

Upholstered chair: French Provincial.

Side table: French Provincial.

Cheval glass: French Provincial.

Secrétaire: French Provincial.

Ladderback chair: French Provincial.

Oak court cupboard: Jacobean.

High chest: William and Mary.

THE TRADITIONAL ENGLISH LOOK

The Mood It Creates: warmth, tranquility, a feeling of stability; can also create an air of formality and elegance.

In England, our "traditionals" include the two periods of **English Baroque:** the massive, ornately carved oak furniture of later **Jacobean;** the lighter, more curved outlines of **William and Mary** furniture, usually made from walnut and lavishly decorated with veneering, marquetry and lacquer. The balanced, beautifully flowing lines of **Queen Anne** furniture followed. Still very much with us is the graceful Queen Anne leg. The eighteenth century, called the "great age" of English cabinetmakers, produced the magnificent designs of **Chippendale, Hepplewhite** and **Sheraton,** as well as the exquisitely refined furniture of the **Adam** brothers. Here, mahogany was "the" wood. **English Regency** furniture reflected England's interest in the classical Greek and Roman revival, but elements adapted from early Egyptian culture were used as well. Eventually, interest in the Regency waned; it was replaced with the lushness of **Victorian.** In fabrics: Velvets, brocades, the more formal chintzes—all of these fabrics complement both English and French traditional furniture.

Settee: Queen Anne.

Bureau cabinet: Queen Anne.

Side chair: Queen Anne.

Detail of cabriole leg: Queen Anne.

Lowboy: Chippendale style (Philadelphia).

Tripod tea table with pie-crust top: Chippendale.

Armchair: Hepplewhite.

Side chair: contemporary adaptation of Chippendale.

Armchair: Adam.

Library table: Regency.

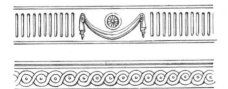

Detail of carving: Adam.

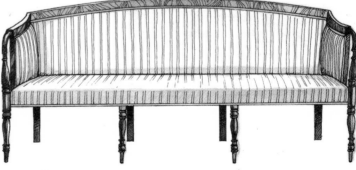

Settee: Sheraton.

THE AMERICAN LOOK

The Mood It Creates: ranges from the cheerful, homey feeling of **Colonial** American to the simple elegance and dignity of the **Federal** period.

The term "Colonial furniture" usually refers to designs inspired by the furniture made in America before, and at the time of, the Revolutionary War. Particularly in the early Colonial period, this furniture was made by individual settlers for their own use, and tended to be rough-hewn, simply designed and confined to the most basic pieces. Maple, oak, pine, ash and fruitwoods were used. As life became less harsh, furniture became more elaborate, particularly in the major American colonial cities. Philadelphia was the center of American furniture manufacture, the designs for which were based on English prototypes, but adapted to American colonial taste. Philadelphia highboys and lowboys became famous; they are still copied today. Other favorites: gateleg tables, the Windsor chair, swing leg tables. American Federal furniture dates roughly from the founding of the federal government in 1789. The English designs of the eighteenth century were copied here; carving, inlay and veneering became popular. **Duncan Phyfe** is the best-known American cabinet-maker of this period. In fabrics: Ginghams, calicos, chintzes and homespun are all traditional with Colonial pieces. Chintzes, printed linens, horsehair, damask and brocades are all suitable with the later Federal styles. Brass handles and brass or glass knobs were the most frequently used hardware on American furniture.

Welsh sideboard: today's colonial look.

Chandelier.

Gateleg table.

Ladderback chair.

Baltimore highboy: Chippendale inspired.

Windsor chair.

Federal sofa: Chippendale inspired.

Table: Queen Anne style.

Fire screen:
Chippendale inspired.

Wingback chair:
Chippendale inspired.

Federal sideboard: Hepplewhite style.

Sewing table:
Duncan Phyfe.

Trestle table and chairs: contemporary adaptation of Shaker.

Lyre-back chair: Duncan Phyfe.

Victorian sofa: Empire style.

Center table with ornate pedestal.

Center divan, covered with plush, featuring fancy center pedestal.

THE VICTORIAN LOOK

The Mood It Creates: lush, elaborate, romantic—unless very carefully handled, a little of this goes a long way!

Victorian furniture styles were very similar in England and America. In both countries, the furniture was characterized by profuse and exaggerated carving that featured a full harvest of naturalistic fruit and flower designs. Individual pieces became progressively heavier and more massive. By the middle of the Victorian age, huge scrolls were being used as feet on tables, sofas and chests. The Victorians wanted display and lots of it. They drew upon all the past periods of furniture design for inspiration and often combined features of two or more periods in a single piece. Typical of **American Victorian** were the boldly curved sofas and chairs. Another favorite: the round or oval upholstered seat placed in the middle of the drawing room and designed to seat several people. Victorian upholstery work was a wonder. It came richly buttoned and tufted, draped, fringed, corded. Often no wood at all was left uncovered. On top of this plushy upholstery went crocheted antimacassars—to grace the backs and arms of chairs and sofas. As a little informal note, tightly stuffed cushions and bolsters were added! Silk, plush and horsehair were favorite fabrics. Today, in more restrained versions, "Victorian" can be fanciful and fun.

Wood-framed bed: Empire type.

Morris chair.

Bentwood rocker with cane back.

Oil lamp.

Combination dressing table and wash stand: Victorian "cottage."

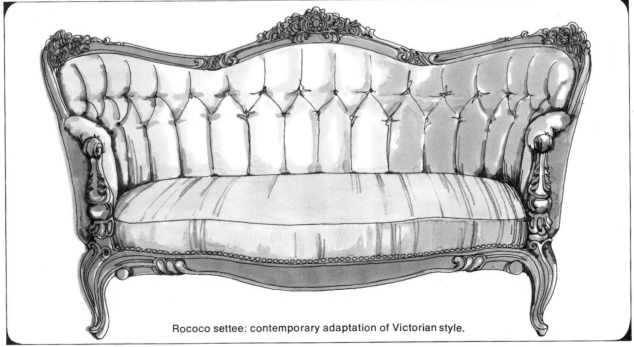

Rococo settee: contemporary adaptation of Victorian style.

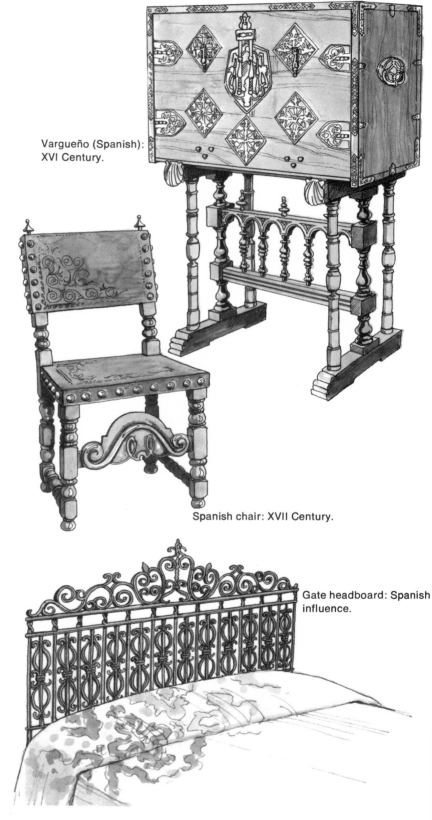

Vargueño (Spanish): XVI Century.

Spanish chair: XVII Century.

Gate headboard: Spanish influence.

THE MELLOW LOOK OF MEDITERRANEAN

The Mood It Creates: suave, sophisticated yet warm; a sense of past and present coming together; shows a strong Spanish influence.

Today's furniture designers have borrowed traditional "looks" from the lands of the Mediterranean, simplified their lines, and interpreted them in warm-colored woods. There is a sense of sunshine tempered with shadow. Individual pieces are solid without being massive. Except for the occasional interpretations of the Spanish-mission folding chair, lines tend to be straight and shapes rectangular. Accessories often include wrought-iron lamps and candlesticks. Ornamental grillwork is sometimes used at windows and in room dividers. Moorish- or Spanish-design area rugs go well here; they're particularly effective over linoleum or asphalt tiles in a ceramic-tile design. Leather, richly toned stripes and Indian-style prints are effective with Mediterranean furniture, although almost any sturdily designed fabrics will suit. Stay away from florals and delicate-looking prints and fabrics.

Writing table and bench: adapted from the Spanish.

Armoire: contemporary adaptation from the Spanish.

Dining table and chairs: Italian Provincial flavor.

Wrought-iron and leather chair: today's Spanish look.

Wall mirror: the Venetian look.

Credenza: influenced by the Venetian style.

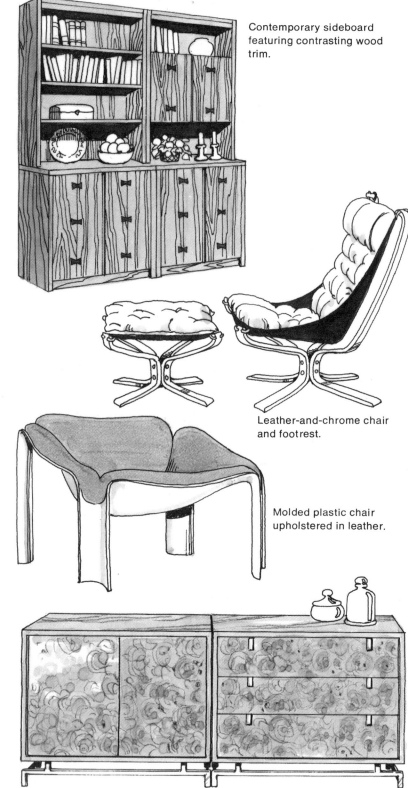

Contemporary sideboard featuring contrasting wood trim.

Leather-and-chrome chair and footrest.

Molded plastic chair upholstered in leather.

Burled wood and chrome chest—contemporary but elegant.

THE MODERNS: SLEEK OR FANCIFUL

The Mood They Create: slick to super-sophisticated; they include the "Scandinavians," the wacky, the works-of-art; most have a high-IQ approach to problems of space and function.

In the hands of talented designers, plastics are revolutionizing our whole concept of furniture. Light and airy Lucite cubes serve as tables, seating space, stackable containers. Bright-colored plastics are molded into fit-together, free-form chairs and tables. Inflatable chairs and stools provide comfortable, bouncy seating—stow flat when not in use or when scheduled for a move. Cubes, rectangles and "S" shapes of plastic foam take stretch-fabric covers for lightweight, inexpensive sofas and chairs. Other materials are being used imaginatively, too. Reinforced cardboard is turning up as stools and occasional tables. Wooden cubes and modular units provide interchangeable seating, storing and serving areas. You'll even find the no-furniture-at-all approach achieved with carpet-covered ledges. These are today's news. Who knows what's coming up next!

Bouncy inflatable plastic armchair.

Sleek Scandinavian dining table and chairs.

Tinted Lucite "mushroom" lamp.

Molded opaque plastic table with tinted Lucite chairs.

Contemporary 4-piece modular upholstered sofa, semi-circular in shape.

Molded plastic chair with leather upholstery.

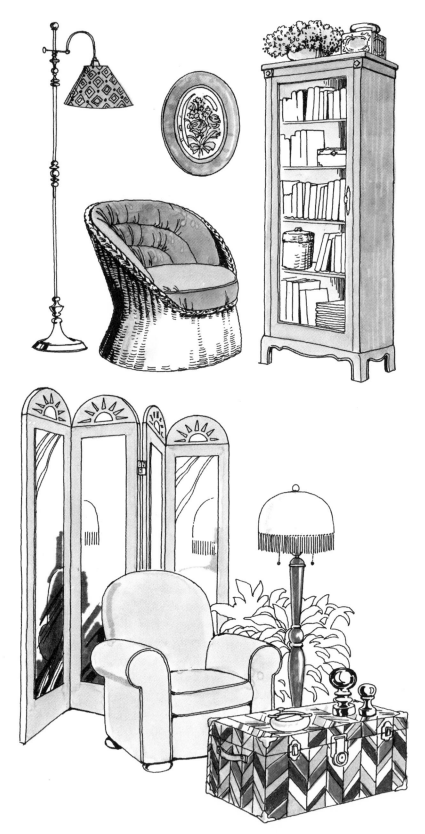

EARLY ATTIC REVIVED

The Mood It Creates: When it is good it is very, very good. When it is bad—forget it!

In its original, unrestored state, it often features broken legs, heavily scratched surfaces, drab fabrics.

Revived, it shows a liberal use of brightly colored paints, often paired with boldly designed fabrics. The latter tend to be used as "throws" rather than as upholstery. Furniture legs are often low, as the easiest way to correct uneven balance in a piece is to saw the legs short-and-even. Handcrafts are much in evidence. Homemade pillows, hand-decorated screens, hand-painted wall graphics—all these are typical of the "look." There is often a blending of indoor and out-door pieces: wicker or wrought-metal furniture standing side by side with wooden items. Large potted plants are often used to complement this mix. Stenciled patterns appear everywhere—on chairs, tabletops, across floors, up walls, around windows. There is an imaginative use of "found" objects: painted or pierced tin cans as lighting fixtures; old windows or window frames as room dividers; discarded auto seats as small sofas.

The general effect can be warm, whimsical, interesting and highly personal. Advantages: lots of look for little money; pieces can be readily discarded.

SPECIAL DECORATING NEWS: THE TREND TOWARD ECLECTIC

You've had a look at some of the major periods in furniture design. Now we'll bring you up-to-date on one of the newer ways to utilize this knowledge in your home. Often called "The Eclectic Look," this approach cuts across the categories of furniture design to combine many styles and types of furniture in one room. Today, we value freedom of choice. We're no longer dominated by what the "experts" say is good style or good fashion. Instead, we're using our own likes and dislikes as a guide. Eclecticism reflects and respects this freedom of choice.

Eclectic, mix-and-match decorating takes a sure eye and a feeling for "what will go together." When it comes off, it is delightful —fun for those who created it and for visiting friends as well. If it doesn't work, it can be a disaster!

How can you make it work for you? Well, here's one basic rule of thumb: It's usually best not to mix too many massive pieces with delicately designed ones. One large armoire or a generously proportioned desk or a big, plump-pillowed sofa might be balanced with an assortment of small tables, open-look chairs and an airy window treatment done in light, pastel-colored fabrics. But suppose you introduce several overstuffed Victorian armchairs *and* an elaborately carved Jacobean-type chest *and* an amply proportioned refectory table into one room. If you then add a glass coffee table and a pair of delicate Adam-design chairs, the lighter pieces will seem to hang in space rather than help to comprise the well-blended whole that marks successful eclectic furnishing.

The old rule of not combining formal with informal pieces seems to be going by the boards. Some eclectically minded people are able to team up a velvet-covered Georgian chair with a wicker table and then fill a corner with an elaborately woven hammock—and somehow, the whole room will work. Often, a strongly defined color scheme is the secret of such success. Or the pieces may have a subtle but definite relationship to each other. In the case of the Georgian chair/wicker table/hammock combination, it might be the intricacy of design in the wood, wicker and woven material that supplies the kinship among the pieces. Unless you *know* that you have this kind of highly refined eye, however, it's probably best to start by mixing styles that are somewhat related: French Provincial and Early American, for instance; or French Empire, English Regency and some modern.

Why try for the difficult-but-delightful eclectic look? If you succeed, you'll have a room that's interesting, pleasantly surprising and that gives a feeling of worldliness and of being "at home" with the decorative arts. It'll be uniquely "you," too!

3 Putting Your Home Together: The Furbishings

3 Putting Your Home Together: The Furbishings

YOUR FINISHING TOUCHES:
MAKE THEM INTERESTING "PERSONALITIES"

Basics are basic to comfortable living. But a home that sticks *just* to those basics is like soup without salt. You need interesting extras to add flavor and verve. Try a diagonal swathe of color running across one long wall, a piece of pottery or a plant dramatically spotlighted, a multicolored pile of pillows—even a simple basket heaped high with balls of bright knitting wools! There are all kinds of ways to introduce exclamation points into your decorating scheme. Call them furbishings, special effects, bright ideas. They're the "personalities" that pull your decorating scheme together and make it sing.

Many of the items that come under this heading serve a serious purpose, too. Good lighting, for instance, is a "necessary." Lighting arrangements that are both sight-saving *and* imaginative really do you proud. The same thing is true of walls, wastebaskets, ashtrays, to name a few more. They can sit there as useful humdrums or you can pick them as carefully as a director picks his cast.

Here's where both of you can really work together, too. One may have a head for color, one the inner eye that sees a length of fabric as a wall mural. Your capabilities may surprise you! And if the effect pleases both of you, it's a successful effort.

On the following pages, we've put together some of the bits of information that can give you a defter touch with finishing touches. There's a section on the general principles of color relationships, for instance. Then we've given you pages of interesting design possibilities you can adopt, adapt or spin off from. Most of them are easy on the budget, none require any unusual ability, and all are open-ended enough to leave room for the kind of self-expression that will make your home an original.

FEATURED IN FULL COLOR: EXTRA-SPECIAL IDEAS TO ADD INTEREST TO YOUR HOME

Make sure you check out the super-specials we've highlighted on our full-color pages. They're a real "idea bank" you can draw on—for interesting color schemes, do-it-yourself designs, decorating hints *and* suggestions for making everyday meals and parties at home easier and more fun. Notice that we've placed the emphasis on *ideas* rather than on rigid, specific how-to information. This leaves you free to adapt our designs to your own home situation. Each drawing includes its own caption—to clue you in on the ideas shown. To make them even more useful, however, we'd like to add some general information here and now.

First of all, we tried to emphasize the "practical and possible" in selecting the ideas. We checked each one to make sure that the materials involved, the amount of space needed and the general effects achieved were all in line with today's budgets and way of life. We think you'll find that all of the materials mentioned are easily available at local stores and that none represent a heavy outlay of money. We also kept in mind the often cramped dimensions of modern apartments and houses. So, many of the drawings illustrate ways to make the most of limited space. And we tried to cover a range of effects—from traditional to contemporary—but all with that special look of easy living that seems to characterize this era.

Secondly, we concentrated on the decorating and design problems, and on the mealtime and entertaining situations you're most apt to experience. How to partition off a pullman kitchen, how to conjure up a dining area where there is none, how to cope with breakfast-on-the-run or snacks-and-punch-for-the-bunch—you'll find all these, and more, covered in "living" color!

And, last but not least, we included thoughts for every room in your home—living room, dining area, bedroom, kitchen, bath. We also tried to make each drawing as idea-stimulating as possible. Those that feature color schemes, for instance, also contain interesting sidelights on other decorating aspects—and those that concentrate on a specific design or decorating idea often include attractive color combinations. So whether you're looking for "inspiration" for a particular room or for solutions to a particular problem, check our "colorama"! Remember, you can abstract the points that appeal from any of these ideas, too. Like one design approach but don't fancy the colors we've chosen? Simple solution! Latch onto the idea, but choose your own color scheme. Like one of the entertaining ideas but prefer a different menu? Again, choose your own. We've planned the pages so they work this way for you!

Look For These "Extras"
When You Check Our Color Pages

☐ The color wheel—page 65. Check the fabric swatches on this page. They'll give you some pointers on how to coordinate a variety of prints and patterns all in one room.

☐ The natural neutrals—pages 66-67. This monochromatic scheme combines many shades of one color. We feature the brown-beige-white range, but you can interpret with any color!

☐ Our red, white and blue room—page 68. This flag-bright color scheme illustrates the wonderful way that white works. Use it to "separate" vivid colors so they'll suit the smallest room.

☐ Featuring fabric on a wall—page 104. Canopies, quilts, wall-to-wall hangings—we show them used in dining areas—but don't forget that the same ideas work equally well in other rooms.

☐ Kitchen drama—page 102. The country charm of copper, brick and wood . . . the drama of a floor-to-ceiling stripe . . . we show these in kitchens, but they'd work in foyers or rumpus rooms, too!

☐ Making a bathroom "grow"—page 185. Even if bathroom space isn't a problem, check out our tricks with pegboard and mirrors. They're great for modernizing an old-fashioned bath.

☐ Unusual "dividers"—pages 186-187. Some interesting "extras" here: using baskets for kitchen storage; styrofoam panels you can "sculpture" yourself; felt draperies (cut out like our panels) that hide an ugly view.

☐ Decorating with plants—page 103. Check out the idea of arranging plants at different heights to add to their interest, or of filling an empty corner with a "hanging" chair.

☐ Showing off things you love—page 101. Here, notice the lighted shelf—a good idea for plants, too? Also, the lucite cube that holds our spoon collection—great for all small treasures.

☐ Hiding those "uglies"—page 188. Note the arrangement of wooden dowels we show—keep it in mind to hide an exposed pipe, an awkward wall jog. Ditto our string "mobile."

☐ Quick and easy eating—page 301. Small quarters? You can still achieve a change-of-place to keep everyday meals interesting —that's the "extra" idea within this color page.

☐ Dinner for two—page 335. We've shown this chafing dish "special" set up on small occasional tables—for two. Want to set it for four? Just add more tables and floor cushions!

☐ Sit-down serving for four—page 302. Check the nifty centerpiece idea shown here—a cluster of small house plants plus three fat candles, grouped in a handsome container. And all reuseable!

☐ Party plans—page 336. Of special interest here—the fact that our serving suggestions keep food and beverages handsomely out of the way, yet still within easy reach when they're wanted!

COLOR: DRAB OR DRAMATIC, IT'S THE ONE ACCESSORY THAT'S ALWAYS WITH YOU

Choose it in pale pastel or deep-and-dark—wherever there's any light, there's color. Peek at a sunbeam through a prism and you'll see the six colors that actually make up light: violet, blue, green, yellow, orange, red. All others are just combinations of these basic hues. Black, white and gray are also designated as colors in decorating circles (although scientists don't recognize them as such).

How important is color? Take a look at the black and white grouping we've sketched here. Then see what happens when we add red. Same elements, but what a difference! Wave color across a room and you wave a magic wand. It can make the tall seem shorter; the narrow, wider. It can warm or cool. It can make the ugly seem to disappear. No other decorating tool will do as much for you, at as little cost. Well-planned and chosen, color will pull a whole room together and make even the oddest assortment of furniture hang together better. On the other side of the coin— we've all seen rooms that seem to have a bad case of the jitters because of color-conflict or that look chronically anemic due to a wishy-washy scheme. Most of us react to color emotionally; we say that color can create a "feeling" in a room. Certainly a red, white and blue room gives off a very different aura from one done in subtle browns and grays. There are some experts who feel that favorite colors are a key to personality—for instance, that warmhearted, impulsive types will favor red, while more intro-verted individuals will prefer blue. Phrases like "a sunny disposi-tion," "a red-hot temper," "having the blues" point up the truth of this association.

Because color is so much with us, learning how to use it well is worthwhile. There are basic rules that can guide you in your choosing. The most important of these: Be sure that you both *like* a color before you decide to use it! Start by noticing colors—in cars, clothing, package designs as well as in the room schemes shown in magazines. Decide which appeal to you, which don't. If the two of you don't agree, cross the color off as a possibility. Once you've worked up a list of agreed-on "likes," use the in-formation on the following pages to start working out color groupings or combinations around these favorites. Helpful hint: Swing into a paint store and pick up some of their little square color samples to experiment with. Don't be afraid to go way out. After all, you're not committed to anything—yet. And as you'll soon see, putting colors together successfully isn't as difficult as you might think.

To Play It Safe:
Pick Up Your Color Scheme From A Favorite "Thing"

Maybe it's a poster that gives you a good feeling—or a piece of handprinted fabric, a favorite painting, even an old plate you picked up in a swap shop. If you respond to it positively, it can be the starting point for a whole color scheme. The finished room is almost sure to please. Why? Well, first of all, you're starting with something that you already know you like. The color combinations are there, right in front of your eyes—a preview of the room itself. Another advantage: You're working with a color scheme created by an expert—an artist or professional designer with a trained eye and a talent for choosing pleasing or dramatic combinations of hues. Benefiting from this kind of expertise doesn't reduce your own creativity at all. You still have a wide area of personal choice when you translate his or her colors and combinations into room furnishings. For instance—the artist's background color doesn't have to be your basic color. You might decide to reverse the scheme, using one of the accents as a basic and the basic as an accent. No matter how you decide to play off the piece, however, there are some sound rules to follow in planning the proportions of colors you put into a room.

The "rule of three": basic, secondary and accent colors. To follow this useful color plan, choose one basic color to cover about 60% of the room. This percentage would probably include walls and the major upholstered pieces, possibly windows and the floor-covering. A secondary color accounts for the rest of the furnishings. Use a third color for accents—pillows, bric-a-brac, a painted table—the smaller, accessory pieces. This approach should give you a planned, put-together look that has interest and verve.

This
useful
rule adapts
to any
color scheme.

Borrowed color schemes in action. Just turn to page 68 and you'll see a colorful scheme built around a favorite poster. The perky bedroom-office borrows its patriotic colors from an Americana poster. This scheme, too, could be reversed so red or blue replaced white as the basic color in a more heavily used area. Or you might retain white on the walls and at the windows, but use red or blue carpeting or a checkered pattern of red and blue floor tiles for a more "practical" effect.

Or maybe you'd like to build a living-dining room color scheme around an old Tiffany lampshade that features red, green and white. Because a living-dining room is a heavy traffic area, we'd suggest using dark red as the basic color (for the floor, too). In a master bedroom you might pull a switch, using pale green on the floor and walls, with red as a secondary, and retaining white as the accent.

Check the following pages for additional facts about color and color schemes, with helpful illustrations as "for instances."

A Dictionary Of Colorful Words

Bone up on this list of basic terms and you'll have some idea of what paint and fabric salesmen are talking about when they discuss matching or mixing colors.

HUE refers to the name of a color (such as blue or red).
INTENSITY refers to a color's purity. There are twelve pure colors. These are the vibrant, high-intensity colors.
SHADES are achieved by adding black to colors.
TINTS are made by adding white to colors.
TONES are produced by adding gray to colors.
VALUE refers to the lightness or darkness of a color. Tints are light-value, high-key colors. Shades are dark-value, low-key colors.

In addition to these terms, you'll hear people talk about:

WARM AND COOL COLORS. Reds and yellows—the colors of the sun and fire—create a feeling of warmth. Blue, blue-green, purple and blue-purple are the cool-looking colors. True green and red-purple are called intermediate colors because they can swing either way. (You'll find these colors on the color wheel.)
COLOR LINKAGE is another special term you may hear. This refers to the flow of color from one room to another. Wherever more than one room can be seen at a glance (in small apartments, for instance), it's often considered desirable to repeat key colors throughout. They can appear as the basic colors in some rooms, as accents in others. It's the repetition, not the proportions, that achieves a feeling of unity.

How To Deal With A Color Wheel

To get the best grasp on the basics of color, work with a color wheel. Use the one included in Chapter Two (see page 65), or pick one up in a local art supply store or from your paint dealer. It's a standard palette of colors that includes the six colors present in sunlight (blue, green, yellow, orange, red, purple) plus blue-green, blue-purple, red-purple, red-orange, yellow-orange and yellow-green. They're shown as full-strength colors on the wheel itself. Bear in mind that there is a tint for each and that all together these give you a wide range to choose from. Here's how it all works:

Note:
See our
color wheel
on page 65.

THE PRIMARY COLORS (red, blue, yellow) are equidistant from each other on the wheel.

THE SECONDARY COLORS are placed halfway between the primary colors. Secondary colors are made by mixing equal amounts of one primary color with another: red and blue for purple; blue and yellow for green; red and yellow for orange.

THE TERTIARY COLORS fill the rest of the wheel. These are made by mixing equal amounts of a primary color with one of the secondary colors on either side of it on the wheel: blue and purple for blue-purple; purple and red for red-purple; red and orange for red-orange; orange and yellow for yellow-orange; yellow and green for yellow-green; green and blue for blue-green.

The discussion of color harmonies that follows will give you an idea of how decorators, color experts (and you!) can use this basic knowledge of color to achieve pleasing combinations.

A color harmony is achieved by putting together particular colors from the color wheel into one scheme. There are several different kinds of harmonies you can work out around each color. These are the tried-and-true combinations. To show you how it works, we'll take one color (red) and see some of the harmonies that can be worked out around it. Remember, you can work these out with any one of the colors on the wheel. The diagrams in the margin will help you figure it out.

A MONOCHROMATIC HARMONY combines tints, shades and tones of just one color. With red, your scheme would run from deep scarlet to palest pink.

AN ANALOGOUS HARMONY combines three to five colors that lie next to each other on the color wheel. For red, use the red through yellow section of the wheel or the red through blue section.

A COMPLEMENTARY HARMONY combines colors that lie directly opposite each other on the color wheel. Green is the complementary color for red. Since this scheme creates sharp contrasts, it's usually best to let one color dominate the room and use its complement only for accents. A touch of black or white is often effective here.

A TRIAD HARMONY combines three colors that are equidistant from each other on the wheel. For red, use red, yellow and blue as your triad.

A NO-COLOR HARMONY moves off the color wheel to combine black, white and gray—or the "natural range" of brown through beige or gray. See page 161 for more information on the "natural" materials; also see the room illustrated on pages 66 and 67.

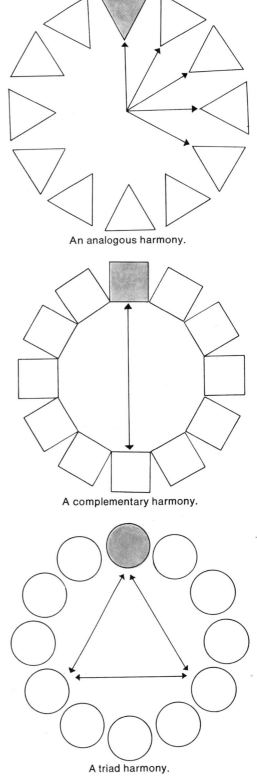

An analogous harmony.

A complementary harmony.

A triad harmony.

Clockwise, from the top: red; red-purple; purple; blue-purple; blue; blue-green; green; yellow-green; yellow; yellow-orange; orange; red-orange.

Working only with the color harmonies we've just outlined, you can achieve a wide variety of different effects. Each harmony offers several combinations of the twelve color-wheel colors and each of those colors also has a paler tint that you can include within your chosen harmony. Twelve full-strength colors, twelve tints—that's twenty-four color elements. And we've described four harmonies (not including the no-color harmony), each of which offers several different possible combinations within its parameters. Obviously, there's plenty of leeway here to accommodate individual likes and dislikes, to vary a mood, to create a formal, informal or in-between decor. Now, what about the "personalities" of the colors themselves?

What Can Colors Do For You?

Colors, like cosmetics, can be the great disguisers; they can make furniture, an architectural feature, even the temperature of a room seem different than it really is. Here are some hints on how to typecast them:

Cool colors recede; they help make small rooms look larger. They also "cool off" the glare in rooms that get more sunlight than you can handle. As mood-setters, they create a soothing, restful effect which makes them popular in bedrooms. Think of them, too, for 1-room apartments or rooms where there's apt to be a lot of hustle and bustle. See page 156 for a description of warm and cool colors.

Warm colors advance; they make objects look larger, rooms smaller. Troubled with a dark room? Warm colors will cheer it up. They look warm and welcoming, so they're good for "people places"—living rooms, dining rooms, kitchens that are "on display."

Light colors "lighten." Because they reflect light, these hues tend to make things look larger, but lighter in weight. They're great in warmer climates because they actually absorb less heat from the sun. If a cheerful look is what you're after, these are for you.

Dark colors contract. They absorb light, so they tend to make things look smaller but heavier. In terms of climate—they absorb *more* heat from the sun than their lighter cousins, so they're really warmer to live with. Caution: Too many "darks" in a room can be depressing, give a somber effect.

Bright colors expand. High-intensity hues like pure red, orange or red-purple are real eye-catchers. They exaggerate the size of objects and close in walls that they're used on. They've got a lot of zing—but handle them with care or they'll end up as distracting intruders.

The no-colors create special effects, too. White does well with brights, tends to lessen their intensity. Touches of black, on the other hand, will oomph up pastels, can help pull a multicolored scheme together. The neutrals—browns, beiges, grays—give nice effects and are easy to use and live with. Just be careful that they don't cross the line between "restful" and "dull." Using a lot of textures or a sharp accent like yellow or orange can help keep their interest high. When you're picking colors for your whole home, try to balance out the warms and the cools. Too much of either one can get tedious after a while. In any one room: If you tend to be conservative, put the most neutral of the colors you've picked on the large areas like walls, floors and major furnishings. Save the brightest colors for the smallest items —pillows, lamps, ashtrays. They're the least painful to replace if you decide they're disasters, or just plain get tired of that particular bright. Another idea: Keep a double set of accent-accessories —one for summer, one for winter. This seasonal switch will help keep the room interesting.

Solving Problem-Rooms:
With Lights, Brights And Cools

We've told you that colors can do wonders in overcoming short-comings. Cast your eye down this list of common decorating problems. If you identify with one of them, you might want to consider the colorful solution we suggest.

Got a cave-room? Small and dark, with a low ceiling—this room makes you feel Neanderthal. Come on with the cools, the lights and the whites. Pale blues, pale greens, pale purples should help expand the area. Lighten the tint as you work your way up from floor-to-walls-to-ceiling, with the last done in a barely-there pastel or light-white.

Want to disguise a horror? Awkward windows, wall pipes and jogged walls! Again, use a "light" as your basic room color and cover the offending area with the same color; use bright, bright accents in other parts of the room to draw the eye away from the Frankenstein. Exception: Paint exposed ceiling pipes (and ceiling) dark-to-black to make those pipes "disappear."

Coping with furniture that doesn't fit? Maybe you've inherited some big, heavy pieces that overpower your rather petite rooms. Cover or color them with pastel tints to make them seem lighter and less oppressive. Use a light, monochromatic color scheme (matching furniture to walls) and you'll hardly know they're there. If you've been lucky enough to find a home with big, big rooms but are shaking along with very little furniture or with pieces that are too small for their environment, use the brightest brights to make the furniture seem more important. Consider a really dazzling print for one piece. Then pick up solids from it for the other furnishings.

The Dark And The Warm Colors: They Can Be Problem-Solvers, Too!

Now that you've seen some of what the lights and brights can accomplish, let's give an eye to the wonders the warmer, darker colors can work. The effects they create can be even more dramatic than those involving the pale, cool or high-intensities. As you'll see, we've used them mainly as secondary or accent colors. Of course, they can be used as basic hues in a room, but you have to be careful with them.

Living under a canyon-high ceiling? The too-high ceiling can be a problem in older apartments or houses. If the room is small to boot, you can feel you're living at the bottom of a well. Solution? Consider painting that sky-high plaster with a deep-and-dark or really warmhearted color. Red, orange, a deep gold—any of these would snug down the ceiling to cozier proportions.

Want to highlight a good feature? Maybe it's a pair of beautiful French windows or a fireplace or mantel. Paint them a light, bright color. Or maybe you *like* those beams in the ceiling. Accent them with a dark or warm color and they'll really stand out. If you want them noticed but not spotlighted, choose a "warm" or "dark" as the room's secondary color, paint your favorite feature to match, and choose a third color for accents.

White walls giving you the willies? Sometimes you're just plain stuck with hospital-white. The landlord refuses to let you paint or paper, or imposes a stiff restoration charge that you just can't handle. Here's where warm to sizzling-hot colors can turn the trick. Grab that color wheel and pick the analogous harmony that runs from yellow through red (and don't spare the red!). Or pair one of the warm colors with its direct complement (its opposite on the color wheel, remember?). Or take another look at that smashing red-white-and-blue room inspired by an Americana poster (see page 68). Those walls are white, yes, but there's nothing drab about them! In fact, follow any of these routes and you may end up believing you *chose* those white walls just to set off that lovely warm color scheme you dreamed up.

Decorating With The Natural Neutrals

Wood, cork, grass cloth . . . unpainted brick . . . leather and fur . . . wicker, cane and bamboo—these are the new neutrals. They bring their own natural colors into a room, and the tonic of texture, too. Stuck with white walls *and* blah-beige carpeting? Plan a white-to-beige-to-brown monochromatic scheme around these "naturals." Add a touch of wood or cork paneling to one wall, invest in a leather- or vinyl-covered chair or a fur throw—then extend these colorings to your other fabrics. (See this scheme in color on pages 66 and 67). You make the most of what's already there! And—the components that make up this scheme will adapt to other arrangements later on. Leather, fur, natural wood—these are things of beauty always and can always be included in another color scheme. Because they add the dimension of texture, however, use them sparingly in colorful rooms. Where several different textures share the limelight with an assortment of colors, confusion results. Confucius didn't say it, but it's true!

Watch the woods you put into a room, too. Chests, desks, inlaid wooden furniture—these all add their own color to a room. If you plan to include several large, all-wooden pieces, keep fabric, wall and carpeting colors to a minimum. Or relate them to the wood-tones in the furniture (as we suggested in our monochromatic white-beige-brown scheme). The woods themselves need not match. In fact, you can get very interesting effects by combining light with darker wooden pieces or by pairing "formal" woods like mahogany with favorite "informals" like cane or bamboo.

Warning: Before you paint or panel, always check with your landlord to make sure he'll go along with your plans. This advice includes painting floors, walls, ceilings or any large area—and any paneling you might be considering. The same goes for replacing carpeting he's provided. Minor "redo's" are usually OK!

Special Note: Always "Sample" Colors Before You Buy!

However you pick your colors—whether you use a color wheel or take an educated guess—always try to get hold of fabric, paint chip or wallpaper swatches; then look at them in the room in which they'll be used. The larger the sample the better. Remember, colors look different under different lighting. The effect they give will also depend on the other elements used with them. The larger the area covered the more intense a color will appear. Even a pastel shade of paint will look darker on the wall than it did as a chip. So bring in those samples, place them around the room, and take a good look at them together before you buy! Careful choosing can help avoid a "losing" color scheme.

DECORATOR HINT
If you can't decide which one of several color schemes you like best, leave all your samples out on display in the room for several days. Eventually, you'll find that one scheme appeals more than the others.

TODAY'S WAYS WITH WALLS
HELP YOU COVER THEM UP OR
SHOW THEM OFF

There are two ways to think about walls. With the "coatrack approach" they just stand there, handy holders for whatever you choose to put up on them. But come on—you can do better than that! Ideally, they should be integrated into your decorating scheme as an attractive framework for it; or they can be one of the important features of the room. Most likely, you'll face walls that are clean and freshly painted—in a sanitary-looking off-white or pallid pastel! You may even be given your choice of three or four equally blah tints to select from. In addition to the non-interest colors, your walls are apt to stand as a monotonous expanse, without a hint of molding or woodwork to relieve the eye. Older apartments or houses may offer more architectural interest, but along with this often come cracks and peeling paint that need to be coped with. To achieve an artistic effect, in either case, will take a little creative thinking and planning on your part.

Fortunately, there are a lot of products and ideas around that can help make the doing easier. We've gathered a fair share of them together in the following pages. We've also included some hard-nosed facts and figures on today's paints and wallcoverings: how they function, how to buy them, how to figure costs and quantities. So read on, and make mental notes of any ideas that appeal or apply. Then start developing your walls' personalities. One important reminder—we've mentioned it before, but it bears repeating. Always check your lease and/or landlord before you paint or put up wallcoverings. The standard lease usually bans deep-toned paints and wallpapers of any kind. Many landlords can be persuaded otherwise, but it's best to check first.

Rx: To Cure the Wishy-Washies,
Paint Up A Storm

Nothing else covers as much surface and creates as much interest and color for as little money as paint! You can settle for the conservative approach: a white or light-colored ceiling, with all four walls in a color that relates to the fabrics or floorcoverings you've chosen. Or you can swing into fancy paint jobs like these:

☐ Paint three walls the same shade and the fourth a contrasting color. Or paint two that match, two to contrast.
☐ Paint it all-to-match: walls, floor, trim—maybe even the ceiling.
☐ Paint on stripes—a whole strip of stripes across one wall; one wide stripe to frame a poster or hanging plant. Or create a modern chair-rail effect with one horizontal stripe along each wall at

chair height. This last adds color and wall-interest to a room.
☐ Paint old floors into a new look—brush on a perky color or
plan out a painted pattern. You can even paint walls and floor
with a single simple graphic design (triangles, squares and rectangles are easiest).

Put Up A "Paper"

Today's wallcoverings are marvels. They come in paper or plastic.
They come scrubbable, dry-strippable, even reusable! You'll find
more facts about how they function on pages 171 through 173.
Here, we'll concentrate on their looks. There are solids and stripes
. . . abstract art and patterns . . . geometrics, foils, florals. They're
often color coordinated, so you can put a solid or floral on one
wall and a stripe that color-coordinates with these on another.

   In choosing a paper, bear these facts in mind. An open pattern
on a light, cool-colored background will open up a room. A big,
bold-colored pattern can hold its own where furniture is a little
skimpy. Vertical stripes and patterns add height; horizontals reduce it. Patterns should be in scale with the furniture and the
size of the room. A small design in pale colors will pull a disappearing act in a large room. Large patterns will suffocate tiny
rooms. Here are some special "paper" tricks:

☐ Use horizontal stripes on the end walls or on one short, unbroken wall of a narrow room. It'll *look* wider.
☐ Heavyweight aluminum freezer-foil gives you a smashing "silver wall." Use double-faced cellophane tape as the adhesive, applied in short strips on the wall. Then smooth on your foil—shiny
or dull side out. It's fantastic on ceilings, too!
☐ Gift-wrap papers can be used the same way. Often, they're less
expensive than wallpaper (although less durable). And you may
prefer the patterns.
☐ Don't overlook the ways in which paper or plastic can dramatize small, awkward areas: filling in the spaces between kitchen
cabinets; decorating ceiling areas between beams; framing set-in
windows. Cover doors and woodwork with the same paper you
use on the walls of a room or choose a wallcovering that comes
with matching fabric for draperies.

Cut Loose With Posters

Posters are current, colorful and usually cheaper than other re-
productions. Another advantage—you can put them up on the
wall in a variety of ways, ranging from simple to sophisticated.
Most direct methods: Put them up on the wall "as is," with
double-faced tape or with artists' push pins (found in art supply
stores and in some hardware stores). You can frame a poster as
you would a regular painting. You can mat posters, using the

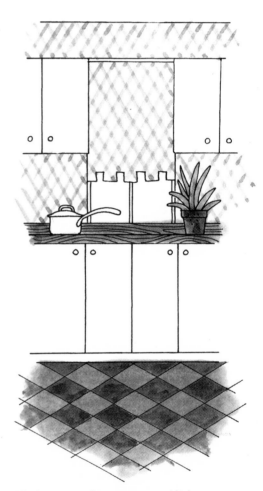

Wallpaper used to spruce up a kitchen:
filling in space between cabinets and
counter and between cabinets and ceiling;
covering a window shade.

standard-size mats from your art supply store or cutting your own from posterboard. For the most unusual effect, buy dayglo posters and spotlight them with black light. The special dayglo inks will glow like luminous watch hands. Some other unusual treatments:

☐ Use a number of posters on one wall. Arrange them in an asymmetrical "broken" pattern like the one we show in the left-hand margin, overlap them, or march them straight across or up and down a wall.

☐ You can mount two, back to back, on a piece of posterboard and hang them from the ceiling like a mobile.

☐ Mounted in picture frames or on posterboard, they can stand up against walls to accent furniture arrangements that feature pillows and low tables.

Whatever you plan for your posters, try to buy ones that have not been rolled up. They'll be easier to work with and won't curl back up on the wall. If a poster has been rolled, try reverse rolling to uncurl it. Or iron it flat! How to: Use your iron at a low setting; place the poster, printed side down, on an ironing board—then run the iron lightly across the back until the poster lies flat.

Frame A Fabric

Dramatically framed, a length of fabric can be as decorative as a painting or poster. For a super-coordinated look: Use a fabric that matches your draperies or upholstery. For do-it-yourself fabric artwork: Frame a large piece of felt, cut out geometric or free-form shapes from smaller pieces (in a variety of colors), and put them up on the background piece in any pattern you please. Felt adheres to felt without any "stickum," so you can rearrange the design as often as you want. Check our sketches and the hints on the opposite page for other ways to frame your fabric. Incidentally, most of these ideas will work well with a panel of wallpaper, too.

Posters in an assymetrical arrangement.

Piece of print fabric in a gilt frame.

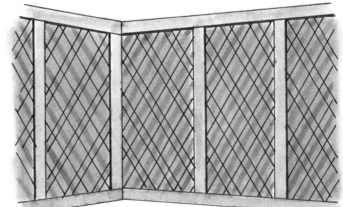

Fabric on wall, with "wooden look" beams added at seams.

☐ Put a rectangle of fabric up on your wall with a staple gun or fabric adhesive. Then frame it with strips of wooden molding cut-to-fit in a hardware store. If you plan to paint the molding, do it before you put it up.

☐ For a warmhearted, country look, "paper" walls with fabric (using fabric adhesive or a staple gun), then cover the seams with molded plastic beams. You'll find these in hardware stores and lumberyards. And you have to look carefully to tell them from the real thing. They come with manufacturer's instructions for gluing or nailing them up.

☐ Instant elegance: Fill in a large gilt picture frame with a piece of cut velvet or other luxury fabric. You can afford to splurge on the fabric because you won't need much of it! Another thought for fabulous fabric: Try an old Paisley shawl, mounted and framed.

Modernize With A Mural

Paint-it-yourself murals aren't as tough as they look, particularly if you settle for a simple shape and not too much detail. A back-of-the-bed mural like the one on this page can be sketched freehand in chalk, then painted in. For alternative ideas, check our other suggestions.

The graph paper approach. Draw or trace the mural outline on graph paper. Use a 1-inch to 1-foot scale. Next, draw a chalk grid on the wall, using 1-foot squares. Now, chalk in your mural outline, following the graph paper miniature, square by square. Then fill in with color.

Don't paint it—project it! For a mural you can change any time you wish, try an inexpensive slide projector and some favorite art slides. Project the image on a wall, on closed blinds or on closed draperies if they're a solid color.

Tape up a mural! Use colored plastic tape to put together a geometric Mondrian-type mural. Plan it out on paper first, then measure it out on the wall with a yardstick and pencil. Then tape away!

"Collage" a mural from cutouts! To avoid defacing walls, paste your mural down on a piece of Fome-Cor (a thin layer of Styrofoam, papered on both sides). Use cutouts from wallpaper, posters, sheets of construction paper. You can even fill in with cutouts from magazines, bits of cloth, pieces of fancy foil wrapping paper. Main idea: Get that layered look, the look of lots going on. You can then mount the Fome-Cor on the wall with double-faced adhesive; or hang it as you would a picture, using screw-in eyes, picture wire and hooks.

Freehand mural on wall behind bed.

PAINT: THE BASIC FACTS AND FIGURES

The chart below describes some of the basic kinds of paints and sealers, defines their advantages, gives some idea of comparative price ranges, and indicates in which rooms or general areas each can best be used.

PAINTS FOR "INSIDE" JOBS

Type	Description	Where Used
Latex primer-sealer (water-thinned)	Simple to apply. Dries quickly and can be re-coated or painted over in about two hours.	On unpainted interior wallboard, plaster, masonry and all types of drywall.
Enamel undercoater (alkyd base, low odor type)	Hard, tight film. Provides good base for enamel. Easy brushing, smooth leveling. Dries in about twelve hours.	Undercoater for alkyd enamels.
Latex wall paint (water-thinned)	The most popular of the interior paints. Durable, good coverage and washability, quick-drying, nontoxic.	Primer-sealer and also finish coat for interior wallboard, wallpaper, plaster. Use on primed wood only.
Flat alkyd enamel	Gives a flat finish. Used same as latex wall paint, but has slightly better washability and abrasion resistance.	Primer-sealer and also finish coat on plaster, wallboard, masonry.
Semi-gloss and full-gloss enamel (alkyd base)	Retains gloss well; resists grease and oil. Better washability and resistance to abrasion than flat alkyd enamel.	On primed plaster and wallboard and on pre-pared wood trim and metal. Good for kitchens, bathrooms and on prop-erly primed woodwork.
Semi-gloss and full-gloss latex enamel (water-thinned)	Combines advantages of latex paints: easy appli-cation and cleanup, rapid-drying, low odor and nonflammable. Good leveling, but lap-ping does not compare favorably with alkyd enamels.	On wallboard, wallpaper, wood and plaster. Good for kitchens, bathrooms and on properly primed woodwork.
Epoxy enamel	Hard film, wide gloss range. Has excellent adhesion and resistance to abrasion, water, sol-vents, greases and dirt. Cost comparatively high, but durability is excellent.	Effective in heavy wear areas: hallways, kitch-ens, bathrooms, laun-dries and on concrete floors.

Type	Description	Where Used
Dripless enamel (special alkyd base)	Does not drip from brush or roller. Easy brushing, self-sealing, excellent color retention. Solvent- and water-resistant.	Decorative enamel for properly primed plaster, wallboard and similar surfaces; also for wood trim and primed metal.
Interior floor and deck enamel	Alkyd and latex used successfully, but polyurethane types provide harder, more flexible and more abrasion-resistant surfaces. When applying polyurethane enamel, follow manufacturer's instructions explicitly and also keep room well-ventilated.	General application to properly primed floors and covered decks.
Clear varnish finishes for wood	Provide durable and attractive finish; seal wood better than lacquer. Show scratch marks. Can be flat, satin, semi-gloss or glossy finish.	For all interior smooth wood.
Shellac	Available in clear and "orange" finishes. Fast-drying. Thinned first coat provides excellent seal for new wood.	For wood walls, trim, furniture or any wood surface requiring only occasional dusting.
Lacquer	Fast-drying. Available in clear and in a variety of color finishes.	Same as above.
Stains	Available in natural finish and in a variety of colors that provide attractive, natural appearance. Several coats are required for bare wood.	As sealers for wood surfaces (especially knots) and as primers for metal surfaces. Good for aluminum and steel windows, heating ducts, radiators and heating pipes.

Figuring Out How Much Paint You Need

Naturally, the amount will depend on the type of paint used and the number of coats needed as well as on the size of the area to be covered. Here, the paint manufacturers have come to your rescue. *Most cans of paint carry this information right on the label: how many square feet the can will cover, and how many coats are needed.* All you have to figure is your square footage. (Measure, then multiply the height of the wall by the width—that's your area in square feet). Remember that the figure you get will apply to one coat only. You'll need that same amount again for each additional coat. If you're in any doubt about quantities, check

DECORATOR HINT
To paint badly cracked walls, try adding some sand to the paint you use. It gives a very flat, matte effect that's attractive—*and* a good disguise! Check your paint dealer for "how-to" advice.

with a paint dealer. They're usually experts in this area. For a basic "wardrobe" of painting equipment, check our list below. You'll find essentials (and some of the possible "extras").

CHECKLIST: HOME PAINTING SUPPLIES

☐ a pair of old shoes; old clothes or coveralls that really cover
☐ paint
☐ paint thinner, if using oil-based paint
☐ extra cans (clean and dry) for mixing paints
☐ stirring paddles
☐ paint strainers—buy them or use an old piece of screening or an old stocking
☐ paint trays, if using rollers
☐ drop cloths (plastic sheets are best)
☐ sandpaper, a scraper, spackling compound or putty, if you are going to do any filling in or smoothing down before you paint
☐ brushes and/or rollers

Note: When do you use a brush rather than a roller? For wide, flat expanses of wall, it's really a matter of personal choice. Some awkward spots (like radiators, baseboards and carved cornices) are best done with a brush.

Basic brushes and where to use them. Using the right brush can make the job easier, so check this list:

SASH TOOL—for moldings, trim, narrow edges, windows.

FLAT PAINT BRUSH—1-inch to 6-inch widths. Use wide ones for walls, floors, ceilings; use narrower ones for sashes, radiators, furniture.

OVAL PAINT BRUSH—in a variety of widths. Use for pipes, rounded furniture legs, some radiator parts.

FLAT VARNISH BRUSH—in a variety of widths. Suit the width to the job.

OVAL VARNISH BRUSH—for rounded legs, pipes. Can be used in place of sash tool (see above).

FOAM RUBBER BRUSHES are also available as flat brushes, in a variety of widths.

PAINT ROLLERS—use 7-inch width for large areas, shorter ones for corners and trim.

Note: For general use, choose a 1½-inch-wide flat paint brush.

Brush and bristle tips—plus advice on rollers. A few extra hints on using and caring for your painting tools:

☐ With a new brush, remove loose bristles by ruffling bristles with your fingers or by running bristles across your palm.
☐ Hang brushes up by their handles or lay them flat; don't stand them up or bristles will be bent.

☐ Wash brushes thoroughly after use with yellow kitchen soap. If you're using oil-based paint, finish cleaning by suspending brush in jar of thinning liquid, then drying on old cloths or paper toweling. Correct thinning liquids: linseed oil or turpentine for paint; turpentine for varnish; denatured alcohol for shellac; lacquer thinner for lacquer.

Warning: Thinners and solvents can be dangerous to inhale and to store. Always check the label for directions on proper use.

☐ Use a roller with a ½-inch nap for plasterboard and other smooth surfaces. Choose a ¾-inch nap for textured plaster, masonry, stucco, brick, or wire fences.

Special Note: Use The "Free" Decorating Services!

Expert advice can be helpful. There's a raft of it available in the form of magazines as well as in the manufacturers' booklets you can pick up in paint, hardware and floorcovering stores. If you're buying furniture or having draperies or slipcovers made in a department store, you can take advantage of their decorating services, too. Most larger stores maintain special consultants in the furniture and/or upholstery fabric departments. They'll be happy to help you with free advice about particular problems. For an overall decorating job: Most of these stores also maintain decorating departments that function as does any regular decorating service. They're staffed with fully trained and accredited decorators who will use both their own store and outside manufacturers as sources. What other kinds of advice are open to you besides a regular decorator? In some cities, there are decorator-consulting services available. Here, you work out a decorating scheme with the service for a flat fee, but do your own buying and use your own painters and upholsterers. "To the trade only": When you see this sign in a furniture, fabric or floorcovering store window (or in a showroom), it means that the store will sell to you only through a decorator.

Check our chart on page 172 to see what's news in wallcoverings.

Note: Be sure that any private decorator you hire is a member of AID (American Institute of Interior Designers) or NSID (National Society of Interior Designers). You're surer of getting trained and competent advice.

Decorators who are members of either organization will include this information on their business cards. Both AID and NSID are nationwide organizations, with members in all major American cities. The headquarters for both are located in New York City. If there doesn't seem to be an AID or NSID decorator in your community, you can always check with "headquarters" and ask them to tell you the name and address of the member or members nearest you. You can also check with them if you have any doubt about the credentials of a decorator.

Rx: To Help Woeful Walls, Consider These Cover-Ups

There are some walls that even spackling and paint won't cure. Or the effort would be so great it wouldn't pay off. Faced with these? Think in terms of a Cover-up Caper. Here, you don't attempt to cope with the wall itself—you put something in front of it! There are a number of ways to accomplish this.

Costume with cloth. The trick here is to keep the price-per-yard to a minimum. Colored or patterned sheets, theatrical scrim, burlap, toweling—these are all good possibilities. You can put the yardage up with a staple gun or with fabric glue. Another idea: Hang it from a ceiling rod just as you would draperies. This can give a very nice effect, particularly if you carry it out around a window as our sketch shows. Or shir it, using top and bottom rods.

Put up pegboard. This can run into money, but the advantages may outweigh the cost. If you're short on space, pegboard offers almost unlimited up-on-the-wall storage. It makes hanging paintings and other wall decor easy. (Don't forget that getting a nail to hold in an old and crumbling wall can be a problem!) It now comes in white, so you don't have to paint it if you want your walls to be white, anyway.

Panel them over—with wooden or plastic paneling, with thin sheets of cork, with adhesive-backed mirrored squares. The last two ideas are best if there's only one wall involved. In general, think of paneling only if you plan to stay awhile because the investment in labor and money is high.

Screen them off. Screens draw the eye down to their level, so you don't have to worry too much about what goes on above them. Screens run the gamut from almost priceless handprinted Oriental jobs to modern decorative ready-mades, inexpensive Shoji paper screens, room-divider panels that can be hinged together as screens and wooden make-your-owns. The latter involve hinging together panels of wood, then covering them with cloth, wallpaper, overlapping posters or paint. Basic procedure: Cover each panel with its decorative "coat" *before* you hinge them all together. If you use cloth or paper, carry it over the top and sides and around onto the back. Otherwise, it'll start to peel at the edges! Poster note: Those ever-handy posters do a good job of covering cracks and "peelies" all by themselves. Put them up on the wall over the worst spots. Usually, they're eye-catching enough to draw attention away from the wall's lesser ills. Mounted without frames, they're light enough to hold on even the sickest plaster walls.

WALLCOVERINGS: THE FACTS AND FIGURES

Any form of wallcovering will probably cost you more than paint. Often, however, it's an investment that pays off in good looks, long wear and low upkeep—and it effects a bigger change in a room than paint does.

What every amateur paperhanger should have on hand. The basic equipment that's necessary to do a good job:

☐ drop cloths (plastic is best)
☐ mat knife (if not using precut papers)
☐ paste and paste brush (if not using prepasted type)—or pan (if using prepasted papers)
☐ chalk and plumb line—to mark first straight guideline
☐ soft, dry wallpaper brush—to help smooth paper over wall
☐ stepladder or step stool—high enough for safe reaching, sturdy enough to take your weight
☐ wallpaper—allow an extra roll for patching and "just in case"

How Wallpaper Is Measured

Wallpaper is available in rolls, panels and sheets. Each is measured a little differently. Check the listing below.

☐ **Paper in rolls.** This is measured and priced by the single roll. Each single roll provides 30 square feet of paper. The most usual dimension sold today is 30″ x 5 yards (untrimmed). Trimmed, each roll offers 27″ x 5 yards of usable paper. Some machine-made and pretrimmed papers are available in rolls that measure 24″ x 6 yards and 18″ x 7 yards.

☐ **Panels of paper.** All hand-screened **stripes** now come in panels and measure 9′3″ x 27″. All **mural papers** also come in panels.

☐ **Sheets of paper.** Some specialty papers, such as book lining papers and jewel-toned squares, are available in sheets. Again, these sheets may vary slightly in size depending on the pattern.

To figure out how much wallpaper you need, follow these steps:

1. Measure all around the room, including any jogs or jut-outs. A 14x18′ room, for instance, would measure 14+18+14+18—or a total of 64 running feet.
2. Then measure the height of the room from baseboard to ceiling. Let's say it's 8 feet.
3. Multiply the running feet of the room by the height to get the square footage to be papered—here it's 64x8′ = 512 square feet.

Note: In general, the precut and prepasted or self-adhering varieties of wallcoverings make good do-it-yourself projects. Ditto the mirror and plastic tile self-adhering squares.

WALLCOVERINGS GALORE

Type	Description	Where Used
Wallpaper: all-paper or fabric-flocked. Available in rolls or in precut, pre-pasted and strippable squares.	Can be plastic-treated or made water-resistant so it's washable. Be sure to ask when you buy, however.	Comes in such a wide variety of colors and patterns (both washable and unwashable) that it can be used in any room. Water-resistant or washable papers are ideal in kitchens, bathrooms, children's rooms, playrooms.
Vinyls or vinyl-coated coverings	Sturdy, scrubbable; available in a wide selection of colors and patterns. Grease, crayon, lipstick and / or other marks wash off easily.	Ideal for kitchens, bathrooms, children's rooms, playrooms.
Linoleum	Washable, grease-resistant. Many colors and patterns.	Same as above.
Wood paneling: in traditional woods, plywood or striated woods.	Warm, handsome appearance. Quite expensive.	Popular for dens, libraries, living rooms, dining rooms, playrooms.
Cork sheets	Handsome; good insulators. The smooth, light-tan variety soils easily, cannot be cleaned. Darker varieties are also available.	Same as above.
Tiles: ceramic, porcelain-covered or plastic.	Smooth, durable finish. Easy to clean. Wide range of patterns and colors.	Bathrooms, kitchens, breakfast nooks, playrooms.
Insulated board	Inexpensive, easy to install. Semi-finished appearance.	Basements, attics, garage rooms.
Fiber board, plastic wallboard	Give a glossy, durable surface. In a variety of patterns, including imitation tile. Applied right over plaster, wood or concrete.	Kitchens, bathrooms, basements, playrooms.

Type	Description	Where Used
Asbestos cement board	Clean, neat appearance; fireproof.	Kitchens, bathrooms, basements, playrooms.
Grasspaper	Handsome texture but expensive.	Not washable, so avoid rooms where there's wear and tear on walls.
Specialty coverings: mirroring, glass, glass brick, fiberglass sheets, natural brick.	Each gives its own effect, serves a special purpose. All of them are expensive.	These are the caviars of wallcoverings—and who's to tell you how to take your caviar!

SLIPCOVERS: NOW THEY'RE ALL-TIME FAVORITES —AND FOR MANY GOOD REASONS

There was a time when slipcovers were thought of only as "summer replacements." You put them on to protect furniture from sunlight and dust, and to make rooms look and feel cooler. Today, they're as important as upholstery—maybe even more so.

Of course, you can still use them to give a seasonal "lift" to rooms. The fact that slipcovers go on and come off easily is their biggest plus. But they have other advantages, too.

☐ They're much less expensive than upholstery work because less time and labor is involved.

☐ They're much easier to clean. When they get soiled just whip them off—and into the washing machine or dry cleaner's with them.

☐ You have a wider range of fabrics to choose from. Even some dress goods can be used for slipcovering (although they won't wear as well as heavier materials).

☐ They're often an inexpensive way of making an ugly old upholstered piece "do." You might be reluctant to pay for reupholstering it. Well, pop on a slipcover and your ugly duckling's transformed! Slipcovers also make it possible to work out a coordinated color scheme for secondhand or inherited pieces.

Slipcovering brand-new furniture. If you know that a piece is going to get very heavy wear or if it's going to be placed where spills and spots are a definite possibility, it might be wise to plan on slipcovers to protect that nice new upholstery. This is particularly true if you select an expensive or fragile upholstery fabric. You can always remove the slipcovers later on—when you're permanently settled or when children are past the messy stage.

Consider the ready-mades—their fit is phenomenal! Stores offer a really staggering assortment of ready-to-buy slipcovers. Gone are the days of the baggy knit in a fudgy color. Synthetic "stretch" fibers and stretch foam backing have revolutionized this field. Today's "stretchies" are available quilted, flocked, printed. Some give a velvet or crushed-velvet look. You can even buy stretch vinyls that have the look of leather! They come in coordinated prints and solids, and the range of sizes gets bigger every day. You can buy them for three or four different types of armchairs; for sofas, sectionals, studio couches, Hollywood beds, sofa beds, recliners.

To sew your own, just pick your pattern! Here again, it's all made easy for you. Most of the major pattern manufacturers offer a good selection of paper patterns for slipcovers. Some publish special supplementary brochures on slipcovering. And if you're a real novice—or have never tried this type of sew-your-own before—you might try one of the special adult education courses in slipcovering. These are offered by various schools and/or community organizations as well as by many of the sewing machine manufacturers.

Easiest of all: Cover up with a "throw." Use an Indian blanket, a length of batik, or hand-dye or stencil your own fabric. Check the stores, too, for their ready-to-buy throws. You'll find quite a little revolution has gone on in this department. Throws now come in shaggy piles, fake furs, slushy-plushy velours. And they're foam backed to minimize slipping! Best of all, you have a choice of sizes to further insure their good fit. Some of the most popular sizes are:

70x90″—for armchairs
70x120″—for conventional sofas
70x144″—for oversize sofas

So—throw them over, tuck them in. Then stand back and admire your handsome results.

HOUSE LIGHTS: THESE NEW VISIONARIES SEE DRAMA IN EVERY ROOM

Lighting has come out from under wraps! Today, it takes its place as an important decorative element—and gives better visibility at the same time. You'll find it in all kinds of forms—strips, spots, tubes, to name a few. Even the look in lamps is changing. There's more emphasis on versatility, on the lamp's ability to adjust to your needs. Lamps are coming off tabletops to stand on the floor, hang from the ceiling, swing out from the walls, tuck in under shelving. Some are almost pure art forms in themselves. And even where the look is traditional, new and better bulbs and lighting controls make lamps more efficient.

Some Bright Light-Ideas

This is kind of a catch-all of do's and dont's and "possibles" that have to do with lighting your home. Most are pretty basic kinds of info you should be familiar with.

Plan work and reading-area lighting first. This is where good lighting is essential (beside chairs and sofas, by beds, on a sewing table or desk, in the kitchen). Once you have these areas comfortably lit, add general room lighting and any special effects you want to achieve.

Work and reading light should be diffused, not glaring. Here, all bulbs should be covered. The new "bare bulb look" is not for these areas. Use shades or frosted or glazed bulbs. Be sure to keep shades and bulbs clean. Economy hint: Fluorescents give almost twice as much light for half the wattage of incandescent bulbs. Tinted bulbs give the least light per watt.

Avoid sharp contrasts in lighting. Suppose you're reading under a good light—but when you lift your eyes up from the page you have to blink because the rest of the room is dark by contrast. You could do damage to your eyes! You don't have to have the same level of lighting in all areas of the room. Just provide some general background lighting to avoid a black-and-white effect.

Efficient shades are important. Ideally, they should be semi-translucent, white or off-white. If you like the look of an opaque shade better, make sure the inside of it is white. Straight or nearly straight-lined shades are better than shades that are strongly curved. Also, look for shades that give a wide spread of downward light as well as some upward light.

Once again, try before you buy! Always try to see a lamp actually turned on in the store before you bring it home. It may not give the kind of lighting you want due to its size and/or shape or the shade it has.

Boning Up On Bulbs

More and more, modern lighting fixtures are featuring exposed bulbs. And every year manufacturers add to the types of bulbs available. So it's useful to know what's on the market. Check a local utility company for recommendations on what's best for your lighting needs.

DECORATOR HINT
Make those double-socket lamps do double duty. Put in one tinted bulb for soft room lighting and one good reading bulb (in the recommended wattage) for reading.

THE LIGHT BULB PICTURE

Type	Description
Incandescent (everyday house bulbs)	Standard types offer a choice of 15 to 300 watts (clear, frosted or colors). Globular, flame-shaped and tubular varieties are also available. Three-way bulbs: available in 30-70-100, 50-100-150, 50-200-250, 100-200-300 watts. Always use base down. (See chart below for suggested wattages.)
Fluorescent tubes	Generally available in 15", 18", 24", 36" and 48" tube lengths. Wattage: 14, 15, 20, 30, 40. (See chart below for suggested wattages in kitchens and baths.) Also available in circular form, in extra-narrow tubes and as regular socket-bulbs.
Indirect white and semi-indirect	Both reflect light upward. Can be used without fixtures.
Neon	Practically heatless; use very little current.
Luminous glass panels	Cold light; soft and diffused for walls and ceilings.

GUIDELINES FOR BASIC HOME LIGHTING

Room	Type of Light	Placement	Wattage
Living room/ den	Table lamp	On end or side table. Base of shade should be at eye level of seated person (approximately 45" from floor).	150 watts for occasional reading, writing, sewing (or a 50-100-150 3-way bulb). 200- or 300-watt bulb for prolonged reading, writing or sewing.
	Floor lamp	To the side and slightly behind chair or sofa so reading or work area is shadow free. Base of shade should measure 43" to 47" from floor.	150 to 300 watts.
Bedroom	Wall lamp	Over beds. Bottom of shade should be 30" above top of mattress.	150 watts is the minimum wattage that should be used for reading.
	Bedside lamp	On night tables. Bottom of shade should be 20" above top of mattress.	Same as above.
Office/den	Desk lamp	Place 15" to left of work area (to right if left-handed), 12" back from front edge of desk. Shade should measure 15" from desk top.	200- or 300-watt bulb for prolonged reading or writing.

Note: Special types of desk lamps include high-intensity models, which feature specialized bulbs and magnifiers; the architectural variety, which have adjustable arms and shades, can be clamped to the desk or hung on the wall.

Kitchens and bathrooms	Fluorescent	On ceilings, under cabinets, beside mirrors.	Two 40-watt or two 30-watt tubes for ceiling and over-sink fixtures; one 20- or 40-watt for counter-top lighting. About half this wattage is needed in bathrooms (check your lighting dealer for specific needs).

Diffusers and shields for lamps. These both work to improve home lighting. Diffusers are available in both bowl and disc shapes—in glass and plastic. They surround the light bulb under the lampshade to scatter and redirect light, soften shadows, reduce reflected glare. Shields (usually made of perforated metal or louvered plastic) are placed above lamp bulbs to help shield passersby from direct glare.

Various lighting arrangements that are contemporary in feeling. From the top: track lighting; a "chandelier" made of 3-way sockets plugged together; hanging light fixture, with cord run across ceiling and plugged into standard baseboard outlet; spotlight focused on plant to give interesting play of light.

Decorating With Light

Lighting can create a mood, accent a room feature, dramatize a background. Lamps and lighting fixtures are important accessories in themselves—"little furnishings" that should complement your general color scheme and decorating style. Choose and place them tastefully and they're a visual delight. If they're out of kilter with your other furnishings, provide insufficient light, or create harsh glare-spots, they're a decorating disaster.

Light is an integral part of color. So keep these color-facts in mind when you choose your home's lighting. Incandescent lights are warm lights. They'll accent the reds, oranges and yellows in the room. They'll also make dark tones look richer. "Cool" fluorescent light brings up the cooler colors, can make blues and greens very dramatic. Usually, it's best to choose a Soft White fluorescent. This has a bit of red in it to soften it. The 3500 White is efficient for work areas, but is less desirable for decorating purposes. Now for some effects you can achieve with light.

Play with light and shadow. We've already mentioned that sharply contrasting dark-and-bright spots are undesirable in a room. But you *can* use soft background light with strongly lit areas. Spotlights will focus attention on a bright-colored rug, a poster, a plant. To create an "indirect lighting" effect with a spot, point it at the ceiling and let the light reflect down. For dramatic shadows, shine a spotlight on a piece of statuary or through a mobile. Today, spotlights come in a variety of forms. Some are designed to be wall- or ceiling-mounted like theatrical lights. Others are attractively designed and can be placed right out in sight on the floor or on a table.

Light dimmers (or rheostats) are useful lighting tools, too. You can hitch up a single lamp—or all the lights in the room—to one. With a dimmer, you can "dial" just the degree of light you want—from barely-there to full reading light. Look for dimmers in any lighting or hardware store.

Have fun with "the bare-bulb look." We've already mentioned the trend toward leaving bulbs and wiring exposed (with a caution not to use this type of lighting for reading). Bare-bulb lighting can extend all the way from a single globular bulb hung from the ceiling to elaborate "chandeliers" composed of 3-way sockets plugged together at interesting angles. To help you achieve this look successfully, lighting equipment manufacturers have come up with an assortment of decorative bulbs—globular, mushroom-shaped, tubular. Also on the market: extra-thick electrical wire encased in round vinyl—comes in white, black or colors.

Another bare-bulb lighting gimmick: Remember the rows of

bare bulbs used around mirrors in theatrical dressing rooms? These are now available in easy-mount strips you can put up anywhere. Run a strip of them down the side of a room divider for dramatic emphasis. Or frame a mirror or poster with them.

Feature a fabulous fixture. They're available in all sizes and shapes. You can get lighting fixtures that are pure art forms: columns of light; sculptural arrangements of Lucite rods and lights; translucent plastic spheres to set on tabletops or shelves. You can get light rods or neon tubes to suspend from ceilings on invisible wires. You can get flexible light tubes to set on a table, like a serpent of light. You can even get occasional tables with inset luminous-panel tops (these can double as furniture-cum-lighting fixtures).

Another big trend in lighting is the hanging fixture. These fixtures can suspend from the ceiling or jut out from a wall. In either case, they're available in traditional or contemporary styles. They put light where you want it, save on floor and table space. You don't have to install wall or ceiling wiring to accommodate these, either. Have them fitted with their own electrical cord and plug, then mount them where you want them and plug the cord into a standard baseboard socket. Hide the cords behind decorative wall hangings or use magic markers to color them to match your walls. Caution: If you want them actually wired into the walls, have this work done by a licensed electrician.

Track lighting is another interesting variation on the mounted lighting fixture. Essentially, this is an electrified track (a long, continuous outlet, really) into which you fit individual swivel lights. Point the individual lights anywhere you want. Use them as spotlights or to wash a whole room in light. With track lighting, you group most of your lighting needs into one system. You don't have to cope with a lot of separate lamps, lamp cords and extension cords.

Swing into the psychedelics. These will take you into whole new combinations of light-color-motion. Often, they create a whole environment in themselves. You might investigate the kinetic lamps that flicker like firelight or change form and color in response to sounds; the color-motion lamps that feature a revolving drum of colored panels to project a constantly changing pattern of colored light; the dimension of black light tubes and bulbs. These last make white fabrics and paint glow like phosphorous. They also lend a luminous glow to the special dayglo paints and posters now available. Never mount black lights where you'll be looking directly into them, however. This can cause serious eye injury.

YOUR ACCESSORIES: CHOOSE THEM WITH TENDER, LOVING CARE

Accessories are probably the most "you" thing about a room. So it pays to choose them carefully. Here again, it's a together thing. If one of you adores pottery and the other hates it, play down the pottery in favor of something else! The same goes for those mementos of the past. Most homes can take limited quantities of football pennants, college beer steins, security teddy bears, ashtrays collected from favorite haunts. They won't look like much in your new surroundings—and they may be resented! Taste is always a matter of personal choice, but there are a few pointers that can help in your choosing and arranging.

Here's How To Be A More Successful "Accessorizer"

The overall rule of thumb is: Make the useful decorative, the decorative useful. How? Remember that accessories have to fit smoothly into your general room scheme. Colors should blend well or contrast smartly with other colors in the room. The same goes for the scale of accessories. You probably won't be happy with massive ashtrays set on small, dainty tables, for instance. So when you're choosing—decide which things have to go into the room for comfortable living, then try to make them decorative!

Another good piece of advice: Kick the knickknack habit if you're addicted. Two or three well-chosen accessories will show up better than a flood of small "things." If you're a born pack rat and plan to stay that way, group your goodies into definite collection areas. Don't strew them around with a lavish hand. (You'll find some suggestions for "housing" collections later on in this chapter.) Also, don't feel that you have to acquire all your accessories immediately. It's more fun to pick them up gradually so they reflect your growing tastes and interests. Once you buy them, though, don't feel you have to hang on to them forever. Accessories go out of style, get tired-looking, are subject to damage. A chipped ashtray looks just as bad in a room as a chipped plate or glass does on a dining table! So take a hard look at those accessories every once in a while and *replace* if you have to.

Using The "Usables" In Interesting Ways

Here's a clutch of ideas on how to introduce some of the more current and useful objects into your life. Many of these may be on your "to buy" list already. But have you thought of using them in these ways?

Join the pillow culture. Today's pillows are to toss, to heap, to use in place of chairs, to furnish with! And they're decorative into the bargain. You can buy them, ready-made, in all sizes—from teensy-weensies to toss on a sofa as color accents to giant-size floor cushions you spread around to serve as extra seating. Within this "throwaround" concept, here are two ideas. Turn a bed into a seating area by covering it with a throw-spread and a healthy helping of pillows in all sizes and shapes. Guests just pile these up behind them as backrests, as the mood moves them. Or make a chair of two large pillows by placing one up against the wall as a "back" and one on the floor in front of it as a seat. Take the pillow culture one step further and you turn pillows into furniture. Use polyurethane "shapes" to create sofas, seating blocks, beds. You can buy this versatile "stuffing" in squares, rectangles, triangles, cubes, cylinders—in department stores or chain stores. Or check your yellow pages under "pillows" or "foam rubber." Covered in your selection of fabric, these shapes can create a "pillow environment." Large rectangles form the basis of bed-sofas; cylinders and triangles act as backrests. For extra seating, pile up a tower of squares or set out an assortment of cylinders. And there are your furbished furnishings—brought to you through the good offices of pillows!

Enter the mirror and mylar dimension. In reflection lies the magic of mirrors. And mylar-mirror (actually a silvered polyester film) has the extra virtues of being lightweight, "bendable" and inexpensive. To make small rooms look larger, to enhance the fairyland quality of lighting, "paper" a wall with mirroring or with mylar. Specifically for mirrors: Turn one into a tabletop; mount mirror "portholes" on a wall with double-sided pressure tape; frame a poster or strew a wall with round, convex rearview mirrors. Take advantage of the self-stick mirrored squares. Cover a wooden screen with them and use as a space-expanding room divider. Cover two screens with them, then place one on either side of a window. They're a wow in place of drapes! Now picture a diamond-studded wall. It's easy. Just paint one wall a deep, dark tone and scatter it with those same mirrored squares (put them up up-ended so they form diamond-shapes).

SPECIFICALLY FOR MYLAR: Drama up a ceiling with a mylar panel (it's safe because mylar is so lightweight). Cut it into strips, then mount them on a wall to dramatize and lighten up a corner. Or make a mirrory sliding door or window-treatment. Just mount those mylar strips on a standard accordion-fold vinyl door or on a set of vertical venetian blinds.

SPECIAL MIRROR MEMO: When buying mirrors, remember that they're available in five grades (AA, A, No. 1, No. 2, No. 3), with AA being as nearly perfect as possible. All grades are usable in

Mirrors are graded,
so check
before you buy.

homes, but No. 3 grade must be examined carefully before buying, as it may have obvious defects. Also: Never hang mirrors in a spot where they'll receive direct sunlight all day long. They may haze over.

Show off your art and artifacts. Paintings, prints, family photos, blow-ups of photos—these are all effective additions to rooms. At the very least, they add color and drama. Often, they'll solve a real problem. Hung at eye level on a wall, they'll reduce the height of a room. Grouped around an awkwardly placed window, they'll tend to make it "disappear." Stand them in front of ugly radiators or use them to fill in bare spaces under windows. Got an ugly door that's in full view? Cut a large photostat or photo blow-up to size and paper the door with it. Turn a hallway alley into an art gallery. Just cover the walls with paintings and photos and light them with a ceiling track. Or cover large squares of posterboard with burlap, pin them full of small prints and photos, attach a standing easel to each, and use them next to front doors or as room dividers.

Now for some hints on how to arrange pictures on a wall. Even one picture can be effective if it's properly placed (see the one-picture arrangement we show). Some ways to maximize a single picture: Balance it with another accessory; feature it by framing it with molding or with a wide stripe of painted wall; or leave it as the *only* eye-catcher on a broad expanse of white wall and spotlight it dramatically. Another idea: Balance pictures against each other—one large one, two or three small ones. The trick here is to have the outside edges evenly aligned. Or use an open "scatter" pattern like the one sketched here. Once again, you mix

One-picture arrangement.

"Scatter" pattern.

Pictures arranged with outer edges lining up.

larger and smaller pictures (in this case, though, there's no attempt to line up edges). Experiment a bit on your own. With just a bit of practice, you'll develop an eye for what makes an interesting arrangement.

The easy way to hang picture groupings—follow these step-by-step directions to put pictures just where you want them on the wall. With this method, you do all the shuffling and rearranging before the pictures go up on the wall!

☐ Gather together all your pictures or hangings and lay them out on the floor on top of a large sheet of paper. (Paper should be the same size as the wall area you want to fill.)

☐ Take the picture hooks you are planning to use and insert them into the pictures, with wire fully extended, just as if they were being hung on the paper.

Special Note: If you use picture hooks, be sure to allow for the length of the hook. If you don't, all the pictures will hang an inch lower than you want them to.

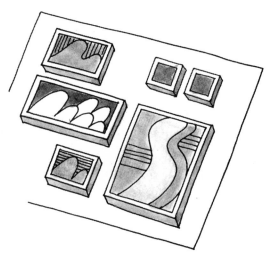

Pictures laid down on a piece of paper on the floor.

☐ Put a pencil mark on each place where a nail should be driven to hold a picture hook. Wise idea: Jot the name or description of each picture next to its dot. This way you won't have wasted your time if you have to fold up the operation before you're finished.

☐ When you've marked each picture, place the paper on the wall over the area where you plan to hang the grouping. Attach it with masking tape or get an "assistant" to help with the holding.

☐ Now, just line up the picture hooks and the dots, and hammer in your nails. Tear off the paper, then hang the pictures.

Note: Follow the same procedure for hangings and/or other types of wall ornaments. (See diagram below.)

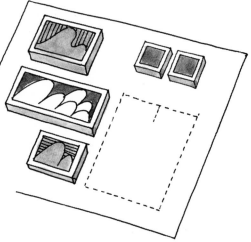

Line drawn around one picture, with mark made to indicate drop when picture is hanging. (Repeat procedure with each picture.)

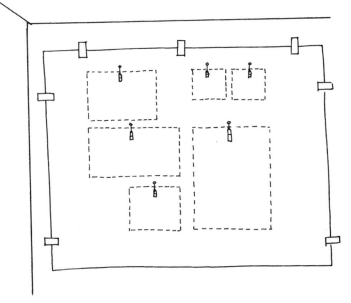

Paper taped on wall, with positions of pictures indicated. Hammer in nails or picture hooks, tear off paper, then hang pictures.

Create a collection. It can be a grouping of related items (interesting bottles, snuffboxes, antique dolls) or a potpourri of favorite things. The secret is to group your items together somewhere where they'll show off to good advantage. If you're really ambitious, you can build a whole collector's wall. Some simpler ideas: Paint an ordinary stepladder a gay color and set out your collection on it. Or stack together a series of wooden cubes in an interesting step-pattern and group your collection inside and on top of these. A windowsill plus window shelves will work, too. Some kinds of items can even be hung from the ceiling on nylon fishing line or invisible wire. (Don't try this with heavy or breakable items!) Really small items like coins can be displayed in curio cabinets or on tables. Another idea: Try to pick up a secondhand store display case from an office-furniture store. Paint it and pop in your things. Or build your own lighted wall display cases with plexiglass. And don't forget the great hanger-upper—pegboard. Special hook-in brackets are available to help you mount small shelves on this.

Make candlelight part of your life. Candles come in all sizes, shapes, colors . . . scented or "plain." For the clearest, most beautiful light imaginable, try natural beeswax candles. Got an urge to make your own? You can buy handy kits of wax, wicks and coloring in most candle shops and department stores. Here again, placement is all-important. Try grouping two or three candles of different heights in front of a piece of mirror propped against the wall. The reflection is magical and you double the amount of light given off. Set a large votive candle (in its glass cup) inside a basket floored with aluminum foil and let its light shine through. For unusual holders, pile up colorful children's blocks and set a large candle smack on top. Or search for an old newel post you can crown with a candle. Tiny floating candles are available. For pure enchantment, float these in a shallow glass bowl. Add a flower if the mood moves you.

Practical note: Most candle holders and arrangements will offer greater safety and convenience if you use dripless candles in them. Hot wax can burn fingers, damage tabletops, stain linens. Opt for dripless and you can avoid all this!

Bring out the best in books. Like pictures and photos, books add to the personality of a room. They're useful decorating tools, too. Frame a window with bookshelves and who needs draperies! Use bookshelves to create a recessed niche for a sofa. Use the same technique to take the bedroomy look out of a guest room-den. Put up your shelving; shove the bed into the niche you've created.

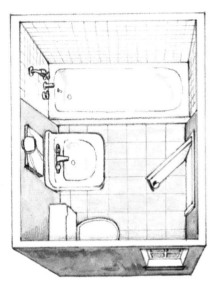

How Does Your Bathroom Grow?
With Pegboard, Mirrors And Imagination.

A standard bathroom floor plan.

Shelves, storage cubes, shaving and makeup lights, a mirror—all hook into a pegboard "wall unit" that frames sink and toilet. A door mirror and more pegboard create a mini dressing room around the door.

Need a den or office that's light, airy and feels really separate? A sculptured wall like this might be the answer. Cut it from lightweight styrofoam panels and cubes. You can even paint it if you want to!

Create a new room or two-rooms-from-one with colorful, dramatic, easy-to-handle hangings of felt. Dowels weight each panel at the bottom. The cutouts create interest, allow light and air to flow through.

Divide—And Conquer Your Space Problems!

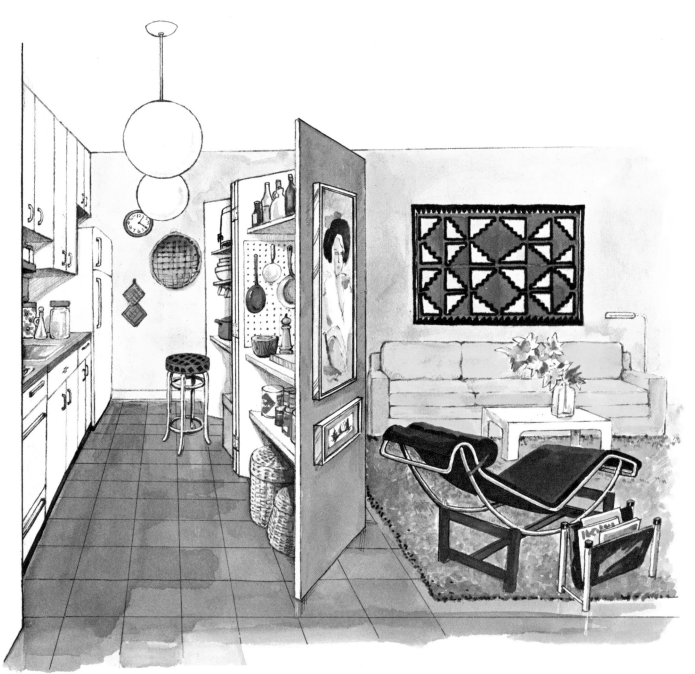

When is a wall not a wall? When it's a clever arrangement of wooden panels hinged together like a screen. Ours separates a pullman kitchen from the living room, provides extra storage and wall space on both sides.

"Uglies" Do A Disappearing Act.

Even modern built-in radiator/cooling units can be ugly. Grillwork panels (sold at hardware stores) will hide them away attractively.

Strands of cord knotted with beads curtain off a window air conditioner. Hang strands from a wooden lathe attached to the ceiling.

The hi-rise radiator's hidden, the heat comes through, the knob's in reach! How-to-do-it: Use wooden dowels nailed to a 2x4 frame and an asbestos-lined window shelf.

Now cover with a throw and pillows. Those versatile cubes make interesting book holders. Fit larger ones with shelves, use the smaller ones "as is." Standing bookcases make good room dividers. Stack one set on top of another if height is needed. Place two back to back if you want the book-look on both sides. For the height of convenience, mount casters on a small bookcase and you'll always have your books within arm's reach! One final idea: Drama the drabs out of your kitchen by adding shelves of jacketed books. Or put in a hutch and fill its shelves with books.

Use "living" accessories. The most common of these are plants and herbs, but if you like fish, a well-kept and well-lighted tank can be an attractive sight. Let's concentrate on plants. You can place potted plants almost anywhere—on windowsills, tabletops, under tables, beside chairs, in hanging planters. Plants thrive in artificial light; try to place your indoor miniature-gardens under a lighting fixture or under specially designed plant-lighters. To start a lighted garden, all you need is one 24- or 25-inch commercial fluorescent fixture designed to hold two 20-watt tubes. It's also best to add a reflector. This unit can be attached to a table bottom, edge of a shelf or bottom of a cabinet. Equip it with metal legs (available where you buy it) and you can stand it on a table. Stand plant pots in plastic trays or put saucers under them. You can create a whole "living wall"—by filling a wall unit with plants and lighting each shelf, by putting up a series of light boxes filled with plants, or by hanging plants in wall brackets and flooding the whole wall with light from a ceiling track. Remember, indoor window boxes also add the gaiety of greenery to a room and take advantage of natural light. A variation on this theme: Buy one of the small window hothouse units available in toy shops and set your mini-garden up in this.

Formal floral arrangements can be expensive and need attention. If you're looking for a touch of "living color" on tabletops, consider still lifes composed of fresh vegetables or fruit (a pineapple, apples, radishes, a cauliflower, an eggplant!). Leave them out while you're entertaining or for a day or two for your own enjoyment; then slice them into a salad or pop them into a pot!

Television and stereo components can be decorative accessories. The word is: Highlight rather than hide them. For TV: Put it "up on the wall" on a shelf all its own, perhaps set off with one other accessory. Or take it out of its case and show it off like a piece of decorative sculpture—on a pedestal or in a plexiglass box. Stereo units, too, can go on the wall—as part of a wall-storage unit or by themselves. Stereo speakers make handy end tables, incidentally. To make a completely "magic of machinery" look,

DECORATOR IDEA
Use a tea wagon as a night table in a bedroom. Put a lamp and ashtray on the top level, books and magazines on the lower shelf.

DECORATOR IDEA
If you don't have a "green thumb," invest in Chinese evergreens. They'll thrive in water with a few pebbles added, need almost no care.

combine TV and stereo components with bookcases, then edge everything with perforated metal strips.

Have Fun With The "Just For Funs"

Put some of the paraphernalia of past and present into your home just because it's amusing. From the past: Wooden cradles or brass coal buckets make great magazine holders; a pottery milk churn can be a handsome vase; and for a paperweight, you can't beat an old flatiron. Use a child's wagon as a coffee table— or press an old bench into use this way. From the other end of the time spectrum: Today's this-and-that stores carry great collections of inexpensive fun items. Papier-mâché is big, comes in the form of gaily painted boxes, desk accessories, kitchen canisters, mirror frames. Marvelous butterfly- or dragon-shaped kites are versatile decorations; try one as a wall hanging or instant mobile. Paper lampshades are available in stark white or colorful imitation Tiffany patterns. Oriental wicker baskets, wind chimes, beaded curtains, pottery tea sets—each of these exotica lends its own distinctive note to a room.

Living In A Furnished Room, Or At Home With Parents? Personalize With Accessories!

It's amazing what a shelf of books, a poster on a wall, a mobile can do to liven up the place. Here's where screens really come into their own, too. Hinge several panels together, decorate them up, add a table, two chairs and a TV set, and you can create a room-within-a-room, as our sketch shows. It can be your own private retreat within which only your own tastes show. Or use individual screens to blot out "furnished room frights." Take down dull, dreary draperies and set a vividly papered screen on either side of the window instead. (Paper draperies are also available, by the way—inexpensive and disposable.) If you can't stand the paint or wallpaper, consider "hanging" the walls with these paper draperies or with an inexpensive cloth. Spotlighting, too, will help blot out the nasties. Draw attention to the "nices" you add to the room through the use of spots, and no one will notice the other unfortunates.

Room-within-a-room, created with hinged panels.

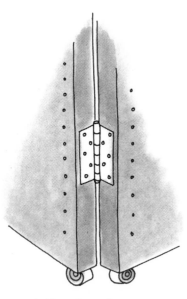

Two panels hinged together.

HANDBOOK OF
Ideas to Stretch Small Spaces and Budgets

Modern houses and apartments often put the squeeze on space—and on your budget. Fortunately, furniture designers and manufacturers are coming to grips with the problem. They're using new materials, developing new concepts in furnishings to help provide successful solutions. Your own ingenuity can help, too.

The general trend is to concentrate on small-scale pieces, multipurpose pieces or on a very few larger ones. The uncluttered look is aesthetically pleasing. Thinking of room space as a whole helps, too. In other words: Don't measure a room by its wall space alone. Consider how you might use the center of the room for furniture placement. Look up! The space from the top of your head to the ceiling can be used—and not just as a wall-storage area, either. The following pages include some clever ways to turn it into actual living space.

If you're faced with a space bind, haphazard furnishings can finish you. To make the most of the room that's there, you have to plan the whole thing out in advance. Then choose each piece with a definite idea of where it will go and what it will do for you. For instance, narrow end tables are good. But using a pair of short, narrow bookcases as end tables might be better because they'll offer shelf space as well as surface area. If you're confined to a 1-room studio—is a small dining room table the best answer? You might be better off putting in a desk instead. Set it up for two when you're dining at home alone. And plan dinner parties as buffet affairs. (The desk then becomes your buffet table.) This is the kind of think-and-think-again that can make tiny rooms more livable. The ideal "buys," of course, are furnishings that can pull their weight now *and* will also be usable when you move to larger quarters.

In this Handbook, we'll try to give you a quick picture of what's available in space-saving furniture and ideas. And we include specific suggestions on how to cut furnishing and decorating costs. You may decide to go your own route—and it may be better than ours. But at least we can save you some shopping and thinking time!

Armoire angled out into room to create foyer.

STORAGE FURNITURE: TRADITIONAL OR MODERN

These days storage furniture includes anything and everything you can put other things into. Traditional designs include the armoire, a large standing cupboard which can be fitted out to hold clothes, dishes, glasses, pots, pans. Angle one straight out from the wall and it can create a dining area or an entrance area where there was none before. The same goes for étagères—those tall, narrow sets of shelves which fit into awkward spaces so handily. Here we show one put to work as a combination bar and buffet-server. Modern version of the armoire: a metal office locker decked out with paint. Spruce up a filing cabinet in the same way and you have an inexpensive end-table-plus-storage-drawer piece. We've mentioned using trunks as bedside tables. Team them with living room couches or chairs for table-cum-storage space, too! Our little mini-dining corner shows two bright ideas. Wooden cubes fitted with casters are used as rollaway stools. They fit neatly under the window shelf, which functions as a serving table. *But*—their tops are hinged so the whole inside is storage space. They're covered in contact paper, topped with cushions.

Modern étagère used as a buffet-bar.

Metal office cabinet painted in an imaginative way.

Cubes (on casters) intended for extra
seating/storage—stored under a window
shelf.

Two dressers angled to form a
reading/study nook in a room.

Footlocker used as a coffee
table (fastened to blocks or
casters to give a more finished
look).

Small trunk used as end table.

Component storage units
stacked to form divider.

Modular upholstered unit with triangular tables
fitted in.

MODULARS
MULTIPLY SPACE

The traditional chair-and-ottoman is a simple example of the modular concept. But how far we've taken it! Today, modular upholstered pieces come armless, one-armed, curved, triangular. Just fit them together in the way that suits you best. Some units include square and triangular tables that can be slotted in as part of the overall unit. Their diverse shapes let you move them away from walls—to curve out into the room, divide it into living and dining areas. Or group them as a circle, smack in the center of the room, around a large coffee table. You've created a conversation pit for entertaining. Use the outside perimeter for TV viewing, reading, other "together" activities. Or compose a unit of low tables and large cushions. Move them around—from a scatter pattern (as we show) to a long, low dining table that will seat and serve a full-scale dinner party. Achieve the same effect with a collection of cubes or wooden boxes. Slipcovered polyurethane shapes are the ultimate in modulars. You can even buy precut, build-your-own modular furniture units. They fit together into "environments" like our super-bed or can be used separately.

Slipcovered polyurethane shapes used in a variety
of ways.

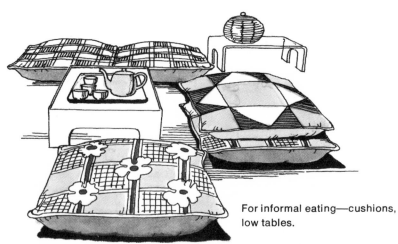

For informal eating—cushions,
low tables.

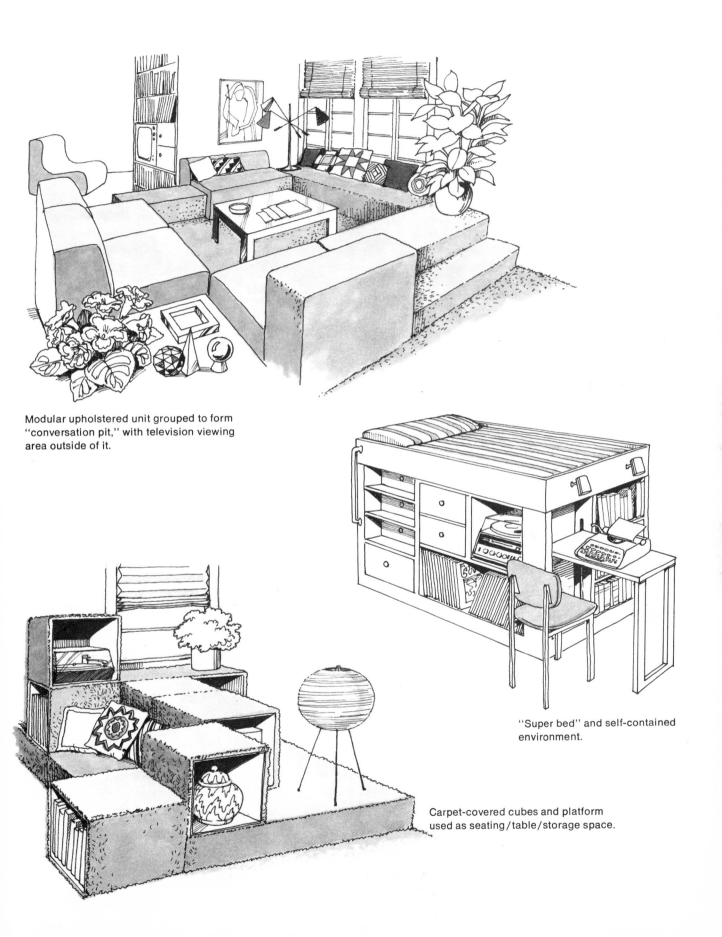

Modular upholstered unit grouped to form
"conversation pit," with television viewing
area outside of it.

"Super bed" and self-contained
environment.

Carpet-covered cubes and platform
used as seating/table/storage space.

FOLD-DOWNS
FIT ALMOST ANYWHERE

And they free up space when they're not in use. They include today's version of the "Murphy bed" (like the one shown here). Essentially, it's a pullman bed that folds up on the wall with special hinges you can buy in hardware stores. Box it around with a wooden casing finished off with wooden shutters, and who knows it's there? Fold-down shelves can function anywhere—as extra kitchen work space, as a hideaway dining table, as a desk or buffet serving space. Chairs, too, come in fold-down versions. Bridge chairs can make serviceable dining chairs. Hang them up on the wall when not in use. And outdoor canvas chairs can make gay extra seating that hides away in closets between parties. And then there's the whole field of drop leaf and extension tables. These offer a lot of seating space in very little living space. Take them in your choice of traditional or contemporary designs, in light or dark woods, even in plastics. Don't forget the good old bridge table, either. It can be a lifesaver if space is really limited. The stackables really belong in this picture, too. Stools, molded wood or plastic chairs, tables—they all share the virtue of piling up neatly on top of each other!

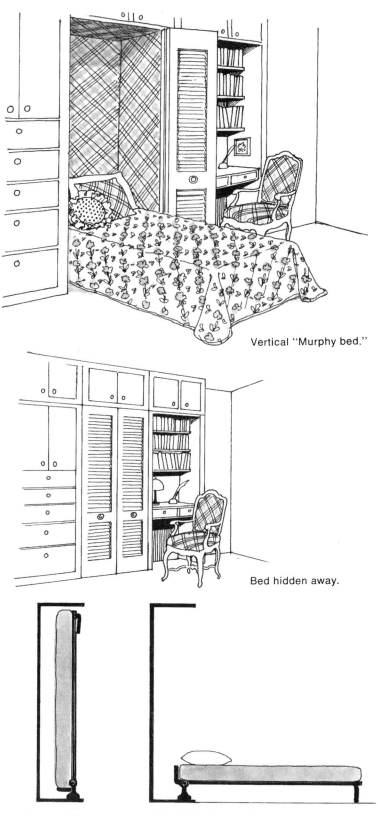

Vertical "Murphy bed."

Bed hidden away.

Diagram of bed folded up on wall.

Diagram of bed pulled down.

Bridge chairs hang on wall when not in use.

Stackable chairs.

Foldable canvas chairs.

Stackable molded tables.

Fold-down shelf used for buffet service.

Table with pull-out extensions.

Yarn used as trimming on pillows, draperies, valance.

EASY, INEXPENSIVE: TRIM THE BLAHS AWAY

"Landlord standard" color schemes are blah. So are the boxlike rooms favored by today's builders. If your funds are limited, you can work wonders with the wide selection of ready-made trimmings available today. Some ideas: "Mantilla" a window with black nylon netting. Tack down a square of black braid right in the middle of that tired tan carpeting (use heavy steel upholstery pins), paint dining chairs and table a glossy black, and set them smack in the middle of your braid "island." Complete the scheme with an edging of matching braid tacked to the tops of walls and around the welting of furniture.

Or make the room Mexican: Tack strips of bouncy ball fringe straight across a window frame (finish with an edging of plastic tape) and across one wall, mount gaily colored straw hats on another wall, sling a serape over a table—and you look as warmhearted as a fiesta! Other ideas: Jazz up a so-so table and chairs with an edging of gingham ribbon! "Gift wrap" pillows, a tired-looking sofa, drab draperies with bright ribbon or trimming yarn! Or stripe them up with sequin stripping sold by the yard! Other ideas: embroidered iron-on butterfly patches on sofa and chairs, or a rickrack-striped wall and sofa. That's for starters!

Iron-on butterfly patches on sofa cushions.

Create a dining area with braid; chairs are painted black.

Rickrack trimming on wall and sofa.

Gingham trim on table and chair cushions.

Narrow display ledges show off collections and other prized or decorative objects.

USING THE SPACE ABOVE

We mentioned "looking upward" for more living space. Here are some of the ways you can bring it off. First, there's the useful loft. This can provide a sleep area or a cozy lounging-reading-TV "room." If you're faced with a tiny sleeping alcove, double the space with a pair of broad built-in "living shelves," one for sleeping, one for lounging. Reach the upper shelf via a ladder, just as you would with a loft. Not so far off the ground, but still a dimensional use of space: a dining platform, stepped up from your living room. Or use a series of cubes and platforms, covered with carpeting, or some of those plushy throws we mentioned (page 174), to maximize seating and table space in a small room. Ceiling-storage is another efficient use of space. It can be as simple as a conventional ladder (as shown) to hold extra blankets, sheets and other fairly light household items. Or you can go all the way, with a storage platform built in with metal supports so it will take heavier objects. Another idea: Build a narrow display ledge right around all four walls to show off a collection or hold party-minded dishes, casseroles, vases and glasses.

Platform arrangements maximize seating and table space.

Dining platform; carpet-covered platform used as table or for seating.

Ladder used for ceiling storage.

"Living shelves"—one for sleeping, one for lounging.

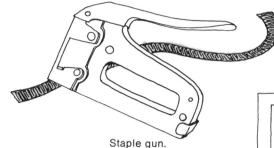

Staple gun.

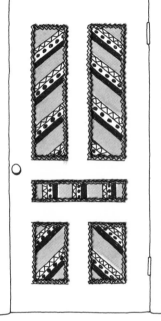

Door decorated with
fabric.

BUDGET-STRETCHER: STAPLE GUN DECORATING

One of the fastest and easiest ways
to refurbish on a shoestring is via
the staple gun. First of all, it offers
almost instant reupholstering. If
you have a chair or love seat with an
exposed wooden frame, you're
golden! Just remove the old fabric
to use as a pattern, cut out your new
covering, then staple it to the piece
and trim with braid to hide the raw
edges. A fast way to get the effect of
draperies: Staple-gun strips of fabric around and over a window.
Again, trim with tape or braid. Turn a
piece of board or an old door into a
headboard by covering it with a gay
fabric applied with staples. Just
stand it up behind your bed and
you're all set in a matter of two or
three hours. Beaten-up old trunks
and wooden chests can be reno-
vated with a quick coating of fabric.
The sketches on the right will show
you how to back-tack to join pieces
of fabric without the staples showing. Again, it's a fast-and-easy way
to cover wooden screens, cover a
bad wall, or cover unpainted furniture if you don't want to paint. You
can also create effective felt wall-
murals with a staple gun. Staple
your pattern to a painted plywood
panel.

Recover a chair by
means of a staple gun—
edge fabric with braid.

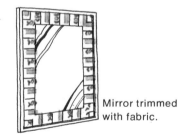

Mirror trimmed
with fabric.

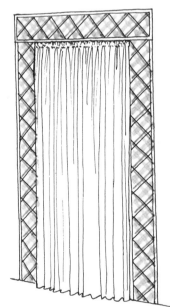

Strips of fabric around a
window—trimmed with tape.

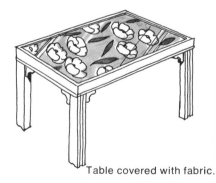

Table covered with fabric.

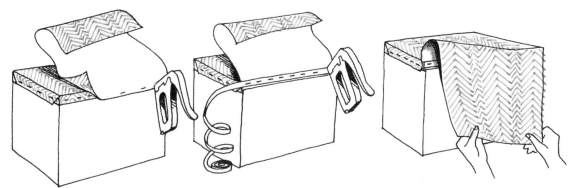

Back-tacking to hide staples—covering a trunk.

Miter corners.

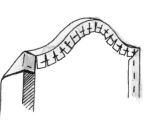

Bring fabric around a curve.

Cover edging with a panel.

Cover staples with trim.

Fabric used as curtain/drapery on wall—stapled taut on other wall and over door.

Board covered with fabric to form headboard.

A build-your-own wall unit.

Create a bookcase with bricks and wooden shelving.

BUILD FURNITURE THE EASY WAY

What do you do for furniture when the budget says "don't buy" and you're not talented at building your own? Put together some pieces without getting into the hammer-and-nails bit. Bookcases made from lengths of shelving and bricks can be very effective. Paint the bricks a bright color. Or use small wooden cubes as the "stackers." A pile of old books covered in matching gift wrap paper or wallpaper need only be topped with lucite to turn into a handsome occasional table. Glue a store-bought fiber board bed board to four wooden cubes, top with a mattress —there's your bed! If you want to combine bed and storage space, shove together some secondhand filing cabinets, drawer sides out, top with your bed board, and you've got it made. If you're really put to it, heavyweight cardboard cartons and packing cases can be useful. Stand a large-size one on end, run a heavy wooden dowel through it (see our sketch at right), and you have a clothes-storage unit. You can use regular flat wall paint to dress it up. Painted liquor cartons can function as bookcases (stack them like cubes) and as storage units for sheets and towels. Any other ideas?

Flowerpots glued together form the base for this lamp.

Cushions strapped together to form a stool or backrest.

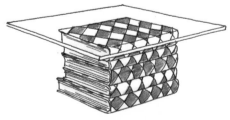

Books covered with gift wrap paper used as the base for a Lucite-topped table.

Table made from a lacquered cardboard carton.

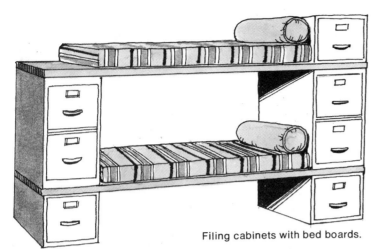

Filing cabinets with bed boards.

Fiber board bed board glued to four wooden cubes, topped with mattress—a "make-your-own" bed.

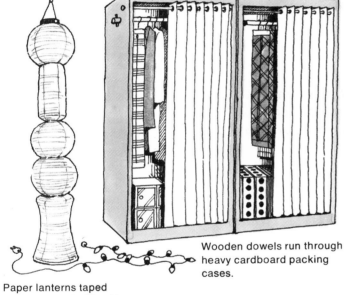

Wooden dowels run through heavy cardboard packing cases.

Paper lanterns taped together, used with white Christmas tree lights.

An easy-to-make table—epoxy cardboard mailing tubes around a fiber barrel or drum.

Fabric used in front of packing cases is reinforced with grommets, held in place with café curtain rod.

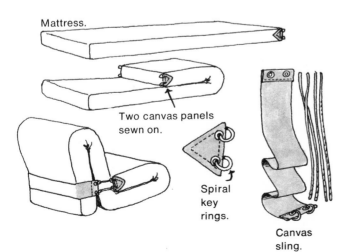

Mattress.

Two canvas panels sewn on.

Spiral key rings.

Canvas sling.

Create a sofa or chair out of a non-foam mattress.

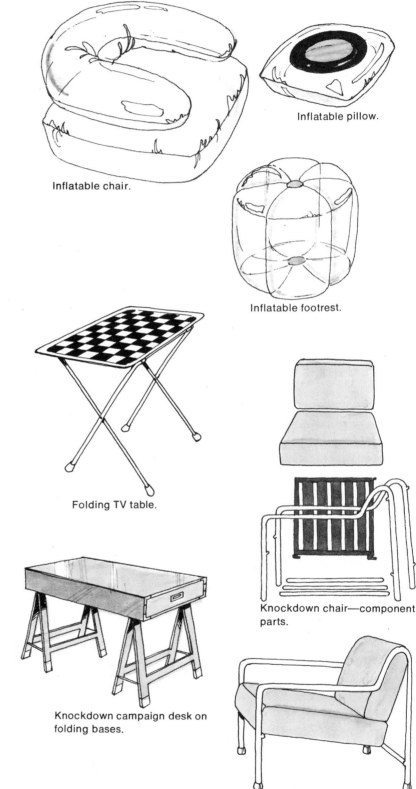

Inflatable pillow.

Inflatable chair.

Inflatable footrest.

TEMPORARIES APPEAR "ON DEMAND"

These are a direct response to today's space-minded and highly mobile apartment dwellers. First, the inflatables! These plastic "blow-ups" appear as pillows, chairs, cylinders that can be used as tables or seating space. They offer a delightfully airy look, deflate to fold away when you don't need them. Knockdown, or KD furniture as it's called, is another good answer for the space-and-budget-bound. This is often made of heavy-duty cardboard reinforced with easels or interior grids. It's inexpensive, can be folded away easily or discarded when no longer needed. Those small, individual TV tables or standing trays are useful, too. Use them as extra chair-side tables as well as buffet tables. Gaily colored shopping bags can be made to serve as "temporary" storage space, too. Hang them on hooks on the back of a closet door. Or paint an old-fashioned coatrack a bright color and hang the bags right on it, out in plain sight! You might consider renting furniture, too. There are several large, countrywide rental services that can provide almost everything you'll need. It can be expensive, but it's often worth it rather than paying for moving furniture long distances—or investing in pieces you really won't need or want later on.

Folding TV table.

Knockdown chair—component parts.

Knockdown campaign desk on folding bases.

Knockdown chair—assembled.

ARRANGING YOUR FURNITURE: MAKE IT LOOK WELL, MAKE IT EASY TO LIVE WITH

When you enter a room that gives off a feeling of order and ease, that you can move around in comfortably, that invites you to sit and chat—it isn't a matter of chance. Thoughtful furniture arrangement has a lot to do with it. And there's really no great mystery to arranging furniture. Planning and common sense will take you a long way.

First and foremost: Know your measurements! Start by measuring each room, including the heights of ceilings. Then draw yourself rough room plans. Graph paper is helpful here. Another helpful idea: Ask your art supply or stationery store for a furniture template. This is a small plastic stencil with the shapes of various pieces of furniture cut out. Use it to pencil in various arrangements of furniture so you get an advance idea of where the larger and smaller pieces will fit best. If you don't want to bother with templates, cut out circles and rectangles from plain paper to represent the various pieces of furniture you think you may want to include. (Our sketches in the margin show you what a template looks like; also shown are some sample cutouts.) Now —measure each piece of furniture before you buy it or move it in. Based on these measurements, you may want to move those pieces of paper around on your floor plan again!

Keep in mind how the room will be used. Are you coping with a 1-room studio? If so, eating, sleeping and entertaining must all be planned for. Is it a living room-dining room combination? Do you have hobbies that require special equipment? Where do you like to watch TV? How do you like to entertain? Remember that you want to be able to move around the room without bumping into things!

On the following pages, you'll find some tips on handling "traffic" in rooms—along with suggestions for coping with some of the more usual "room problems." Of course, we can't cover every situation. But the suggestions will give you ideas on how furniture can be used to break up space, change the visual effect of a room, create special-interest corners. Unfortunately, very few of us are blessed with rooms that are ideally designed— gracefully shaped, with windows and doors well-spaced and with attractive architectural features like mantels and moldings to add a spice of interest. Most of us have to cope with at least one room that is too small, too long and narrow, or that has an awkwardly placed window or door. So—artful furniture arrangement is a useful talent to acquire!

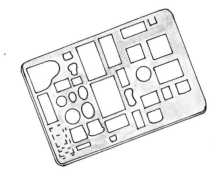

A template.

Sample cutouts.

BASIC SOLUTIONS TO MANY SITUATIONS

The sketches here and on the facing page present some ideas for using pieces of furniture as design elements in a room. We've also included a room arrangement that indicates some of the basic rules of good traffic flow. (You'll find this room diagram discussed on the final page of this section.)

☐ Positioning furniture vertically. There's nothing that says furniture has to sit parallel to a wall. Sofas, tables or chairs can be positioned coming away from a wall. Three advantages to this arrangement: Visually, it will help shorten a long, narrow room; it can make more efficient use of a short wall; last but not least, furniture placed vertically can act as a room divider.

☐ Using the diagonal. As our sketch shows, furniture can be placed on the diagonal in a room. What does this achieve? You take advantage of a long stretch of space in the room *and* create two interestingly shaped areas on either side. This will also help shorten a long, narrow room.

☐ "Clumping" furniture. This too can be a handy technique to keep in mind. Two armchairs side by side can assume the weight and importance of a sofa. Two small, low tables placed side by side, or even at right angles to each other, become the focus of a conversation grouping. Use the same principle with bookcases, hassocks, even floor pillows (pair two of these side by side and you create the effect of a sofa sans legs).

Tables and chairs "clumped" to create a conversation area. Note "L"-shaped table arrangement, pairing of chairs.

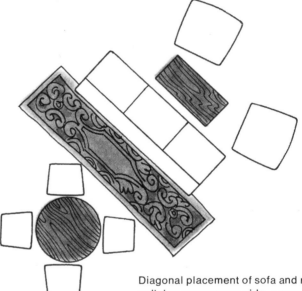

Diagonal placement of sofa and rug creates a dining area on one side, a conversation area on the other.

Vertical arrangement of sofa and chairs makes maximum use of wall space.

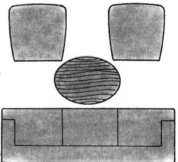

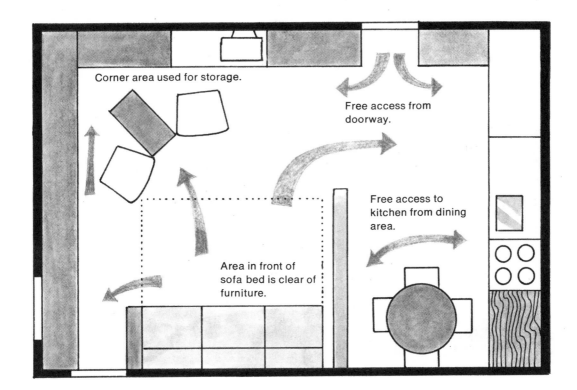

Corner area used for storage.

Free access from doorway.

Free access to kitchen from dining area.

Area in front of sofa bed is clear of furniture.

Closeup view of part of the wall unit.

THE ART OF AVOIDING TRAFFIC JAMS

Good "traffic flow" is important to any room. In small rooms and in multipurpose areas, it's essential—and sometimes hard to achieve. On the previous page, we've diagrammed furniture placement and traffic flow in a 1-room studio. Here, sleeping, eating and living space must all be provided for—and in such a way that one activity doesn't get in the way of others.

One answer is the open-center furniture arrangement, a solution that can apply to almost any size room. This particular arrangement also illustrates these basic traffic rules:

☐ Don't block doorways. Instead, create traffic lanes to them.

☐ Arrange furniture so it can "stay put" for daily living, needs to be shifted only for special-occasion activities.

☐ Consolidate shelf and storage areas into large single units placed out of the way of general traffic.

☐ Take advantage of natural light for work areas when you can —and isolate those work areas from general traffic lanes.

☐ Make the most of corner space. Try not to cut it off as "dead space."

Our 1-room studio locates the dining area at the end of the room where both pullman kitchen and bath are also located. The dining table is placed to one side of the kitchen entry, near enough for easy serving, but leaving free access to both kitchen and bath. An open-shelved divider stands vertically to the wall on the other side of the dining table—blocking the dining area from view *and* providing extra shelves to serve from. Notice that the sofa bed is flanked by the room divider on one side and a low bookcase on the other. Both provide surface area for ashtrays and glasses, and take the place of a coffee table—which would have to be moved each time the sofa was opened for sleeping.

Two small easy chairs flank a game table. Facing the sofa bed, they form a conversation grouping for entertaining—but they can be swung toward the game table for a quiet evening of backgammon or reading-at-home.

The prize feature is the wall unit which wraps the long wall, corner and part of the adjoining wall. It's a marvelous combination of standard pieces of furniture, ready-made bookcases, cubes and shelves. Into it fit a small TV, stereo components, a 3-drawer dresser, floor cushions for extra seating, a coat rod for guests (so the room's one closet can be reserved for "family use") and a multiplicity of space for books, games, records and general paraphernalia. Grouped this way, these diverse elements create an eye-appealing wall and a sense of order and organization. (See our closeup view of part of this unit on page 209.) Incidentally, this whole furniture plan could adapt to a living room or den as well.

4 Keeping Your Home Well-Groomed

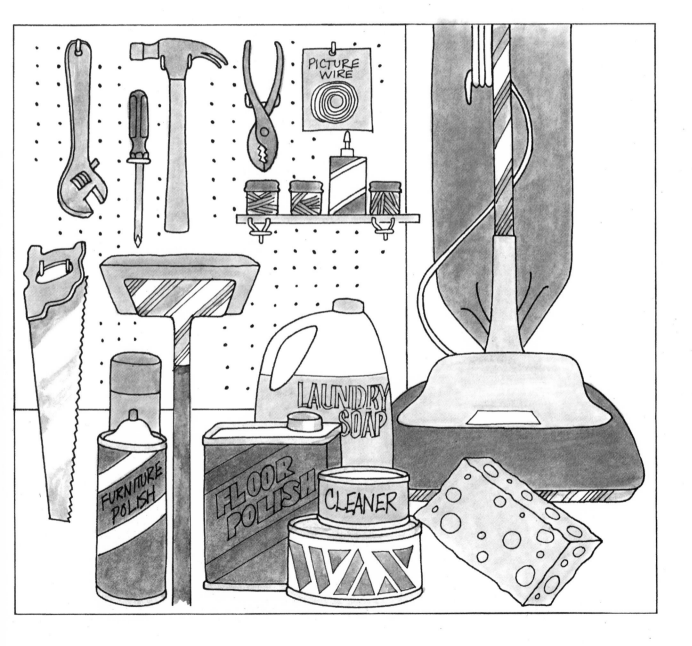

4 Keeping Your Home Well-Groomed

TRY FOR A HAPPY BALANCE BETWEEN NASTY-NEAT AND CARELESS-CASUAL

Your home should match many moods—it should be a place for quiet moments together, a place in which to share with friends your love of living, a work and grow place. It will meet all your moods better if you keep it well-groomed. How do you define well-groomed? Well, let's think about these two "for instances."

Scene #1: "Hey, I asked the Johnsons to stop by tonight."

Scene #2: "Let's start sorting out the new slides—I'd like to get them labeled."

Face it! There are moments when either of these scenes could throw you into a mild panic. Maybe the place is a real *mess*. Or maybe you've just finished tidying up and don't feel like seeing slides and labels spread out all over the place. An occasional inability to cope is everyone's privilege. But if your home *always* needs a whirlwind digging out before friends can walk through the door or if you squelch hobbies that create mild disorder— yours is not a "living" home.

Successful housekeeping strikes a happy balance between too-neat and too-casual. It also provides a middle path for you two as keepers of the home. Neither of you should feel driven by an unending series of chores. But total neglect won't make for comfortable living, either. The more sensible approach is to decide on what both of you agree is the necessary amount of house care and cleaning; then figure out who'll do what, and when. You may have to change your schedule from time to time, but that's to be expected.

Actually, today's home-technologies make upkeep easier than ever before. New and better appliances, more effective cleaning supplies, new soil- and spot-resistant finishes—they all help with the job. The trick is to use each of these most efficiently. And that's what the following pages will help you to do. They'll also give you pointers on how to organize your time best. So don't panic about housework. Read on and remember: You've got a lot of things working for you when it comes to keeping your home in shape!

HOME CARE AND CLEANING: WHAT DOES IT REALLY BOIL DOWN TO?

Highly paid efficiency experts are often called upon to do what's called a "job analysis." That is, these experts break down a particular job into the number and types of activities it entails. They then know exactly what skills a person must have in order to perform that job efficiently. We regard homemaking as important work. And we know that people handle work better when they understand what they're doing and why. So we've taken a leaf from the experts' book and analyzed home care and cleaning in terms of the major activities you'll be getting involved with. We've even gone the experts a step better. We've added some input from experienced homemakers, input based on practical know-how that they've worked out "on the job." Here's the list—with a basic procedure and some bright ideas for each area:

Picking up, putting away, throwing out—to keep rooms looking tidy, to make it easier to find things when you want them.

BASIC PROCEDURE

Get used to doing small jobs as you go along; don't let things pile up!

BRIGHT IDEAS

Plan your storage areas carefully, particularly if space is tight. Invest in extra hooks, shelves, brackets to make maximum use of the space. Try to provide storage space in each room, even if it's only a large box or basket for "quickie" tidying.

Line your trash baskets and garbage pails with disposable bags. You can swoop these out and dispose of them on your way out in the morning, when you're leaving on an errand, or first thing when you get home at night.

Put things away as you finish using them. Then they're back where they belong, you know where to find them the next time, and they're not lying around as clutterbugs.

Keep down the magazine and newspaper pileup. Clip the articles you're interested in, file them, and pitch the rest. Check those filed articles at least once a year, too. You'll probably find many of *them* can go!

Dusting and vacuuming—to get rid of fingermarks, dust, grit, animal hairs. Today, you can often dust-and-polish in one operation.

BASIC PROCEDURE

Let your vacuum do as much of the work as possible!

BRIGHT IDEAS

Vacuum wooden floors before polishing them. Vacuum bathroom and kitchen floors before polishing them, to help prevent buildup of corner dirt. Use the proper attachments for these jobs and for other special jobs as well. For example: Use the soft brush for dusting off baseboards and tabletops; the crevice tool for getting dust and crumbs out of corners, off stair risers, out of the crack between backs and seats of sofas and upholstered chairs; the upholstery nozzle for sucking dust from upholstery, draperies, even heavy clothing. If you go about it the right way, you can get the dust off almost anything in a room with your vacuum—walls, pictures, lamps and appliances, as well as floors and carpets.

Use treated dustcloths if you can; they leave a dust-resistant finish. Or spray rags or paper toweling with a dust-resister spray and then dust.

Caution: Check manufacturers' instructions before using cloths or sprays. Some should be used only on oiled (not waxed) surfaces.

Keep a duster tucked away in each room for quick tidy-ups. Or make "dusting mitts" from pieces of old toweling and keep one of these in each room for those "once-over-lightlies."

Washing up, wiping and waxing—to remove grease, fingermarks, food spills; in the case of waxing, to provide a protective and easier-to-clean surface.

BASIC PROCEDURE
Use wax to make wiping up easier.

BRIGHT IDEAS
Wax windowsills and other woodwork for easier wash-ups. You can also wax small, frequently handled objects like lamp bases, candlesticks and kitchen appliances to make them easier to wash off. Use either liquid or paste wax, but make sure to read the directions on the wax before using it, and thus prevent possible mishaps.

Use those special cleaning preparations available for glass, marble, porcelain, laminated surfaces and natural-wood finishes. They're designed to make cleaning wooden kitchen cabinets, mirrors, bathroom fixtures and counter tops as effort free as possible.

Frequent "little wipe-ups" in a bathroom save on major clean-up time. Get in the habit of wiping up sink surfaces, the toilet cover and the floor area around tub and sink after you bathe or shower.

Little wipe-ups in the kitchen help, too. A spill on counter top or range? Wipe it up right away. While you have that sponge in your hand, cast a quick glance at the refrigerator and cabinets. Fingermarks? Give them a quick swipe.

Remember that household ammonia is a great grease-cutter. A small amount added to a pail of cleaning water makes mopping up more efficient. Or put a drop on a wet sponge when you're doing those bathroom and kitchen wipe-ups. It smells strong, and it's effective!

Caution: Never combine ammonia with a chlorine-base bleach (even in a washing machine). Also, never combine it with a toilet bowl cleaner. Either combination causes the release of chlorine gas, which can be deadly.

Laundry—to keep clothing and washable household rugs and fabrics clean and wrinkle free.

BASIC PROCEDURE
Get as much mileage out of a washing machine as you can.
BRIGHT IDEAS
Invest in two laundry bags so you can sort soiled laundry as you stow it away. Whites, colorfast pastels and light-colored towels go in one. Dark-colored, heavily soiled and heavier-weight items go in the other. This pre-sorting is particularly useful if you're using a launderette rather than your own washer and dryer. Your soiled clothes come out of the bags ready to pop into the machines.

The newer washer and dryer models can usually handle smaller items like bras, socks and stockings without snarl-ups—particularly if you use the "slow wash" setting. If you run into problems, invest in a couple of nylon mesh laundry bags to avoid tangles. Helpful hint: Always check your machine for the correct setting for these smaller items, as they tend to be fragile. Also— hook bras before putting them through the machine to help keep them from catching on other clothing.

When you're sorting soiled clothes, pile them on a clean surface or spread a sheet out on the floor as a sorting area.

Note: You'll find additional details on these general categories of home care and cleaning as you read further on in this chapter. But this quickie overview gives you the general idea of what it's all about.

TIMETABLE THOSE CLEANING JOBS: WHAT TO DO AND HOW OFTEN

Your cleaning schedule really depends on your own point of view and life-style. What is important, though, is to work out some kind of timetable and stick to it! Otherwise, you won't be running your home—it'll run you. The chart on the next page is meant as a guide only. If you're not super-tidy, you may switch some of our weeklies to things to do occasionally-if-ever. But at least the chart gives you a starting point for drawing up your own list. So don't feel guilty if you do end up switching ours around a bit. Look through it and then plan the jobs according to what suits your own time best. After you've tried your own schedule for a week or so, you may want to revise it a bit, too.

SUGGESTED CLEANING SCHEDULE

Daily	Weekly	Monthly	Occasionally
Make beds.	Thoroughly dust furniture, windowsills, lamps, telephone (use vacuum if possible).	Wipe off bric-a-brac; dust backs of books (if necessary).	Wash or clean draperies and/or curtains.
Straighten up living room and bedroom (hang up clothes; pick up books, records; plump up pillows; run dustcloth over tabletops if they look dusty).	Vacuum or carpet sweep rugs; dry mop or vacuum wooden floors; wash kitchen and bathroom floors.	Vacuum thoroughly (including draperies, ceiling corners, baseboards).	Clean furniture coverings, bedspreads, blankets.
Tidy up bathroom; wipe off sink and tub.	Clean kitchen (counter tops, cabinet doors, refrigerator doors, range top and doors).	Defrost freezer and clean refrigerator (if necessary).	Clean walls, ceilings. Wash blinds. Wax floors.
Wash dishes.	Clean bathroom (tub, toilet, sink, mirror).	Clean range thoroughly (including oven if necessary).	Shampoo rugs or carpeting (do it yourself or have it done professionally).
Dispose of trash and garbage.	Laundry (sort and wash it or take to laundry; iron clothes if necessary).	Wash off fingermarks (walls, doors, sills).	Straighten closets.
Do one or two items from the weekly schedule.	Take and/or pick up dry cleaning, shirts, shoes.	Turn mattresses.	Clean cupboards and drawers.
	Change sheets and towels.	Polish furniture (if necessary).	Clean light fixtures.
		Wash out garbage cans and trash cans (if necessary).	
		Sweep outside porches and walks.	

Arranging for exterminator service. There are times when you may need the services of an exterminator. In older city apartments, you may want to have one come in once a month.

Some buildings provide a visiting exterminator at no extra charge to you. However, you'll have to find out what days each month he'll be in the building and arrange for him to have access to your apartment. In your own home and in some apartment buildings, you'll have to freight the cost of an exterminating service yourself and make all the necessary calls and arrangements. In either case, be sure to mention which type of pest you're bothered by (mice, roaches, waterbugs, fleas). Ask about any possible aftereffects the sprays may have and what safety measures you should take—particularly important if you have pets.

When the seasons change, so does clothing—and sometimes draperies, slipcovers and bedspreads. You can store out-of-season items in your own home or use professional storage facilities.

☐ If you store them yourself, be sure to clean all woolens. Then spray them with moth spray or sprinkle them with moth crystals. Next, seal them in airtight plastic bags or in clean boxes closed up with masking tape and place them in a closet that you have vacuumed thoroughly.

☐ Professional storage facilities are safe and convenient. Many dry cleaners offer this service "free." However, they will charge you for dry-cleaning each item stored. It's usually worth it for heavy outdoor clothes and woolens. You might compromise (and cut costs) by storing these professionally and coping with smaller, lighter and moth-safe items at home.

☐ Experts usually recommend professional cold storage for furs —to prolong the life of the fur and protect against moths.

EARLY BIRD OR NIGHT OWL: PLAN YOUR DAILY MUSTS TO SUIT YOUR PERSONALITY

Let's face it: You can't force yourself to be something you're not. If your energy level runs low toward the end of the day—or if you really resent interrupting leisurely evening hours with chores —no amount of expert advice is going to set you to tidying up before bedtime. The reverse is true, too. If it takes two alarm clocks to wake you up and you make it to the office in a semi-sleepwalking state, early morning chores are not for you! Your intentions may be good, but your performance won't be. So size yourself up realistically and then plan to do the daily "musts" at the times of day when you function best. Look at the two sample schedules on the following page. They'll show you how to divide your work—depending on what type you are.

DAILY SCHEDULES: FOR MORNING TYPES AND NIGHTTIME TYPES

To Do	Morning Type	Nighttime Type
Tidying up: clothes, books, records, newspapers, magazines quick dusting plumping pillows	Do in the morning before leaving the house.	Do before going to bed.
Washing dishes	Do them together—breakfast dishes and last night's dinner dishes (if you really are a morning type).	Leave breakfast dishes rinsed and stacked to be done with the dinner dishes.

If you have a dishwasher, it's better ecology—and more economical—to rinse and store dishes in the washer until you have a full load. You can turn the washer on anytime. Just remember: You have to unload it before you can start refilling it. That's the job you'll want to plan out according to your own best time schedule.

Making beds	Turn back to air while you dress and have breakfast. Make beds before leaving the house.	Leave turned back to air. Make them when you first get back into the house (if you don't find it depressing to face an unmade bed).
Taking out trash and garbage	Collect and throw out on your way out the door.	Collect and throw out the last thing at night.

If you have a garbage-disposal unit, use it as you scrape and rinse your dishes before stacking them in the dishwasher or sink. Don't let food scraps sit in the disposal unit. At the very least, unpleasant odors will develop.

Wiping up bathroom	Wipe up after morning shower or bath.	Wipe up when you get back home or after your evening shower or bath.
Preparing meals	Make breakfast in the morning. Take frozen foods for dinner out of freezer and leave in refrigerator to defrost before you leave the house.	Before going to bed: Fill juice glasses, cover and leave in refrigerator. If using separate timer for your electric coffee maker (or timer outlet on range), set timer! Also, take frozen foods for next night's dinner out of freezer and leave in refrigerator to defrost.

THE ONCE-A-WEEKERS AND THE OCCASIONALS

Here again, your plan of action will probably depend on how your personality is put together. Are you the methodical type or one who favors the "Pike's Peak or bust" approach?

If you're methodical, you'll probably try to space out these heavier cleaning jobs—do one weekly task each day and one or two of the "occasionals" each month. That way your home is reasonably clean at all times.

If you favor the all-out type of operation, you'll do all the weekly cleaning once a week, and all at once. And you'll set aside one or two days a year for the really big jobs—a super dig-out! Most experts warn that this approach tends to leave you exhausted and bad-tempered. But if it's really your thing, you'll probably come through it with a sense of exhilaration and accomplishment. And the house *does* look great when you finish! Just remember that your days may be filled with work and study, so these cleaning bouts will have to take place in the evening or on a Saturday morning or afternoon.

How to use professional cleaning help most efficiently. If you really dislike housecleaning or if your free time is very limited, you might try to work some professional help into the budget. This isn't being self-indulgent—it's being realistic. Outside help is costly, however, so it pays to organize a little ahead of time to save wasting their time (and your money). Here's a starter list of things you can do to help make the work go faster:

☐ Make sure you know exactly what you want done and can explain it to others. Don't think in general terms like "clean the kitchen." Make a list of the specific jobs to be done: Defrost the refrigerator, clean the oven, wash and wax the floor, wipe fingermarks off walls and cabinets.

☐ Set out any cleaning equipment and/or supplies you expect to have used.

☐ If your list of jobs includes doing laundry in a coin washing machine and dryer, have the necessary change ready.

☐ Strip beds ahead of time so they'll be ready for remaking when your bedroom is being cleaned.

The large professional cleaning services will usually ask you exactly what you want done before they will quote a price. Most of them will send in two or three people, with their own equipment.

These services are particularly useful for once-a-month cleaning or heavy spring or fall cleaning, although some people do use them weekly. They'll do general cleaning as well as the harder jobs like washing walls, waxing or polishing floors, and vacuuming floorcoverings and draperies with a heavy-duty commercial vacuum. This can be expensive, but it's sometimes worth it.

In addition to these general cleaning services, you'll find

specialists available, particularly in the larger cities—window washers, floor and/or furniture refinishers, rug and upholstery cleaners, specialists in cleaning and repairing blinds. You'll find such services listed in your Yellow Pages.

The question of salaries and fees. Professional cleaning services (and the specialists) usually charge a flat fee, which includes transportation and insurance. If you hire individual cleaning help, you will probably pay by the hour and will have to add carfare and, possibly, provide lunch. You'll also be responsible for arranging Social Security payments if the total salary earned within a quarter year adds up to $50 or more. Social Security quarter-years are figured from January through March, April through June, July through September, and October through December. Contact your local District Director of the Internal Revenue Service and ask for Circular H; it contains all the details on Social Security. It's also a good idea to check your insurance broker and ask him about coverage, in case anyone is injured in your home. The cost for this coverage isn't too high and it's a valuable protection.

YOUR HOUSEHOLD HELPERS AND HOW TO STORE THEM

Meet the cast of characters who can help take the trauma out of housework. Cleaning tools and supplies—they've never been so diverse, they've never been better. But you do have to know them to fully appreciate what they can do! This means: Be a label and tag reader. Manufacturers go to a great deal of trouble to tell you just what their products will and will not do. Yet time after time these labels are blithely ignored. So do take a few minutes before you wipe on that cleaning preparation. Start your cleaning the right way—read, absorb, then use the product!

Modern Cleaning Tools Rate High For Looks And Good Behavior

Designers these days are busily at work producing cleaning tools that are more comfortable to handle and easier to use than ever before. Even gaily colored cleaning tools are with us. They lift the spirits and invite use. So all other things being equal, opt for the decorator look in the equipment you choose. Here's a starter list of essentials:

BASIC EQUIPMENT
- [ ] broom
- [ ] dustpan
- [ ] vacuum cleaner and/or electric broom (see page 125 for details on choosing one)

□ dry mop and squeegee mop
□ pail
□ step stool
□ brushes (for upholstery, lampshades, et al.—if you don't have vacuum attachments)

IMPORTANT INCIDENTALS
□ dustcloths
□ sponges (assorted sizes and shapes)
□ toilet brush
□ rubber or plastic gloves
□ paper towels

NICE BUT NOT NECESSARY
□ special brushes for radiators, blinds, etc. (if your vacuum doesn't have necessary attachments)
□ window squeegee
□ electric broom (in addition to a vacuum)
□ wax applicators
□ basket, cart or caddy for carrying cleaning supplies
□ electric rug shampooer/floor polisher

Note: Rug shampooer and floor polisher are usually combined in one appliance. Some models are available with special brushes for scrubbing tile and vinyl floors. If you invest in one of these, make sure the model you choose has a motor heavy enough to take the additional strain of floor scrubbing. This usually means buying in the middle-to-higher price bracket.

Hints on how to care for tools. Brooms should be hung up by their handles, ditto for brushes. Wash brushes frequently with warm water and detergent. Wash mops (both wet and dry) often enough to keep them clean and odor free. Hang by the handles to store. Dusters and sponges also need washing. Idea: Wash a load of them together in the washing machine, but don't mix them in with clothing. Rinse scrub pail after each use to prevent dried cleaning powder or soap from building up at the bottom. Vacuums and/or electric brooms: Check the manufacturer's instructions for care and cleaning. If trouble develops, call a manufacturer's service representative or vacuum repairman.

Note: Cleaning equipment that's hard to get at or that's messily stored can discourage you from using the equipment at all. There's a real advantage to planning efficient, easily accessible storage areas for household cleaning equipment. Well-planned storage areas don't have to take up a great deal of space, either. If your kitchen is equipped with a "broom closet"—or if you can spare a clothes closet for this purpose—that's great. But often

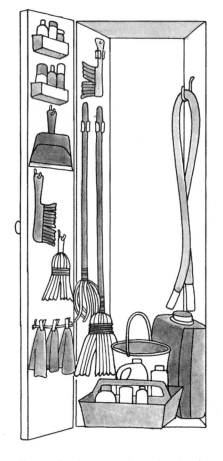

A well-organized storage closet for cleaning tools.

spare wall space or a screened-off corner in a living room or bedroom will do as well. We describe two efficient storage setups below.

TWO BASIC BLUEPRINTS FOR STORING YOUR CLEANING TOOLS AND AIDS

Ideally, the "perfect" cleaning closet should run 1 foot deep, 3 feet wide and 8 feet high (or the full height of your ceiling). It should be divided into an upper and lower section, the lower section measuring 5 feet (to accommodate brooms, mops and long-handled brushes). Closet floor should be flush with the room floor so you can roll the vacuum out without lifting it up.

Organizing Tips: To Use Space Most Efficiently

☐ Spring-clip holders on side walls of closet hold brooms, mops, brushes.
☐ Small utility shelves on back of closet door hold cans, bottles, jars.
☐ Wire utility rack on back wall of closet holds vacuum cleaner attachments (if these don't store away right on your vacuum).
☐ Large hook holds vacuum hose where it's easy to find.
☐ Cup hooks on side walls of closet hold dustpan, dust brushes, whisk broom.
☐ Mini-clothesline (with clothespins) on back of closet door holds dustcloths.
☐ Utility basket used for carrying supplies to rest of house.

Safety note: It's best to dispose of oily or cleaner-soaked cloths; they can be combustible. If you must store them, choose a well-ventilated area.

The Pegboard Storage Unit: Hints On How To Arrange It

☐ Brooms and mops hang from spring-clip hooks.
☐ Clean rags and dusters store away in nylon mesh bag.
☐ Used dusters hang on mini-clothesline.
☐ Bottles, jars and cans rest on utility shelves.
☐ Vacuum hose hangs on a large hook.
☐ Vacuum stores away at base of pegboard or in the nearest available closet.

IDEAS FOR ORGANIZING CLEANING SUPPLY CENTERS

Even a small household can accumulate a surprising number of bottles, jars and cans that contain one type of cleaning preparation or another. Under the kitchen sink is really not the best place

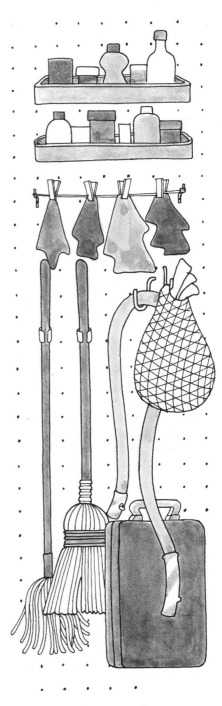

A pegboard storage unit.

to store laundry and cleaning supplies. Most of these preparations are poisonous, so it's wise to get into the habit of providing safer storage space for them. At most, try to store only those supplies you use right at the sink. Also—if your budget can handle it, it pays to have more than one container of some of these items so you can keep them close at hand for bathrooms or bedrooms as well as for the kitchen (or upstairs and downstairs if you're into two-level living). Here are some ideas for organizing your cleaning supply centers:

Creating Storage Areas: Three Ideas

1. Invest in a small metal or plastic wall cabinet to hold cleaning supplies. Hang it on the bathroom wall or in a hallway.
2. Outfit a carryall wicker basket to hold those extra supplies. You can store it in a closet. Thread narrow hemming tape through the sides of the basket to create pockets that will hold bottles and jars. You'll end up with something that looks rather like a fitted picnic basket. Or use one of those handy wicker wine baskets that are already divided into compartments.
3. Add extra utility shelves to the sides of a kitchen cabinet for polishes, waxes, laundry aids.

LET YOUR AUTOMATIC WASHER AND DRYER DO MORE OF THE WORK FOR YOU

Used properly, an automatic washer and dryer can do almost anything in the way of laundry. The new settings are designed to provide the right water temperature, degree of agitation, spin speed and drying setting for even the most delicate fabrics. Here are some extra-smart tips for using these modern "laundries" to their utmost:

Work-Saver Ideas: If You Own Your Own Machines

☐ For really heavily stained items—fill the machine with water, detergent and bleach. Stop the cycle. Add stained items and let soak for the length of time indicated on the bleach package. Then advance the dial so normal cycle will be completed. Many machines include a soak cycle, but this is sometimes not long enough to bleach out very heavy stains.

☐ For drip-dry items—stop the cycle before the final spin. Lift out the "drip-dryers," put them in a plastic dishpan or pail and carry them over to a spot where you can hang them up to drip and dry—over a laundry or bathroom tub, usually.

☐ Keep a batch of hangers near your dryer. When permanent press shirts, blouses, dresses and pants come out of the dryer, hang them on the hangers—immediately. Smooth out collars, cuffs and hems. Shape shoulders, pleats and pants creases by hand.

If you own a washer and dryer, take note of some of these work-saving ideas.

This can mean you don't even have to do once-over-lightly ironing.

☐ Invest in three large, sturdy shopping bags labeled "yours," "mine" and "linen closet." Sort socks, underwear, sweaters, sheets, pillowcases and towels into the appropriate bags as you take them out of the dryer. This makes for easy carrying to the appropriate drawers and shelves.

Work-Saver Ideas: If You Use A Launderette

☐ Invest in a small-size shopping cart and liner. It's the best way to transport laundry in an apartment building.

☐ If you're transporting laundry by car, invest in one or more plastic laundry baskets. They fit neatly on auto seats, and clothing can be folded tidily into them to prevent wrinkling.

☐ Use those folding counters provided in most launderettes. The more folding you do the less ironing you'll get involved in.

☐ Use "yours" and "mine" paper bags to sort small items like socks and underwear straight from the dryer.

Special note: check the label before washing or ironing. New labeling practices make proper washing and ironing of all items much easier. Now, sewn-on manufacturers' labels give you specific laundering instructions, also indicate whether dry cleaning is preferable. The instructions are usually included right under the manufacturer's name.

Laundry Products And How To Use Them

When using any laundry product, follow this rule of three: First, read the label carefully to see if it's the right product for the job. Second, check the label to see how much of it you need. Third, measure amounts carefully (using a measuring cup if necessary). Since most people do most of their laundry in an automatic washer, we've checklisted some basic steps for using these machines—and we've included information on the basic laundry products themselves.

CHECKLIST: TO WASH BY AUTOMATIC WASHER

☐ Check clothes—fasten hooks, close zippers, empty and brush out pockets. Remove pins, ornaments, heavy buckles. If you notice any rips or tears, now's the time to mend them!

☐ Check for ground-in dirt on collars and cuffs, socks and pants knees. To loosen heavy soil like this, use one of the spray-on pre-wash preparations. These are particularly effective on greasy stains and on man-made fibers (which tend to hold grease stains longer than natural fibers). Or make a paste of soap or detergent mixed with a little water, dampen the soiled areas, and gently rub in the solution. Or apply a little liquid laundry detergent to these areas. Or use one of the enzyme presoaks, following package directions.

A little organization goes a long way if you use a launderette.

IF YOU PREFER
You can add washing products after the wash cycle has started. Some manufacturers' instructions suggest this for their particular machines. If you have any doubts, check your dealer or appliance store.

☐ Measure out and add washing products to the machine. Many of the newer phosphate-free detergents do a better job if they're dissolved in the wash water before the clothes are added. Choose an all-purpose detergent for general laundry, a light-duty one for delicate, lightly soiled fabrics. For front loading washers or washer-dryer combinations, use a low-sudsing detergent. Top loaders will take normal, intermediate or low-sudsing detergents.

☐ If you use bleach, you have your choice of two types—chlorine (liquid or dry) or dry oxygen bleach. Oxygen bleaches are milder than chlorine bleaches and can be used on all washable fabrics. Chlorine bleaches can be used on white and colorfast cottons, linens, synthetics and permanent press items. Don't use them on silk, wool, mohair and some types of spandex. To use liquid chlorine bleach safely, measure it, dilute it with at least 1 quart of water, and add to the load after wash load has been agitating for three or four minutes. Dry bleaches should not be poured directly onto colored fabrics in the washer.

☐ Put clothes in washer. Check to see that they're distributed evenly and that machine is not too full.

☐ Select wash and rinse temperatures, type of washing action, spin speed and washing time on control panel of washer. See the charts below and on the following pages for hints on proper settings for different types of fabrics.

☐ Start the machine.

☐ If you use a fabric softener, check clothing labels carefully. Some fabrics can be damaged by these. Different types of softeners are available. The liquids are usually added to the final rinse water. Some products, however, can be added to the wash water. Some are even designed to be used in a clothes dryer. Read the package directions to make sure you're using yours correctly.

☐ If you use starch—once again, read the package instructions carefully. Some starches must be dissolved in water before they can be used. The newer spray types can be applied while you iron. Sometimes, starching can be done in the automatic washer.

LAUNDRY DO'S AND DON'TS FOR TODAY'S MOST COMMON FABRICS AND FIBERS

Fabric or Fiber	Item	Laundry Do's and Don'ts
Permanent press	Table linens	Presoak and/or remove any stains before washing. Wash in warm water or use permanent press cycle. Tumble-dry and fold right from dryer. If you're fussy, give them a light pressing with your iron, at the correct setting.

Fabric or Fiber	Item	Laundry Do's and Don'ts
Permanent press	Sheets	Machine washing is recommended. Wash whites and pastels in hot water, dark colors in warm water. Wash darks separately the first few times (until excess dye is eliminated). Bleach can be used on lights and whites. A fabric softener can be used occasionally. Tumble-dry and fold immediately.
	Clothing	Wash at permanent press setting. Tumble-dry and remove from dryer immediately. Collars and cuffs may need a light pressing if you're particularly fussy. Ditto the creases in pants legs.
Cotton	Sheets and table linens	Wash in hot water. Bleach whites when necessary. Iron at high temperature (have table linens very damp).
	Clothing	Same as for cotton sheets and table linens. You may want to starch some items, such as shirts.
	Towels	Wash in hot water. Use water softener in hard water areas. Use fabric softeners sparingly, as they tend to build up a non-absorbent finish. For fluffy towels, tumble-dry (never iron).
Wool	Blankets	Always follow manufacturer's instructions. Some blankets can be washed and dried on delicate cycle. The majority should be dry-cleaned. Electric blankets, however, should be washed and *not* dry-cleaned in most cases.
Synthetics	All items	Wash in warm-to-hot water, rinse in cool. Or use cold water with special cold water detergent. Wash frequently in small loads. Wash whites separately, as they tend to pick up color. Use a short washing time and slow spin if possible.

HOW TO CHOOSE THE PROPER SETTINGS ON YOUR AUTOMATIC WASHER

Type of Load	Wash Temperature	Rinse Temperature	Action Setting	Time
Sturdy whites and color-fasts	Hot (140°)	Warm or cold	Regular	10-12 minutes
Sturdy permanent press and wash-and-wear:				
heavy soil	Hot (140°)	Cold	Permanent press	6-8 minutes
normal soil	Warm (100-110°)	Cold	Permanent press	6-8 minutes
Sturdy, non-colorfast	Warm (100-110°)	Cold	Regular	6-8 minutes
Man-made fibers (nylon, polyester)	Warm (100-110°)	Cold	Delicate or gentle	4-6 minutes
Woolens, silks, delicate fabrics, loose knits, hand washables	Warm (100-110°)	Cold	Delicate or gentle	4-6 minutes
Lightly soiled items, extra-sensitive colors that fade easily	Cold (80° or cooler)	Cold	Delicate or gentle	4-6 minutes

Ironing: Today It's Once-Over-Lightly

Mention ironing and a common reaction is, "Who needs it?" If you really get into wash-and-wear and permanent press, the answer is: "Not you." If you like a spic-and-span look, however, or occasionally fall for an item in a natural fiber, here are a few hints to make the pressing easier:

The iron itself can be one of three types. Steam and spray-steam irons do just what the names imply. They create moisture in the form of steam and/or a light spray. This is usually enough to handle all fabrics and fibers without any other dampening. Possible exception: regular cottons that have been thoroughly dried—you may have to dampen these before ironing. Dry irons can be used to press synthetics and permanent press without additional dampening. Other fibers will probably have to be dampened. All three types indicate the proper setting for each type of fiber.

If you have to dampen fabrics, the usual method is to sprinkle the item lightly with warm water, roll up, and let stand for an hour or so before ironing. If you get caught short with a batch of dampened items and no time to iron, stick them in a plastic bag and then into the refrigerator until you can complete the job. You can keep them this way for a day or two without their mildewing or drying out again.

Hang drip-dry items properly and you'll cut down on ironing. Always hang the article up dripping wet. If possible, use those special inflatable drip-dry hangers. An alternative: large wooden coat hangers. Both of these will give a better shape to shoulders in clothing. Smooth out collars, cuffs, seams, hems.

When you're ironing items with straight edges—like napkins, handkerchiefs, tablecloths—start from the outside corners and work toward the middle of each edge. Do this all the way around each side. Then fold in half and iron the middle part, again working from the edges in. Repeat this last procedure each time you fold the item over. This will keep edges straight and the whole item "squared up." Try to avoid ironing in a crease, as this eventually weakens the fabric.

To touch up permanent press blouses and shirts, start with collars and cuffs. Lay them out flat on the ironing board and press from the outside edges in. Iron on both sides. Then press the back and front, if necessary.

With sheets, careful folding replaces ironing in the case of permanent press. For regular cotton sheets, many people prefer to use a commercial laundry.

HINTS FOR THE APPRENTICE HANDYMAN (OR WOMAN)

If you're already an expert do-it-yourselfer, skip this section. If you're in the ready-and-willing-but-beginner class, read on. We'll give you a few basic tips that can help you cope with small or stopgap home repairs. With labor costs soaring, you'll probably find you'll be tempted to do some of your own work even if you're not bucking for the title of "expert in home repairs." First of all, those legends about people who repair anything from leaking faucets to sick TV sets with a hairpin are just that—legends. Proper tools (good-quality ones) are important, particularly if the job is new to you. You can buy a basic tool kit in any one of several price ranges. Or you can assemble what you need piece by piece. If you opt for the latter, be sure to include a toolbox or

CHECKLIST:
YOUR BASIC TOOL KIT
☐ claw hammer (for driving and pulling nails)
☐ assorted screwdrivers, including a Phillips
☐ pliers
☐ electric drill or hand drill with bits
☐ flexible steel tape measure
☐ penknife
☐ adjustable wrench
☐ mat knife (the type that holds a heavy-duty razor blade)
☐ all-purpose glue
☐ machine oil
☐ assorted nails, screws, hooks
☐ picture hooks and wire, or picture hangers
☐ assorted wall hangers
☐ crosscut saw

other receptacle to house your tools. They'll scatter and disappear otherwise! Another good idea is to scratch your initials on each tool or label it in some way. This helps borrowed tools find their way back! Check our starter list in the margin.

This assortment will enable you to make simple repairs and do some simple carpentry like building shelves or putting up pegboard. If you get into more complicated jobs, you can add to your tool kit as the need arises.

Note: For one-time jobs that require special equipment, consider renting. It's usually quite inexpensive and easy to arrange.

About apartment dwellers and the superintendent. If you live in an apartment building, the superintendent is supposed to handle minor repair jobs and/or arrange for an outside workman to do them. In actual practice, you may have quite a wait! However, always report what's wrong to the "super" and give him a fair chance to cope before trying it yourself.

Emergency Fix-Ups For Minor Breakdowns

These problems are bound to occur sooner or later (probably over a weekend or in the middle of the night); they can be real annoyances, but, happily enough, are easily taken care of.

A leaky faucet. Wrap a wet washcloth around the top of the faucet. Twist the ends downward so the water will trickle down the cloth. This is purely a temporary measure, but it will stop that drip and preserve your sanity until you get professional help.

A running toilet. First, try jiggling the handle several times. If this doesn't work, the problem is probably with the flush ball. It may not be properly sealing the hole through which water flows from the flush tank into the toilet bowl. To correct, lift off the tank cover carefully. Examine the flush ball (see diagram). If the chain, lift wires or rod attached to the flush ball are tangled, just disentangle them so the ball again sits squarely, fully covering the hole. Or the flush ball may be misaligned. The guide arm (which keeps the ball in place in many toilet models) may be out of line. To correct, loosen the small screw holding the guide arm to the overflow tube (see diagram) and jiggle the guide until the flush ball is in line properly. If the flush ball itself is damaged, just unscrew it from the rod or wire it's attached to and buy a new one at your plumbing supply or hardware store. If none of these remedies work, turn the shutoff valve that feeds water into the tank. You'll find it under the tank or nearby. The noise will stop immediately and you can empty the toilet later, if necessary.

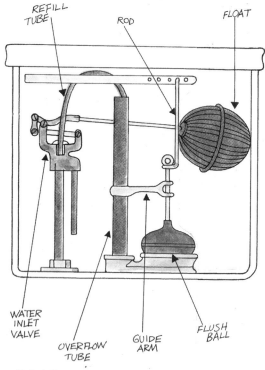

Toilet diagram.

Emergency note: Follow this same turn-off procedure if toilet starts to overflow.

Squeaky hinges. The squeak usually means that a squirt of oil is needed at the friction points. Use soap, starch or talcum powder if you're caught without oil.

Electric appliances that go dead. Check to see that the electric cord is fully plugged into the outlet. Try reversing the plug. Check the appliance, too, to see that the cord is tightly connected at that end. Check for breaks in the cord. Make sure you haven't blown a fuse. If this has happened, other appliances or lights may also be out. If none of these approaches work, the fault is with the appliance itself. Have it repaired professionally; don't tamper with it yourself.

Window shades that won't roll back up. Try gently pulling the shade down and then quickly releasing it. If this doesn't do it, remove the shade from the window frame and reroll by hand. If it's still balky, you may have to rewind the spring, located near the flat tip at one end of the wooden roller. This simply involves turning the flat metal tip around and around until the spring feels tight. It's really just like winding a watch! To make the job easier, insert the metal tip between the tines of a fork, then turn. Or insert the metal tip into a keyhole and turn.

Blown fuses or circuit breakers. The first thing to do is to turn off all affected switches and unplug any appliances that have stopped. Locate the fuse or circuit breaker box. *If it's a blown fuse:* Unscrew it (it will look blackened and you may be able to see where the fuse wire has melted through in the glass section of the base). Replace with a fuse of the same amperage. *Never try to replace it with a higher-amperage fuse.*

If it's a circuit breaker: You'll see which circuit breaker has flipped out of place. Push it all the way to the right, then back into normal position (toward the left). When it lines up with the other circuit breakers, it's in the operating position. If a fuse or circuit breaker blows regularly, you are overloading it and should check to see what's wrong.

Note: Don't wait for an emergency before you locate your fuse or circuit breaker box. Check to see where it is when you move in! Also, try to figure out just which lighting fixtures and appliances are controlled by each fuse or circuit breaker. List them and post the list near the fuse or breaker box.

Dull scissors. Just cut up a piece of sandpaper with the scissors. The blades will sharpen as they come in contact with the abrasive.

Unclogging drains with a plunger. This is the easiest way to clear a clogged drain and it works almost every time. Basically, the plunger is a large rubber suction cup at the end of a stick. You simply place the rubber cup over the drain opening in the sink and pump the handle up and down. When you hear a sucking sound, you know it's working. To unclog a stopped-up toilet with a plunger, stick the plunger straight down into the toilet bowl so that it covers the narrow opening at the bottom of the bowl and pump the plunger up and down.

Note: If your drains clog up regularly, you'd better consult a plumber. Something serious might be wrong.

Leaking sink stoppers. We're talking about those metal sink stoppers that you open and close via a handle placed between the faucet knobs. Usually, the leaking is caused by the stopper getting clogged with hair and grease. To cope: Just put the stopper in the "open" position, turn it to lift it out, and remove the accumulated gunk with a tissue.

Warning: Always call a professional if you notice that your lights are dim. It means you're leaking current and this can be extremely dangerous. Before you call, turn off all appliances that run on their own motors (like the refrigerator) because the lowered current can cause the motor to burn out. In fact, most electrical repairs are better left to the experts. Ditto for boiler and furnace problems.

ALSO EFFECTIVE FOR DRAINS
Try an aerosol spray drain cleaner—you upend can over a drain and push down hard on it. The spray that's forced out flushes out the drain.

A SAFE HOME IS A HAPPIER HOME

Statistics show that we are often extremely careless about taking the most basic safety precautions in our homes. The result? An incredibly high percentage of accidents occur right there. You don't have to be a worrywart. But you will feel more at ease in your home if you know that you have safety-checked each room and eliminated any obvious hazards. Also, it's nice to know that you have basic emergency supplies on hand to cope with minor accidents. We've put together several safety checklists to help you make yours a more secure home.

CHECKLIST: GENERAL SAFETY MEASURES

☐ Check out each room in your home for possible safety hazards. See the specific do's and don'ts checklisted on pages 233 to 234.

☐ Keep your medicine chest locked; stock it and/or a first-aid kit with basic emergency supplies.

☐ List important phone numbers and keep the list near the phone:

• fire department
• police
• ambulance service
• doctor
• poison control center

☐ List important medical facts about both of you and keep a list in each of your wallets, another one near your phone at home:

• your blood type
• any allergies you have (this includes medicines to which you have reacted badly)
• what vaccinations and inoculations you have had
• any operations you have had
• any physical conditions you may have that could affect the emergency medical measures you might be given (diabetes, heart condition, chronic sinus, etc.)

In an emergency, information like the above can save invaluable time and can prevent medical mishaps.

CHECKLIST: SAFETY DO'S AND DON'TS FOR YOUR HOME

☐ Check all doormats and small area rugs. Do they all have non-skid backing?

☐ Keep traffic paths clear of clutter. This includes furniture that has angular or protruding parts.

☐ As safety insurance, use the nonskid strips, designs or mats in bathtubs and stall showers.

☐ Never smoke in bed. Never leave a lit cigarette on the edge of an ashtray, counter or other surface and then walk away from it.

☐ Keep matches in a safe place.

☐ Keep kitchen and bathroom floors clean and dry. Never touch a telephone or other electrical appliance with wet hands.

☐ Never replace burned-out light bulbs without turning the light switch to "off."

☐ Never use an appliance that has a frayed or damaged cord, broken or split wires. Ditto for lamps.

☐ Make sure there are no electrical cords or appliances on or near the tub or sink. Be particularly careful with small electric heaters.

☐ Get into the habit of keeping all poisons, cleaning fluids, bleaches, drain cleaners and other potentially harmful substances in a safe place. Always read and follow all directions on such products. Never mix chlorine bleach with a toilet bowl cleaner, ammonia, lye or oven cleaner. The resulting fumes can be fatal.

☐ Try to buy nonflammable kinds of household cleaners such as dry-cleaning fluids, furniture polish and window-cleaning spray. Be sure to use these in a well-ventilated room. Never smoke while using flammable liquids and never use them near an open flame.

☐ Don't store paint- or oil-stained rags. Throw them away.

☐ Keep a fire extinguisher in your home. Check with your fire department for the proper type.

☐ Keep a first-aid kit in your home. You can buy kits at your drugstore in a variety of sizes and price ranges. Choose a well-stocked one (and replace when contents are outdated).

HOME EMERGENCIES: WHAT TO DO

Just remember—the first thing not to do is panic. Keep your head and you'll be able to cope.

If fire breaks out and it's a small cooking or grease fire, use a fire extinguisher. Or turn off the heat and smother flames with salt or baking soda. *Never throw water on a grease fire—you'll only spread it!* For other small fires (in wastepaper baskets or curtains), use a fire extinguisher or put out with water.

If the fire begins to spread or is a serious fire to start with, get everyone out of the house, then call the fire department. Don't return to the house or apartment for valuables or anything else.

Wise precaution note: Ask your fire department for literature on other safety procedures for coping with fires, smoke, etc. They'll probably have material they'll be happy to give you.

If you suspect a gas leak, do not strike a match. Do open all available windows and turn off any open flame (such as pilot lights on range and water heater). Then leave the house. Report the leak to the police or your utility company. Exception: If you can rapidly ascertain that the leak is coming from a range burner that has blown out, it is not necessary to leave the house. Observe the other precautions we've listed and then turn the burner knob to "off" to shut off the flow of gas.

If a break-in occurs, police departments recommend the following: Should you awaken during the night and suspect that an intruder has entered your home, do absolutely nothing! Pretend to be asleep. When you are sure the intruder has left, call the police. Don't try to phone while the intruder is there. If you have a weapon in the house, don't try to use it. Don't scream for help unless you are actually attacked. Don't try to get out of the house. Any action on your part may provoke an attack.

IF AN ACCIDENT OCCURS

1. Call a doctor immediately.
2. Make certain that the injured person is breathing and that his airway is clear.
3. Stop the bleeding, if any. Most external bleeding can be controlled by applying direct pressure over the wound. A first-aid manual will describe pressure points and the use of tourniquets.
4. Don't make the injury worse: Avoid unnecessary movement of the injured person.
5. If a head, neck or back injury is suspected, don't move or lift the patient.
6. If the patient vomits, turn his head to one side, so that he will not aspirate the vomitus.

Wise precaution note: Get yourself a good first-aid manual and read through it! The American Red Cross has an excellent one. Better yet, enroll in a first-aid course and learn the lifesaving techniques, including mouth-to-mouth resuscitation.

HANDBOOK OF
Cleaning How-To's

Congratulations—that happy moment has arrived. You've worked the hassles out of daily housekeeping and your home is running along quite smoothly. Best of all, you both have leisure hours left over for fun, for being together. And guess what? Even when one of those "special situations" comes up—and it will—you'll be able to handle the job confidently and efficiently. Removing water stains from a tabletop? Putting the range back in shape? Don't tense up. This handy-helper Handbook is packed with information on "how to do it."

There's a knack to every trade, including homemaking. We've tried to gather together practical tips that can help cut down on cleaning time *and* prevent mistakes that might damage equipment or furnishings. Modern appliances, fabrics and furniture materials can be a bit tricky to cope with. Some of the highly specialized cleaning preparations on the market today should be handled carefully, too. Used properly, they're great time- and energy-savers. But you have to know just how and when to apply them.

As you read through our Handbook, you'll find frequent reminders to read directions and check manufacturers' tags and labels. We've really pressed the point because there's just no substitute for a manufacturer's know-how about his product. Also, checking labels is a good habit to acquire. New materials and products appear all the time. The only way to keep up with what they'll do is to read those instructions!

Here's something else to keep in mind. Most of the big cleaning jobs you'll be reading about don't have to be done often. Usually, you'll be able to schedule them for a time that's convenient for both of you. If you get really bogged down and feeling frantic about it, call for help! Maybe you two can swap jobs with a neighbor. Maybe a pal will lend a hand. And there's always professional cleaning help to fall back on. Sometimes it's worth cutting a corner somewhere else to work this kind of "assist" into the budget.

WHIZ QUIZ: HOW TO COPE WITH SPECIAL PROBLEMS

Here's an easy way to check out your housekeeping know-how. There's a lot of misinformation to be found on how to cope with special housekeeping problems. Some of the suggestions you may hear are simply ineffectual. Others can cause actual damage. So replace fiction with fact! Take the little Whiz Quiz we've listed below. Then check your answers against the information presented at the right. Give yourself a pat on the back *and* 5 points for each correct answer you come up with. (A score of 35 qualifies you for the title of Practically Perfect Housekeeper; 25 to 30 points marks you as Better Than Most.) Wrong guesses? No problem —just reread our "how-to" information on this page and check out the rest of this Handbook for additional useful tips.

1. What common household substance can you wipe out your refrigerator with to help prevent odors from forming?
2. What type of wax is safe for vinyl floors, what type for rubber or asphalt floors?
3. How can you protect furniture legs from damage when you shampoo carpeting at home?
4. What special treatment will make plastic furniture surfaces easier to keep clean?
5. How can you help prevent drip marks when you're washing a wall?
6. What is the first and most important thing to do when you want to clean a lamp?
7. What are the three common food substances that can damage silver?

1. Refrigerators
Using a solution made up of 2 tablespoons of baking soda to a quart of water is helpful in preventing odors from forming in your refrigerator.

2. Floor Waxes
Either water-base *or* buffing-type waxes are safe for most vinyls. But only a water-base wax can be used on rubber or asphalt tile floors. Other types can damage the finish.

3. Furniture Legs
The simple precaution of wrapping furniture legs with plastic wrap or aluminum foil will help protect them when you shampoo carpeting at home.

4. Plastic Furniture
There's a special antistatic treatment that can be applied to acrylic and most other plastic furniture surfaces. This will help keep dust to a minimum.

5. Washing Walls
Wring out your cloth or sponge as tightly as you can when you wash a wall or ceiling. This will help minimize those drip marks.

6. Lamps
The cardinal rule when cleaning a lamp or any electrical appliance or fixture is—unplug it first! This is a safety and an efficiency measure it doesn't pay to ignore.

7. Silver
Try to keep any silver flatware or serving pieces you may have from coming in contact with eggs, salt or vinegar. All three substances can damage the silver.

Note: You'll find additional information on all of the topics above spelled out on the following pages of this Handbook. Each special area of cleaning is headlined (refrigerator, range, floors, furniture, etc.) to make the information easy to find and use. Once you've read and absorbed the information, you can always refer back to a specific topic for a quick "refresher course" when the need arises. Hope you found our Whiz Quiz interesting. It's just a sampling of the kind of know-how we've included here—read on! If you didn't qualify as a Practically Perfect Housekeeper this first time around, you may by the time you've finished!

In fact, we had a particular goal in mind when we set up this introductory Whiz Quiz. We hoped it would act as a kind of ambassador-of-goodwill for the specialized cleaning information included here. So much of the information available on these topics ends up by making the jobs sound like the dreariest chores imaginable, much worse than they really are. We thought that something in a lighter vein would help you keep an open mind on things until you could judge for yourself.

TAKING CARE OF YOUR REFRIGERATOR

Three basic types of refrigerators are in use today:
- manual defrost
- automatic defrost
- frostless refrigerator-freezer

With a manual defrost, you set the control to "defrost" and then dispose of the water as the accumulated frost melts. With an automatic defrost, the water is disposed of by the refrigerator mechanism itself. (In some models you may have to start the defrost cycle manually, but the refrigerator mechanism will restart automatically when defrosting is complete.) In a frostless model, the mechanism defrosts itself when necessary. There's no visible frost. Be sure to check and see which type you have.

Apart from the defrosting process, all three types require about the same general care. Here are the basic steps to take to keep your refrigerator in good shape:

☐ Keep an eye on what's in it. Check regularly and remove any food that isn't fresh. This is a safety as well as a sanitary measure.

☐ Wipe up all spills promptly. They'll be much harder to clean up if you let them harden or set.

☐ Wipe out the inside of the refrigerator occasionally with a solution of 2 tablespoons of borax or baking soda to a quart of water. Make sure that your sponge or cloth is well wrung out. If you have a side-by-side model, wipe out the freezer when you defrost it—using the same solution. This cleaning will prevent odors from forming.

☐ When necessary, shelves, chrome parts and the outside of the unit can be washed with a mild detergent. Never use scouring powder or any abrasive on the outside—you'll destroy the finish. Final grooming note: Polish the exterior occasionally with a cream wax. The extra finish will make wipe-offs easier.

Efficient freezer-defrosting technique. If you have the type of freezer unit that requires defrosting, try to defrost whenever frost in the freezer compartment is about ¼ inch thick. With side-by-side models or models that have a pull-out freezer drawer, the freezer itself will not have to be cleaned nearly as often as the refrigerator. Cleaning technique: Wrap frozen items in sheets of newspaper or place them in a picnic cooler. Another alternative: See if friendly neighbors will let you store frozen foods in their freezers. Remove food from trays or compartments that are directly below the freezer compartment. If you're facing a really heavy defrost job, it's better to remove all food from the refrigerator. Turn the control to "off" or "defrost." Adjust deflector flap on drip tray so it extends outward. Place a pan of hot water in the freezing compartment and keep replacing it with more hot water as it cools. Leave the refrigerator door open. When all frost has melted, empty the drip tray, clean the freezer compartment and inside of refrigerator; wipe dry. Wash shelves, containers and ice cube trays in your kitchen sink, dry them, and replace. Turn the control to the regular setting and replace foods. Note: Never try to loosen heavy frost by chipping with a knife or sharp object. You may cause damage to the freezer unit.

TAKING CARE OF YOUR RANGE

Whether you have a conventional gas or electric range or a model with a self-cleaning oven, here are the basic steps necessary to keep the top of the range and the exterior working efficiently and looking bright:

☐ Wipe up all spills and grease spatters before they harden or burn on.

☐ Wipe off the surface around the top burners and the exterior with a damp cloth or sponge wrung out in a solution of warm water and detergent. Do this as often as necessary.

☐ If you have a gas range, clean grates and burners once a week, if possible. Wash them in hot water with detergent. Use a steel pad on stubborn spots. If burners are clogged, clean with a wire. (If you have an electric range, this won't be necessary—burner units are self cleaning.)

☐ Clean your broiler pan after each use.

If you have a conventional oven: Try to wipe it out while it's still slightly warm, after each use. If you use an oven cleaner for heavier cleaning, *follow the directions exactly.* These cleaners are quite effective, but they can be dangerous if handled carelessly. They can cause damage to eyes and hands as well as to equipment.

If you have a self-cleaning oven: Just take out any cooking utensils, set the special control to lock the door, and start the high heat cleaning cycle. Follow manufacturer's instructions exactly. When the cycle is completed, wipe out the resulting ash. Unless manufacturer specifies otherwise, you can put the drip pans (from under the burners) in the oven to clean as part of the self-cleaning cycle.

TAKING CARE OF YOUR FLOORS

How you clean and care for your floors depends upon the type of flooring material that's involved. On the following page, you'll find some useful and effective cleaning hints for the major types of flooring available today.

Wood floors. When you first move in, be sure to ask whether the floors are waxed or have been treated with a urethane plastic finish. *If they have been treated, don't use wax on them.* Just vacuum or dry mop them as part of your weekly cleanup. Go over them occasionally with a damp mop wrung out in warm water and a mild detergent. If there's a light film left after cleaning, go over the floor with a mop well wrung out in warm water to which a little vinegar has been added.

If you have waxed wooden floors, vacuum or dry mop as above. If a spill causes spotting, remove the spot with a liquid wax designed for wood flooring, then buff that area with a hand buffer or electric floor polisher. To maintain sheen, polish floors occasionally with an electric polisher or hand buffer. (Electric polishers can be rented quite inexpensively.) For thorough cleaning, experts recommend using one of the liquid cleaning waxes that clean and wax in one operation. Caution: Make sure you use one designed for wood floors, not a water-base wax. Apply it with a cloth, then polish with an electric polisher, if possible. If you do not use a liquid cleaning wax, clean the floor with a commercial solvent, then wax with paste wax and polish with an electric polisher or hand buffer. Note: Don't use water on waxed wood floors. You may cause them to warp and they may eventually dry out and crack.

Painted floors. Protect and clean them with wax as you would regular wood floors. See above.

Smooth surface floorcoverings. Sweep them regularly and wipe up spills promptly. Once a week, if possible, wash them with warm water and detergent. Or use one of the cleaner-polishes. You can also use a water-base self-polishing wax or liquid buffing wax on most *vinyl* floors. There are some vinyls available with a permanent finish that requires no waxing. You just wipe them with a mop dipped in warm water and detergent. For rubber or asphalt floors: Never use anything but a water-base self-polishing wax. Buffing-type waxes will destroy the surface completely! If you're in doubt about which type of floorcovering you have, check with your superintendent, manager or builder.

Carpets and rugs. Vacuum rugs and carpets regularly—at least once a week (more frequently if they're in areas of heavy traffic or if you get a lot of gritty soil in your home). Grit and dust not only make your carpets and rugs look dingy, but they can cause wear and tear through abrasion. Some people use a carpet sweeper or electric broom for between-vacuum cleanings. These will pick up surface dust, but they don't have the type of deep suction that a regular vacuum has. Spots or stains should be removed as soon

as possible. Use a mild soap and warm water or a commercial stain remover designed for this purpose. If you use a commercial cleaner, know your rug or carpeting fiber! If you've rented an apartment that comes complete with carpeting, ask the superintendent or manager about the fiber content. Then check the commercial cleaner you're using for specific directions for that type of fiber.

Both rugs and carpeting should be given a really thorough cleaning about once a year—more frequently if they get heavy wear. You can have this done by professionals, either in your home or in their plant. Or you can do it yourself, using one of the commercial products available at your hardware store. You have a choice of two types: a shampoo liquid or a sawdust-type substance that is impregnated with cleaning fluid. If you choose the shampoo method, it's best to rent a shampoo machine (also usually available at the hardware store). If you select the sawdust-type cleaner, you'll need a vacuum with good suction to pick it up. In either case, wrap furniture legs with plastic wrap or aluminum foil to protect them from the cleaning substance. Be sure to cover those metal buttons sometimes found on the bottoms of furniture legs. Keep them covered until carpet is dry. They may cause rust marks otherwise.

Warning note: Always make sure that the type of cleaning method you use is suitable for your rug or carpeting fiber. If a rug is not colorfast, for instance, shampooing may cause the colors to run. Read the directions on the product container; ask the hardware store clerk if you have any doubts. It's even a good idea to call a professional rug cleaner and ask his advice. Rugs and carpeting are expensive and it doesn't pay to take chances with them.

You'll reduce the strain on rugs and carpets—and make cleaning jobs easier—if you turn them occasionally so that all sections receive equal wear. In the case of installed carpeting, try to rearrange the furniture from time to time to reroute the major traffic patterns. This will somewhat equalize wear and soiling.

TAKING CARE OF YOUR FURNITURE

Once again, the kind of care you must give your furniture depends on what the furniture is made of. We've covered most of the usual materials you'll find. If you're not sure what material has been used for a particular piece of furniture, check with the store you bought it from before using any cleaning substance on it.

Wood furniture. Dust it regularly with a clean, dry cloth or duster. Wipe up all spills immediately. As preventive medicine, try to use coasters and/or mats on wooden tabletops to prevent spots and rings. Many of the newer furniture-care products enable you to dust, clean and polish in one operation. This is a real time-saver! Pick the cleaner according to the type of finish on your furniture—high gloss, satin finish or low gloss (such as the oiled woods). Follow the directions on the container.

Occasionally, wood furniture should be thoroughly cleaned, then rewaxed or oiled. Use a clean cloth dampened with mineral spirits or with an oil-base synthetic turpentine. (You'll find both of these at your hardware store; either one will remove the old wax and clean the wood.) Then rewax with a paste or liquid wax. Use cream polish or oil instead of wax if your furniture finish requires it. If you've had any special finish applied to tabletops or if a piece is topped with wood-grained plastic, check the store where you bought it for special cleaning instructions.

Painted or enameled wood. Dust it regularly. Wipe it off occasionally with a solution of detergent and warm water. Applying furniture wax will also help keep surfaces clean and bright.

Plastic furniture. Acrylics and most other plastic furniture surfaces can be given an antistatic treatment to help keep dust to a minimum. Ask about this when you buy the piece. The general care for plastics is then easy. Just wash off occasionally with warm water and detergent and dry with a lint-free cloth. A thin coat of silicone-base spray wax (or a low-luster cream polish) will also help keep them looking bright. If the surface becomes badly scratched, try using automobile polish to gloss over the scratches.

Caution: Solvents, cleaning fluids, nail polish and nail polish remover contain substances that can mar or dull plastic furniture. Try not to use them near your plastic pieces.

Chrome and glass furniture. Dust it regularly. When necessary, wipe it off with a soft, damp cloth. For sticky or greasy spots, use warm water and a mild detergent. Using a furniture wax designed for high-gloss furniture will help keep the sparkle on both the metal and glass. It'll also reduce those fingermarks and smudges to a minimum. Just make sure that any cloth you use (either for wiping or waxing) is soft and free of "scratchies" like buttons or seams. In fact, it's safest not to use torn-up rags at all. Get some regular dustcloths or pieces of cheesecloth (by the way, these are really best for all furniture).

TAKING CARE OF WINDOWS AND MIRRORS

We've already mentioned that liquid glass cleaners are the easiest products to use for cleaning window glass or mirrors. If windows

---

IF YOU DON'T KNOW WHAT STORE IT CAME FROM
You're probably reasonably safe if you wash off the piece with a sponge wrung out in mild soapsuds, then wax it lightly with a good furniture wax.

are particularly dirty, you can use hot water with a detergent, or a solution of 1 quart of water with 2 or 3 tablespoons of vinegar, ammonia or denatured alcohol. Use the same solution for mirrors. Wipe surfaces dry with paper toweling, a lint-free cloth, a small squeegee or crumpled sheets of newspaper. This last does a surprisingly good job because printer's ink contains a substance that cuts grease easily.

When you're doing the insides of your windows, it pays to do the job right. Clear the windowsills of any plants or bric-a-brac. They'll only be in your way and reaching over them can create an accident hazard. If your windows are the small-paned variety (with a pattern of wooden strips between the panes), it's helpful to vacuum them first, using your dust brush attachment or a hand vacuum. This will suck away loose dust and make the washing easier. When you've finished the windows, give the sills a good washing off, too. There'll never be a better time!

Special safety note: When it comes to doing the outsides of windows, we recommend using a professional. Most big-city apartment buildings forbid doing the outsides yourself. Even in a single-story house, the danger of an accident exists. And really, the pros can do a better job. They have all the right equipment and the know-how. Unless you're awfully fussy, it's a job that has to be done only a couple of times a year at most. When the windows need cleaning, check out the curtains, too. Take them down if they need to be cleaned.

UPHOLSTERY AND DRAPERY FABRICS

Never before has there been such a wide variety of upholstery and drapery fabrics available; you can just about name your wish in terms of weave, fiber content and special finish. Many of these processes make care and cleaning easier. But they also mean that you have to know what you're doing in caring for them. Once again, we urge you to *read those tags and labels* on pieces of upholstered furniture and draperies; they contain special cleaning do's and don'ts. Ask about the upkeep when you buy, too. This is your best safeguard against making costly mistakes. The following pages will give you some general pointers on care, but they're no substitute for specific instructions from a manufacturer.

General care of upholstery fabrics. Here are some basic guidelines for the care of upholstered pieces, regardless of the fiber or finish. Other "specifics" are given on the following pages.

☐ Even though they may not show it, upholstery fabrics absorb room dust, which will eventually soil or damage them. So—you should vacuum or whisk-broom them weekly. If you vacuum, use the soft brush or special upholstery attachment. If you don't have attachments, invest in a small hand vacuum.

☐ Remove all spots as soon as possible, even on specially treated fabrics.

☐ Pay special attention to arms and headrests; they tend to get dirty more quickly than the rest of the upholstery. You can usually clean them with detergent suds. To clean, whisk the detergent up in warm water until you have a good thick batch of suds. Scoop up a little of the suds (suds only!) with a damp cloth, then sponge off the soiled area. Repeat until the area is clean. If body oils or grease have soiled the piece heavily, you can use a dry-cleaning solution—but check out those manufacturer's tags first!

Fabrics with a protective finish. One of the most important things to remember here is that even those special finishes won't allow you to spill liquids around with gay abandon. Even if the fabrics are listed as stain resistant or waterproof, reasonable care is still needed. What the finishes do mean, however, is that you can *promptly* blot up a stain or spill and get a much better result than you would on an untreated fabric. Notice the emphasis on the word "promptly"! Some fabrics have also been treated for soil resistance and this adds greatly to their practicality. Now for some details on the two most common finishes:

☐ Scotchguard brand and Zepel are two leaders in this field. Both are now available with a special soil-resistant ingredient. In this case, they're labeled "Extra Soil Defense" or "ESK" (Scotchguard) or "Total Action" (Zepel).

☐ Fabrics treated with either will repel water, oil and grease stains as well as general soil.

☐ To avoid staining, you must blot up the spill immediately, before it sets or has a chance to permeate the finish. If you do get a slight residual stain, you can usually remove it with soap and water. Make sure you sponge off all traces of soap because a film of soap affects the performance of the finish. You can also use a good dry-cleaning solvent.

☐ Dry-cleaning these finishes too often may tend to lessen their effectiveness.

☐ If you're interested in a piece of upholstered furniture that doesn't feature a protective finish, you can spray one onto it yourself. Do-it-yourself versions are available in spray containers at your hardware store. If you're choosing an untreated drapery or upholstery fabric, you can have it treated by a professional service before the yardage is put on the furniture or sewn into draperies. Ask your fabric dealer about this. He'll tell you how to go about having it done.

Again, we repeat—the finishes available today aren't a license to be extra messy. They're worth investing in (particularly for fabrics that get heavy wear), but they do have their limits.

Wise-bird precaution: If you know that a particular piece is going to take a real beating, it might be worthwhile to slipcover it with a washable fabric. As we've already mentioned, slipcovers are easy to keep clean.

Fabrics made of olefin. Herculon, Polycrest and Vectra are all trademarks for olefin fabrics. These fabrics have a built-in resistance to stains, sunlight, acids and alkalis, rot and mildew. They are becoming more and more popular as the styles and colors in which they are available continue to expand. Here are some general hints on how to care for them:

☐ Wash them with soap and water or a mild detergent.
☐ If they're very soiled, you can clean them with any water-base agent or foam.
☐ Dry cleaning is not recommended for these fabrics. However, some commercial cleaners will service olefin-covered furniture that has been in use for a long time or is very soiled.
☐ Blot up all stains or spills immediately with a tissue or paper towel. Most water-based stains can be cleaned with a detergent solution. Oil- or wax-based stains can usually be cleaned with ordinary household spot remover. Stubborn stains may require a special solvent (always test a solvent on an inconspicuous area of the fabric first).

Leather. Dust it regularly with a clean, untreated cloth. To clean, wipe it off with a cloth moistened with a mild soap-and-water solution, then rinse with a cloth dampened with clean, warm water. Buff to dry. Never soak leather with water or use strong detergents, solvents or oily substances. Paste wax will help keep the leather supple and in good condition. When leather needs a thorough cleaning, use one of the patented leather soaps that are available at your hardware store. Or have the cleaning done professionally. Given proper care, leather will last indefinitely.

TAKING CARE OF WALLS AND CEILINGS

To keep walls and ceilings free of dust and cobwebs, vacuum them occasionally, using the soft brush attachment. Or dust them with a soft cloth tied over a clean dry mop or broom. If you plan to wash them, here's what to do:

☐ If they're painted, test a small area first. If you're afflicted with poor-quality paint, you're better off repainting (otherwise, you're apt to wash off some of the paint, leaving a permanently streaked surface).
☐ If the paint will stand up under washing, use a special paint cleaner or a mild soap. Use two pails—one filled with your soap solution, the other with clear rinse water.

☐ For walls, work from the bottom up; otherwise, you may create streaks that are difficult to get rid of. Wash and rinse a 3-foot area at a time, using a circular motion and overlapping the clean areas to avoid rings or streaks.

☐ For ceilings, cover the furniture first. Then proceed as above, working from one side of the ceiling to the other.

☐ In both cases, wring out your sponge or cloth as tightly as you can to minimize the drips.

☐ Wash vinyl or vinyl-coated wallcoverings the same way, using detergent with lots of suds.

TAKING CARE OF LAMPS AND LIGHTING FIXTURES

Dusty bulbs, reflectors and shades cut down the amount of light you get. So check out your lamps occasionally. Do the shades seem soiled, the bulbs dusty or dark? If so, here's how to cope:

☐ First, unplug the lamp. This is the cardinal rule when cleaning any electrical fixture or appliance.

☐ Take off the shade and the reflector, if any. Unscrew the bulb, wipe with a damp cloth, and replace just before you're ready to replug the lamp. If the bulb looks dark, however, replace it with a new one. Almost-used-up bulbs pull current but give little light.

☐ Wash reflectors in sudsy water or wipe off with a damp cloth. Make sure every lamp part is dry before replacing on the lamp. The list below outlines how to clean a variety of lampshades.

How To Clean Lampshades
Different types of lampshades require different kinds of care. However, all of them are fairly easy to clean if you give them the proper treatment. Some useful cleaning tips are listed below.

Painted silk, linen, cotton. These shades must be dry-cleaned.

Plain silk, rayon, nylon. These can be washed if they are sewn (not glued) to the frame and if trim is colorfast. Otherwise, dry-clean. To wash, dunk in a tub of sudsy water, rinse twice in cool water, set outside to dry quickly. Never set silk shades in full sun, however.

Plastic or metal. Wipe these with a cloth dipped in cool, soapy water, rinse with a damp cloth, and dry.

Fiberglass. Wipe with a damp cloth.

Real parchment. Dust these regularly. Apply neat's-foot oil or castor oil occasionally to keep them from drying out.

Imitation parchment. Clean these with liquid wax.

TAKING CARE OF PEWTER AND STAINLESS

Pewter can be washed regularly in warm, sudsy water. Polish it occasionally with special pewter polish or silver polish. This is a soft metal, so you should never use harsh cleansers on it. If pewter is very soiled, send it to a professional metal cleaner. Stainless steel flatware does not tarnish and does not need polishing. It's dishwasher-safe—but don't put it in the dishwasher basket along with silver flatware. This can pit the stainless.

TAKING CARE OF SILVER

If you give silver proper day-in and day-out care, you can cut down on the polishing needed and keep pieces looking better.

☐ Use silver as often as possible, washing it after each use. This helps keep it clean and develops a soft glow (patina).

☐ Store it in a lined silver chest or in specially treated cloths.

☐ Dust and wash decorative pieces frequently. Use hot, sudsy water for all silverware. Rinse with hot water and dry immediately. Dishwashers are okay for silver. Possible exception: old, hollow-handled knives. The modern ones are dishwasher-safe.

☐ Use one of the commercially treated silver-cleaning cloths or mitts to wipe off silver in between polishings. These cloths contain a tarnish-retarder; it's quite effective.

☐ Never wrap silver in plastic—if any moisture is present, the plastic may stick to the silver and damage it. Also—never use rubber bands around silver, even if the bands are put on over a silver storage cloth. Rubber can damage silver—even through paper or cloth!

☐ Eggs, salt and vinegar are all hard on silver. Try not to use silver serving pieces for foods that contain these. Always use a glass liner for silver flower bowls. For fresh fruit, line your bowl with paper toweling.

When it's time to polish, roll up your sleeves, collect all the pieces that need doing, and dig in.

☐ First, wash each piece in hot, sudsy water.

☐ Apply the polish with a soft cloth or sponge. Use a silver brush for molded trimming or heavily embossed pieces. Don't rub too hard with either, particularly if you're cleaning plated pieces.

☐ Wash each piece again in hot, sudsy water. Be sure to get all the polish off. Otherwise, it will build up in the crevices.

Remember—your home is a background for both of you and it reflects both of you. The more attractive it looks the better it shows you off. Any home requires some care just to keep it livable. A little extra effort can achieve that special look that marks the well-cared-for home!

5 Making the Most of Your Money

5 Making the Most of Your Money

BEING A GOOD MONEY-MANAGER: HOW DO YOU DO IT?

Meet Joe and Mary. They're both into fields in which, so far, the main reward is self-satisfaction. Joe works with disturbed kids; Mary's trying to make it as an illustrator. Impractical? Dreamers? Well, it's a funny thing. That garage apartment they're leasing is very attractive—and the rent's always paid on time. Their parties are fun, too: good food, with a friendly jug of wine. And they did take that bicycle tour of the British Isles many of their friends are still just thinking about. Guess they're proof that it isn't *how much* money you have to work with—it's *how you handle it.*

While some people may be "born" money-managers, for most of us it's a matter of learning: first, learning that good financial practices are important; next, learning what's involved in handling money efficiently. It's a cold, unpleasant fact that money heads the list of troublemakers in marriages. Granted, in some cases serious personality problems may underlie the money troubles. Usually, though, it's a matter of not understanding what's involved in handling money and not knowing how to arrive at workable financial arrangements.

This chapter aims at acquainting you with the basic factors involved in establishing a good personal-finance equation—i.e., a situation where you do more than just "break even" at the end of each month. We deal with setting up and maintaining a budget; using credit advantageously; understanding the financial world of banks, investments, insurance plans. These aren't far-in-the-future skills. They're abilities you need as soon as you start earning and/or spending your own money.

Having these skills is like being able to read road signs. They help you decide where you want to go. Then they help you to get there. They pay off in other advantages, too—like getting more value for your dollar and avoiding that frantic feeling of never quite catching up with the bills. Usually, you're able to finance more fun, too. With this knowledge, you're in control of your own affairs. Without basic money-skills like these, you're driving blind and apt to end up "off the road" entirely.

THE GOOD BUDGET POINTS OUT
WHERE TO SPEND YOUR MONEY

Budget—ugh! A dirty word, right? Wrong! You turn your nose up at a budget only when you don't understand what it's all about. Right now, you're probably thinking of complicated bookkeeping, pinching pennies, having to keep track of every cent. This just isn't so. No sensible person would advocate living like a miser. The money you have available should buy you as comfortable a life-style as possible.

A budget is not so much a matter of saving; rather, it's a *plan for spending*. It needn't be complicated and it shouldn't be a straitjacket. It should help give you a clear picture of where you stand financially. Above all, it should help you get the things you really want to have: maybe a sports car, a ski trip, a stereo system. Any or all of these can be part of your budget if any or all of these are what *you* happen to want. And that's another important point about your budget, or "plan-for-spending," as some prefer to call it. It should be as personal as your initials—tailored to fit *your* life-style as completely as the furnishings in your home do.

Books on personal finance often set up "ideal" budgets. These are great as examples of what a budget can be. But they're really not meant to be absorbed lock, stock and barrel. The same goes for budget advice given by friends or family; it's helpful as a broad outline but not as an actual blueprint for you. Trying to live someone else's budget is like trying to live someone else's life. It will never really satisfy you. To work, that's what a budget must do—satisfy *you,* meet *your* wants and needs. Otherwise, you'll start to slide away from it and you might as well not have one at all.

We'll show you some sample budgets later on in this chapter. But please remember that they're just samples. The real basis of this section consists of the "how-to" advice—the step-by-step outlining of how to get a budget started, how to maintain it, how to adjust it if it seems out of whack. Read through the samples, of course. They're interesting and informative, particularly as comparisons if you're already following a budget. But we advise spending more time on the nuts and bolts stuff—and the most time of all in thinking about how the guidelines apply to you.

And remember, you're budgeting for two now! Even if you have a double salary to cover double costs, you'll still have the problem of two points of view. Here's where differences in value judgments become really crucial. Do you do extra entertaining—or save for a trip-for-two? If one feels one way, one the other, you'll have to thrash the difference through to a compromise you can both accept.

The Basic Budget Is A Four-Point Plan

With any project, the details fall into place more easily when you have the big picture clearly in mind. That goes for your budget, too. Start out with a well-defined outline of its major components and the specifics will fill in more easily. Essentially, your budget plans out four kinds of spending for you. Each type of spending provides its own reward.

Spending for comfortable daily living. This includes having enough cash on hand to pay regular weekly or monthly bills for rent, food, clothing, transportation, telephone—the basic items that keep you going from day to day. Regardless of what scale you live on, you won't be really comfortable unless you can maintain your life-style without a hassle. Getting dunning letters from local stores, scrounging around to come up with the rent, serving spaghetti four nights in a row because you're short on food money —crises like these aren't comfortable for anyone. And a good budget will help avoid them. No amount of planning can provide steak on a hamburger income—but you can at least make sure of the hamburger!

Spending for major purchases. A house, a car, a special vacation, new stereo equipment—you should build a compartment into your budget that will make "big buys" like these possible. How rapidly they become possible depends on the overall size of your income and the share-of-income you allot to this "big buy" section. Here, the secret of success is to think in terms of very specific goals. Decide what you want, find out how much it will cost you. Then plan out how quickly you can, or want to be able to, buy it.

Spending for financial security. You may never have thought of it this way before, but savings accounts, insurance and investments are a form of spending—one of the most rewarding. You're buying security, peace of mind, the ability to borrow money cheaply. And you're getting extra value for every dollar spent: the interest that banks, insurance companies and corporations pay you for placing your dollars with them! In effect, you're using money to buy money.

Splurge spending. Yes, the sensible budget includes even this type of spending! There's an occasional "throw caution to the winds" buy in each of us. Why grit your teeth and resist? With splurge spending planned for, you can dine in that superb little restaurant or put racing stripes on the wagon. And you won't blow the rest of the budget! (Just remember—you have to keep this splurge spending category in proportion to your overall budget.)

Saving on a regular basis can make that longed-for vacation a reality.

CHECKLIST ANY BUDGET FOR "THE BASIC FOUR"

- ☐ living expenses
- ☐ big buys
- ☐ long-range security
- ☐ splurge spending

Cover these four areas and you'll have your money well in hand.

A Budget Is A Good Thing—"Okay, Where Do I Start?"

At the beginning—that's the very best place! It's not as difficult as you might think, either. We'll give you a short list of what to do as starters, then go into the more detailed "whys."

A CHECKLIST TO BEGIN YOUR BUDGET

- ☐ open a checking account
- ☐ start a savings account
- ☐ total up your net income (income after taxes)
- ☐ list all your expenses (those that are constant, those that can change)

That's a nice pat list—but you need to know more about each item before you can make a start. So here are the details:

A checking account: the whys and wherefores. Your budget will work best if your money is where you need it when you need it. Checking accounts have several advantages. You won't have to keep a lot of cash with you or in your home. Cash-in-the-hand has a habit of dribbling away. And there's always the danger of theft. Checks are also the most convenient way of paying bills. You don't have to make special stops to buy them, as you do with money orders. This convenience can encourage you to pay bills promptly, while the money's available and before you incur late-payment charges. And most importantly, checks give you a written record of how and where you've spent your money. They also serve as receipts of payment. What goes into your checking account? Usually, whatever amount you need to cover your regular living expenses.

Note: In some areas, employers and banks offer a plan under which your payroll checks can be automatically deposited in your checking account. You can then make your own arrangements for transferring funds from the checking account to savings funds.

A savings account: how it helps. As we've just mentioned, some budget arrangements call for keeping occasional and emergency-expense money in a savings account. There are definite advantages to this approach. You collect interest on the money and

See pages 266 through 268 for more details on checks and checking accounts.

the temptation to nibble into it for living expenses is lessened. A savings account is useful, too, as a collection point for money you intend to invest. Again, you're earning interest while your capital builds up to the amount you need or while you're waiting for the right investment to come along. Finally, there's something about a savings account that seems to encourage putting money into it. Maybe it's seeing those interest-paid entries. Maybe it's the sight of that growing balance. Whatever the appeal, savings increase faster in savings accounts than in piggy banks.

Note: Generally speaking, the longer you are willing to leave your money on deposit the higher the rate of interest you will earn. Therefore, after you have determined the purpose of your savings, you should pick the savings plan that best suits your needs. Some of the different types of savings plans available are described later on in this chapter.

For more info on savings accounts, see pages 262 and 263.

Totaling up your net income. Obviously, you can't decide how you want to spend your money until you know how much you really have to spend. How do you arrive at a total figure? Start with your take-home pay—the actual amount you receive each week or month after all deductions have been withheld. (This is called your *net* income. Gross income is your income before any deductions are taken.) Then add in additional income you're 100% sure of getting (e.g., interest, dividends or profit sharing). Don't include bonuses, gifts, winnings and the like. These are windfalls, not certain income. If you're both working, obviously you'll include both salaries—but after taxes, please! Got your total? Now it's time to total up your expenses.

Adding up expenses: set up three lists. Basically, you face three types of expenses and should list each type separately.

- ☐ fixed expenses
- ☐ flexible expenses
- ☐ occasional and emergency expenses

Each of these categories will include several items. Breaking down your expenses into three separate lists shows you exactly which costs you *must* handle on a regular basis and which you can play around with a little.

Obviously, those fixed expenses are the bedrock of any budget. They're the costs that must be met first—and on a regular basis. They bear careful thinking about before you assume them. Flexible expenses are often cash items and are usually paid for on a daily or weekly basis. How much you spend on any one item, or on the category as a whole, is a matter of personal choice. You can adjust up or down as you work with a budget. Occasional and emergency expenses lie in between the first two types. They will occur—that you can count on! Exactly how much you will have to pay out is a variable figure. Clothing, vacations, education, gifts—these costs you have some control over. Real emergency expenses are difficult to estimate. Here are some experts' views on what is a safe minimum:

A minimum emergency fund—here are the experts' opinions.

SUGGESTION #1: Always have three to six months' salary on hand as a cushion against emergencies.
SUGGESTION #2: Save approximately 10% of your take-home pay to build up an emergency fund large enough to cover six months' living expenses.
SUGGESTION #3: Saving at the same rate as above, build a fund large enough to meet three months' living expenses.

Although the details vary, you can see that specialists in financial planning consider the emergency fund of prime importance!

TYPECASTING YOUR EXPENSES

Fixed	Flexible	Occasional and Emergency
Rent	Food	Uninsured medical and dental bills
Insurance (life, auto, health, tenant's or homeowner's)	Lunches	
	Laundry and cleaning	Home appliance and auto repairs
	Entertainment	Large clothing outlays
Repayment of credit or loans	Carfare and general transportation	Vacations
Dues (union, club, fraternal organizations)	Newspapers and magazines	Gifts
Regular contributions	Personal (clothes, grooming, etc.)	Continuing education
Utilities (gas, electricity, telephone)	Household operating expenses	Note: Preplanning in this category can really help avoid panic and emergency borrowing.
	Savings	
Note: These expenses remain fairly constant, so you know almost exactly what your outlay will be.	Miscellaneous Note: Books, records, hobby equipment and sports can be included here or can be listed separately.	

How Much Should You Spend In Each Category, On Each Item?

How much you spend—and on what—is completely your own business as long as your total outlay doesn't exceed your income. It's not a matter of ethics or morality but of personal choice and circumstance. There are various factors that will influence how you spend your money. For instance:

Where you live makes a difference in your budget. Life in big cities like New York, Boston or Los Angeles is expensive—particularly when it comes to rent costs. As a general rule, it costs more to live on either the western or eastern seacoasts (or near any metropolitan area), less in non-metropolitan areas and least of all in the rural South.

The type of work you do makes a difference, too. Certain fields require a large wardrobe and some expensive lunching, which isn't always reimbursed by the company. Casual clothes and lunch in the company cafeteria are the style in other jobs.

Personal tastes and hobbies can weigh heavily on a budget. A fondness for eating out will bump your food or entertainment category, for instance. Hobbies like skiing or photography will bite into the budget more than bird watching. This doesn't mean you shouldn't enjoy these pleasures; it just means you'll have to take up the slack someplace else in your plan. It also means that *your* spending plan may look different from the sample budgets you'll be seeing on the next few pages. That's to be expected—people are different, too!

That first budget. To make it most useful, base it on what you're actually spending, not on what you think you should be doing. If this is your first go-round with budgeting and paying bills, you'll probably have to live through two or three months before you know how much you tend to spend on most items. Keep all your sales receipts and bills—and try to keep some kind of record of your cash outlay. Just chuck the sales slips et al. in a box or a file folder if you're not dedicated to this type of record-keeping. It'll get easier as you go along.

THE NEXT STEP: Go over all your check stubs and all those receipts and bills you've saved. Do some adding up, then put down a figure for each item on your budget list. If you have no entries for some items in the "flexible expenses" list, you know they're not going to be "biggies" in your budget, so don't worry about them.

THE FINAL CHECKUP: Now that you've got some actual figures down, take a good look at them. Figure out what *percentage* of your total income the highest outlays represent. Then ask yourselves: Are these the things that are most important to us? Is this really where we want to spend a lot of our money? You may reach an instant agreement that "Yes, these are important to us," or

FIRST-BUDGET TECHNIQUES
(1) Keep track of expenses.

(2) Add them up by category.

(3) Look the figures over—are you spending where you want to?

"No, they're not." Or you may have to talk them out a bit, maybe do a little horse trading. One agrees to cut down on magazines, the other on taxis in order to boost the food or entertainment fund a little. If your fixed-plus-flexible expenses are using up all your net income, with nothing left over to put in that important "Occasional and Emergency" expense column, you know you'll have to cut down the flexibles somewhere.

Here's where taking a look at the statistics can help. Checking out sample budgets and the "averages" can help give you a clearer picture of where your budget may be running heavy—perhaps too heavy, even allowing for personal preferences. Example: You find that your food bills come in consistently at 10 to 20% above most averages. Why? Are you really a gourmet cook who enjoys fine food? Do you both like entertaining at home and do a lot of it? Or are you just a careless shopper? Are your laundry bills running almost as high as the average totals for general household maintenance? Maybe you should skip that commercial laundry and plan to do-it-yourself. Switch to drip-dry shirts and use a launderette—or invest in your own machine. Sample budgets are useful for this kind of comparison-checking. But don't use them for orgies of self-doubt or guilt—the "No one else is spending money on records, why are we so frivolous?" type of thing.

FACTS AND FIGURES THAT SHOW CHANGING INCOME

These statistics may be useful as financial signposts—helping to show you where your budget might be headed in the long run.

Working Wives: You're on the increase!

1950	1970	1973
21%	39%	45%
	(52% in families with incomes over $10,000)	

Percentage of husband–wife families with the wife in the labor force.

Projection: Average family income is on the rise!

1968 average family income	1971 average family income	1980s projected average family income
$8,600	$10,971	$15,000

And it's projected that half this additional buying power will be in the hands of young and middle marrieds!

Thought-provoker: It looks like you'll have an increasing amount of money to spend. You'd better get used to spending it efficiently!

SAMPLE BUDGETS DON'T ALLOW FOR CHANGING FINANCIAL CONDITIONS, VARIATIONS IN LOCALE

Most sample budgets are based on averages—average family size, average income, average expenses. They don't actually tell a real-life individual too much. However, here's one that indicates, within percentage ranges, how a great many "average" families might spend net income:

Item	Percent of income
housing	27 – 30
food	19 – 25
transportation	14 – 17
clothing	9 – 13
medical care	6 – 7
recreation	4 – 5
personal care	2 – 3
tobacco and alcohol	3 – 4
education	1 – 3
miscellaneous	3 – 6

Here, the wide ranges allow for variations based on geography, type of occupation, personal tastes and all the other variables. If your budget falls within these averages, you're doing all right. (Note that savings are not included in the percentages as spent.)

MEET BARBARA AND JOHN HOOPER: YOUNG MARRIEDS WHO SETTLED IN NEW YORK CITY

Like so many resident New Yorkers, Barbara and John Hooper came to the city as young marrieds. Both native Virginians, they met during their sophomore year in college. After graduation, John was offered a position as a junior executive with a clothing manufacturer in New York City; both he and Barbara decided they'd like to try big-city life. After a hectic month that included getting married, moving north to New York, and a stay with a college classmate while they hunted for an apartment, John and Barbara settled into housekeeping on their own. Once settled, Barbara joined a large insurance company as a claims examiner.

In talking about their first year together, Barbara says, "I guess we were fairly typical of most big-cityites starting out. We did get lucky with the apartment. The neighborhood wasn't so great and it was a walk-up, but it did have a separate bedroom and a pretty good-sized living room." John adds, "We may have gone heavier than most on spending for clothes and furniture. But we didn't want to move anything with us so we had to start from scratch when we got here. And both of us needed big-city clothes. In college we'd gotten by pretty much on jeans and shirts. I *did* work weekends and summers during college—but my job was playing guitar with a rock group, and you don't need a gray flannel suit for that!"

Here is a typical month's budget from their first year:

Total yearly net income	**$11,750.00**	
Total monthly net income	**$ 979.00—**	**100%**
Monthly expenses:		
Payments on bank loan (to buy furniture)	$ 52.61—	5.3%
Repayment of educational loan	$ 50.00—	5.1%
Rent	$ 180.00—	18.3%
Food	$ 100.00—	10.1%
Lunches	$ 120.00—	12.2%
Utilities	$ 20.21—	2.0%
Telephone	$ 39.57—	4.0%
Transportation	$ 40.00—	4.1%
Household and personal expenses	$ 20.70—	2.1%
Department store charges	$ 91.60—	9.3%
Credit card charges	$ 39.70—	4.0%
Recreation	$ 30.00—	3.1%
Savings	$ 200.00—	20.4%
Total	$ 984.39—	100%

Note: Medical insurance was paid for by their employers. Their monthly savings included dollars set aside for any uninsured medical expenses. They carried no other type of insurance. Also, this month's budget did not reflect any outlays (or separate budget categories) for vacations, dues, contributions or gifts.

"That month we came out a bit short," John admits, "but we called home a lot. So we decided to watch that phone bill."

Your budget may end up looking different—but this one does give you some idea of how one city couple spent their income.

AFTER THE FIRST FEW MONTHS: IS YOUR BUDGET A SUCCESS OR SAD NEWS?

You've listed your expenses, you've planned out your spending on paper—you're all set. Well, not quite. First budgets don't always work out exactly as you've planned them, so it's important to know just how yours is doing. Here's how:

For the first few months, eagle-eye all your spending. Save all sales receipts and bills. Just for these few months, try to keep cash expenditures to a minimum. Use checks wherever possible. But keep track of whatever cash you do lay out. Carrying a little memo book with you is helpful here. You may be gritting your teeth already at the mere thought of this kind of tallying, but just remember—it's only for two or three months and it will make for smoother sailing later on.

When your checkup period is over, total up what you've spent, using the same headings you've set up in your budget. Now, take a deep breath—and compare! All right—which of the following story lines describes the situation?

Love at first sight: budget and outlay are matchmates. Those spending figures come pretty close to what you've planned out for them. It doesn't have to be a penny-for-penny match; that's almost impossible to achieve. If your average expenditures come within a few dollars (more or less) of what you've budgeted, you have a healthy little plan going there. Stick with it. From now on, you can get by with checking out total expenditures vs. budget once a year—perhaps at tax time. Go back to careful, daily record-keeping only if you feel you are spending more than usual.

Hey! The lifeboat is leaking! What's happened? Your fixed expenses are running close to what you figured. But your cash expenditures are running much higher. If this "leak" is just a dribble —a matter of a few dollars—ignore it. You're probably just buying newspapers, magazines or other small items that are hard to keep track of. If your cash expenses are running consistently $10 or more per week over your budget, that "leak" can sink the boat! It could run into hundreds of dollars per year and just swamp your savings. What to do about this dilemma?

First, locate the leak. Write down absolutely everything you buy for the next few weeks. Then look over these expenses. If you find you're buying things you really need, but have forgotten to write into the budget, you're okay. Just add them in and cut down elsewhere in the plan if you have to. You may find, however, that you're just frittering money away. In this case, talk sternly to yourselves, try to carry less cash with you, and have another go at sticking to the original plan.

When savings accounts are the losers. Here's how this plot goes. Your fixed and flexible expenses are running fairly true to what you've estimated. But your security and occasional/emergency spending fund isn't building up the way you'd like it to. In fact, it looks pretty sick. Non-budgeted spending (buying clothes on impulse or dining out frequently, for instance) is eating into that savings plan. What's wrong? Often, it's a question of motivation. You're not saving because you don't really want to. We can all understand the need for a cushion against emergencies. But after that, it gets tougher. Saving toward specific goals can help. We've mentioned this before, but it's really a useful tip and bears repeating. If you can decide on certain clearly defined objectives like a house, a car, a vacation, the saving usually comes easier. Remember, too—savings widen your life-choices. They get you out of the hand-to-mouth trap. With savings, you can move to another state, continue your education, start your own business, spend several months traveling. Try to keep this in mind: A closetful of clothes can add up to a down payment on a house. Or you could be eating out in Paris for the cost of a six-month round of local restaurants and other entertainment. If these examples don't appeal, just remember: Chances are there will be something "big" you'll want—and soon. Savings are the way!

All is lost—the regiment is wiped out! The budget is a bust: Your paycheck is spent two days after you get it; you never have enough in your checking account to pay your rent; your account is often overdrawn. This is a time for stern, even drastic, measures. First: Put your money where it's harder to get at. For instance, if you've been keeping your occasional/emergency expense money in your checking account, transfer it to your savings account. Next: Spend your weekly cash allotment for food, laundry and other necessities. Then put aside enough money for daily workday expenses. Then put a few dollars into that emergency savings fund. Whatever's left over is what you have for weekend entertainment. *For you, a notebook or budget envelope book is a must.* Use it to keep track of every expense. You're right—this kind of strict budget is neither easy nor fun. You have to think about money practically all day, every day. But face it—your money is doing a vanishing act because you haven't thought about it at all! Usually, a few weeks on a super-strict budget can train you to the middle path. You're aware enough of money by then to keep track of it almost automatically and can return to a looser form of budget. If even these drastic measures don't do it, you're in for a big rethink. Maybe your overall income just isn't enough and one or both of you will have to think about bringing in extra money. Or you've got a hangup about money and should look for some professional help. Many communities offer group therapy sessions for the addictive spender (some larger employers do, too). The important thing is to realize that you are facing financial problems that will only get worse if you don't get income and outlay back into balance. That first budget, even if it doesn't work, can still be helpful in pointing out your money difficulties before they become completely crippling.

TO KEEP YOUR BUDGET RUNNING SMOOTHLY: GIVE IT PERIODIC CHECKUPS

There's nothing less useful than a tired old budget—one that's out-of-date, no longer reflecting your true income or spending habits. Keep yours in good condition! Give it an overhaul every time there's a change in your income. That's a must. But over and above this basic care, take a look at that budget once or twice a year, even if there've been no radical changes in your life-style. Fluctuations in the cost of living, changing interests on your part —both of these can create a gap between the spending plan you've worked out on paper and your actual spending habits. Here's a little checkup questionnaire you can use when you haul your budget out for "servicing":

Budget Need A Tuneup?
Check These Possible Trouble Spots

☐ Is it up-to-date? Take a quick look at check stubs and receipts, particularly in the "flexible expenses" area. Do the "real" figures jibe with the budget projections? If not, revise the plan to fit your current spending pattern. Just remember that when you build an increase into one category, you have to shave somewhere else (if your overall income is still the same).

☐ Has your spendable income increased? If you've gotten a raise in salary, paid off a credit purchase or loan, or are receiving interest on investments—add this extra money into your budget, and quickly. Decide how you want to spend it or you'll end up just frittering it away.

☐ Has your spendable income decreased? Perhaps you've taken a temporary cut in pay or removed money from a savings account or other interest-producing investment. Maybe it's higher rent or additional insurance coverage. If your spendable income has decreased for any reason, refigure that budget to see where you can take up the slack. Get the new figures down on paper. Don't settle for a mental note to "cut down all around." You may end up in real trouble.

Keeping a budget book is a help. You can write your budget down on any old scrap of paper and stick it in a bureau drawer. If you're really budget minded, it doesn't make any difference what form your version takes. Usually, though, it's easier to use a little memo book. The loose-leaf variety is handy because you can add extra pages if you need them. Use the same book to keep track of expenditures (when this kind of record-keeping is necessary) and you'll have all your budget statistics in one place.

SOME HIGH-INTEREST FACTS ABOUT BANKS AND BANKING

The days of money-in-the-sock hidden under the mattress are over. Modern banks offer a range of services that are both useful and profitable for you—even if your income is small. You don't have to become an expert overnight. But understanding some of the fundamentals about banks and banking practices will help you use bank services more efficiently. Essentially, this is what you look for in a bank:

☐ a convenient location—near either your home or office
☐ a maximum return on your savings
☐ the type of checking account and other services that best meet your needs
☐ safety

When you're deciding on a bank, you usually have two choices: to concentrate most of your banking business under one roof and maintain your checking and savings account (and safe-deposit box if you use one) at the same bank—or use one bank for checking and another for savings. The first makes it easier to transfer funds from one account to another. The second can help prevent your dipping into a savings fund too easily.

Sometimes, people decide to maintain a checking account with a commercial bank and then shop around for a savings institution that combines the best rate of interest with the greatest degree of convenience.

Where Should You Bank?
Check These Questions And Answers To Help You Decide

Here's a brief rundown on the different types of banking institutions that are generally available today:

What is a commercial bank?

Full-service (commercial) banks are chartered by state or federal law. They are designed to serve the financial needs of business and industry. However, in recent years they have tailored their services to meet the needs of the individual customer as well and now offer a wide range of these services. Deposits are insured by the Federal Deposit Insurance Corporation (FDIC).

What services does it offer?

All offer checking and savings accounts and personal installment loans, and some offer safe-deposit box rental. Most also offer other types of personal loans, home mortgages, personal investment services, trust administration and traveler's checks. These banks will also transfer funds to out-of-state or foreign banks and issue letters of credit.

Interest rates?

Ceilings on interest rates are determined by government regulation. Commercial banks' interest ceilings generally are lower than those of other financial institutions because the agencies regulating these ceilings set them at a lower rate.

Mutual savings banks (state chartered) were established specifically to provide a safe place for family and individual savings. They operate in eighteen states, primarily in the Northeast. Technically, they are owned by their depositors and not by stockholders (as would be the case in a nonmutual savings bank). Most carry some form of deposit insurance. More than two-thirds of them belong to the Federal Deposit Insurance Corporation. This means that should a bank fail, you would recover your savings (up to the amount insured by the Federal Deposit Insurance Corporation). You would receive them back in cash or in the form of a new account in a solvent bank.

Mutual savings banks offer nonbusiness savings accounts, mortgage and home improvement loans, passbook loans, safe-deposit box rentals, money orders, traveler's checks and bank checks. They also offer banking by mail and payroll deduction savings plans.

The interest rates (set by FDIC regulation) on savings accounts usually run higher than rates set for commercial banks.

What is a savings bank?

What services does it offer?

Interest rates?

Savings and loan associations use the savings accounts that are on deposit with them to make home mortgage loans for buying, building or repairing homes. They are chartered by either the state or federal government; accounts on deposit with them are insured, up to specified amounts, by the Federal Savings and Loan Insurance Corporation or by private insurance agencies. These associations are also called savings and loan companies, cooperative banks or Homestead Associations.

They offer passbook loans and banking by mail in addition to savings accounts, home mortgages and home improvement loans.

They usually pay a higher rate of interest than commercial banks because the ceiling rates set by the Federal Home Reserve Bank Board allow them to do so. These interest rates usually run about the same as those allowed for mutual savings banks.

What is a savings and loan association?

What services does it offer?

Interest rates?

Credit unions are nonprofit corporations formed by employees of the same company, members of a union or fraternal organization, or residents of a small, tightly knit community or group.

They are set up to accept savings deposits and make loans to members. Some also offer life insurance.

Generally, they offer the highest interest rates on savings and the lowest rates on loans of any of the banking institutions. Why? Because they are set up as nonprofit corporations, they do not pay any federal income tax. They also operate with a limited overhead, which reduces costs still further.

What is a credit union?

What services does it offer?

Interest rates?

What About Compound Interest:
What Does It Mean, Does It Make A Difference?

How you feel about compound interest depends upon whether you take the long view or the immediate point of view. Essentially, compounding means paying interest on interest. For example: If you have $100 deposited in a savings account at 5%, the simple interest rate on that is $5 per year. At the end of the first year, you have $105.00. If interest is compounded annually, the second year's rate of interest would be based on $105 rather than on the original $100. If the interest is compounded quarterly, the 5% is divided into four parts, yielding 1¼% interest every three months. This means that your $100 will earn about $5.08 by the end of the first year. Your $100 will double itself in about fifteen years if you maintain a 5% interest rate compounded quarterly. And that goes for every $100 you save at that rate!

There's one immediate advantage to having interest compounded frequently. If you do withdraw a large sum of money before the interest period is over, you will have earned some money on it. Banks that offer day-of-deposit to day-of-withdrawal accounts guarantee that you won't lose any interest earned on any sum you have banked with them.

Know what your bank's interest-payment dates are and try not to withdraw money just before those dates. You may be losing interest if it's not a day-of-deposit to day-of-withdrawal account. Some banks offer *days of grace* at the end of each interest period. If you deposit your money within this grace period, you draw interest on it from the first day of the entire grace period.

Consider a passbook loan if you need money and prefer not to withdraw savings (which may never be replaced). This is a loan in which you offer the savings in your savings account as collateral. It's usually the cheapest type of loan you can get—and your savings go on earning bank interest while they act as collateral. This means, in effect, that you can deduct the interest paid in the savings account from the interest you are paying on the passbook loan.

Some Other Special Services Your Bank May Offer

We've already talked about "regular" savings accounts and the compound interest they usually provide. Here are other forms of savings that are commonly used:

Savings certificates or time deposits. These are useful when you have a fairly large sum of money you know you won't be using for a while and want to stash away—anything from several hundred to several thousand dollars. Don't laugh, it does happen!

You deposit your money at the bank and agree to leave it there for a specific length of time, from several months up to several years. Because the bank knows it will have the use of that money for a long period of time, it will pay you a higher rate of interest than it will on regular savings accounts. Be sure to check the penalties for early withdrawals, however. They can be hefty.

Christmas, Chanukkah or other "special" savings clubs. With these, you agree to deposit the same amount each week, then withdraw the total at the holiday season or when you have reached a specific amount. In addition to holiday gifts, you can save for a vacation or for a new automobile this way. While some banks have started to pay interest on this type of account, it's usually a lower rate than on regular savings deposits. And sometimes, no interest is paid at all. Obviously, if no interest is paid, it's better to use a regular savings account unless you don't trust yourself not to dip into it for other purposes. In this case, you're paying for "safety." The coupon book you receive with these types of clubs *does* tend to encourage regular savings!

"Automatic" savings plans. Under one plan, you set aside a portion of your paycheck and deposit it in your savings account. Or you can arrange for your bank to transfer a specific sum (every week or month) from your checking to your savings account. Some companies provide *payroll savings plans* with which you automatically buy U.S. Savings Bonds. What about Savings Bonds, by the way? How do they work?

SERIES E BONDS are bought at a 25% discount—i.e., you pay $18.75, get back $25 at the end of five years and ten months. If you keep them to maturity, they pay about $5\frac{1}{2}\%$ interest— less if you cash them in before maturity. For tax purposes, interest may be deferred until redemption.

SERIES H BONDS are called "current-income" bonds. You buy them in denominations of $500, $1,000, $5,000 or $10,000. You pay the full face amount of each bond, but you receive the interest during the tax year.

Safe-deposit boxes. For a very small fee, a bank will rent you a box in its vault in which you can keep important papers and other small valuables like jewelry. Tax records, stock certificates, bonds—these are the kinds of documents that are better off in a safe-deposit box than kept at home. Your will should not be kept in a safe-deposit box. Instead, keep one copy at home, in a fireproof box, and one copy at your lawyer's office. This way, you are making sure that it will then be readily accessible to you and to the other members of your family if it is needed.

Checking In On Checking Accounts

There are two standard types of checking accounts: regular checking accounts and special checking accounts. It usually pays to do a little figuring and shopping around to find which type will serve you best—and which bank offers the most advantageous deal on that type. Basically, here's what's involved:

Special checking accounts are designed for people who write a relatively small number of checks each month. There is no minimum balance needed. The only requirement is that you keep enough in the account to cover the checks you actually write. You'll pay a small fee for each check that you write and (usually) a monthly service charge as well. Some banks skip the service charge for any month in which you write more than a given number of checks. Some banks also offer special checking accounts designed especially for students. Shop around to determine the best type of account for your needs.

Regular checking accounts usually require you to maintain a minimum balance. This can range from $100 or $150 up to over $1,000, depending on the bank and the area in which you live. Monthly charges on this type of account vary from one bank to another. You may be charged a flat monthly service charge in addition to maintaining a balance. Or you may be charged a monthly fee only when and if your balance dips below the required minimum. Some arrangements offer unlimited transactions without any monthly fee if you maintain a balance above a specified amount. If you're a heavy check-user, this type of account may be for you. Here again, it pays to shop around for the plan that best suits your needs.

Regular or special: how to choose between the two. The fly in the ointment is that minimum balance needed for a regular account. Remember, that money won't be earning the interest that it would be pulling in if it were in a savings account. To decide which type of checking arrangement pays off for you: Figure out the amount of interest the minimum balance would earn as savings. Then estimate how many checks you write per month and what those checks would cost you with a special checking account. If the interest on savings comes to more than the charge for checks, you're better off with special checking.

Joint or individual accounts: which will it be? Both regular and special checking accounts can be held jointly or as single accounts. If you each maintain an individual account, you'll have to pay two service charges. With a joint account, you don't pay the double charge, but the bookkeeping can get complicated. If

SPECIAL CHECKING   REGULAR CHECKING

you keep separate checkbooks and you both write lots of checks, you'll have to adjust the balance in *both* books each time one of you writes a check! Or you'll have to keep separate balances and compare from time to time (with the risk that you may end up overdrawn). The best solution for most couples: Establish a joint account with one checkbook. Appoint one of you to be the "check-writer." The other half of the team then carries one or two blank checks in case of emergencies. Keep a little cushion in the account so that these emergency checks won't result in an overdrawn account.

Remember: You pay for checks that bounce and they don't do much for your image with the local merchants or your credit rating! Some banks offer overdraft accounts that allow you to write checks for more than the balance in your account without a penalty fee. However, these are really automatic loans on which you'll pay interest.

A Good Balancing Act Keeps The Bounce Out of Your Checkbook!

You may not enjoy this job, but putting it off only makes it harder! Actually, balancing your checkbook is just a matter of adding and subtracting. Here's what you have to work with:

- ☐ the bank statement and the balance it shows
- ☐ your canceled checks and checkbook
- ☐ the balance your stubs or book show

Here's a step-by-step outline of what to do:

Step 1. Arrange all the canceled checks in order, by number or date.

Step 2. Check off the canceled checks against your own stubs.

Step 3. Total up the outstanding checks that show on your stubs (checks written that have not been returned with the statement). Remember to include the fee charged for each of these checks if you have a special checking account.

Step 4. Add up any deposits shown on your stubs that are not shown on the statement. Then add this amount to the final balance shown on the statement.

Step 5. Subtract the total from Step 3 from the total you got as the result of Step 4. The figure you get is your current true balance.

If the current true balance agrees with the balance you show in your checkbook—congratulations! If it's off by a few cents, just correct your balance and forget it. If it's off by a large amount, take the following additional steps:

Step 6. Check off the canceled checks against the debits shown on the statement.

Step 7. Recheck off the canceled checks against your own stubs.
Step 8. Check the deposits shown on the statement against those entered on your check stubs.

This should show you where the error is. If you still can't get the two balances to agree, go back and recheck the figures all the way 'round. We know that this may all sound a bit complicated, but it's really easier than it sounds.

A Quick Rundown On Some Special Types Of Checks

In addition to the standard checks you usually write, there are others available to meet particular circumstances. Just in case you may have to use them, here's a brief description of each:

A certified check is one written on your account that you then take to the bank. The bank establishes the fact that you have enough money in your account to cover the check, sets that amount aside, and guarantees the amount and signature on the check by stamping "certified" on it. A certified check is as good as cash and is usually required for real-estate transactions and the like. It's best to write a certified check out to yourself, then endorse it over to the other party. If the deal falls through, you don't have to cancel the check—just redeposit it in your account.

Cashier's checks are checks issued by the bank and are usually drawn against savings accounts. If you only write a few checks a year, you might use these instead of maintaining a checking account. Some savings banks offer a limited number of them free each month; others make a small charge for them.

Bank money orders are bought from the bank in any amount you want and are made out to any third party you name.

A bank draft is a check drawn by your bank on the account that bank maintains in another city. Bank drafts are made payable to the person you name.

Traveler's checks are designed to provide a safe way of replacing cash in situations where your own personal check might not be accepted. Here's how they work: You buy them in denominations of $10, $20, etc. Each check is numbered and a record is kept of those numbers. You sign the checks when you purchase them. The checks are invalid until they are signed a second time by you in the presence of the person cashing them. If you lose them, you just report the loss and they can be replaced. Usually, you'll have no trouble in getting stores or hotels to accept traveler's checks.

HANDBOOK OF
Credit Do's and Don'ts

"Fly now—pay later!" "Drive it while you pay for it!" "The charge account you open now, you can use before you leave the store!" We're bombarded with offers to borrow and/or buy on credit. If you took the ads and commercials at face value, you'd think the world was peopled with bankers and merchants who, out of the goodness of their hearts, wanted to put extra money or goods in your hands. Unfortunately, this just isn't so. In the midst of all the rosy offers lurks a hard fact. *You always pay for credit!* Nobody, repeat nobody, extends credit without being repaid in some way for the service. A straight interest rate—a carrying charge—an additional markup on the merchandise. One way or another, you'll end up paying more for goods and services bought on credit or via a loan than you would if you paid cash.

Does this mean that you avoid credit like the plague? Not necessarily. In our highly commercial and complicated society, credit is often necessary. Used wisely, it doesn't have to end up as a crushing burden. Nor do those extra charges have to represent a foolish waste of money. What is essential, though, is that you understand what you're doing when you borrow money or buy on credit. You must understand the terms you're being offered, know exactly how much extra you're paying. And above all—you should shop around for credit the same way you do for a "good buy" on sheets and bedding or an automobile.

Unfortunately, many people really don't know how to go about making credit work for them instead of against them. You're just starting out. Your expenses are apt to be heavy. The temptation (or even necessity) to use some of that credit-buying that's being shoved at you is intense. We hope the information in this Handbook will help clue you in on the most important paths to follow—and the pitfalls to avoid. This is a time when you need to squeeze the last bit of buying power out of every dollar. Being smart about credit is a major way to achieve this. So bone up on our do's and don'ts—then put them into practice!

CAN YOU FIND THE HIDDEN CREDIT COSTS?

Loan and credit contracts often use complicated and unfamiliar phrases and it's easy to get lost in the jargon. There are many different types of loan and credit contracts available; they can get confusing. Just to give you an idea of how complicated it can get, we've incorporated in the drawings facing you some of the phrases that you'll hear bandied about when you start to look into this question of loans and credit. For fun, see if you know just what the credit phrases we've shown in these drawings mean. Then read on to find out more about these particular loan and credit situations.

Remember, it's not true that "one is just as good as another" when it comes to choosing these kinds of services. Both loans and credit should be tailored to the situation and your needs as exactly as possible. The way you finance an automobile might be quite different from the way you pay for a new coat, for instance. And the real question is—should you "buy ahead" on semi-luxury "consumables" like clothing at all? If you don't tailor the credit to the type of goods or services you're buying, you can be almost certain of paying more in carrying charges than you have to!

PITFALL #1
Don't think
"credit
isn't like
borrowing."
It is—
and you
pay for
it at the
rate of
12 to 30%!

WHAT IS THIS THING CALLED CREDIT?

All credit is really a form of borrowing. We tend to think of borrowing only in terms of borrowing actual cash. This is one of the pitfalls in buying goods or services on credit. We just don't put it in the same class as going to a bank and negotiating a loan. If we did, we might be more careful about how often, and for what, we took these trips to the credit-well. Make no mistake about it. The retail store that allows you to buy goods "on credit" is actually lending you the money you would otherwise have had to pay for those goods. With some credit-buying (which we'll go into on the next few pages) the store is also "lending" you the merchandise until you have paid off the amount owed. And they can take their property back (all of it) if you miss one payment! Sound horrendous? Some forms of credit-buying are, as you'll soon see. The true annual interest rates allowed by law are surprisingly high, too. With all of this in mind—is there anything *good* about credit? Absolutely.

ON THE BRIGHT SIDE: WHAT CREDIT CAN DO FOR YOU

There are three ways in which buying on credit can be useful. Under some circumstances, these forms of credit can even work to save you money.

You can use the merchandise while you pay for it. For certain kinds of goods and under some conditions, this is a real boon. If the item to be purchased is a "must," it's probably to your advantage to buy this way.

A GOOD USE: You replace a faulty refrigerator with a new one bought on credit. You effect savings on the utility bill, possibly also on food and/or milk. The savings help offset the carrying charges on the loan.

A FOOLISH USE: You treat yourself to a bang-up dinner on your credit card and can't pay within the billing date. The heavy carrying charges on that unpaid balance can really hurt!

As a general rule of thumb: Credit is best used to buy major items, items that will help save money in some way, items that will be around for a while, are necessary and are not "consumables."

You can budget your purchases over a length of time—again, a distinct advantage. If you're faced with a large expenditure and don't have a very healthy emergency fund, one heavy outlay could disrupt your budget for several months. And fractured budgets have a way of never getting back together again.

A GOOD USE: You've been offered a larger sales territory, but need a car to get the job. Buying the car would "total" the emergency fund. Obviously, you finance the car and leave the emergency fund intact as protection against real trouble.

A FOOLISH USE: You charge a group of records you can't afford to pay for now—and figure you'll catch up later on.

Obviously, the secret here is common sense and self-restraint.

You can take advantage of sales and make credit-buying pay off. The fact that you need something, and it's on sale, doesn't always mean that you have the ready cash to buy it with.

A GOOD USE: You need sheets, it's May, and the white sales are on. But the budget's depressed because of that April 15th income tax payment. You charge the sheets and get the savings-advantage of the sale.

A FOOLISH USE: You have plenty of sheets, but can't resist that sale! You rack them up on the charge card and pay heavy interest. Have you really saved anything?

ON THE NEGATIVE SIDE:
WHAT CREDIT CAN DO TO YOU

Just check the little list below to see if easy credit has ever given you any of these financial aches and pains.

OUCH! A high-pressure salesman talked you into that electric organ. And it was so easy to sign that contract.

OUCH! That contract included a hidden service charge!

OUCH! Your credit debts are biting into food and rent money.

Any or all of these ailments are only too possible with credit.

FINDING YOUR WAY TO THE MAJOR SOURCES OF CREDIT

Where	Type of Credit	Interest Rate
Major retail stores	30-day charge accounts.	No interest is charged.
	Budget accounts.	You may pay your bill over a period of 3 to 6 months. Usually, a small interest-charge is added.
	Revolving accounts.	You can charge up to a given amount, and you agree to pay in monthly installments. No interest charged if entire amount is paid when due. A 12 to 18% rate is charged on any unpaid balance.
	Installment-sale credit for major items.	If geared to monthly unpaid balance, can run from 12 to 42% annually.

FINDING YOUR WAY TO THE MAJOR SOURCES OF CREDIT

Where	Type of Credit	Interest Rate
Small retail stores	Charge and credit programs sponsored by banks or other finance organizations.	Usually same terms as revolving accounts (see page 273) or bank charge cards described below.
Credit cards	Travel and entertainment cards.	Annual membership fee. Entire bill must be paid each month.
	Bank charge cards.	Annual interest rate of 12 to 18% on any unpaid balance.
Full-service banks	Personal loans for cars, home improvements, other purposes.	True annual interest rates range from 12 to 16%.
Savings banks	Passbook loans.	A low annual interest rate. Deduct from this the interest the savings account continues to earn.
Insurance companies	Loans made by the company against cash value built up in an insurance policy.	Usually a fairly low annual interest rate. Policies written recently allow for a scaling rate of interest to keep these rates in line with prevailing rates.
Finance companies	These private institutions offer loans based on credit rating or collateral. Because they take bigger risks, their interest rates are higher.	Annual rate can run as high as 33%.
Small-loan companies	These private institutions offer small cash loans at high interest rates.	Rates range up to 42% annually.
Credit unions	These membership groups offer savings-account holders personal loans at relatively low rates.	Rates range from 9 to 12%.

FINDING OUT THE TRUTH
ABOUT INTEREST CHARGES

"Appalling" is the word for many types of interest charges—if you look at them from the consumer's point of view. Here are some examples of how interest is computed on various types of unsecured loans (i.e., loans for which you put up no collateral). Remember that most credit arrangements are really unsecured loans! In general, interest rates vary depending upon state laws, the types of financial institutions involved and the individual's financial condition and ability to pay.

Interest on the unpaid balance. This is the unlovely baby you'll probably be coping with most often if you're dealing with charge cards, retail credit plans or finance companies.

Here's the scale of *true annual simple interest rates* based on three typical monthly rates. These rates vary slightly from store to store, depending upon whether the interest is applied from the day of purchase or after the first payment has been made.

1½% monthly . . . . can work out to 19.56%
2% monthly . . . . can work out to 26.8%
2½% monthly . . . . can work out to 34.49%

You arrive at these staggering figures because the interest you're paying monthly is actually being compounded twelve times, because there are twelve months in a year.

To dope out what a true annual interest rate is, read the next item on our list!

PITFALL #2
interest
that's
compounded
monthly.

Discounted interest. Here, the lender will deduct the interest from the principal before you receive the loan and you will repay in installments. The kicker: You're charged interest on the full amount of the loan, not on the amount you actually receive. For instance: If you borrow $300 at a quoted rate of 6½%, to be repaid in twelve monthly installments, the bank will deduct $19.50 (which represents 6½% of $300) immediately. You get $280.50—but you will repay at the rate of $300 divided by 12. That's $25 monthly. Now, to figure out what interest rate you're actually paying by-the-year: Deduct $25 from $280.50, which leaves $255.50. Now deduct $25 from $255.50. Continue this process, of deducting $25 from the previous total, twelve times. (You'll end up with $5.50 as a final figure.) Now add up all twelve figures (from $280.50 down to $5.50) and divide by 12. You'll get $143.00, the actual amount of money that you'll

PITFALL #3
interest
that's
deducted
from the
principal.

have effective use of throughout the year. And if you divide $143.00 into $19.50, you'll arrive at the annual interest rate you're really paying—13.64%! The Truth in Lending Laws require that the true annual interest rates be quoted.

Monthly repayment. This works the same way as an "interest on unpaid balance" loan except that you are usually repaying in equal monthly installments.

Add-on interest is often used by banks. Here, the add-on interest rate is added to your principal and you pay interest on the whole amount. On $300 at 7% interest, $21 is added to the principal—so you repay at the rate of $321 divided by 12, which works out to an actual 14%.

SOME DEEP PITFALLS TO WATCH OUT FOR IN INSTALLMENT BUYING

Keep an eagle eye out for these in any installment credit contract you sign:

Wage assignment. This gives your creditor the power to garnishee your salary if you miss an installment payment. Legally, it obliges your employer to withhold part of your salary until the debt is paid off.

Acceleration clauses. Here, all installment payments are immediately due and payable if you default on one payment, whatever the reason. If you can't pay the total unpaid balance, the merchandise is repossessed—but even this may not absolve you from future liability. This is what we meant when we talked, earlier, about merchandise being "lent" to you until the total cost is paid off. You don't actually own the item until you've made all the payments.

HOW DO YOU ESTABLISH A GOOD CREDIT RATING?

The old joke used to go this way: You can't get a credit rating unless you borrow money. And it's true! If you live a completely cash-and-carry life, without even the use of a checking account, you won't establish any rating. And no credit rating is almost as crippling as a bad credit standing. Fortunately—or unfortunately, in our credit-oriented society— it's usually not necessary to go to the lengths of taking out a loan you don't really need and repaying it promptly in order to establish a desirable credit profile.

Even the monthly rent you pay is a form of credit—actually, the full amount is due on signing the lease, but under the terms of the lease, the landlord agrees to accept the full amount in a series of installment payments called rent.

Here are some concrete steps you can take, in the normal course of your life, to help establish a good credit rating:

☐ Pay your rent promptly—remember, it's a form of credit!

☐ Don't job-hop; most loan or credit institutions require that you be in one job for at least a year before you're eligible for credit.

☐ Keep up your department store charge accounts.

☐ Don't overdraw your checking account.

☐ Don't get over-extended on credit—most banks advise that your credit commitments should not exceed 15 to 20% of your net income.

☐ If you run into temporary trouble in meeting bills, notify your creditors that you'll be late—but you will pay. Or make a partial payment with an accompanying explanation. This lets them know you haven't "run out!"

SOME REALLY VITAL DO'S AND DON'TS OF CREDIT

When you're figuring out credit possibilities, remember that some alternatives are tougher than others. These credit hints should steer you away from the worst binds and, we hope, point out the easier paths to follow.

Figure out what credit is costing you. We've given you definitions of most of the credit jargon you'll run into. We've also shown you how some of the most common kinds of credit arrangements really work—what the hidden costs are. Use the information. Ask what kind of credit arrangement you're getting into. Figure out the actual rate of interest.

Play the percentages. Recognize the fact that some kinds of credit arrangements work better for one kind of purchase than another. Example: The same item costs slightly more at store A than at store B, but store A offers regular monthly charge accounts and store B only revolving credit accounts. It might make sense to charge the item, at the slightly higher price, at store A because it will cost you less in carrying charges to charge it there. And the difference in credit costs may more than make up for the difference in the price of the item.

Never borrow more than you need. You're paying for every dollar and if it's there, it's likely you'll spend it!

Don't sign anything you haven't read or don't understand. Take your time reading through material; ask questions. If the salesman gets impatient or can't answer your questions, forget that store. There's always another credit deal available.

Don't multiply charge cards. There's a thriving black market business in stolen credit cards. The more of them you have the easier it is to lose—and use—them. Always report a loss immediately, by phone, and follow up with a report in writing sent via registered special delivery mail. Such notification clears you of responsibility if the card is ever used illegally.

Keep tabs on your credit rating. If you're turned down for credit, go to the central credit bureau in your city, ask to see your file, and find out what the problem is. Insert explanations for any information in your file you feel is incorrect or inaccurate.

Understand to whom you owe your money. In some cases, a retail store may "sell" its bills to a collection agency. This is called "factoring." The danger to you? The finance company has no obligation to you for the quality or performance of the merchandise. And the retailer couldn't care less because he's already collected his money from the finance company. You're out of luck if you have any problems with the merchandise.

Remember: Credit is rather like an automobile. There's nothing intrinsically bad about either. Both exist to be used. If the car is driven wisely and safely, there is small risk involved and the car adds much to the comfort of daily living. The same is true of credit. When used intelligently and knowledgeably, credit can be a boon—otherwise, it can spell "broke!"

MAKING SURE WITH INSURANCE: IT'S A MATTER OF POLICY

Insurance that is wisely chosen provides invaluable protection against sudden loss of income, heavy medical and hospital bills, lawsuits. But don't kid yourself. Being able to separate the bona fide from the ballyhoo is essential in the whole area of insurance. A good agent is your best hedge against ending up with policies that don't do what they claim to or that don't really fill your particular needs. You'll find some tips on how to choose an agent on page 285 of this chapter. But first, let's take a look at the field in general.

For Complete Protection: Follow This P*A*T*H

Here's an easy way to remember the basic types of insurance most people should carry—just think of the word *path*. It stands for:

Personal insurance
Automobile insurance
Tenant's or homeowner's insurance
Health insurance

There's a wide variety of policies available within each of these categories—and some pitfalls connected with each, too. There's no question, however, about the importance of being covered in all these basic areas. We won't try to play agent. No one, including yourself, should try that game. But we will give you the kind of rundown that will help you understand what each kind of insurance can do for you—and what it can't.

Personal Insurance

For those who depend on you—financial security in case of your death. That's the primary purpose of personal, or life, insurance. That's what you want to be able to depend upon. In terms of "fringe benefits," it may also build up funds toward retirement or other goals and provide a cash reserve from which you can borrow. Personal finance experts, however, advise that you plan your life insurance policies to meet that primary goal and pay less attention to the fringe-benefit features, which are desirable but not really essential.

Basically, here's what you're doing when you take on any life insurance policy:

You agree to pay the insurance company a certain amount of money regularly. } **the premium**

The company agrees to pay back a lump sum in one of two ways: } **the face value**

In case of your death, they pay the lump sum to someone whom you name in the policy; } **the beneficiary**

Or they will repay the lump sum at some specified future date. } **the maturity date**

In addition to knowing what the terms "premium," "face value," "beneficiary" and "maturity date" mean, there are two other phrases you should know about because we'll be referring to them further on.

A NONPARTICIPATING POLICY is a policy on which you receive no dividends. The premiums cover the projected cost of the protection offered. They also pay the "handling costs" of the policy and provide a profit for the company.

A PARTICIPATING POLICY is one in which the company builds a "cushion" into the premiums—i.e., the premiums come to slightly more than the cost of the protection offered, plus handling costs. Usually, the policyholder receives a partial refund of these over-charges in the form of dividends paid after the first one or two years.

Most insurance policies fall within one of three broad categories that we'll describe—although there's a wide range of options available within each of the three. If you understand what the basic types are, however, you'll be surer of choosing the type (or combination of types) that will provide dependable protection for your own situation.

What are the three types of life insurance policies available?

A basic rule: policies with cash value cost more. Each of the three types of policies offers death protection. Some, however, also build up a cash value, which means you get money back if you give up the policy. The premiums are higher for this type of policy. And the faster the cash value builds up the higher the premium will be. Actually, you're buying a partial savings plan—but you're getting less death protection for each dollar you spend. Now for some details on the three basic types of policies available.

Term policies

Term insurance: lower premium outlay initially, no cash value. Here, you're buying pure death protection. You buy this protection for a specific period of time—usually from five to fifty years. If you die within that period, your beneficiary collects. You get nothing back when the policy expires. The premium on the policy remains the same throughout the life of the policy. At the end of the term, you can renew the policy at a higher premium. One comedian described term insurance as a gamble between you and the insurance company. If you live out the term—they win. If you die before the term expires—you win!

THE ADVANTAGES: In the early years, it offers the maximum amount of death protection for a minimum outlay of premium. It can be tailored to fit changing family situations. During the early years of raising your family, you can carry heavier amounts of term insurance. As your income increases, your children grow older, and your other forms of savings and retirement plans increase, you can decrease the amount of term you carry.

Term vs. ordinary life insurance: a comparison. An ordinary life insurance policy is designed to level out your premium rate over a period of years. Your premium doesn't increase in relation to a decreasing life expectancy. The premiums on a term insurance policy, on the other hand, do increase as your life expectancy decreases. So, while term is less costly initially—the premiums on a $20,000 policy for a twenty-five-year-old man run approximately 17% less for nonparticipating term than for ordinary life—the term becomes more and more costly in relation to the ordinary life policy the longer you hold both. A good agent can help you work out an insurance plan that's completely geared to your own needs, income and estimated investment potential.

Ordinary life insurance: higher premiums initially, growing cash value. This type of policy is sometimes referred to as a whole or straight life insurance policy. This type not only pays the face value in case of your death, but also builds cash values. Every year you hold the policy means an increase in the amount you are guaranteed to get back should you cash it in. The cash value is stated in your contract. You can also borrow this amount from the policy at fairly low interest rates—interest rates the insurance company guarantees. If you borrow against the policy and die before the loan is paid back, the outstanding amount is deducted from the face value. The premium remains the same throughout your lifetime. In effect, you can carry a policy like this for as long as you need maximum protection. When your needs change, you can cash it in or replace it with a policy for a lesser amount, and get back the cash value that has built up. You won't get back all of what you've put in, but that's the price you're paying for the death protection it offers. To put it in that comedian's terms: You're hedging your bet with the insurance company via those cash values. You're also hedging your bet in terms of your insurability. Certain physical conditions that may develop can bar you from getting insurance. With a straight life policy, you're insured for as long as you choose to maintain the policy.

THE ADVANTAGES: It can provide lifetime protection, even if you develop a physical condition that would otherwise make you uninsurable. It's also a form of enforced saving. If you're not a

Ordinary life policies

"saver" by nature, that higher premium may be worth the additional security you gain.

Endowment policies

Endowments: highest premiums, primarily a savings plan. These savings policies are written for a specific period of time—usually twenty or thirty years—or to a certain age (for instance, sixty-five). Premiums are divided into equal payments, paid over this period of time. If you die within that period, your beneficiary gets the full face value. If you live to its end, you get it. The premiums are very high because the cash value quickly builds to almost 100% of the face, or protection, part of the policy. The cash value of ordinary life insurance usually builds only to 60%. The higher premium is what builds this cash value.

THE ADVANTAGES: An endowment policy can be a useful way of saving for retirement, a second home, children's college education or any other long-range goal. But these policies are really valuable only if you're reasonably sure you wouldn't be saving that same amount in some other way that yields a higher rate of interest.

As we mentioned earlier, there are a number of variations within the three categories of term, ordinary life and endowment insurance. Here's a quick glance at some of the most common:

Group insurance

Group insurance: lowest-cost protection available. You buy this insurance through your job, fraternal organization, labor union or other group. Often, your employer or the group pays all or part of the premium. Basically, it's term insurance—bought on a yearly basis and renewed from year to year for the time you're associated with the group. It's the cheapest insurance you can get. If you can buy extra coverage at your employer's group rates, grab it! You'll be much better off than if you buy term insurance on your own.

Level nonrenewable

Level nonrenewable term: fixed premiums, not renewable. It's usually written for a term of five to fifty years. While not renewable, you can usually convert it to another type of policy at the end of the term.

Level renewable

Level renewable term: renewable without a medical exam. You'll pay fixed premiums for the five- to fifty-year term it's written for. And you'll pay a higher premium when you renew it—but at least it is renewable, even if you've developed an "uninsurable" medical condition in the interim.

Family income plans

Family income plans: combinations of term and ordinary life. These are designed to give your family an income during the years when it most needs income protection. The amount of term insurance in the package gradually decreases as your children grow older and are less dependent on the insurance you'll leave behind should you die. The ordinary life part of the package remains in effect unless you terminate it.

Modified whole life: term insurance that converts to whole life. This starts out as low-cost term, then automatically converts to ordinary life (with higher premiums). It's often bought by doctors and other professionals who have a small income at the beginning of their careers or while they're still training. They're sure, however, of higher earnings later on and are willing to pay the higher whole life premium in order to build cash value into their policies.

Modified whole life

Limited payment life: builds cash value faster than ordinary life insurance. The premiums are paid up over a specified number of years, usually twenty to thirty, or to a specific age, usually sixty-five. The premiums are higher than those for ordinary life. It's most useful for people who are going to have a peak income for a relatively few years.

Limited payment life

Buying Insurance: How Soon And How Much

Years ago, people believed that everybody should be insured for enough to cover burial costs. Sounds a bit gruesome, but it's essentially true—particularly in these days of rising funeral costs! If you have no dependents, a low-cost term insurance policy for a few thousand dollars is really part of being a responsible citizen. There are reasons for taking on more comprehensive insurance coverage at this stage, but they are mainly precautionary.

If you have no dependents

☐ A policy that guarantees your insurability at a later date is a good idea. Diabetes, heart disease or another medical condition just might make you uninsurable in later life!

☐ If you're not good at other forms of saving, an ordinary life policy will guarantee you some cash return later on. The lower premium you'll pay now, however, will probably be offset by the additional years you'll be paying it, so there's no great advantage to "buying young."

If you have anyone in the family who depends mainly on you for support—elderly parents or children, for instance—then you definitely need insurance. Ideally, you should buy an amount that will cover any funeral or other expenses and that will provide an adequate life-style (in today's inflated economy) for your dependents for as long as they need financial help. Given these circumstances, you really should have the help of a trained insurance agent. He'll work out the best plan for *your* needs and *your* income.

If you have dependents

EXTRA FEATURES: EACH TYPE OF POLICY INCLUDES SOME OR ALL OF THESE

Feature	Description	Advantages and/or Disadvantages
Double indemnity	The company pays double the face value of the policy if you die of accidental causes rather than of natural causes.	Costs little, but some experts question how helpful it really is. If you need the extra face value it provides, why not buy that much insurance to begin with? If you don't, why pay for it?
Nonforfeiture values	These are the *payback benefits* that an insurance company guarantees to give you even if you discontinue a permanent policy.	You have a choice of three possible benefits: 1) taking the cash value in cash or as income; 2) taking a paid-up permanent policy for less than the original face value; 3) taking extended term insurance for as long a period as the net cash value of the original policy will buy.
Waiver of premium for disability	The company forgoes its rights to premiums if you are disabled and cannot pay them.	The policy continues in effect even though you cannot pay the premiums.
Guaranteed insurability	The company will sell you a second policy in addition to the original contract, for any amount up to the face value of the original policy, without a medical exam.	You can get additional insurance even if you develop a medical condition which might otherwise mean that you were uninsurable.
Convertibility	You can change the policy to another type without a medical exam.	You can adjust insurance to your family's current needs even if you have a medical condition.
Automatic premium loan	The company automatically lends you the price of the premium, at a guaranteed rate of interest, if you can't pay the premium.	You are able to continue the policy even though you can't pay the premium. You can repay the loan at a later date.
Grace period	You can delay paying the premium for a certain period, usually 31 days, after it becomes due.	You are able to continue the policy even if you're temporarily "strapped."

What's An Insurance Agent And How Do You Find One?

Agents are sales representatives of insurance companies. They work on a commission basis, the commission being paid on each policy they sell. A competent agent can be invaluable in helping you work out an insurance plan that will grow with your needs.

In choosing an agent, there are two factors to consider: the reputation of the insurance company he represents and his own reputation as a capable underwriter. Start by checking out both—with your local Better Business Bureau and/or your state's insurance commissioner. It's also wise to check with parents, friends of parents or even with your own employer. They may be able to recommend an agent they have dealt with or know of.

It's also a good idea to choose an agent who's been in business for a while. This is a good indication that he has satisfied his clients. Don't choose an underwriter just because he's a relative or a classmate—check out his qualifications.

Two Special-Situation "Buys" In Insurance

If you've served in the armed forces, you may be eligible for low-cost GI Life Insurance. Contact your nearest Veterans Administration office for details.

If you live in New York, Connecticut or Massachusetts, you can buy your insurance at savings banks. The cost is lower than if you bought the same type of policy through an agent.

Automobile Insurance: The Whats, Hows And Whys

Some states—New York, Massachusetts and North Carolina, for instance—require car owners to be insured. Even if you live in a state where insurance is not required, however, we strongly urge you to carry at least a minimum-liability policy. Auto insurance is the best and surest way of avoiding problems that can arise from an accident or lawsuit.

How are the rates set? How do you get the best "buy"? Insurance companies base their rates on your age, marital status, driving record, type of car and how you use it, and on the area in which you live. Younger drivers and drivers who use their cars for work traditionally pay a higher rate than others. Here are some things to look for to help you get the best possible rate:

☐ A company that offers lower rates for younger drivers. Some companies are beginning to advertise these special "younger drivers" plans.

☐ Discounts to drivers who have had no accidents in the past five years, who have taken accredited driver-education courses, or who have a good scholastic record.

☐ Auto clubs in your area that may offer lower rates.

It pays to comparison shop for auto insurance, *but*—don't overlook the insurance company's reputation for paying claims promptly and fairly. Ask other drivers what their experiences have been with the various companies. A low rate won't mean a thing if every claim is a hassle! Also, make sure you know exactly what coverage you're paying for. The chart we've included below will give you an idea of the types of coverage available. Read it through and you'll be better equipped to compare one company's offer with another's. This is particularly important in the case of auto insurance "packages." Another thrift note: It usually costs you a little less if you pay your insurance premium in one lump sum each year. There are multi-payment plans available, but there's usually a slight carrying charge for them.

AUTO INSURANCE POLICIES: WHAT THEY COVER

Type of Coverage	Description
Bodily-injury liability	Referred to in two-number groups, such as 10/20, 25/50, or 100/300. The first number is the maximum amount (in thousands of dollars) the company will pay any one person involved in an accident. The second number is the maximum total amount (in thousands of dollars) the company will pay out to all the people involved in the same accident.
Property-damage liability	Covers damage to other cars, houses, buildings, telephone poles—any property except your own car.
Medical payments	Covers medical expenses for you and your passengers, no matter who is at fault in the accident.
Protection against uninsured motorists	Protects you and your passengers if you're hit by a motorist who cannot pay damages or by a hit-and-run driver.
Comprehensive physical damage	Includes fire, theft, flood, vandalism, hitting an animal—just about anything that could happen to your car except hitting another car.
Collision	Covers your car if it hits or is hit by another car or object. Comes with a deductible amount which varies according to the policy you choose. Typically, you pay the first $25, $50, $100 or $250 in damages.

No-fault insurance. Some states have enacted "no-fault" laws to guarantee speedy and fair settlements of auto accident claims. Under no-fault laws, the insuring company automatically covers medical expenses and lost income (up to a specified maximum) for any people injured in the accident. This eliminates the need for lawsuits to establish "whose fault" the accident was before settlement can be made.

Tenant's And Homeowner's Insurance: The Whats, Hows And Whys

You're not an art collector and you don't own any antiques! Why do you need tenant's or homeowner's insurance? Think about it. What would it cost you to replace all your clothes, books, records and other property? You're right—homeowner's insurance is a good thing to have.

Inventory before you invest. To figure out how much coverage you need, make a list of all your possessions, estimate what they cost, and file away any sales receipts or other data you used in arriving at the estimates. It's also a good idea to take some photos of each room in your home and file them away, too, as extra proof in case you ever have to file a claim. Don't underinsure yourself; a total loss is always possible. In fact, many companies insist that you insure at least 80% of the actual value. There's no point in overinsuring, either, because the company will pay only what the property is actually worth—not an inflated estimate.

Factors that affect the rate you pay. Where you live, the amount of coverage you buy, and the deductible amount—these all affect your rate. Non-fireproof buildings, high-crime areas, high-cost-of-living areas—these will bump your rate, too. For instance: In major cities in the Northeast, $10,000 worth of coverage might cost you over $100 per year. The same coverage would cost considerably less in southern cities. In some high-crime areas in large cities, you might have trouble getting theft insurance if you both work. The federal government now has an arrangement whereby one large company in each area will give theft insurance to anyone who agrees to put in certain security precautions—special locks and/or a "peephole" on the front door, for instance. Twenty-one states also have a FAIR (Fair Access to Insurance Requirements) plan in effect. This assures fire insurance to anyone who wants it and lives in an insurable building. Any knowledgeable insurance agent, or your state's insurance commissioner, can tell you how to obtain insurance coverage through these plans.

If you own expensive jewelry, paintings, antiques or other valuable collections, you'll need supplements, or riders, on any policy you buy. Special items like these should be appraised professionally and insured separately.

Insurance companies offer special policies for people who rent apartments. They're package policies that cover a range of different types of insurance. The chart immediately following shows

If you
rent an
apartment:
See page 288.

you what you get if you decide on this kind of arrangement. Again, a reminder: Dealing with a reputable insurance company through a competent agent is additional insurance—that your dollar will buy the best coverage and that claims will be fairly and promptly settled.

TENANT'S PACKAGE POLICIES: WHAT THEY COVER

Type of Coverage	Description
Fire and theft	Protection against loss due to fire, theft, vandalism, lightning and other perils. The policy carries a specified deductible amount. You're paid the current market value of your property, less the deductible. The higher the deductible the lower the premium. An added clause will protect your property away from home.
Liability	If someone trips on your rug or gets hit on the head by something you drop out a window, this pays for damages awarded them.
Medical payments	Situation: A friend trips and falls in your home. He doesn't want to sue, it isn't clear who's at fault, but you feel morally obligated to pay his medical bills. This policy pays actual medical costs no matter who's at fault.

Health Insurance: Immunizes Your Income Against Soaring Medical Costs

This isn't a maybe—it's a must! One uninsured illness can throw a family into lifelong debt. It's so important that most employers, especially large companies, offer you some kind of group health insurance. Some employers pay the total cost—more often, though, an employer will freight part of the premiums. This group insurance is the lowest-cost health protection you can get. Take all the extra options and benefits your group plan offers even if you have to pay for them yourself. They'll cost you much less than if you bought them individually. For couples: If only one of you has group insurance, you can usually switch the policy to a family plan that will cover both of you and may include maternity benefits. This is cheaper than one of you buying a second policy. If you both have group health insurance, keep both policies if one or both are free. It pays to be grabby here! Otherwise, compare policies; keep the one with the most comprehensive coverage.

Blue Cross/Blue Shield: your next-best buy if no group health insurance is available to you. They're government regulated and nonprofit, so they can offer lower premiums than most private plans. Here again, buy the most comprehensive policy you can!

ADVICE FOR COUPLES
Keep all company-paid policies.

Switch an individual policy to a family plan.

Compare policies and keep the better one.

Beware! The mail-order insurance plan—it rarely offers even minimal coverage, much less anything spectacular. Let's analyze a few of those great-sounding claims.

The Claim	The Reality
Up to $250 per week or $600 to $1,000 per month	This averages out to roughly $20 to $35 per day for hospital expenses—yet $80 to $100 per day (and up) is the room-rate in many hospitals!
	Doctors' fees, drugs and other expenses aren't covered.
Tax-free	Almost all health insurance payments are tax-free. But check the premiums. For most other health plans, they're deductible—for mail-order plans, *they're not!*
No medical exam	This appeals to older people, who tend to have more medical problems. As a younger insurer, this makes your premiums higher because you're sharing the risk of insuring the others.
	The big loophole: You don't collect benefits for the first two years of a policy for a pre-existing condition such as heart trouble—even if you didn't know you had it at the time. Mail-order insurance companies use this loophole to the fullest, have a high rate of claim rejections.
Up to $50,000	Most don't start paying benefits until after the fifth day in the hospital. The average hospital stay is about a week. To reach the maximum, you'd have to stay in the hospital for years at a stretch, and this just doesn't happen!

Check the following chart to get an idea of the major types of protection that health plans offer.

**HEALTH INSURANCE PLANS:
THE MAJOR TYPES OF PROTECTION**

Type of Coverage	Description
Hospitali-zation	Benefits may meet all, or part of, hospital costs up to a maximum number of days in the hospital.
Cash indemnity policies	Pay specific amounts for specific illnesses—so much per day for hospital room and a maximum for all other hospital and doctor bills. No time limit is set.
Surgical	Payments are made according to a set scale in the contract. If your surgeon charges more, you pay the difference. Some policies will cover preoperative and postoperative visits to the surgeon's office.

HEALTH INSURANCE PLANS:
THE MAJOR TYPES OF PROTECTION

Type of Coverage	Description
Service-benefit contracts	Pay the entire basic cost of hospital room for a specified length of time, plus most in-hospital expenses.
General medical	Covers some nonsurgical costs: doctors' visits to home or hospital; patient's visits to doctor's office. Benefits vary widely.
Major medical	Designed as protection against long illnesses or serious accidents. Most carry a deductible amount of from $50 to $1,000. The company guarantees to pay a certain percentage of all costs above that amount. The deductible can be applicable per year or per illness. The higher the deductible the lower the premium.
Income protection	Called loss-of-income, accident-and-sickness indemnity, or disability policies. They pay weekly or monthly cash benefits while you're not working because of illness or accident. There is usually a waiting period before payments begin. The longer this "elimination" period the lower the premium.
Comprehensive	Package policies that combine basic coverage and major medical. Usually cheaper than two separate policies because the major medical is tailored to cover a percentage of the costs above those covered by the basic hospitalization part of the policy. There's no overlapping coverage.
Dental insurance	A relatively new development, usually available only as a group plan. Sometimes it's entirely paid for by the employer. If you pay for it yourself, premiums might amount to almost what your yearly dental bills would be, so it's more of a savings-toward-dental-care than insurance. Nevertheless, it does mean your payments are spaced out evenly over the year.
Prepaid group practice plan	In effect, you divide up a year's average medical costs into a series of regular premium payments. This entitles you to use the services of the doctors and hospitals that are part of the plan. Useful for families with small children, who may run into a year of almost constant "ailments."

TAXES: THEY'RE A YEARLY EVENT—
SO LEARN TO LIVE WITH THEM!

The single most important point to remember about taxes is that they must be paid. The corollary to this is: Always figure your income *after* taxes when you plan out your year's spending. Most working people come under the withholding tax system. Your employer withholds a certain percentage of each paycheck and turns it over to the federal government for you. Some states also have a withholding system for state income taxes.

Filling out tax forms: the long and the short. It's really not as mysterious as it seems. If you have no unusual deductions and the main portion of your income is earned salary, you can probably fill out your own return. Use the instruction booklet included with the tax form. Have any questions? Check your nearest Internal Revenue Service office for personal advice and/or helpful information booklets. Or buy one of the many tax workbooks that are on the market.

USE THE SHORT FORM 1040A—if your income is under a specified amount, if all but $200 of it was reported on your W-2 (withholding) form, and if you take the standard deductions.
USE THE LONG FORM 1040—if your income is higher than the amount specified for form 1040A, if you have sources of income that are not subject to withholding, or if you prefer to itemize your deductions rather than accept the standard amounts.

Separately or jointly: how should you file? If you're married and both earn about the same salary, it usually pays to file a joint return. Many experts suggest filing a joint return. There are certain tax benefits available on a joint return that usually make it advantageous to do so. If your incomes differ widely or if one has unusually large medical or other deductions, you just might come out ahead by filing separately. The only way to find out is to estimate both totals with an actual tax return or consult a tax expert.

Keep those records—and keep them straight! There's nothing more frustrating than sitting down to figure taxes and finding that you have only a hit-and-miss record of what you've spent or of what you've taken in. You can use a safe-deposit box for important records. Or treat yourself to an accordion file folder as an in-home filing system. File checks, bills and dividend receipts by the month or under separate categories like "medical," "interest payments," "contributions."

Note: If you have any income in addition to salary (from investments, savings accounts, free-lance work), it's particularly important to keep track of it. Failing to report additional income is a serious offense. Another point: If your return is ever audited, you may have to produce the actual bills to prove expenditures. The Internal Revenue Service may not accept canceled checks alone as proof of expenses. Use the checklist on page 292 to help you in setting up your filing system of "save for tax time" items.

CHECKLIST: THE ITEMS YOU OR YOUR ACCOUNTANT NEED TO FIGURE TAXES ACCURATELY

☐ the actual bills for all deductible items
☐ receipts for cash expenditures and contributions
☐ record of earned income
☐ record of additional income (dividends, interest on savings, extra earnings)
☐ record of stock or bond sales (when you bought it, what you paid for it, when you sold it, the profit or loss involved)
☐ record of taxes paid (federal, state, city, sales tax)
☐ record of losses due to theft or casualty
☐ record of alimony or child support payments

Want help with your taxes? Here's what's available. As we've already mentioned, the IRS will provide free tax advice in the form of personal help or informative pamphlets. If you just want to get the whole thing off your mind, however, there are three routes you can take.

A PERSONAL TAX ACCOUNTANT. He should be a CPA with a record of having been in business for a while. You can work out a variety of ways to use his services. These range from the once-a-year visit (when you bring him your records and discuss your return, and he makes it out and files it) to a complete accounting service, under which he keeps your records and makes out any returns that are due. The more frequently he reviews your records in any one year the higher his fee will be.

THE STORE-FRONT CHAINS. These are opening all over the country. Generally, they offer useful help and will guarantee to pay for any mistakes in figures that are their fault. They'll also go down to the IRS with you to explain your return if it's questioned. Always get this guarantee in writing, however!

LOCAL BANKS. They're beginning to offer computer-run tax services; they offer guarantees similar to those offered by the store-front chains.

Caution: Beware of free-lance tax-return helpers who are not qualified and who may have disappeared if you ever find you need their help in explaining a return or checking back on figures. The IRS tends to turn a very deaf ear to sob stories of any kind. And fines for late or incorrect returns can really hurt!

INVESTMENTS: A BRIEF PORTFOLIO OF PLANS, PRECAUTIONS AND BASIC TERMS

The wisest words ever uttered about the investment market: Never put in money you can't afford to lose. There's just no such thing as an absolutely surefire investment. For every fortune made in real estate, land, commodities, stocks or bonds, there's been a fortune lost. Money you invest will never be as safe or easily accessible as it would be in a savings account. On the other hand, money sensibly invested acts as a hedge against inflation and can yield a higher rate of return than interest on savings. Those who don't try to "make a killing," but rather are satisfied with small but steady gains and a reasonable rate of return, can find the investment world a satisfactory venture.

At What Point Are You Ready To Invest?

Before you even think about investments, there are two basic obligations you should have fulfilled.

☐ AN ADEQUATE AMOUNT OF SAVINGS. This is usually defined as having an amount equal to three to six months' salary in the bank.
☐ AN INSURANCE PLAN that will provide adequately for any dependents you may have.

When these provisions are met, you can feel comfortable about investing any extra cash you may accumulate.

How Do You Go About It? Where Do You Start?

You wouldn't put a canoe into a river without some idea of where you were headed and what kind of conditions lay ahead—rocks, rapids, waterfalls. You'd check a map—maybe even take an experienced hand with you. The same is true of the investment trip.

Learn the route! Research any investment area you're considering. Some of the more common investment fields include Certificates of Deposit (or CD's), bank paper, treasury bills, treasury notes, stocks and bonds. Your bank is a good source of information about all these areas. In the case of stocks or bonds, however, here are some additional steps you can take. Get annual reports of companies you're interested in. Check the market quotations listed in your newspaper. If there's an investment seminar being given in your area, sign up for it!

Consult qualified professionals! Choose a recommended broker —one who works for a respected brokerage house or who comes well recommended by friends. Even the professionals can't guarantee that you'll make money—but they can save you from making stupid mistakes. Most competent brokers will lean toward the conservative side in their advice. Steer clear of any deal that isn't funded and handled by established sources. This is your best protection against buying "pie in the sky" certificates that may turn out to be totally worthless. Cast a wary eye, too, on investments that offer an unusually high rate of return. Usually, the higher the return the greater the risk.

Some Investment Plans That Are Useful For The Small Investor

If you're interested in the stock market, there are several investment programs that you might find useful.

Monthly investment programs like the Monthly Investment Plan offered by the New York Stock Exchange let you choose the stocks you want to buy and invest in them on a regular basis. Here, you can invest small, specific amounts—as little as $40 per quarter.

Mutual funds offer another route for the small investor. These funds are investment companies that purchase many different stocks. You, in turn, buy into the company. The advantage? You attain more diversified investments than you could hope to achieve on your own. There are two types of mutuals sold. Always know which type you're investing in.

A NO-LOAD MUTUAL FUND charges an investment advisory fee but no brokerage fee. You buy shares *net* from the fund and sell them *net*. A few have a redemption fee.

A LOAD MUTUAL FUND, on the other hand, charges a fee (usually about 8½%) that includes a salesman's or broker's commission. A front end load payment means that you pay the entire amount due at the time you invest. With this type of fund, be sure you plan to continue in the fund long enough to make the initial payment worthwhile.

Mutual funds also offer monthly plans, in which you invest small amounts each month over a period of years. Many mutual funds exist. Look over annual reports and earnings records of several funds and know what each one's major goals are before you invest in one.

Traditionally, the funds are considered to be conservative investments. They don't move up or down as rapidly as more speculative stocks do. However, keep this in mind: There's no guarantee even with a mutual. Be sure to check the record of the fund you're doing business with. And remember that your rate of return tends to be lower with a mutual than on other forms of stock investment. You're trading a possible higher return for the additional safety mutuals offer.

Investment Lingo: Some Basic Terms

Here's a small glossary of stock market terms you're apt to run across when you're reading up on stocks and bonds.

Common stock. Holders of common stock are entitled to share in the net profits of the corporation in which they are shareholders to the extent that the board of directors distributes such profits in the form of dividends. Common stock holders' rights to dividends come after those of the holders of preferred shares.

Preferred stock. Holders of preferred stock are entitled to share in the net profits of the corporation in which they are shareholders to the extent specified in their shares, and are generally entitled to receive their dividends before the holders of common stock.

Note: The percentage of dividends paid on preferred stock *is* specified and cannot exceed that amount regardless of how well the corporation does. There are no limits on the amount of dividends that can be paid on common stock—it's simply a question of how well the corporation does in any one year.

Bonds are certificates of indebtedness. A company has borrowed money from you, agrees to pay interest, and is obligated to pay . back your investment. They're similar to a savings investment, but the price of bonds fluctuates—both up and down. You can make an additional gain if your bonds go up.

Dividend—the share of earnings paid out on common and preferred stocks.

A growth stock is one that has had an outstanding record of increased earnings—perhaps 10 to 15% a year—and there is reason to believe it will continue to go up at this same rate.

Par value is the price at which the stock is carried on the company's books as opposed to the actual value (the price it commands in the open market).

It's a good idea to have separate wills (see page 296).

YOUR WILL: HAVING ONE CAN CUT INHERITANCE COSTS AND COMPLICATIONS

Wills are one of the most unpopular topics of conversation around. Yet they're necessary and useful instruments. Having a will provides three major advantages.

It makes sure that you determine how your estate will be distributed (rather than the state doing so).

If you have children who are minors, it gives you the opportunity of naming a guardian. Without a will, this decision can be made by the court, in a purely impersonal way.

You can make your own choice of executor, guardian, trustee and lawyer—and make your own arrangements with them as to how they'll be reimbursed for time spent working on your estate. If you die without a will, the fees paid to court-appointed functionaries may be higher than fees you arranged for yourself.

It's advisable for a husband and wife to have separate wills. Otherwise, there may be a question as to "who owned what" in the event of one partner's death. Or there may be a question of "intent" if both die at the same time.

Lawyers are an invaluable help in drawing up even the simplest will. They are familiar with the state and federal laws governing inheritances and inheritance taxes, and can save you from making costly mistakes. The fee for drawing a simple will is usually not exorbitant and is well worth the security it provides. A good lawyer will also be able to advise you on ways to distribute part of your estate before your death so that your heirs pay as little as possible in the way of inheritance taxes.

THE FAMILY LAWYER: THE VALUE OF HAVING ONE

It's a wise idea to choose a "family lawyer" early in life. Make sure you choose someone competent whom you get along with and trust.

How to choose your lawyer? Here, the advice is very much the same as that we gave you for choosing an insurance agent. Consult your family and/or family friends—their advice can be useful. Another approach is to consult the firm you work for or your local bank. Either may be able to suggest a lawyer or law firm with whom they have had dealings. The state bar association might also be helpful. A personal recommendation from someone whose judgment you respect is the safest course.

6 Cooking Like an Expert: From the Start

6 Cooking Like an Expert: From the Start

YOU CAN'T LIVE ON LOVE

FOOD FACTS AND FADS

"THE FIFTH DIMENSION"

A MOMENT ON THE LIPS:
A LIFETIME ON THE HIPS

THOSE VITAL VITAMINS

HANDBOOK OF SHOPPING,
MEAL-PLANNING AND COOKING

    THE METHOD BEHIND SHOPPING LISTS

    HOW TO WIN AT THE
    GROCERY-SHOPPING GAME

    SUPERMARKET LABELING AND DATING

    HOW TO STORE FOODS SAFELY
    AND EFFICIENTLY

    PUTTING MEALS TOGETHER

    BASIC METHODS OF COOKING

    HOW TO READ A RECIPE

RECIPES THAT SUIT OUR CHANGING TIMES

SCHEDULE SOME "QUICK AND EASIES"

SPECIAL RECIPES FOR TWO

SPECIAL RECIPES FOR GUESTS

ASK FRIENDS IN FOR DINNER

SPECIAL OCCASION PARTIES

YOU'RE OFF TO A GOOD START

YOU CAN'T LIVE ON LOVE . . .

But you do want to love the life you're living. Good health starts with good nutrition—and you're certainly going to enjoy life more if your health is good. So it's important to get in the habit, right off the bat, of planning and serving meals that are nutritionally sound. Entertaining is an important part of your "good life," too. Whether you're sharing a casual potluck supper or serving a fully planned sit-down meal, the pleasures of gathering friends around your table are very real. Just don't fall into the trap of fussing over meals for "company" and skimping on your own everyday eating. The home that features super-specials for the Saturday-night crowd and shakes along on TV dinners and franks-and-beans because it's "just for us" is in for trouble!

Poorly planned and poorly cooked meals can be surprisingly expensive in terms of the dollar. At the least they produce boredom—at worst, they can be a health hazard. This chapter rounds up the most important food-facts and planning-pointers you need —to put together a fast-and-easy that doesn't scream "quickie," to balance a budget meal so it's full of food value. It also shows you how to read and use a recipe so both everyday meals and party stroganoffs end up as credits instead of expensive ruins. We've also tucked in some appetite-appealing recipes of our own —to please you two, to wow a crowd! *Plus* a special Handbook of Shopping, Meal-Planning and Cooking. And don't listen to any pessimistic talk about "the problems of cooking for two." It doesn't have to limit you. Dinners *à deux* can include glamour-items like mushrooms, an imported cheese and fresh fruit. Convenience foods are a boon for twosomes. Frozen, prepared and packaged specialties aren't always more expensive, and they certainly save time and effort.

The change in roles of "homemaker vs. breadwinner" means "cooking together" makes sense, too. Maybe one of you shops for the food, the other prepares it. If one of you is great at salads, then serve a hefty main-course salad occasionally. One of you hates to cook? Then plan party menus so one handles the main dish, the other prepares Irish coffee as an easy dessert and after-dinner drink combined. That's good we're-a-twosome planning!

PUT FOOD FACTS AHEAD OF FADS

Cholesterol . . . calories . . . carbohydrates. Organic. Macrobiotic and microbiotic. Food and diet have almost replaced the gossip column as party chitchat. All of us have easy access to information about food. Magazine articles, advertising commercials and newspaper articles publicize new facts and findings almost daily. Food labels do a good job of informing us about the nutritional value of their contents—if we take the time to read and use them, that is. Most of us have become weight-conscious and vitamin-oriented. Does all this mean we're eating better?

Not necessarily. Studies by the United States Department of Agriculture show that, for many of us, there's still room for improvement. The very fact that we *are* more food- and weight-conscious has raised a whole crop of questionable diets. Some don't seem to agree with the facts as we know them at present. You'll find a full rundown on the Basic Four Food Groups on pages 304 to 305. But first—what about those food fads?

Some Important Questions That Relate To Popular Food Fads

No one knows all the answers; however, those given here are based on recent data from government authorities and other reliable sources.

The how-many-meals-a-day controversy

Is it really necessary to eat three-a-day? Not at all. It's more a matter of what you eat than when. Some people do better on two larger meals a day, some on four or five smaller meals. Most nutritionists consider breakfast important because, soundly planned, it helps maintain your energy level through the morning, which tends to be a busy time of day. Without it, you'll have a tendency to droop by midmorning. It doesn't have to be a conventional breakfast, however. (See pages 323 and 324 for some new but nicely balanced breakfast recipes.)

If you can get vitamins and minerals from pills, why worry about foods? A balanced diet will give you a wider variety of needed nutrients—and it'll cost you less. Unless, of course, your doctor feels you need a boost.

The vitamin puzzle

Can you take in too many vitamins? Can it be dangerous? Your body has a knack for knowing what it can use, then disposing of the excess. There are a few exceptions! Example: Overload your system with much too much vitamin A or D concentrate and you risk the possibility of uncomfortable and even serious toxic disorders. Generally, it's considered unwise to down vitamin pills indiscriminately. Always check with your doctor first.

This strawberry blender-breakfast looks as good as it tastes. Served right in the kitchen, it cuts cleanup to a minimum, too. (Recipe on page 324.)

Brunch in the bedroom—what could be cozier on a no-rush morning? Our Omelet Puffs are ideal for electric griddle or skillet cooking. (Recipe on page 326.)

Dinner at your desk—it's fun when it means intimate, easy eating for two. Our salmon skillet recipe makes it even simpler. (Recipe on page 329.)

302

Dinner For Four? A "Sideboard" Makes The Serving Easy!

Here, a room divider serves as "silent butler" for an Oriental-style main dish. A two-in-one vegetable course and a chilled dessert help make the serving relaxed, too! (Recipes on pages 338 and 339.)

Do chemical fertilizers, hormones and pesticides have a harmful effect on the food we eat? Chemically fertilized fruits and vegetables are not harmful—and they cost much less than the organically grown ones. The hormones and pesticides now in use are deemed safe when used according to government directives. Under present conditions, we just couldn't have enough food to go around without an assist from chemicals.

The health-food mystique

Do preservatives "kill" the nutrients in food? Preservatives are the "safe-keepers" of foods, preserving them along with their nutrients. *All* such additives are carefully studied for safety and effectiveness by the food industry and by the government agencies involved.

What are food additives all about? What do they add? An additive is *anything* that is put into food that adds to such qualities as flavor, freshness, texture, color, keepability, ease of preparation or nutritive value. Some are natural, some manufactured. All are chemicals. Why let that word frighten you? Our bodies are actually made up of chemicals. Every protein, carbohydrate, fat or other nutrient we consume is really a chemical! What's with wheat germ, whole grains, kelp, alfalfa sprouts? There's nothing wrong with these or any other "natural" foods as long as you take in enough of them, in the right proportions, to supply established daily nutritional needs. They tend to be budget-busting in price, however. And it's never been proven that "natural" foods offer any special protection to make up for that extra cost.

What about diets that include, or stress, only one group of foods? Whether they're geared toward weight-loss or a mystical belief in the special properties of certain foods, any of the basic diets that exclude categories of food are cheating on nutrition-needs and can be harmful in the long run. Nutrients are the chemical substances in food that keep our bodies alive and working well. No one nutrient can do it all. You need a combination to perform these three essential jobs: to grow and repair tissues; to furnish energy; to regulate body processes. Nutrients can be grouped as proteins, carbohydrates and fats—all of which provide energy (or calories)—and vitamins and minerals, which do not. To furnish all the nutrients needed, a healthful diet must include foods from the Basic Four Food Groups shown on the following page.

The nothing-but-this diet

Variety Can Put More Zip In A Menu, More Zing Into You

It's not just a matter of academic interest. We really are what we eat! All the cosmetics in the world won't replace sensible eating as a beauty-booster—nor put back the bounce you lose through poor diet. Fad foods can be boring, bad nutrition and hard to prepare. To feel tip-top, look to those Basic Four Food Groups.

Now—think of a dream meal. Rosy-cold shrimp followed by a rare roast ringed with herbed rice and small carrots. A crisp salad, a chocolate sundae, coffee-just-right—the picture is complete! This great dinner includes choices from the Basic Four Food Groups.

YOUR MENU-MAKERS: THE BASIC FOUR FOOD GROUPS

Group	Foods It Includes	Number of Servings	What Do They Do for You?
Meat Group	Meat Poultry Fish Eggs Dried beans, peas or lentils Peanut butter, nuts Note: These are the protein-rich foods.	2 servings or more daily.	Build and repair body tissues; help to regulate vital body processes; help to convert food into energy.
Fruits And Vegetables Group	All fruits and vegetables Note: Include a citrus fruit or other good source of vitamin C every day; include a dark green or deep-yellow vegetable or fruit—for vitamin A—every other day.	4 servings or more daily.	Help to maintain healthy gums and tissues; help to maintain normal night vision and healthy skin.
Cereals And Breads Group	Cereal Bread Cornmeal Macaroni, noodles or spaghetti Rice Note: These should all be whole-grain, enriched, restored or fortified.	4 servings or more daily.	Provide energy; help to regulate vital body processes; help to convert food into energy.

Group	Foods It Includes	Number of Servings	What Do They Do for You?
Milk Group	Milk Note: The following may replace part of the daily requirement as a source of calcium: Cheese Yogurt Milk beverages Milk desserts	Children under 9 —2 to 3 cups. Children 9 to 12 —3 or more cups. Teen-agers—4 or more cups. Adults—2 or more cups. Pregnant women —4 or more cups. Nursing mothers —4 or more cups.	Help to build healthy bones and teeth; help to build and repair tissues; help to convert food into energy.

WHERE DID ALL THE OTHERS GO? INTO THE FIFTH DIMENSION!

Some foods in the Fifth Dimension: butter, margarine, oil, salad dressings, gravies, sauces, sugars, jams, jellies, candies, syrups, sweet desserts. You don't have to ignore these foods, even though they're not part of the Basic Four. Instead, use them to add variety —and extra calories where they're needed.

Note: The Fifth Dimension also includes sweetened and alcoholic beverages.

Brainstorms! Some Surprisingly Good Ways To Get The Basic Four Into Your Eating

Maybe you're a Prejudiced Picker—you love two or three of the famous Four, can't stand the others. Yes, you'll settle for an occasional vegetable. Or choke down a glass of milk (usually after a trip to the dentist and a little lecture on the value of calcium). But every day? Ugh! Or maybe it's your partner who's busy resisting one or more of the Basic Four. You'd be surprised at how many different ways there are to present foods from each of the groups. We put on our thinking caps and came up with quite a list, just to get you started. You'll probably come up with a few of your own once you start. Even if you don't have anything against our groups, you'll find some of our brainstorms make a refreshing change from the usual.

Be protein-wise. Most Americans eat more protein than they need. But if the food budget's tight—or you can't find time for a sit-down dinner—you might substitute these ideas for steak:

☐ Slather breakfast toast with peanut butter (it comes under the Meat Group, remember?).

☐ Be Bostonish—have baked beans for breakfast (they're part of the Meat Group, too).

☐ Cook extra drumsticks next time you serve chicken. Serve them, cold, for breakfast with juice and toast.

☐ Try the new vegetable protein products on the market. Sprinkle them on salads and sandwiches.

☐ Top soups or salads with chopped hard-cooked egg.

☐ Serve a hot hors d'oeuvre: meat spread or peanut butter on crackers, topped with a dab of catsup and run under the broiler.

☐ Add canned meatballs or cut-up franks to soups.

☐ Add anchovies or a small amount of canned tuna or sardines to a green salad.

Be clever about fruits and vegetables. This may be a bit more difficult, but it's not impossible. Witness these:

☐ Try vegetables raw instead of cooked—sneak zucchini, cauliflower, green pepper, even raw string beans or peas into green salads.

☐ Try sandwiches with a layer of coleslaw, a slice of tomato or shredded carrot—then a slice of green pepper.

☐ What about melon with a scoop of ice cream for breakfast or as a snack?

☐ Investigate pickled or dried fruit as garnishes for meats—try apricots, pears, peaches.

☐ Try adding fresh or dried fruits to cream cheese sandwiches—sliced bananas, apples, pears.

☐ How about ice cream or sherbet in fruit juice—or fruit juice with ginger ale as a thirst-quencher?

☐ If you've got a real diehard on your hands, remember that fruit juices are featured in some exotic tropical drinks. Substitute them for more usual pre-dinner potions. Something's better than nothing!

Fresh ideas for serving cereals, breads, rice and pasta. It's easy to get away from humdrum ways of serving foods in this category. Here are some bright ideas for starters—remember to choose enriched or fortified varieties.

☐ Try buttered noodles or the packaged rice mixes as substitutes for potatoes.

☐ Add rice, noodles or macaroni to vegetable soups.

☐ Have a fling at serving hot and hearty fried cornmeal mush as a breakfast cereal. It's great topped with syrup.

☐ Flavored croutons add a special crunch to soups or salads. So—toss in a handful of the handy packaged variety.

☐ Don't forget about macaroni or rice salads. Make your own or get it at the nearest deli.

☐ Why limit your pastas to spaghetti? There are a lot of good recipes around for lasagna, manicotti, cannelloni. It might pay to branch out a bit!

☐ Garnish hot cereals with a variety of toppings to make them more tempting—brown sugar, raisins, chopped dates, walnuts. There's a wide range of possibilities.

☐ Try serving corn bread along with chili. Serve it on the side or shortcake style.

☐ Waffle and pancake mixes make these foods "easy as pie." (Incidentally, pie isn't a bad breakfast dish, either.) Top them with ice cream, fresh fruit or jelly, for a change.

☐ What about biscuit strawberry shortcake for breakfast? A delicious way to start the day!

Grade A ideas for the Milk Group. This can be a real toughie because those who don't relish a glass of milk often resist it in other forms. But there are ways around everything.

☐ Homemade ice cream or a good-quality commercial variety can be a real help here. Try the whole range of flavors.

☐ Try cottage cheese and fruit for breakfast.

☐ Try adding cubes of cheese to salads, grated Parmesan over buttered vegetables.

☐ Serve a grilled cheese sandwich as a breakfast surprise—or grilled cheese mini-squares as a pre-dinner hors d'oeuvre.

☐ We've already mentioned ice cream with melon. What about a scoop on top of cereal, in coffee for those who normally take it black?

☐ There are special ways with yogurt, too. Try yogurt with melon or green grapes. Add a dollop to a favorite salad dressing. Or top a baked potato with a spoonful.

☐ Don't forget about cocoa as a cold weather alternate to tea or coffee. This often has great appeal.

☐ Cook hot breakfast cereal in milk instead of water, stirring in a little extra fortified dry milk.

A MOMENT ON THE LIPS: A LIFETIME ON THE HIPS

Insurance statistics, health and beauty columns and medical reports all warn us of the undesirable effects of overeating. We're all conscious of weight, but still there's a tendency to overdo. Sometimes it's snacking in the Fifth Dimension area. Sometimes it's a matter of taking in more than we really need from one of the Basic Four Groups and slighting one or more of the others. Under average circumstances, you need only two 2- to 3-ounce servings from the Meat Group, for instance.

When you start counting or cutting calories, however, you want to make sure you keep the nutrition! There's little to be gained health-wise by swinging from overeating to a situation in which you're depriving your body of nutrients it really needs.

The Calorie Countdown: How Much Is Enough?

The number of calories you can handle (or actually need) daily is really a personal matter. Remember, it's unused calories that build up extra weight! So maintaining an even weight is really a matter of balance. It amounts to balancing out the amount of food energy (or calories) you expend against the number you take in.

age
height
weight
build
physical activity

these are the factors that affect your calorie needs

Just to give you an idea of how the calorie-count can run, here's a mini-chart of the estimated number of calories needed daily by so-called "Average Citizens." (This is based on age, height and weight.) The counts are also based on an average amount of physical exertion and average climate and environmental conditions. (People living in extremely cold climates, or at very high altitudes, tend to burn up calories faster.)

	Age	Height	Weight	Average Number of Calories Needed (Daily)
Males	19-22	5'9"	147 lbs.	3,000
	23-50	5'9"	154 lbs.	2,700
	51 +	5'9"	154 lbs.	2,400
Females	19-22	5'5"	128 lbs.	2,100
	23-50	5'5"	128 lbs.	2,000
	51 +	5'5"	128 lbs.	1,800

Note: Data from the Recommended Daily Dietary Allowances (revised 1973) Food and Nutrition Board, National Academy of Sciences, National Research Council.

How do the Basic Four add up, calorie-wise? The minimum number of servings of foods in the Basic Four Groups totals a daily intake of 1,200 to 1,600 calories per day. That's without butter, margarine or any foods from the Fifth Dimension. Now—how can you adjust a Basic Four menu "up and down"? Just glance at the facing page and you'll see how easy it is!

THE BASIC MENU

Meal	Foods	Number of Servings From the Basic Four
Breakfast	Grapefruit (½)	1 serving (fruits and vegetables)
	Fortified cereal (1 cup)	1 serving (cereals and breads)
	Enriched white bread (2 slices)	2 servings (cereals and breads)
	Fortified milk (1½ cups)	1½ servings (milk)
Lunch	Ham (2 oz.)	1 serving (meat)
	Carrot sticks (1 carrot)	1 serving (fruits and vegetables)
	Whole wheat bread (2 slices)	2 servings (cereals and breads)
	Fortified milk (½ cup)	½ serving (milk)
	Ice cream (½ cup— equals ¼ cup milk)	¼ serving (milk)
Dinner	Beef (2 oz.) in pepper steak	1 serving (meat)
	Vegetables in pepper steak	1 serving (fruits and vegetables)
	Tossed green salad	1 serving (fruits and vegetables)
	Enriched rice (½ cup)	1 serving (cereals and breads)
	Upside-down cake with whipped cream	*from the Fifth Dimension

*Note: Other foods in the Fifth Dimension include sugar, butter, honey (breakfast); mayonnaise or butter, potato chips (lunch); butter, French dressing (dinner).

Total Servings From The Basic Four

Here's how the menu plan detailed in the chart above rates in terms of daily nutritional needs. It includes: 2 servings of meat (minimum total 2 or more); 4 servings of fruits and vegetables (minimum total 4—including citrus fruit or other good source of vitamin C every day and a dark green or deep-yellow vegetable or fruit every other day); 6 servings of cereals and breads (minimum total 4 or more); 2¼ cups of milk (minimum total 2 cups for adults).

To Cut Calories:

☐ Slice off any extra servings of bread for the day.

☐ Skip the rice at dinnertime.

☐ Take your milk "skim" instead of whole.

☐ Use a low-calorie dressing on salad.

☐ Skip the upside-down cake and other foods in the Fifth Dimension.

Result: You've reduced the calories, but the basic nutrition is all there!

To Add Calories:

☐ Increase the intake in the Milk Group by adding a cup of milk at dinner, a custard or yogurt snack during the afternoon.

☐ Add an extra serving or two in the Meat Group by including eggs or sausage with breakfast.

☐ Add an extra serving in the Cereals and Breads Group by serving dinner rolls made with enriched flour.

See how easy it is? It's just a matter of juggling around within the four groups, and of adding generous amounts of Fifth Dimension foods. A difference of 500 calories a day equals a pound a week, lost or gained.

THOSE VITAL VITAMINS: THEIR REAL-LIFE STORY

No other area of nutrition has built up quite the mystique around it that vitamins have. They're touted as cure-alls, sold almost like candy. What are they, really? They're a group of substances that are musts for life and growth. They play a part in releasing the energy from foods. In addition, each individual vitamin has a special function or functions that make it a vital link in the chain of nutrition.

And Then There's The Matter Of Minerals

Like vitamins, minerals do not provide energy in the form of calories, but are just as essential to good nutrition. That's why we've included a listing of the most important minerals, and the foods that supply them, in the chart on "Important Substances" on the following two pages.

What do minerals do for you? Some give strength and rigidity to certain body structures, like teeth and bones. Some help with numerous vital body functions, like the building of red blood cells. Minerals, like vitamins, are well supplied by a balanced diet.

Note: Even water is important to a well-balanced diet. Check our chart to see what it does and what foods help supply it.

IMPORTANT SUBSTANCES AND THEIR SOURCES

Substance	What It Does	Important Sources
Vitamins:		
Vitamin A	Helps maintain healthy skin and tissues, normal night vision.	Liver; egg yolk; deep-yellow and dark green leafy vegetables; tomatoes; apricots, peaches, cantaloupe; whole milk, cream; cheeses made from whole milk; vitamin A-fortified skim and low-fat milk; margarine, butter.
Thiamin (B1)	Helps change food into energy.	Pork; liver, heart, kidney; nuts; dried beans and peas; whole-grain and enriched cereals and breads; wheat germ; dry yeast.
Riboflavin (B2)	Needed for healthy skin; helps turn food into energy.	Liver, heart, kidney, tongue; leafy green vegetables; milk, cheese, yogurt; enriched breads.
Niacin	Helps convert food into energy; aids normal functioning of digestive tract and nervous system; helps to keep skin healthy.	Meat, fish, poultry; liver; peanuts, peanut butter; mushrooms, peas; whole-grain and enriched cereals and breads.
Vitamin B6	Helps the body use protein.	Meat, fish, chicken; liver, kidney; egg yolk; peanuts, peanut butter; bananas; potatoes, corn; whole-grain foods; wheat germ.
Vitamin B12	Needed for the functioning of all cells.	Meat, fish; liver, kidney; eggs; milk and cheese.
Folacin	Needed for the formation of blood cells.	Liver; dried beans; peanuts, walnuts, filberts; dark green vegetables.
Vitamin C (Ascorbic Acid)	Needed to keep tissues healthy.	Citrus fruits; strawberries, raspberries; cantaloupe, watermelon; tomatoes; broccoli, Brussels sprouts, green pepper, potatoes, cabbage.
Vitamin D	Helps absorb calcium and phosphorus needed for healthy bones and teeth.	Liver; egg yolk; herring, mackerel; canned salmon, sardines; vitamin D-enriched milk.
Vitamin E	Needed for stability of substances in body tissues.	Liver; eggs; whole-grain cereals and breads; whole milk; margarine, salad oil and dressings, mayonnaise.

IMPORTANT SUBSTANCES AND THEIR SOURCES

Substance	What It Does	Important Sources
Minerals:		
Calcium	Needed for maintenance of healthy bones, teeth.	Canned salmon, sardines; collards, kale, mustard greens; milk and milk products.
Phosphorus	Necessary for formation of bones and teeth.	Meat, fish, poultry; eggs; dried beans; peanuts, peanut butter; whole-grain cereals and breads; milk.
Iron	Helps build red blood cells.	Lean meat, poultry; liver, heart, kidney; clams, oysters, sardines, scallops, shrimp, tuna; soybeans, dried beans and peas; egg yolk; dried fruits; watermelon; tomato juice; beet greens, Swiss chard, dandelion greens, spinach; whole-grain and enriched cereals and breads; wheat germ.
Magnesium	Needed to activate chemical reactions in the body.	Dried beans; nuts, peanut butter; dark green vegetables; whole-grain cereals and breads; wheat germ.
Iodine	Needed to help regulate many body functions.	Iodized salt; seafood.
Water:	Needed to regulate body temperature, aid in the excretion of body wastes, sustain the health of all cells.	Drinking water; fruits, vegetables; milk; soups, juices; tea, coffee.

HANDBOOK OF
Shopping, Meal-Planning and Cooking

An afternoon of golf or tennis—helping with the decorations for the community bazaar—a full day at the office. None of these need create crisis situations with dinner if you bring know-how and a little organizing-in-advance into play. Of course, there'll be times when the clock runs out and that trip to the store doesn't materialize. Or plans change and the dinner you'd scheduled has to be scrapped in favor of something fast and easy. But once you know the general pattern your life shakes down into, you can begin to plan and shop intelligently.

This doesn't mean that you have to set up a rigid meal-plan and then jam your life into that schedule, come what may. You can project a week's menus at a time. If you end up shuffling the order in which you serve them—well, that's fine. The makings will still be on hand. You can also learn some simple pointers about making up a shopping list—how to keep it current, how to set it up so it pares down the time you spend in the store. You can cut down on spoilage by learning to buy wisely and store properly. *And* you can maintain a shelf of emergency supplies. Abilities like these will make life run more smoothly.

You'll find some good, sound, practical advice packed into the pages of this Handbook. We've concentrated on the basic approaches to different aspects of food shopping and meal-planning. Once you understand the methods, you can easily adapt them to your own menus and to the storage space you have available.

Here's another important point. Learn to make intelligent use of the available stores. Supermarkets certainly have their advantages. But if you tend to be an impulse buyer, maybe you'd be better off with a smaller store that will fill telephone orders—at least until you learn to curb that tendency to buy everything you see! Again, you pay more at a delicatessen—but there are times when the convenience is worth it. Just don't get in the habit of doing the week's grocery shopping there. Common sense and flexibility are the keys to success here, too.

THE METHOD BEHIND SHOPPING LISTS

Your shopping system has to work for *you*! But here are some pointers that are helpful for almost everyone:

☐ Plan menus by the week. You save time, forget less, cut waste by planning leftovers.

☐ Keep a running list going— jot things down as you see you need them. Use a memo pad or wallboard, then transfer to your shopping list.

☐ Organize your list by supermarket departments (meat, dairy, etc.) or by the various stores you'll be using. This saves unnecessary running around. Incidentally, try to do your shopping at times when the store isn't crowded. You'll save on time and temper.

☐ Check the newspapers and try to include the advertised budget-wise specials in your week's plan. But don't get trapped into buying what you don't need or want. P.S. It's rarely worth running from store to store to stock up on specials, either.

☐ To be super-efficient, type up a basic shopping list, make copies, then just check off the items you need each time you shop.

☐ If you're "shopping together," whack up the list between you. Make two lists or tear one in half. Divide the work!

HOW TO WIN AT THE GROCERY-SHOPPING GAME

Here's some know-how that can help you get more value and more nutrition for the food dollars you spend. To make it most useful, we've arranged the information as a series of checklists.

CHECKLIST: MEAT VALUES
Most Important!

☐ What's the cost per serving? This is what really counts, not the price per pound. Figured this way, you'll often find that boneless cuts of meat and chicken parts are the best buys even though they may cost more per pound than bone-in cuts or whole chickens. This is particularly true for small families and busy couples who are not going to use the bones for making soups.

☐ How much should I buy? Figure out how much you need ahead of time. "Over-buying" (without a specific plan for the leftovers) can make for costly waste. Here are some rough estimates on how much meat to allow per serving:

Boneless cuts: ¼ to ⅓ lb. per serving
Boneless roasts: ⅓ to ½ lb. per serving
Medium bone-in: ½ to ¾ lb. per serving
Large bone-in: ¾ to 1 lb. per serving

☐ Is it in season? There are seasons in meat as in fruits and vegetables. There are times when certain meats are more plentiful, and usually cheaper, than at other times: lamb in the spring, beef and pork in the winter, for instance. The advertised specials are a good clue to what's "in season."

☐ Can I use a cheaper cut? There's no difference in nutritional value between cheaper and more expensive cuts. Braising and stewing are cooking methods that make the most of cheaper cuts. (Here's a good place to use a pressure cooker to cut down on your cooking time.) Using commercial tenderizers or marinating these cuts can sometimes make them suitable for broiling.

☐ Are there any unadvertised specials in the meat case? Always check out the whole meat case before you buy. You may find an unadvertised or midweek special that's a better buy than what you'd planned.

CHECKLIST: FRUITS AND VEGETABLES
Most Important!

☐ Is it in season? Produce that's plentiful because it's in season is almost always cheaper than out-of-season items. Check the food columns in your newspaper for news on what crops are coming in for the week ahead. If a recipe calls for an out-of-season item, consider using frozen rather than fresh.

☐ Is it really "fresh"? You'll get better flavor, more nutrition and less waste if you learn how to "pick 'em fresh"! Here are some pointers:

Vegetables should be free of blemishes, feel crisp, show a bright color. Check the leafy tops on vegetables that have them (carrots and beets, for instance). If these look wilted or dry, the vegetable itself is probably not too fresh.

Fruits should be free of blemishes or bruises; are generally ripe when you can "smell the fruit" right through the skin.

CHECKLIST: DAIRY ITEMS
Most Important!

☐ How does it rate nutrition-wise? Margarines can be substituted for the more expensive butter. Skim milk and fortified skim-milk products can also be a better buy than whole milk—unless you need the extra fat content for some reason.

Processed cheeses are cheaper than natural cheeses, but don't offer as much flavor. They keep better, however. Block cheese is the least expensive, individually wrapped slices the most costly (but they keep better).

There's no difference in food value between white and brown eggs, Grade A or Grade B eggs. If you're watching pennies, choose whichever is cheaper. Large, medium and small eggs vary in price according to how plentiful they are. Here's a guide to minimum weight egg sizes:

Jumbo	—30 oz. per dozen
Extra Large	—27 oz. per dozen
Large	—24 oz. per dozen
Medium	—21 oz. per dozen
Small	—18 oz. per dozen

Generally speaking, if there is less than a 7¢ price spread per dozen eggs between one size and the next smaller size in the same grade, you will get more for your money by buying the larger size.

CHECKLIST: BREAD AND BAKERY VALUES
Most Important!

☐ What's on the day-old shelf? Often, it pays to seek out day-old breads and rolls. With packaging what it is today, there's rarely a loss in freshness—and the price is often really slashed!

CHECKLIST: CANNED GOODS
Most Important!

☐ Am I buying it in the most economical size? The rule of thumb is that the larger the can the better the buy! It pays to do a little figuring here. Check the label to see how many ounces or pounds it contains. Then divide that amount into the price of the item and you'll see how much you're paying per ounce or pound. (See information on unit pricing on the opposite page.) Compare different brands, too.

☐ Am I buying it in the most economical form? When it comes to canned fruits and vegetables, those packed as "wholes" are usually more expensive than those packed as "pieces." Unless appearance is important, you're better off buying the less expensive types. The same goes for the cheaper grades of canned goods. There's no difference in safety or food-value. Why pay for the fancier grade canned tomato, for instance, if you're going to include it in a casserole?

CHECKLIST: CONVENIENCE FOODS
Most Important!

☐ It is timesaving enough to be worth the extra cost? Many times the answer can be "yes" for a busy working couple. Prepared foods can make the difference between variety and monotony, good nutrition and poor nutrition, in a diet. Just remember, though: the greater the degree of pre-preparation the higher the cost. At times, you may want to settle for the semi-prepared mixes rather than the more expensive "fully prepareds."

☐ Is it really costing me more? Here, the answer may well be "no." Take the mixes, for instance. Sometimes they're cheaper than making-it-from-scratch. Many of the convenience foods are really designed for two. And there's no waste in preparing them! Example: Packaged frozen vegetables come already peeled, pared and trimmed of stems and outside leaves. Everything in the package is edible!

THE LOWDOWN ON SUPERMARKET LABELING AND DATING

There've been several "giant steps" taken in the field of labeling and dating. All work to put more information in the hands of the consumer. Here's how some of these work for you:

Nutritional labeling: The nutrition information panel appears on food labels to the right of the principal display panel. It provides information on the nutritional composition of the food.

Under FDA regulations, this information must appear on foods that are enriched and fortified and foods for which a nutritional claim is made. Other food labels may voluntarily contain nutrition information.

All nutrition information must follow a standard format. The information includes the size of a serving and the total number of servings in the container.

The number of calories and the weight in grams of protein, carbohydrate and fat are listed per serving. Optional information is the fat content by degree of saturation and the amount of cholesterol. The sodium content may also be listed.

Every nutrition information panel gives the percentage of the U.S. Recommended Daily Allowance (U.S. RDA) for protein, five vitamins and two minerals. Percentages of the U.S. RDA for an additional twelve vitamins and minerals may be listed.

Unit pricing. Some stores have unit pricing. This means the store tells you how much the products cost per ounce or pound or other unit of measurement. This gives you a way of comparing costs between different size packages and different brands.

HOW TO STORE FOODS SAFELY AND EFFICIENTLY

Make no mistake about it—spoiled foods or foods that have been improperly stored or refrigerated can be dangerous! It pays to know what you're doing in this area. Here are some pointers:

How to store meats. Fresh, frozen or cooked, all meats should be refrigerated as promptly as possible.

☐ Pop already frozen meats into your freezer "as is." Freeze fresh meat, fish or chicken in the original store wrapping if you plan to use it within one week. Otherwise, tuck the original package into a heavyweight plastic bag or overwrap it with freezer foil.
☐ Meats you'll use within a day or two: Leave in the original wrapping; store in the meat section of your refrigerator.
☐ Use liver and other organ meats the same day (or the day after) you buy them. Ditto for fresh fish (or freeze it immediately).
☐ Cooked meats and leftovers: Either cover and refrigerate immediately, or cool rapidly and then refrigerate. See note below.

Note re cooling: Hot foods can be placed right in the refrigerator provided they don't raise the refrigerator temperature above 45°. A large quantity of hot food should be cooled in a big bowl (or a sink), filled with cold water and ice that almost reach the top of the food container. Replace ice as it melts.

Check this special note on how to cool foods rapidly.

Storing other "spoilables." Here again, the word is "caution."

☐ Store opened canned goods in the refrigerator in their original containers. Use promptly.
☐ Dishes made with milk, cream, mayonnaise or eggs: Cool rapidly, refrigerate immediately, and don't keep them longer than twenty-four hours!

☐ Fresh greens and vegetables: Wash and trim them, then store in plastic bags or in your refrigerator crisper. Fruit info: Don't wash berries before storing them—wait until just before you use them.

☐ Wrap cheese tightly and refrigerate. Use soft cheeses promptly.

☐ Wrap all breads and cakes tightly. In warm weather, store in the refrigerator to prevent mold.

Storing canned and packaged goods. In general, store them in a cool, dry place. Check canned goods for signs of swelling or bulging; discard them immediately if you notice this.

Storing frozen foods. Tuck store-bought "frozens" into your freezer immediately. Check the list below to see how long suggested storage times at 0° F are.

Beef	6 to 9 mos.	Poultry	6 to 9 mos.
Ground beef	3 to 4 mos.	Fish	3 to 9 mos.
Pork	4 to 5 mos.	Eggs	6 to 9 mos.
Sausage	2 mos.	Breads and cakes	2 to 8 mos.
Veal	6 to 9 mos.		
Lamb	6 to 9 mos.	Citrus fruits	3 to 4 mos.
Cooked hams	3 to 4 mos.	Other fruits and vegetables	1 year
Most other cooked meats	2 mos.		

Note: Don't freeze canned hams!

PUTTING MEALS TOGETHER: HOW TO SAVE ON TIME AND TEMPER

Some simple meals seem to take forever to put together—or leave a pile of pans behind them—or just won't come out on time. Situations like these will ruffle the most even temper. And in most cases, they can be avoided if you do just a bit of thinking ahead.

Plan the preliminaries. Read the recipes ahead of time and make sure you have all the ingredients and equipment you need. Make a note of anything you're lacking so you'll be sure to shop for it. If you plan your meals by the week, it pays to check all the recipes you'll be using that week. Then make up your shopping list. (You'll save extra trips to the store.)

☐ The ingredients in a recipe: In what order will you use them? It pays to think ahead here, too—to make sure you have everything out and ready to be used when you need it.

☐ The equipment: Can you reduce the number of pans needed? Example: Brown meat and onions in the same pan in which you'll oven-cook them. Cook two items in the same pan—team up frozen vegetables, for instance. Cook them together, serve them together. (Frozen cauliflower and green peas are one good combination.) Just remember to check the cooking times listed on the packages, start one and then add the other, or choose go-togethers that need the same cooking time.

☐ Are there any particular preliminaries needed—heating the oven, boiling water for rice, setting the temperature gauge on an electric skillet, heating fat for deep frying? Check on this kind of preparation first and you'll save hassle later.

Put time on your side. First, check all cooking times. The item that takes the longest cooking and/or preparation time will set the pattern for the meal. Baking a ham? You have time during which you can prepare the rest of dinner. And that's the lead time you need before serving!

☐ Work out a cooking-time schedule for the whole menu. Put it down on paper until you become good at keeping these "figures" in your head.

☐ Use your timer! It'll save ruined food and pans. Even experienced cooks rely on timer-reminders.

☐ Start one item, prepare others while it's cooking. Example: Potatoes can bake while you wash and tear up salad greens and make dessert.

☐ Don't load up a menu with last-minute items. You'll be frantic if you do. Instead, plan menu-mates that can cook along on their own or keep warm in a pan, in combination with food that demands last-minute attention.

☐ Use your warming oven or hot tray if you have one. They allow you more flexibility in timing and mean that it needn't be exact.

Work out canny combinations. Pair frozen or canned vegetables with start-from-scratch meats, or vice versa. Choose menu-partners you can cook together—baked ham with baked, instead of candied, sweet potatoes. Or oven-fry chicken parts while you bake the ham; serve the chicken cold the next night. Concentrate on one-dish meals, too. Combine "hots" and "colds"—delicatessen cold cuts with a hot vegetable, chilled canned vegetables (marinated in oil and vinegar) with a broiled meat. This kind of balance in the cooking department usually works out well in terms of taste complements, too. It's all a matter of thinking things through logically.

SOME BASIC METHODS OF COOKING: OR WHAT'S UP WITH THE PAN OR SKILLET?

You're bound to be a better cook if you know what's really going on on top of that range, under the broiler or in the oven. So we've charted some of the basic cooking processes.

A ROUNDUP OF COOKING METHODS AND TERMS

Mainly for meats

Term	What's Actually Happening?	Advantages
Roast	A dry heat method of cooking meat in the oven. Place meat fat side up on a rack in a shallow roasting pan so heat will reach sides of meat. Do not cover. Do not add water. Check recipe for time, temperature, degree of doneness.	Full flavor is retained in the meat. Recommended for large, tender cuts of beef, veal, pork and lamb.
Broil	A dry heat method of cooking meat in which the surface of the meat is placed 2 to 5 inches from the heat source. Broil until top side is brown, then turn and cook to desired degree of doneness.	Surface of meat turns brown, fat crisps, center stays tender. Recommended for tender steaks, chops (at least ¾ inch thick), sliced ham (at least ½ inch thick), bacon or ground meat.
Panfry	Done on top of the range in a heavy pan or skillet, over medium heat. Unless the pan is coated with a non-stick substance, add a small amount of fat to the pan or allow fat to accumulate as meat cooks. Brown meat on both sides; turn occasionally until done. Don't cover.	Suitable for thin, tender pieces of meat or those made tender by scoring, cubing or grinding. This method cooks pieces quickly enough so they won't toughen or burn.
Braise	Brown meat slowly in a heavy pan on top of the range. Pour off drippings, season, add a small amount of liquid if necessary. (Tender cuts may not need liquid.) Cover tightly and simmer on top of the range or in a 325° oven until tender.	Recommended for smaller budget cuts and for certain tender cuts, particularly pork. Here, meat cooks through thoroughly, tenderizes as it cooks.
Cook in liquid	If desired, brown meat on all sides on top of the range. Cover meat with liquid as directed and season. Cover the pan and simmer until meat is tender. Do not boil.	Used for large, less tender cuts and stew meat. Tenderizes as it cooks.

Term	What's Actually Happening?	Advantages	
Cook and stir	Done on top of the range. Cook ingredients until they're tender, stirring occasionally to keep them from burning or browning too quickly.	For this method, ingredients are usually cut into fairly small pieces. They cook quickly but gently to tenderize or soften—but retain flavor.	**Some general terms**
Brown	Done on top of the range, over moderate heat. Cook until food changes color, usually in a small amount of fat.	Improves the appearance of meat by turning it a rich brown color. Prepares food for further cooking. Many stew recipes call for browning ingredients first as they then give the gravy a richer color.	
Simmer	Can be done on top of the range or in a low (325°) oven. Cook in liquid kept just below the boiling point. Bubbles form slowly and collapse *below* the surface.	Food cooks through slowly and gently. Often used to tenderize cuts of meat.	
Boil	Done on top of the range. Heat until bubbles rise continuously and break on the surface of the liquid (rolling boil—same as above but bubbles form rapidly).	Usually used to heat ingredients rapidly to the point where they'll start cooking. Recipe then often calls for reducing heat so ingredients simmer. Can also be used to reduce the quantity of liquid in a recipe, through evaporation.	
Stir-fry Note: A Chinese wok is ideal for this type of cooking.	Typical of Chinese cooking. Done on top of the range over very high heat. Preheat pan, add any cooking oil other than olive oil, heat oil until very hot. Add food to pan, then stir rapidly to make sure it is coated with the oil. Continue to cook over high heat, stirring constantly, until food is tender.	Very quick cooking. Vegetables retain their color, become tender with a hint of crispness. Very little food value is lost. Meat cooks rapidly, remains tender and flavorful. All food must be cut into small, uniform pieces for this type of cooking.	**Some special methods**
Clay-bake	Place meat, poultry, vegetables into special baker (should be almost full). Cook in the oven following manufacturer's directions for time and heat.	Food cooks in its own juices, without burning. Tenderizes, prevents loss of nutrients. You can substitute a Dutch oven for the clay baker.	

Also available: A variety of special cooking aids, such as oven cooking bags and film, and non-stick pans and skillets. Some offer quicker cleanups after cooking, others do away with the need for using fats or oils. Check out housewares departments.

HOW TO READ A RECIPE

There's more to reading a recipe than just a quick once-over. Actually, you have to think about it in terms of:

- ☐ the ingredients
- ☐ the type of cooking involved
- ☐ the equipment needed
- ☐ the timing

Check the main ingredients first. They're the heart of any recipe. Size them up quickly and you'll know whether you want to make the dish at all. Think about the price of those "main makings," too. Are they in the always-expensive category—one of the better cuts of beef or veal, for instance? Or are they out-of-season items?

Include spices and seasoning in your reasoning. Here again, a recipe may call for a particular herb or spice that's not a big favorite. Even if they all sound appealing, don't forget to do a little figuring. How many seasonings are involved and how exotic are they? Will you have to go out and buy two or three special ones? This could jack up the cost considerably.

Itemize all ingredients as "haves" or "have nots." Transfer the "have nots" to your marketing list. Pre-inventory and you won't get stuck with this monologue: "Now for the cornstarch. Cornstarch? I don't have any!"

Size up the cooking process and the pans you'll need. If the recipe calls for a large, covered skillet—do you have one? Ditto items like a meat grinder, grater, garlic press.

Timetable the recipe. How long is the cooking time for this particular dish? How does it fit into the timetable of your overall menu? If this item needs exact timing at a specified oven temperature, and a second item you're planning needs oven-time at a different temperature—you could be in for trouble. Suppose it calls for long, slow simmering and occasional checking? Cook it on a day when you'll be busy around the house.

CHOOSING RECIPES THAT SUIT OUR CHANGING TIMES

Grandma's cookbook just won't do it for today—no matter how much sentimental value it may have. You need recipes that take full advantage of today's wider range of ingredients, that capitalize on new work-saving and timesaving cooking methods and appliances, that are geared to current food costs and up-to-date knowledge of nutritional values. Most of all, you want recipes that match up with the kind of life you lead.

Light breakfasts-on-the-run are the rule rather than the exception. Dinner is often delayed because of work schedules and/or classes at night. This can make nutritious coffee breaks and tide-over snacks a necessity. It also puts the quick dinner of heros, chili or pizza into the picture. Relax—none of this has to be a dietary disaster! There's a wide selection of good, up-to-date cookbooks available as well as a monthly round of magazine articles and recipes. To help you get started, we've included a batch of recipes on the following pages, too. They're as contemporary as this minute and geared to particular situations.

RECIPES: "QUICK AND EASIES" THAT LIFT OFF ON SCHEDULE

Here's a recipe collection designed to meet today's tight countdown style of living. Each offers a different-and-delicious way to handle "clock-watch cooking" situations. You'll find ideas for breakfasts, lunches and dinners. The range includes stir-fry dishes, casseroles, extra-special sandwiches. And we've included a supersmart group of budget-savers that are bound to come in handy any time.

Quickie Breakfasts...Give You What You Need

Practically painless to make and to take! Here are breakfasts sound enough to satisfy the "big breakfast" eater who's run out of time, cool enough to suit the "nothing but coffee" crowd. And each provides one fourth of your daily nutrition needs!

BLENDER BREAKFAST: CHOCOLATE CHIP

1 pint chocolate ice cream, slightly softened
2½ cups fortified whole wheat flake cereal
1 cup milk
2 tablespoons chocolate-flavored syrup

If you have "no time for breakfast," try breakfast in a glass! A few seconds in the blender and your meal is ready. Serve with an orange as accompaniment.

Place all ingredients in blender container; cover. Blend on high speed until mixed, about 30 seconds. 2 servings (1½ cups each).

BLENDER BREAKFAST: STRAWBERRIES 'N CREAM

1 pint strawberry ice cream, slightly softened
1 cup milk

2 envelopes strawberry-flavored instant breakfast drink mix
1 package (10 ounces) frozen strawberries

Place all ingredients in blender container; cover. Blend on high speed until mixed, about 10 seconds. 2 servings (2 cups each).

Add buttered toast and you have another complete breakfast—ready in a wink!

FRENCH-TOAST SANDWICH

Prepared mustard
6 slices French bread, ½ inch thick
3 slices canned pork luncheon meat, ¼ inch thick

⅓ cup milk
2 tablespoons flour
2 eggs
Dash of salt
1 tablespoon butter or margarine

Spread thin layer of mustard on one side of each slice of bread. Place meat between bread slices. Beat milk, flour, eggs and salt until smooth. Soak sandwiches in egg-milk mixture until saturated.

Heat butter in skillet. Carefully transfer each sandwich to skillet. Cook over medium heat until golden brown, about 12 minutes on each side. Serve sandwiches with citrus fruit and glasses of milk. 3 sandwiches or 2 servings.

Try a French-toast sandwich for breakfast! Or try a regulation hamburger. The message: Don't skip breakfast—eat anything you like (so long as it provides one fourth of your daily nutrition needs).

BREAKFAST SOUP

1 can (11 ounces) condensed Cheddar cheese soup

½ cup tomato juice
½ cup milk
½ teaspoon dill weed

Mix all ingredients in 1½-quart saucepan. Heat to boiling; remove from heat. Serve soup in mugs with buttered rye toast. 2 servings.

Soup for breakfast beats a sweet roll and coffee every time. You don't even have to sit down for this one. Just pick up the mug and enjoy your breakfast . . . with a piece of buttered rye toast on the side!

Extra-Quick Dinners For A Busy Twosome

Maybe you get stuck late at the office or get trapped in one of those "rush hour" traffic jams. Or maybe you suddenly discover that movie you plan to see starts a half hour earlier than you thought. There are always times when special circumstances put extra hurry into your meal schedule. Don't panic—we can help!

Here are some dinner recipes to keep tucked up your sleeve for times when the timing's really tight. The hurry-up's built in—but so is the health aspect.

STIR-FRY TUNA

1 teaspoon vegetable oil
¾ cup thin diagonally sliced carrots
¼ cup thin strips green pepper (1 inch long)
2 green onions with tops, sliced ¼ inch thick
1 can (6½ ounces) tuna, drained

1 can (6 ounces) sliced bamboo shoots, drained
2 teaspoons instant chicken bouillon
½ teaspoon salt
1 cup water
1 tablespoon plus 1 teaspoon cornstarch
Chow mein noodles or hot cooked rice

Heat oil in 10-inch skillet; add carrots, green pepper and onions. Cook and stir over medium heat until vegetables start to brown, 3 to 4 minutes. Stir in tuna, bamboo shoots, bouillon and salt. Cook, stirring constantly, until hot, about 2 minutes; remove from heat.

Mix water and cornstarch; stir into vegetable mixture. Heat to boiling. Boil and stir 1 minute. Serve Stir-fry Tuna over chow mein noodles. 2 servings.

Call this an Orient Express—you can stir it together faster than you can order in a Chinese dinner. And the quick cooking carries with it an added bonus —it helps keep the vegetables crisp. Use a wok or electric skillet, if you have one, for this easy one-pot dinner.

BAKED BEAN SOUP

1 can (16 ounces) baked beans (not tomato base)
⅓ cup milk
¾ teaspoon instant beef bouillon

¾ teaspoon dry mustard
½ teaspoon salt
½ teaspoon dried marjoram leaves
¼ teaspoon mint flakes
⅛ teaspoon lemon-pepper

Place all ingredients in blender container; cover. Blend on low speed until smooth, about 40 seconds. Pour mixture into 1½-quart saucepan. Heat to boiling, stirring occasionally. Serve soup warm or cold with Cheesy Sandwich (below). 2 servings.

Our soup-and-sandwich combo is a real meal, incorporating foods from each of the Basic Four. Whip the sandwiches together while the soup's heating.

CHEESY SANDWICH

2 slices provolone cheese, cut to fit bread
2 slices tomato
2 thin slices Bermuda onion
2 slices Italian bread, toasted

Crumbled provolone cheese, if desired
Crumbled crisply fried bacon or bacon-flavored vegetable protein chips, if desired

Heat oven to 350°. Place cheese, tomato and onion slice on each slice of toast; sprinkle with crumbled cheese and bacon. Place on ungreased baking sheet. Bake sandwiches until cheese is melted, about 3 minutes. Serve with soup (above). 2 servings. Make three sandwiches if one of you is really hungry!

When You're Busy Minding The Budget

These unusual main dishes rate high on every count but cost! They spare the meat but don't spoil the flavor. No matter which one you choose, you'll end up with a double winner—on both the flavor and the money end!

ZUCCHINI SPAGHETTI

For second meal—remove zucchini sauce from freezer; dip container into very hot water just to loosen. Place zucchini sauce in 2-quart saucepan. Pour ½ cup water into saucepan. Cover and heat over medium-low heat, stirring occasionally, until hot, about 35 minutes. Serve zucchini sauce over spaghetti with grated Parmesan cheese. 2 servings.

3 tablespoons vegetable oil
1 pound zucchini (about 3 medium), cut into ½-inch cubes
1 can (28 ounces) peeled whole pear-shaped tomatoes (Italian style)
1 can (12 ounces) tomato paste
½ cup dry red wine
1 can (4 ounces) mushroom stems and pieces
3 tablespoons instant minced onion
2 teaspoons dried oregano leaves, crushed
1 teaspoon sugar
1 teaspoon salt
¼ teaspoon garlic powder
8 ounces spaghetti, cooked
Grated Parmesan cheese

Heat oil in Dutch oven over medium-high heat. Cook and stir zucchini in oil until golden brown, about 7 minutes; drain. Stir in remaining ingredients except spaghetti and cheese. Break up tomatoes. Heat to boiling; reduce heat. Cover and simmer 45 minutes, stirring occasionally.

Pour half of the zucchini sauce (about 3½ cups) into 1-quart freezer container; freeze for later use. (Store no longer than 4 weeks.)

Pour remaining zucchini sauce over hot spaghetti. Serve spaghetti with cheese. If desired, garnish with parsley. 2 servings.

OMELET PUFFS

2 eggs, separated
2 tablespoons water
2 tablespoons flour
¼ teaspoon salt
4 slices smoked corned beef, cut into ½-inch pieces

Beat egg whites in small mixer bowl until stiff but not dry.

Beat egg yolks until thick and lemon colored, about 5 minutes. Beat in water, flour and salt gradually; beat until smooth. Stir in corned beef pieces. Fold egg yolk mixture into egg whites.

Heat greased griddle or skillet to 400°. (Griddle is hot enough when a few drops of water dropped on it "skitter" around.) Drop egg mixture by ¼-cupfuls onto hot greased griddle.

Cook puffs until golden brown on bottoms, about 3 minutes; turn. Cook until golden brown on other sides, about 3 minutes. 2 servings.

Extra-Dividend Dinners: You Get Two From One

One of the most precious possessions you have is *time*. So when you decide to invest it, you want the best return possible. These help you invest cooking time extra wisely. While you're stirring up our savory stew or baking a meaty ham, you're laying the groundwork for another meal from each. That's really playing it smart—because it means you've gained extra time when you get ready to serve those "dividend dishes"!

DOUBLE-DUTY MEAT AND VEGETABLES

1 pound beef stew meat, cut into 1-inch pieces	¼ teaspoon garlic powder
Meat tenderizer	Dash of ground sage
2 cups water	Dash of pepper
1 tablespoon Worcestershire sauce	2 teaspoons cornstarch
¾ teaspoon dry mustard	⅔ cup water
	1 package (10 ounces) frozen Brussels sprouts
	Hot cooked rice

Tenderize stew meat as directed on meat tenderizer package. Cook meat in 10-inch skillet over medium-high heat, stirring occasionally, until brown. Stir in 2 cups water, the Worcestershire sauce and seasonings. Heat to boiling; reduce heat. Cover and simmer, stirring occasionally, until meat is tender, about 1 hour.

Mix cornstarch and ⅔ cup water; stir into meat mixture. Cook, stirring constantly, until mixture thickens and boils. Boil and stir 1 minute.

Pour half of the meat into 1-quart freezer container; freeze for later use. (Store no longer than 3 months.) Add frozen Brussels sprouts to remaining meat. Heat to boiling. Cover and simmer until sprouts are tender, 12 to 15 minutes. Serve meat and sprouts over rice. 2 servings.

For second meal—remove meat from freezer; dip container into very hot water just to loosen. Place meat and 1 package (10 ounces) frozen sliced carrots in 2-quart saucepan. Pour ⅓ cup water into saucepan; cover. Heat over medium-low heat, stirring occasionally, until carrots are tender, about 20 minutes. Serve over noodles. 2 servings.

GLAZED BAKED HAM

½ cup currant jelly	¼ teaspoon onion salt
2 tablespoons prepared mustard	1 can (1.5 pounds) ham

Heat jelly, mustard and onion salt to boiling over low heat, stirring constantly. Boil and stir 3 minutes; keep warm.

Bake ham as directed on can. Brush ham with glaze every 15 minutes. Serve any remaining glaze as a sauce. 2 servings—with leftovers. (Use leftovers for Oven-easy Ham with Rice.)

A celebration dish for two that plays a return role in a casserole.

OVEN-EASY HAM WITH RICE

¼ cup uncooked regular rice
½ cup boiling water
½ teaspoon seasoned salt
1 cup diced cooked ham
½ package (6-ounce size) frozen pea pods, thawed

½ can (8½-ounce size) water chestnuts, drained and sliced, or ½ cup thinly sliced celery
½ cup pasteurized process cheese spread

Heat oven to 350°. Sprinkle rice in ungreased 1-quart casserole. Stir in water and seasoned salt. Cover and bake casserole until liquid is absorbed, 20 to 25 minutes; remove from oven.

Stir in remaining ingredients. Cover and bake until bubbly, about 20 minutes. 2 servings.

Dinner-Winners From Your Pantry Shelf

Sophisticated but simple—this kind of recipe for canned or packaged foods is like finding hidden treasure. Here are three unbeatable main dishes in the hidden treasure category. Take the pasta casserole below, for instance. When it's a busy day with no time for shopping, or dinner-out is suddenly canceled—here's the tasty answer to your problem waiting right on your cabinet shelves for you to put together. The main ingredients are simple, but the seasonings make it "sing."

CASSEROLED PASTA

1 cup cavatelli or seashell macaroni
2 tablespoons butter or margarine
1 tablespoon flour
1 tablespoon instant minced onion
⅛ to ¼ teaspoon caraway seed

Dash of ground allspice
1 cup milk
1 jar (2½ ounces) sliced dried beef, cut into 1-inch pieces*
1 tablespoon finely chopped pimiento
1 teaspoon parsley flakes

Heat oven to 350°. Cook cavatelli as directed on package; drain.

Melt butter over low heat. Stir in flour, onion, caraway seed and allspice; remove from heat. Stir in milk. Heat to boiling, stirring constantly. Boil and stir 1 minute.

Mix hot cavatelli, seasoned sauce, dried beef and pimiento in buttered 1-quart casserole. Sprinkle parsley flakes on top.

Cover and bake casserole until bubbly, about 35 minutes. 2 servings.

*If dried beef is too salty, pour boiling water over it and drain.

CHILI CASSEROLE

1 can (15½ ounces) chili without beans
1 tablespoon instant minced onion

1 can (7 ounces) vacuum-packed whole kernel corn, drained
½ cup grated American cheese food

Heat oven to 350°. Pour chili into greased 1-quart casserole. Top with onion and corn; sprinkle with cheese.

Bake casserole uncovered until bubbly, about 25 minutes. Serve with corn chips and shredded lettuce. 2 servings.

The easiest of ingredients, a winning taste. Takes about 35 minutes from start to finish! So keep this one in mind for those really hectic days when you dash in late and are absolutely down to the wire on dinner. There's nothing about the way our chili looks or tastes to give away its fastback design.

SALMON SUPREME

1 tablespoon shortening or bacon fat
¼ cup finely chopped onion
½ head lettuce, coarsely shredded*
1 teaspoon soy sauce
½ teaspoon salt
    Dash of pepper

1 can (7¾ ounces) salmon, drained and flaked, or
1 can (7 ounces) tuna, drained and flaked
1 tablespoon bottled lemon juice
2 cups hot cooked instant rice
    Paprika

When drop-in guests stay on for dinner, don't panic! This recipe puts together makings you already have on hand—and gives them an interesting oriental twist. Just double the recipe and you're set!

Melt shortening in 10-inch skillet; add onion. Cook over low heat, stirring occasionally, until onion is tender, about 4 minutes.

Stir lettuce, soy sauce, salt and pepper into onion; layer salmon on top. Sprinkle lemon juice over salmon. Layer rice over salmon.

Cover and cook over low heat until hot, about 10 minutes. Sprinkle with paprika; serve from skillet. 2 servings.

*¼ head cabbage, finely shredded, can be substituted for the lettuce. Mix 2 tablespoons water with the lemon juice.

MAKING IT SPECIAL: JUST FOR YOU TWO

Not every moment is a busy one. Weekdays will probably be hectic, but the weekend gives you a chance to slow the pace, set up something special, sit down to a simple but superb little meal. Brunch, lunch, a late dinner—you pick the time. We've put together recipes that'll show you care. We feature three main dishes and an absolutely delicious dessert for two that serves up neatly in individual "cups." We've carefully tailored some of the world's really famous dishes to suit dinner-for-two. You'll find a Beef Bourguignon, for instance—savory as ever but styled for eating together at home.

BEEF KABOBS

½ pound beef stew meat, cut into 1-inch pieces
¼ cup dry red wine
2 tablespoons vegetable oil
1 teaspoon soy sauce
1 clove garlic, finely chopped

½ teaspoon dried rosemary leaves, crushed
1 can (8 ounces) pineapple chunks, drained
8 cherry tomatoes
½ green pepper, cut into 1-inch pieces

Place beef pieces in shallow glass dish. Mix wine, oil, soy sauce, garlic and rosemary leaves; pour over beef pieces. Cover tightly and refrigerate 24 hours, turning beef pieces occasionally.

Thread beef pieces on two 12-inch skewers, leaving a small space between each cube. Alternate pineapple chunks, cherry tomatoes and green pepper pieces on two 12-inch skewers, leaving a small space between each.

Set oven control to broil and/or 550°. Broil beef kabobs 5 inches from heat 5 minutes; turn. Broil pineapple-vegetable kabobs 5 inches from heat 3 minutes; turn. Continue to broil beef and pineapple-vegetable kabobs until done, about 2 minutes. Kabobs are nice served with bulgur or rice pilaf. 2 servings.

Our kabobs-for-two come out "just right" because you cook the meat separately from the other makings.

CORNED BEEF HASH QUICHE

1 can (15 ounces) corned beef hash
2 tablespoons flour
3 eggs
1 cup light cream (20%)
½ cup shredded natural Swiss cheese

3 tablespoons finely chopped green onions (with tops)
¼ teaspoon salt
2 drops red pepper sauce
Paprika

Heat oven to 400°. Mix hash, flour and 1 egg thoroughly. Press mixture firmly and evenly against bottom and side of ungreased 9-inch pie plate.

Bake meat crust 10 minutes; remove from oven. Reduce oven temperature to 375°.

Beat 2 eggs; mix in remaining ingredients except paprika. Place crust on oven rack. Carefully pour egg-cream mixture into crust; sprinkle with paprika.

Bake quiche until knife inserted 1 inch from edge comes out clean, about 40 minutes. Cut half of quiche into 2 wedges. Refrigerate remaining quiche and serve cold as an hors d'oeuvre. Cut into thin wedges; cut wedges into bite-size pieces. Insert picks through meat crust. 2 servings plus leftovers.

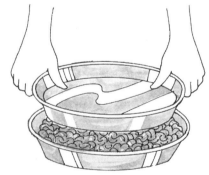

Distribute hash in 9-inch pie plate, then press 8-inch pie plate onto meat mixture. Meat crust will be shaped evenly in pie plate.

BEEF BOURGUIGNON

¾	pound boneless beef chuck or rump, cut into 1-inch pieces		1	sprig parsley
1	tablespoon plus 1 teaspoon flour		1	slice bacon, diced
			6	small white onions
2	teaspoons vegetable oil		1	tablespoon catsup
½	clove garlic		⅛	teaspoon dried thyme leaves
½	cup red Burgundy About ¾ cup water			Dash of pepper
¼	bay leaf		1	tablespoon butter or margarine
½	teaspoon salt		6	mushrooms, sliced Crusty French bread

Heat oven to 325°. Coat beef pieces with flour. Heat oil in skillet. Brown beef pieces on all sides in oil; add garlic. Cook garlic and beef pieces 1 minute. Remove garlic and discard; drain beef pieces. Place beef pieces in ungreased 1½-quart casserole; add Burgundy and just enough water to cover beef pieces. Stir in bay leaf, salt and parsley.

Cover and bake casserole 2 hours. Fry bacon just until limp; add onions. Cook and stir until onions are light brown; add bacon and onions to casserole.

Cover and bake until beef pieces are tender, about 40 minutes. Stir in catsup, thyme leaves and pepper. Cover and bake 10 minutes.

Melt butter in skillet; add mushrooms. Cook and stir until mushrooms are tender; arrange on top of casserole. Serve bourguignon in bowls, with crusty French bread for dipping. 2 servings.

Note: Elegant go-withs for your Beef Bourguignon would be tomato slices marinated in oil-and-vinegar dressing or dressed with plain oil and sprinkled with finely minced onion, parsley and any other herbs you wish. To top it all off, have Pot de Crème au Chocolat or any of the delicious desserts described in the next section.

Another thought: You probably won't need a whole loaf of French bread for dipping. So why not cut that loaf in half—serve one half with your Beef Bourguignon, wrap the other half in foil and pop it into the freezer until needed. When you do decide to serve it—remove from the freezer, open the foil, and let the bread thaw. To serve as a delicious "hot bread": Slice it into 1-inch slices, spread each generously with softened butter or margarine, reassemble the half loaf, reseal the aluminum foil, and pop the whole thing into a preheated 400° oven for about 15 minutes. If you wish, you can cream the butter or margarine with 2 tablespoons minced onion or snipped chives.

For brunch, a formal midnight supper—or the most elegant accompaniment ever of the late, late show! Try it for yourselves first. Then double the recipe and ask another couple in to share the wealth.

POT DE CREME AU CHOCOLAT

⅓ cup semisweet chocolate pieces
½ cup half-and-half
1 tablespoon butter or margarine, softened
1 egg
1 tablespoon plus 1½ teaspoons packed brown sugar
1 tablespoon rum (optional)
Dash of salt

Heat oven to 350°. Heat chocolate pieces and half-and-half, stirring constantly, until chocolate is melted. Cool slightly. Beat remaining ingredients; stir into chocolate mixture gradually. Pour into 2 ungreased 6-ounce custard cups or 2 ovenproof pot de crème cups.

Place cups in baking pan on oven rack. Pour boiling water into pan to within ½ inch of tops of cups.

Bake pot de crème 20 minutes; cool slightly. Cover and refrigerate until cold, at least 4 hours but no longer than 24 hours. 2 servings.

MAKING IT SPECIAL: FOR GUESTS

Spur of the moment or perfectly planned, successful entertaining really boils down to a sense of sharing. But it's the sharing of yourselves that counts. Your ideas, your humor, your interests. Never turn down a chance to be with friends just because you haven't got a special dinner planned. You can always run out for a pizza, expand one of our dinner-from-the-shelf ideas to meet the need, or all share potluck.

How do you get started? Until you've had a little experience at putting menus together, better start off your "invitation entertaining" rather simply. Invite another couple in to watch a football game, listen to records, or just talk. This is a good way to get to know new neighbors, too. We've rounded up several good menus for casual gatherings of various sizes.

RED-EYE COCKTAILS

**Red-eye Cocktails
Peanuts and Seasoned Popcorn
TV Sandwiches
Vegetable Relishes**

1½ cups chilled tomato juice
2 cans (12 ounces each) chilled beer
Red pepper sauce
Salt
Pepper
4 green onions

Mix tomato juice and beer; divide among 4 chilled glasses.

Serve cocktails with red pepper sauce, salt, pepper and green onion stirrers. 4 servings.

TV SANDWICHES

⅓ cup butter or margarine, softened
3 tablespoons dried snipped chives
1½ teaspoons prepared mustard
¾ teaspoon poppy seed

6 hot dog buns, split
12 strips (4x1½ inches each) Swiss cheese
1 to 2 packages (3 ounces each) wafer-thin sliced smoked ham

Heat oven to 350°. Mix butter, chives, mustard and poppy seed. Spread on both halves of buns.

Place cheese strip on each bun half; divide ham slices among buns. Wrap sandwiches individually in aluminum foil. Bake 25 minutes. 4 servings.

"For Dessert and Coffee": A Friendly Invitation

Ask several couples in for a scrumptious dessert and coffee. Any one of these special desserts will help to build your reputation as a hostess. And they're simpler than they seem!

FRUITED MERINGUE KISSES

3 egg whites
¼ teaspoon cream of tartar
¾ cup granulated sugar
1 cup chilled whipping cream

¼ cup powdered sugar
1 package (16 ounces) unsweetened assorted frozen fruit, thawed and drained

Heat oven to 275°. Cover baking sheet with heavy brown paper.

Beat egg whites and cream of tartar until foamy. Beat in granulated sugar, 1 tablespoon at a time; beat until stiff and glossy. (Do not underbeat.) Spoon meringue into 16 mounds on brown paper; flatten slightly with spatula or knife.

Bake meringues until they are ivory color and can be lifted easily from paper, about 1 hour. Crush the smooth bottom sides of warm meringues with thumb; cool completely.

Beat whipping cream and powdered sugar in chilled bowl until stiff; fold in sliced fruit.

To serve, fill shells with fruit-cream mixture and put together in pairs. Serve on sides (yo-yo fashion). 8 servings.

Note: These were inspired by a famous Swiss confection that's served on special occasions in even the tiniest Alpine towns. You can make the meringues the day before, the filling an hour or so before your guests are due to arrive.

DESSERT IN A CUP

⅓ cup semisweet chocolate pieces
¼ cup light corn syrup
¾ cup half-and-half

¾ cup milk
Vanilla, chocolate or mint ice cream

Heat chocolate pieces and corn syrup over low heat until chocolate is melted. Stir in half-and-half and milk; heat until hot.

To serve, pour chocolate mixture over scoops of ice cream in large cups or mugs. 4 servings.

DOUBLE FUDGE PIE

Fine dry bread crumbs
¼ cup granulated sugar
2 teaspoons instant coffee
⅛ teaspoon salt
½ cup water
8 eggs, separated
2 packages (4 ounces each) sweet cooking chocolate, broken into pieces

1 teaspoon vanilla
¼ cup granulated sugar
¾ cup chilled whipping cream
2 tablespoons powdered sugar
1 teaspoon vanilla

Butter 8-inch pie plate; dust with bread crumbs.

Mix ¼ cup granulated sugar, the instant coffee and salt in 2-quart saucepan; stir in water. Beat egg yolks slightly; stir egg yolks and chocolate pieces into coffee mixture.

Cook over medium heat, stirring constantly, *just* until mixture boils; remove from heat. Stir in 1 teaspoon vanilla; cool.

Heat oven to 350°. Beat egg whites in large mixer bowl until foamy. Beat in ¼ cup granulated sugar, 1 tablespoon at a time; beat until stiff. Fold chocolate mixture into egg whites. Fill pie plate with chocolate mixture until level with edge. Reserve remaining chocolate mixture; cover and refrigerate.

Bake pie 25 minutes. Turn off oven; leave pie in oven with door closed 5 minutes. Remove from oven; cool on rack 2 hours. As pie cools it sinks in the center; fill with chilled chocolate mixture. Refrigerate until cold, at least 2 to 3 hours but no longer than 24 hours.

To serve, beat whipping cream, powdered sugar and 1 teaspoon vanilla in chilled bowl until stiff. Spread whipped cream evenly over pie. If desired, garnish with chocolate curls (see sketch in margin). 6 or 7 servings.

To make chocolate curls, use a vegetable parer or thin, sharp knife. Slice across block of sweet milk chocolate with long, thin strokes.

Tables For Two—All Set Up For A Leisurely Dinner At Home.

Beef Bourguignon and Pot de Crème au Chocolat are on the menu, bright fake flowers are on the tables, and your favorite show is on television. Enjoy yourselves! (Recipes on pages 331 and 332.)

Party Plans—Try These "Casuals" Instead Of A Formal Dinner.

New viewpoint for a party—dessert and coffee are sitting pretty on a windowsill. Feature our Fruited Meringue Kisses. (Recipe on page 333.)

Kitchen-casual, our buffet sets up in the tiniest apartment, stars "make 'em yourself" Meat Roll Sandwiches. (Recipe on page 342.)

It's open house—and the more the merrier, with our all-star lineup of snacks and punch ready on the sidelines. (Recipes on pages 343-345.)

BRANCH OUT A BIT:
ASK FRIENDS IN FOR DINNER

You're ready to offer a full-fledged dinner invitation. Perhaps you'll start by asking another couple in to a sit-down meal. Then, work up to a slightly larger dinner for six, buffet style. The serve-yourself setup makes it possible to handle a large group without panic.

On the following pages you'll find two menus, plus recipes— one for a sit-down dinner, one for a buffet. Both break away from the traditional a bit—enough to be interesting without being nervous-making.

Another helpful feature: Our menus are planned so you can do a lot of the preparation ahead of time, leaving you calm and collected on Party Day.

For serving suggestions, check out the new-and-different ideas shown in color on pages 302 and 336.

Bright ideas about buffets. The basic idea behind any buffet setup is to make the serving as easy as possible for both you and your guests! You can have a buffet table that's formal or informal. In fact, you don't have to use a dining table at all. A card table, a desk top, a serving cart, even the top of a dresser—any of these, if set attractively, can function as your buffet "server." But keep that convenience factor in mind. Note our drawings on page 336 for some suggestions for the arrangement of serving dishes, plates, silver and glassware. And here are some more hints to help keep the traffic flowing smoothly:

☐ If you have the space, place your buffet table in the center of the room. This means guests can reach both sides of the table easily. If space is limited, place the table at one side of the room —but pull it far enough away from the wall so that you'll be able to slip in behind it. Then you can replenish serving dishes, add extra napkins, and help guests as they serve themselves without getting in their way.

☐ Don't overcrowd the table. Keep the decorations compact. Don't make the menu too complicated. Be sure there's enough room beside each serving dish for guests to rest their plates on the table as they help themselves.

☐ Arrange your setup so it follows a logical progression: dinner plates at one end, then the main dish, the side dishes, the condiments, the napkins and silver at the other end. If possible, use a small extra table for the beverage and glasses.

Dinner For Four: Different And Delicious

Most of the work can be done a day ahead! Here's all you do on the day of the party. An hour or so before the guests arrive, put together the Honeydew Fruit Bowl (except for the apple slices).

Fifteen minutes before serving, the pork dish goes into the oven to bake, the snow peas and carrots cook on top of the range.

While one of you clears the table, the other slices apples into the fruit bowl, turns the heat on under the coffee (if you opt for coffee instead of Chinese tea). That's organization for you!

PORK AND NOODLES—CHINESE STYLE

**Pork and Noodles—
Chinese Style**

**Snow Peas and
Carrot Nuggets**

Marinated Cucumbers

**Honeydew
Fruit Bowl**

**Chinese Almond
Cookies**

2 pounds pork blade steak, trimmed of bone and excess fat
1 cup catsup
¼ cup soy sauce
2 tablespoons sugar
1 tablespoon dry sherry
½ teaspoon salt
⅛ teaspoon instant minced garlic

1 package (7 ounces) vermicelli or very thin spaghetti
1 tablespoon vegetable oil
5 cups water
2 tablespoons instant chicken bouillon
2 tablespoons soy sauce
1 turnip, very thinly sliced, cut into 1-inch pieces*
Watercress
Chinese onions**

Place steak in shallow glass dish. Mix catsup, ¼ cup soy sauce, the sugar, sherry, salt and instant garlic; pour over steak. Cover and refrigerate, turning steak occasionally, at least 3 hours but no longer than 24 hours.

Heat oven to 375°. Place steak on rack in shallow roasting pan. Roast steak, brushing with marinade every 15 minutes, until tender, about 1 hour. Cut into 1-inch pieces.

Prepare vermicelli as directed on package; drain. Toss vermicelli with oil; place in ungreased baking dish, 13½x8¾x1¾ inches. Place steak pieces on vermicelli. (Can be refrigerated covered at this point no longer than 24 hours.)

Place remaining ingredients except watercress and Chinese onions in saucepan. (Can be refrigerated at this point no longer than 24 hours.)

Heat oven to 375°. Place watercress on top of steak pieces. Heat ingredients in saucepan to boiling; pour over vermicelli and steak pieces. Bake casserole uncovered until bubbly, about 15 minutes. Garnish with Chinese onions. 4 servings.

*1 can (8½ ounces) sliced bamboo shoots, drained, can be substituted for the turnip.

**Chinese onions: Trim root ends and green tops from green onions, leaving white and some green, about 4 inches long. With small sharp knife, slit each end through 5 or 6 times, leaving 1 inch in the middle intact. Drop into bowl of ice water for at least 2 hours; ends will curl slightly.

SNOW PEAS AND CARROT NUGGETS

1 package (7 ounces)
  frozen Chinese pea pods*

1 package (10 ounces)
  carrot nuggets frozen in
  butter sauce in cooking
  pouch
2 teaspoons lemon juice

Cook each vegetable as directed on package.

Drain pea pods; turn into serving dish. Add carrots and lemon juice; toss. 4 servings.

*One package (9 ounces) frozen Italian green beans can be substituted for the frozen Chinese pea pods.

HONEYDEW FRUIT BOWL

1 honeydew melon*
1 can (15 ounces) loquats,
  chilled and drained, or
  1 can (20 ounces) litchis,
  chilled and drained

1 can (11 ounces)
  mandarin orange
  segments, chilled and
  drained
1 unpared apple, thinly
  sliced

Cut melon in half; scoop out melon balls. Scallop edges of melon halves; place on serving plate. Mix all fruits; mound into melon halves and on plate. If desired, garnish fruit with fresh mint. 4 servings.

*If honeydew is out of season, substitute 1 can (13½ ounces) pineapple chunks, chilled and drained, for the melon balls. Serve fruit in glass bowl.

CHINESE ALMOND COOKIES

1 packet or 2 sticks pie crust
  mix
1 cup powdered sugar
1 cup ground or very finely
  chopped almonds

1 egg
3 teaspoons almond extract
  Granulated sugar
36 blanched whole almonds

Heat oven to 400°. Mix pie crust mix (dry), powdered sugar and ground almonds. Stir in egg and almond extract; gather dough into ball.

Knead on lightly floured cloth-covered board until smooth. Shape into 1-inch balls; roll in granulated sugar.

Flatten balls on ungreased baking sheet until ½ inch thick; gently press a whole almond in center of each cookie.

Bake cookies until edges are light brown, 8 to 10 minutes; cool on rack. About 3 dozen cookies.

To be really authentic, serve Chinese tea. This is available loose and in tea bags in many supermarkets. To brew tea, start with clean china, glass or earthenware teapot. Warm pot by filling it with boiling water for a few minutes, then pour water out. Heat cold water to a rolling boil. Put tea or tea bags into warmed teapot (1 teaspoon of loose tea or 1 tea bag per cup) and add boiling water. Let tea steep 3 to 5 minutes to bring out the full flavor. Stir once. Strain loose tea or remove tea bags.

Buffet For Six: Ultra-Casual, Lots Of Fun

Once again, do-it-ahead is the name of the game. Both the main dish and the mushroom topping for rounds are mostly made the day before. How to divvy up the last-minute items: One of you covers the kitchen to start the green beans baking, pop mushroom rounds into the oven while the bouillon heats. The other brings the Tossed Salad with Artichoke Dressing (page 346) to the buffet table and tosses the salad while chatting with guests.

SPICY BOUILLON

This is good served either as a first course, or in mugs as a go-with drink.

5 cups water
2 tablespoons instant chicken or beef bouillon
1 tablespoon lemon juice
½ teaspoon Worcestershire sauce
½ teaspoon horseradish

Heat all ingredients to boiling. Boil bouillon uncovered, stirring occasionally, 5 minutes. 6 servings.

MUSHROOM ROUNDS

If you're feeding a large or especially hungry group, double this recipe.

Eighteen 1½-inch rounds, cut from white bread
3 tablespoons butter or margarine, melted
1 tablespoon butter or margarine
1 cup very finely chopped mushrooms (about 7 medium)
⅛ teaspoon ground thyme
½ teaspoon salt

Heat oven to 400°. Brush both sides of rounds generously with 3 tablespoons melted butter; place on ungreased baking sheet. Bake rounds until brown on bottoms, about 5 minutes; turn. Bake until brown on other sides, about 3 minutes.

Melt 1 tablespoon butter in skillet; add mushrooms and thyme. Cook and stir over low heat until mushrooms are brown; sprinkle with salt. Spread about ½ teaspoon mushroom mixture on each toasted round. (Can be refrigerated covered at this point no longer than 24 hours.) 6 servings.

Note: To serve reheated, heat oven to 350°. Place rounds on ungreased baking sheet. Bake until hot, about 2 minutes.

JAMBALAYA

2½ - to 3-pound broiler-fryer
    chicken, cut up
1 tablespoon salt
¼ teaspoon pepper
8 pork sausage links
2 cans (16 ounces each)
    stewed tomatoes

1 large clove garlic, finely
    chopped
¼ teaspoon ground thyme
⅛ to ¼ teaspoon cayenne
    red pepper
1 cup uncooked regular rice
    Snipped parsley

A great flavor combination—chicken and sausage—with a hint of New Orleans.

Place chicken in Dutch oven; add just enough water to cover chicken. Sprinkle with salt and pepper. Heat to boiling; reduce heat. Cover and simmer 45 minutes.

Remove chicken from broth; reserve. Strain broth, reserving 2 cups. Brown sausage in large pan or Dutch oven. Spoon off fat, reserving 2 tablespoons.

Return reserved fat to pan; add chicken. Stir in reserved broth, tomatoes, garlic, thyme and red pepper. (Can be refrigerated covered at this point no longer than 24 hours.)

Heat to boiling; stir in rice. Cover and simmer 25 minutes. Serve Jambalaya in large bowl; sprinkle with parsley. 6 servings.

GREEN BEANS DELUXE

2 packages (9 ounces each)
    frozen French-style green
    beans, cooked and drained

1 can (10¾ ounces)
    condensed cream of
    mushroom soup
1 can (3½ ounces) French
    fried onions

Heat oven to 350°. Mix cooked beans and soup. Pour into ungreased 1-quart casserole. Bake beans uncovered 10 minutes; sprinkle with onions. Bake until onions are hot, 5 to 10 minutes. 6 servings.

Give A Biggie: Plan A Make-Your-Own Menu

Problem: How do you serve dinner to a dozen or more people without calling in extra help? Solution: Plan dishes the guests can put together for themselves! You set out an array of makings —for sandwiches, salads, sundaes, for instance. Each guest chooses the fillings and "finishing touches" that appeal the most. This is a worksaver for you, but it also means that each guest gets a "custom-made" dinner. And most people are delighted with this casual arrangement.

With our menu, you make the sandwich filling (most of the work done the day before), heap a bowl with salad greens, heat the Cherry Fudge Sundae sauce. The guests bring good appetites, then help themselves!

**Meat Roll
Sandwiches**
**Salad Bowl with
Assorted Dressings**
**Cherry Fudge
Sundaes**

MEAT ROLL SANDWICHES

5 pounds ground beef	2 packages (3 ounces each) wafer-thin sliced smoked ham
5 eggs	
1 cup dry bread crumbs	1 package (8 ounces) shredded Cheddar cheese (about 2 cups)
¾ cup milk	
⅔ cup catsup	
1 tablespoon salt	3 to 4 packages (10 ounces each) brown and serve French rolls
½ teaspoon pepper	
½ teaspoon ground oregano	

Heat oven to 350°. Mix ground beef, eggs, bread crumbs, milk, catsup, salt, pepper and oregano.

Divide ground beef mixture into 3 equal parts. Pat each part on aluminum foil into rectangle, 12x11 inches. Arrange ham on each rectangle; sprinkle each with ½ cup of the cheese.

Roll up each rectangle carefully, beginning at one 12-inch side, using foil to lift meat. Press edges and ends of rolls to seal. Place rolls on rack in jelly roll pan, 15½x10½x1 inch. (Can be refrigerated covered at this point no longer than 24 hours.)

Bake meat rolls uncovered until done, about 1 hour 10 minutes. Sprinkle remaining cheese on top of rolls. Bake until cheese is melted, about 3 minutes.

Prepare French rolls as directed on package; cut in half. Serve ground beef roll with French rolls. (Two 1-inch slices of ground beef roll fit nicely on each French roll.) 12 to 16 servings.

Note: You can substitute 12 to 16 individual hard rolls for the French rolls.

CHERRY FUDGE SUNDAES

1 can (21 ounces) cherry pie filling	1 tablespoon light corn syrup
1 can (16½ ounces) milk chocolate frosting	2 quarts vanilla ice cream

Heat all ingredients except ice cream, stirring occasionally, until frosting is melted and coats cherries. Serve warm sauce on scoops of ice cream. 12 to 16 servings.

Snacks And Punch: Telescope To Treat A Group Of Any Size

Big group, smaller troupe—you're never at a loss for entertaining ideas with this tempting spread of appetizer recipes and our punch-for-the-bunch idea. Double the quantities of each when you expect a real crowd—cut out one or more of the side attractions when the guest list is shorter.

TAKE-YOUR-CHOICE CHEESE BALL

3 packages (8 ounces each) cream cheese, softened
2 tablespoons grated onion
½ teaspoon dry mustard
4 or 5 drops red pepper sauce
3 ounces crumbled blue cheese (about ½ cup)
¾ cup chopped pimiento-stuffed olives
1 package (8 ounces) shredded Cheddar cheese (about 2 cups)
½ teaspoon paprika
¼ cup snipped parsley
¼ cup finely chopped walnuts

Beat cream cheese, onion, dry mustard and red pepper sauce in large mixer bowl; divide in half. Mix blue cheese and olives into one half; mix Cheddar cheese and paprika into second half. Cover each half and refrigerate until firm enough to shape.

Shape each cheese mixture separately into half a ball. Cover and refrigerate until firm.

Roll blue cheese half in snipped parsley; roll Cheddar cheese half in walnuts. Press the halves together to form a ball. Serve cheese ball with assorted crackers. 16 to 20 servings.

Here's our main attraction, sure to be the center of admiring attention at your get-together.

SALAMI WEDGES

1 package (3 ounces) cream cheese, softened
10 slices salami (4½-inch diameter)

Spread cheese over 9 of the salami slices. Stack and top with plain salami slice. Cover and refrigerate at least 3 hours.

Cut stack into 12 wedges. 12 servings.

Choose any of these sidekicks to accompany the Take-Your-Choice Cheese Ball.

GINGERED ALMONDS

1 cup blanched almonds
2 tablespoons butter or margarine
1 teaspoon salt
½ teaspoon ground ginger

Heat oven to 350°. Place almonds and butter in shallow baking pan.

Bake almonds, stirring occasionally, until golden brown, 20 minutes; drain on paper towels. Toss salt and ginger with nuts. Serve warm. About 12 servings.

INSTANT CHICKEN DIP

1 cup dairy sour cream
2 teaspoons instant chicken bouillon
1 teaspoon parsley flakes
¼ teaspoon celery seed

Mix all ingredients. Cover and refrigerate at least 1 hour. 1 cup.

DIP CONTAINERS

☐ Onion Shell—Cut off top and scoop out center of large white or red onion.

☐ Green Pepper Shell—Remove top and seeds from large green pepper. If pepper cup is uneven on bottom, cut small slice from base.

☐ Scalloped Grapefruit Shell—Scallop edge of grapefruit half; remove pulp and membrane.

☐ Seashells—Fill small baking shells with dip (especially appropriate for a seafood dip).

MARINATED SHRIMP

2 cups water	1 cup oil and vinegar salad dressing
1½ teaspoons salt	
1 package (12 ounces) frozen cleaned raw shrimp	1 bay leaf, crushed

Heat water and salt to boiling; add shrimp. Heat to boiling. Cook until shrimp are tender, 1 to 2 minutes. Rinse quickly with running cold water to cool.

Mix shrimp, salad dressing and bay leaf. Cover and refrigerate at least 2 hours but no longer than 1 week. About 8 servings.

Note: You can substitute 2 cans (4½ ounces each) medium shrimp, rinsed and drained, for the raw shrimp; mix with salad dressing and bay leaf.

FRUIT NIBBLERS

½ cantaloupe	2 tablespoons orange-flavored liqueur or orange juice (optional)
½ honeydew melon	
About 3 pounds watermelon	6 to 8 small clusters seedless green grapes

Scoop balls from melons or cut melons into 1-inch cubes. Place 3 balls on each of 12 bamboo skewers; arrange on serving plate or tray.

Sprinkle liqueur over balls. Garnish tray with grape clusters. 12 nibblers.

Note: You can substitute 1 jar (17 ounces) fruits for salads for the melons.

CELEBRATION PUNCH

2 packages (10 ounces each) frozen strawberries, thawed
2 cups vodka (optional)
1 cup bottled lemon juice
1 can (6 ounces) frozen orange juice concentrate, thawed
½ cup water
2 trays ice cubes
2 quarts chilled ginger ale
    Mint sprigs

Mix strawberries, vodka, lemon juice, orange juice concentrate and water. Refrigerate uncovered until cold.

Pour cold mixture over ice cubes in punch bowl. Stir in ginger ale gently. Garnish punch with mint sprigs. 28 to 32 servings (½ cup each).

SPECIAL OCCASION PARTIES

Picnic to potluck supper—special ideas for special occasions!

Hot And Hearty Picnic

Here's a picnic menu that's good for tailgate picnics, skating parties, after-ski gatherings—any occasion when you decide to "bring along a picnic lunch."

QUICK CASSOULET

3 tablespoons butter or margarine
1½ pounds Polish sausage, cut into 1½-inch slices
1½ cups diagonally sliced celery
¾ cup chopped green pepper
½ cup chopped onion
⅛ teaspoon finely chopped garlic
1 can (16 ounces) pork and beans
1 can (about 15 ounces) chili with beans
1 can (17 ounces) lima beans, drained

Melt butter in 4-quart Dutch oven. Cook and stir sausage, celery, green pepper, onion and garlic in butter until sausage is light brown; drain.

Stir in pork and beans, chili with beans and lima beans. Heat to boiling; reduce heat. Simmer cassoulet uncovered until hot, 10 to 15 minutes. Carry to picnic in two 1-quart widemouthed vacuum bottles. 6 servings.

Quick Cassoulet

Pickled Beets and Eggs

Tossed Salad with Artichoke Dressing

Apple Pie or Cheese and Fruit

Pack picnic foods so that the hot foods stay piping hot and the "colds" keep icy cold. This is a health-insurance measure as well as a gourmet tip!

PICKLED BEETS AND EGGS

1 can (16 ounces) small whole beets, drained (reserve liquid)
1 cup white vinegar

⅓ cup sugar
2 tablespoons pickling spice
¾ teaspoon salt
9 hard-cooked eggs, shelled

Heat beet liquid, vinegar, sugar, pickling spice and salt to boiling; reduce heat. Cover and simmer 10 minutes.

Place beets and eggs in large bowl. Pour vinegar mixture over beets and eggs. Cover and refrigerate at least 12 hours but no longer than 1 week. Carry beets and eggs to picnic in covered bowl or jars. (Keep cold.) 6 servings.

TOSSED SALAD WITH ARTICHOKE DRESSING

Take this to the picnic in a plastic bag —toss it with the dressing "right in the bag."

1 large head lettuce, torn into bite-size pieces
4 ounces fresh spinach, torn into bite-size pieces

½ cup drained pitted ripe olives
1 jar (6 ounces) marinated artichoke hearts
½ cup bottled herb dressing

Place greens in large plastic bag. (Can be refrigerated at this point no longer than 24 hours.)

At the picnic, add olives, artichoke hearts (with liquid) and dressing to greens in plastic bag. Close bag tightly; shake salad vigorously. 6 servings.

Let's Go Back To Our House

After the game, when the flick is finished or the cocktail party's breaking up—feel free to ask people in. You can be this relaxed because you're ahead of things with a warmhearted dish you make ahead of time, then reheat and eat when everybody's ready. What is this "wonder" you can prepare hours before, then serve with pride? It's our Pocket Bread, filled with a zesty meatball stuffing. And one reason it reheats so well is that you make the bread and stuffing separately, ladle the meatballs into the bread at the last minute. Nothing gets soggy while waiting—or tastes "reheated" when it's actually served! Check the recipe on the opposite page.

A good salad accompaniment for our Pocket Bread would be the Tossed Salad with Artichoke Dressing on this page. Dessert is an optional extra, but fresh fruit or sherbet might be nice.

If you have a crowd of people, double the Beef-Filled Pocket Bread recipe and serve our Beet and Fresh Mushroom Salad (page 348) as a delightfully different accompaniment. It's a hearty combination of beets, mushrooms and the greens of your choice—try spinach for an extra-colorful salad. Like the pocket bread, this is an ideal do-ahead recipe; if you prepare and chill the greens ahead of time, all that's left is a quick tossing together of greens and vegetables when you're ready to eat.

BEEF-FILLED POCKET BREAD

1 package active dry yeast	1 tablespoon vegetable oil
1⅓ cups warm water (105 to 115°)	1½ cups whole wheat flour
1 teaspoon salt	1½ to 2 cups all-purpose flour*
¼ teaspoon sugar	Cornmeal
	Beef Filling (below)

Dissolve yeast in warm water in large bowl; stir in salt, sugar, oil and whole wheat flour. Beat until smooth. Mix in enough all-purpose flour to make dough easy to handle. Knead on lightly floured surface until smooth and elastic, about 10 minutes. Place in greased bowl. Turn greased side up. Cover and let rise in warm place until double, about 1 hour.

Punch down dough; divide into 6 equal parts. Shape each part into a ball. Cover and let rise 30 minutes. Sprinkle 3 ungreased baking sheets with cornmeal. Roll each ball on lightly floured surface into circle ⅛ inch thick. Place 2 circles in opposite corners of each baking sheet. Cover and let rise 30 minutes.

Pocket Bread—torn, ready for filling.

Heat oven to 500°. Bake breads until puffed and light brown, about 10 minutes. Tear each pocket bread lengthwise in half while warm. If not serving immediately, place in plastic bags.

Prepare Beef Filling; use to stuff pocket bread.

*Do not use self-rising flour in this recipe.

BEEF FILLING

2 pounds ground beef	½ teaspoon crushed red pepper
1 package (2⅜ ounces) Italian-flavored coating mix for chicken	⅓ cup milk
1½ teaspoons salt	1 can (12 ounces) tomato paste
¾ teaspoon ground oregano	2 cups water
	1 teaspoon sugar

Mix ground beef, coating mix, salt, oregano, red pepper and milk; shape by rounded teaspoonfuls into 1-inch balls. Brown half of the meatballs in large skillet over low heat; remove from skillet and drain on paper towels. Repeat with remaining meatballs.

Heat tomato paste, water and sugar to boiling in 3-quart saucepan, stirring occasionally. Boil and stir 1 minute; add meatballs. Heat to boiling; reduce heat. Cover and simmer meatballs until done, about 20 minutes. Cover and refrigerate no longer than 18 hours.

To serve reheated, heat to boiling over medium heat, stirring occasionally. Spoon meatballs and sauce into pocket bread. 6 servings.

BEET AND FRESH MUSHROOM SALAD

Mushrooms darken and gain flavor when marinated. If light color is desired, do not marinate mushrooms. Slice mushrooms into salad just before serving.

⅓ cup olive oil
3 tablespoons red wine vinegar
1 tablespoon Dijon mustard
1½ teaspoons salt
½ teaspoon freshly ground pepper

8 ounces fresh mushrooms, sliced
1 can (16 ounces) baby beets, drained
4 green onions with tops, thinly sliced
12 cups salad greens (iceberg or leaf lettuce, spinach, romaine), torn into bite-size pieces

Mix oil, vinegar, mustard, salt and pepper; pour over mushrooms, beets and onions. Cover and refrigerate vegetables, stirring occasionally, at least 2 to 3 hours but no longer than 18 hours.

Pour dressing and vegetables over salad greens; toss. 12 servings.

Cold-Weather Brunch: Everybody Helps With The Waffles

Ask two or three friends to lend their waffle irons; put out pitchers of batter, bowls of toppings (see next page)—and go! This is planned as a brunch for eight.

RAISED WAFFLES

Legend has it that the first waffle came into being during medieval times. A serving maid had mixed a container of batter and set it by the fire to rise. A careless knight, who'd been warming himself at the fire, sat in the batter. When he arose, presto—the first waffle ever was baked to the back of his chain mail. We prefer the modern waffle iron!

1 package active dry yeast
¼ cup warm water (105 to 115°)
1¾ cups lukewarm milk (scalded then cooled)
2 tablespoons sugar
1 teaspoon salt
3 eggs

¼ cup butter or margarine, softened
2 cups all-purpose flour*
Finely chopped walnuts
Raspberry Cream, Creamy Sauce and Fruit (page 349), and warm syrup and honey

Dissolve yeast in warm water in large mixer bowl; add milk, sugar, salt, eggs, butter and flour. Beat until smooth. Cover and let rise in warm place 1½ hours. Stir down batter. Cover and refrigerate 8 to 12 hours.

Stir down batter. Pour batter** from cup or pitcher onto center of hot waffle iron; sprinkle with walnuts.

Cook until steaming stops, about 5 minutes; remove waffle carefully. Grease iron as necessary.

Serve waffles with Raspberry Cream, Creamy Sauce and Fruit, and warm syrup and honey. 3 to 6 waffles.

*If using self-rising flour, omit salt.

**Use about ½ cup batter in 7-inch round waffle iron or about 1 cup batter in 9-inch square waffle iron.

BROWNIE WAFFLES

1 package (22.5 ounces)
fudge brownie mix
¾ cup water
2 eggs

1 tablespoon vegetable oil
Raspberry Cream,
Creamy Sauce and Fruit
(below), and warm
syrup and honey

Mix brownie mix, water, eggs and oil. Pour batter* from cup or pitcher onto center of hot waffle iron, spreading batter evenly over grids.

Cook waffles until steaming stops, about 3 minutes. Open iron; leave waffle on iron until set, about 1 minute (waffle will be soft). Grease iron as necessary.

Serve waffles with Raspberry Cream, Creamy Sauce and Fruit, and warm syrup and honey. 3 to 5 waffles.

*Use about ⅔ cup batter in 7-inch round waffle iron or about 1⅓ cups batter in 9-inch square waffle iron.

RASPBERRY CREAM

1 package (about 2 ounces)
dessert topping mix
¼ cup cold milk
¼ cup cold orange-flavored
liqueur

2 cups slightly sweetened
frozen raspberries,
slightly thawed
½ cup powdered sugar

Beat topping mix, milk and liqueur in small mixer bowl as directed on topping mix package.

Mix raspberries and powdered sugar; fold into whipped topping. (Can be served immediately.) Cover and refrigerate cream no longer than 3 hours.

CREAMY SAUCE AND FRUIT

½ cup powdered sugar
½ cup butter or margarine,
softened
½ cup chilled whipping
cream, whipped

1 package (16 ounces)
frozen unsweetened
blueberries, slightly thawed
1 package (16 ounces)
frozen unsweetened
strawberries, slightly
thawed

Mix powdered sugar and butter in saucepan until smooth and creamy; fold in whipped cream. Heat the mixture to boiling, stirring occasionally.

Serve creamy sauce immediately as a topping for waffles over blueberries and strawberries.

Year 'Round Brunch: A Buffet Soufflé

Who could resist this unusual soufflé? Deliciously brown on top, this non-sweet brunch dish combines Cheddar cheese with cauliflower and green pepper. A brightly flavored tomato sauce is a complementary accompaniment, ready to be spooned over each helping. Here's a dish that combines foods from three of the Basic Four Food Groups—protein-rich eggs; milk and cheese; vegetables. To complete your menu, offer grapefruit halves as a first course, buttered toast as a go-with. Best of all—there's almost no cleanup afterwards!

CAULIFLOWER-PEPPER SOUFFLE

½ teaspoon salt	¼ teaspoon red pepper sauce
1 small cauliflower, broken into flowerets	3 tablespoons vegetable oil
1 medium green pepper, cut into strips	1 medium onion, finely chopped
1½ cups milk	1 clove garlic, finely chopped
½ cup cornmeal	6 tomatoes, peeled and diced
½ cup shredded Cheddar cheese	1½ teaspoons salt
2 eggs, separated	½ teaspoon dried basil leaves
2 teaspoons baking powder	¼ teaspoon red pepper sauce
1 teaspoon salt	Buttered toast

Heat oven to 375°. Heat 1 inch water and ½ teaspoon salt to boiling; add cauliflower and reduce heat. Simmer uncovered 5 minutes; add green pepper. Cover and simmer 5 minutes; drain. Place cauliflower and green pepper in greased 2-quart casserole.

Heat milk to boiling. Stir gradually into cornmeal; add cheese. Stir until mixture is cool. Stir in egg yolks, baking powder, 1 teaspoon salt and ¼ teaspoon red pepper sauce.

Beat egg whites in small mixer bowl just until stiff but not dry; fold into cornmeal mixture. Pour evenly over cauliflower and green pepper; spread to edge of casserole.

Bake soufflé uncovered until brown, about 40 minutes. Prepare sauce while soufflé is baking: Heat oil in skillet; add onion and garlic. Cook and stir until onion is tender. Stir in remaining ingredients except toast. Heat to boiling; reduce heat. Simmer uncovered about 15 minutes. Serve soufflé with sauce and buttered toast. 5 or 6 servings.

Gourmet Potluck Party: Great Eating For Six Couples

Here's an idea that's growing in popularity all the time—a group party where all share the work and the expense. One couple provides the place (and possibly one course). The others each bring "a dish." It works out best when the menu is planned ahead and each couple knows just what food they're responsible for. Starting below, we give menus and recipes for two such "bring your menu contribution with you" parties.

Since everybody brings something, and since each couple only has one dish to worry about, each course can be something very special.

CHEESY ARTICHOKE

1 artichoke	¼ cup dry sherry
3 quarts water	2 teaspoons Dijon mustard
2 tablespoons vegetable oil	1 teaspoon Worcestershire sauce
1 tablespoon lemon juice	Dash of garlic powder
1 clove garlic, quartered	1 pound Cheddar cheese, shredded (about 4 cups)
½ teaspoon salt	
1 package (8 ounces) cream cheese, softened	

Trim stem even with base of artichoke; slice 1 inch off top and discard. Snip off points of leaves with scissors.

Heat water, oil, lemon juice, garlic and salt to boiling; add artichoke. Heat to boiling; reduce heat. Simmer artichoke uncovered, rotating artichoke occasionally, until leaves pull out easily and bottom is tender when pierced with a knife, 30 to 40 minutes. Drain artichoke upside down.

Beat cream cheese in small mixer bowl until smooth; beat in sherry, mustard, Worcestershire sauce and garlic powder gradually; beat until mixed. Stir in Cheddar cheese.

Cover a 6-ounce tomato paste or juice concentrate can with aluminum foil. Place can on serving plate. Mold cheese mixture around can in the shape of an artichoke. Starting at top, carefully push artichoke leaves into cheese mold so that they overlap (to resemble a large artichoke). Secure leaves with wooden picks when necessary.

Cover with plastic wrap and refrigerate at least 12 hours. Carefully remove wooden picks. Let stand at room temperature 1 hour before serving. Serve artichoke with cheese knives so that guests can scoop additional cheese onto artichoke leaves and Crunchy Cornmeal Thins (page 352) if desired. 12 servings.

**Cheesy Artichoke
Crunchy Cornmeal Thins
Dill Pumpernickel Rolls
Stuffed Ham Slices
Beet and Fresh
Mushroom Salad (page 348)
Individual Grasshopper Soufflés**

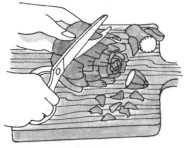

Snip artichoke leaves.

Push artichoke leaves into cheese mold.

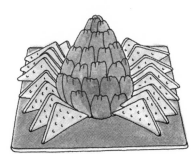

Cheesy Artichoke with Crunchy Cornmeal Thins.

CRUNCHY CORNMEAL THINS

½ cup milk	¾ cup cornmeal
3 tablespoons vegetable oil	¾ cup all-purpose flour
¼ teaspoon Worcestershire sauce	1 teaspoon salt
	½ teaspoon garlic salt
⅛ teaspoon red pepper sauce	¼ teaspoon baking soda

Heat oven to 350°. Mix milk, oil, Worcestershire sauce and red pepper sauce. Mix remaining ingredients in 1-quart bowl; stir in milk mixture gradually until dough forms a ball.

Knead on very lightly floured surface 5 minutes.* Divide dough in half; place each half on greased baking sheet. Roll each half into 12-inch square. (Place a damp cloth under baking sheet to prevent it from slipping while you roll out dough.) Cut into 3-inch squares; cut each square in half to form a triangle.

Bake thins until edges are light brown, about 15 minutes. Cool slightly before removing from baking sheet. 5 dozen thins.

*Flour surface only as dough begins to stick.

STUFFED HAM SLICES

For a party for twelve, two couples prepare this recipe—the hosting couple and one of the guest-couples.

¼ cup thinly sliced celery	2 fully cooked center ham slices, ½ inch thick (about 1½ pounds)
2 tablespoons finely chopped onion	
3 tablespoons butter or margarine	1 tablespoon butter or margarine, melted
1 cup packaged herb seasoned stuffing mix	½ cup orange marmalade
1 orange, peeled and diced	½ cup orange-flavored liqueur
3 tablespoons water	

Heat oven to 325°. Cook and stir celery and onion in 3 tablespoons butter over low heat until onion is tender; remove from heat. Stir in stuffing mix, orange and water.

Place 1 ham slice in ungreased baking dish, 11¾ x 7½ x 1¾ inches. Spread stuffing mixture over meat; top with second ham slice. Brush top ham slice with 1 tablespoon butter.

Cover and bake ham slices 30 minutes; remove from oven. Heat marmalade and ¼ cup of the liqueur to boiling; brush top ham slice with half of the mixture. Bake uncovered 30 minutes.

Heat remaining marmalade mixture; float remaining ¼ cup warm liqueur on top, being careful that it does not mix together with heated marmalade. (Mixture is enough even if ham recipe is doubled.) Ignite; pour over ham. If mixture does not ignite, reheat to boiling. Ignite. 6 servings.

INDIVIDUAL GRASSHOPPER SOUFFLES

½ cup sugar
2 envelopes unflavored
 gelatin
¼ teaspoon salt
1¼ cups water
6 eggs, separated

⅓ cup green crème de
 menthe
⅓ cup white crème de
 cacao
½ cup sugar
1½ cups chilled whipping
 cream

Extend depth of 12 individual soufflé dishes 1½ inches above each dish with band of double thickness aluminum foil; secure foil by folding ends together, taping or fastening with paper clips. Or use dessert dishes (the foil extension may not be necessary).

Mix ½ cup sugar, the gelatin, salt and water in saucepan. Beat egg yolks slightly; stir into gelatin mixture. Cook over medium heat, stirring constantly, *just* until mixture boils. Stir in crème de menthe and crème de cacao.

Chill pan in bowl of ice and water or in refrigerator, stirring occasionally, *just* until mixture mounds slightly when dropped from a spoon, 20 to 30 minutes (mixture should be slightly thicker than unbeaten egg whites). If mixture becomes too thick, place pan in bowl of hot water, stirring constantly, until mixture is proper consistency.

Beat egg whites in large mixer bowl until foamy. (Egg whites should be at room temperature for best volume.) Beat in ½ cup sugar, 1 tablespoon at a time; beat until stiff and glossy. (Do not underbeat.) Fold in gelatin mixture.

Beat whipping cream in chilled bowl until stiff. Fold whipped cream into egg white-gelatin mixture. Carefully turn into soufflé dishes. Refrigerate until set, about 8 hours but no longer than 24 hours.

To serve soufflés, run knife around inside of foil bands and remove bands. Garnish with whipped cream and shaved chocolate or chocolate curls if desired. 12 servings.

Note: A delicate green in color and exquisitely light in texture, these dessert soufflés are of special interest on several counts. First of all, they're a truly "individual" ending to your gourmet supper— each one is a complete soufflé (and one complete portion) in itself. This makes them easy to serve buffet style. Next—they're chilled, so they don't depend on split-second timing for success. They can be made ahead of time and they travel easily. And, best of all, they can serve as dessert and after-dinner drink all in one—especially if you team each up with a demitasse on the side.

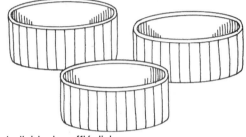

Individual soufflé dishes.

Secure foil by folding ends together.

Tying the foil insures that it will stay in place.

Casual Potluck: Easy Entertaining For Four Couples

On these two pages, you'll find this same potluck party idea translated into a more casual menu. It's the kind of gathering you might plan for a Friday or Sunday evening when nobody wants to fuss too much.

The main dish (prepared by the home-base couple) practically cooks itself in the oven. The cheery cheese bread (second couple) is already baked and needs reheating only. Crunchy coleslaw (third couple) and a maple-flavored fruit dessert (fourth couple) complete the menu.

Beer Stew
Cheese Bread
Coleslaw
Maple Apple Bake

BEER STEW

3 tablespoons vegetable oil	⅛ teaspoon ground thyme
1½ pounds boneless smoked pork hock or shoulder roll, cut into 1-inch pieces	⅛ teaspoon dried basil leaves
	6 carrots, cut into 1-inch pieces
1 pound beef stew meat, cut into 1-inch pieces	3 potatoes, cut into 1-inch pieces
Water	1 medium onion, thinly sliced
1 can (12 ounces) beer	½ cup cold water
1 tablespoon instant beef bouillon	¼ cup all-purpose flour
1½ teaspoons salt	¾ cup walnut halves (optional)
½ teaspoon garlic salt	1 tablespoon butter or margarine, melted (optional)
⅛ teaspoon ground marjoram	

Heat oven to 325°. Heat oil in Dutch oven; add pork hock and stew meat. Cook over medium heat, stirring frequently, until stew meat is brown, about 8 minutes; drain.

Add enough water to beer to measure 2 cups; pour over meat. Add bouillon and seasonings. Heat to boiling. Add carrots, potatoes and onion slices.

Cover and bake meat until tender, about 1½ hours; remove from oven.

Shake ½ cup cold water and the flour in covered jar; stir into stew. Cover and bake 10 minutes.

Stir walnut halves in melted butter; sprinkle stew with walnuts. 8 servings.

Note: The beef in this recipe will assume a pink color (because of the smoked pork).

CHEESE BREAD

3 cups biscuit baking mix	1 cup shredded Cheddar cheese
2 eggs	
½ cup milk	1 tablespoon sesame seed
1 cup shredded Cheddar cheese (about 4 ounces)	¼ cup butter or margarine, melted

Heat oven to 400°. Mix baking mix, eggs, milk and 1 cup cheese. Divide dough in half; pat each half in greased 9-inch pie plate. Sprinkle dough with 1 cup cheese and the sesame seed. Pour butter evenly over tops.

Bake breads until golden brown, 20 to 25 minutes. Cool completely. Wrap breads in heavy-duty aluminum foil and store at room temperature no longer than 24 hours.

To serve reheated, heat oven to 375°. Heat wrapped bread on oven rack until hot, about 15 minutes. Cut into wedges.

COLESLAW

4 cups finely shredded or chopped cabbage (about ½ medium head)	¼ cup mayonnaise or salad dressing
¼ cup chopped onion	½ teaspoon seasoned salt
½ cup dairy sour cream	½ teaspoon dry mustard
	Dash of pepper

Combine cabbage and onion in large salad bowl. Blend remaining ingredients; pour over cabbage and toss. If desired, sprinkle with paprika. 8 servings.

MAPLE APPLE BAKE

8 medium cooking apples, cored, pared and sliced	⅔ cup packed brown sugar
⅔ cup maple-flavored syrup	½ cup all-purpose flour
¼ cup packed brown sugar	½ cup quick-cooking oats
¼ teaspoon ground cinnamon	⅓ cup butter or margarine, softened

Heat oven to 375°. Heat apple slices, syrup, ¼ cup brown sugar and the cinnamon to boiling. Pour into ungreased baking pan, 9x9x2 inches. Mix remaining ingredients; sprinkle over apples.

Bake uncovered until apples are tender and topping is golden brown, about 30 minutes. (Can be served warm and, if desired, with light cream or ice cream.)

To serve reheated, heat oven to 375°. Cover and bake 10 minutes. Uncover and bake until hot, about 10 minutes.

YOU'RE OFF TO A GOOD START

In this chapter, we've tried to help you solve most of the meal-planning situations you'll face at first. Breakfasts-on-the-run, dinners for two, budget-saving dishes, some interesting ways to play host and hostess—they're all here. But the actual recipes and menu suggestions we give are just the beginning. This chapter can serve as much more than a collection of recipes—aside from how intriguing or easy-to-follow they are. We've designed the material included here to act as "starter" information—and "starter" thinking—that can stimulate *your* ideas and increase *your* abilities. For instance, with the basic facts about nutrition you gleaned at the beginning of this chapter—and our Handbook on Shopping, Meal-Planning and Cooking—as a basis, you can keep adding healthful and tasty dishes to your repertoire. You'll have enough information at your fingertips to judge, from the recipe alone, which of the Basic Four Food Groups the dish itself includes—and which must be added via the accompanying dishes. And, extended over a day, a week, a month, this adds up to wiser eating in terms of nutrition and cost.

Remember—neither of you has to be a gourmet cook to insure satisfying food. All it takes is interest and the kind of know-how we've presented here.

In fact, that's really what this whole book is about. We've given you a foundation for finding, furnishing, furbishing, financing and keeping up that home-of-your-own. Whether you become dedicated homebodies or settle for running your household efficiently—with a minimum investment of time and effort—is a personal choice. Either way, we've provided the information you need. We also hope we've given you an idea of what's involved in developing sensible approaches in two other important areas—food and finances. Now we want to offer our congratulations as well—and our best wishes to you in your new life—as you're starting out together.

Index